Get the eBook FREE!

(PDF, ePub, Kindle, and liveBook all included)

We believe that once you buy a book from us, you should be able to read it in any format we have available. To get electronic versions of this book at no additional cost to you, purchase and then register this book at the Manning website.

Go to https://www.manning.com/freebook and follow the instructions to complete your pBook registration.

That's it!
Thanks from Manning!

Building Web APIs with ASP.NET Core

Building Web APIs with ASP.NET Core

VALERIO DE SANCTIS

MANNING
SHELTER ISLAND

For online information and ordering of this and other Manning books, please visit
www.manning.com. The publisher offers discounts on this book when ordered in quantity.
For more information, please contact

Special Sales Department
Manning Publications Co.
20 Baldwin Road
PO Box 761
Shelter Island, NY 11964
Email: orders@manning.com

Manning Publications Co.
20 Baldwin Road
PO Box 761
Shelter Island, NY 11964

Development editor: Doug Rudder
Technical editor: Mwiza Kumwenda
Review editor: Aleksandar Dragosavljević
Production editor: Keri Hales
Copy editor: Keir Simpson
Proofreader: Jason Everett
Technical proofreader: Emanuele Origgi
Typesetter: Dennis Dalinnik
Cover designer: Marija Tudor

ISBN: 9781633439481
Printed in the United States of America

brief contents

v

contents

preface

I still remember the first time I was asked to implement a web API. I was working as a junior developer (actually, I was the sole developer) for a small radio station that did only one thing: broadcast music 24/7. It was one of the first radio stations in Rome to switch from CDs to digital files (MP2, WMA, RealAudio, and the like; MP3s were yet to come), but the daily programming was still done locally, using the workstations that were installed on the radio station's premises.

I was the one who made the audio player (imagine something like VLC or Winamp, but much worse) that the radio station used to broadcast the content. My software was used not only to reproduce the songs, but also to insert advertising messages and the real-time contributions of the radio broadcasters who took turns managing the live broadcast. I was 19 years old at the time, and I really liked that job. I was paid decently, I had the chance to study and learn several new technologies, and (most important) it was a lot of fun.

One day, all the radio broadcasters fell ill at the same time. No one could come to the radio station to manage the programming of songs and advertising messages. That single event, more than 20 years before COVID-19, led that small radio station to understand the importance of being able to manage an entire business remotely.

You can imagine what happened next. The radio manager—an old yet authoritative guy who looked a lot like Jack Lemmon in the movie *Glengarry Glen Ross*—asked me to do "something" that would allow radio broadcasters to do their job from home in the near future. I somehow managed to do that, making Jack Lemmon happy, earning a salary increase, and stripping away all my colleagues' paid sick leave! (I'm joking.

They were happy to experience remote work more than 20 years ahead of time. If you were working in a company during the 2020 pandemic, you know what I mean.)

Jokes aside, after a lot of effort I was able to pull off that project by using a rudimentary, custom-made XML-based RPC implementation. (Imagine something like SOAP, but much worse.) But I happened to lose a lot of time creating the client and getting it to work. I was determined to build it by using Visual Basic 6, but I wasn't prepared for the huge amount of work that would have been required to remotely install, update, and debug such a client for every user. Eventually, I decided to stop trying to reinvent the wheel and started studying, until I figured out that the best possible way to overcome my problems was to replace the VB6 client with an HTML form (handled by a PHP script). Then I had to make the server able to receive the HTTP requests coming from that form in a standardized fashion and act accordingly—in other words, create a web API. I never stopped doing that for the next 25 years. (That's another joke, but I think you get the point.)

A few years later, when the first version of .NET Framework came out, I was working for a different company as a backend web developer. I didn't fall in love with it immediately—PHP and Java were my trusted languages in those days—but I was lucky enough to see the huge potential of the new stack for web development purposes and to start using it for my projects, thus becoming one of the few ASP.NET early adopters in my country. The framework evolved steadily over the next 20 years, mostly in a better way, up to the current installment: ASP.NET Core, which in my opinion is a great web development framework for building any kind of modern, cloud-aware, internet-connected web app.

This, in a nutshell, is what you will find in this book: a brief summary of what I was able to achieve with client-side forms, HTTP methods, and backend services powered by ASP.NET Core after 25 years of decently paid jobs, continuous study, technology updates, and (most important) a lot of fun.

acknowledgments

Writing this book was a huge task, which would not have been possible without the constant support of several important people who have been close to me. First and foremost, I'd like to thank my wife, Carla, for always taking care of me and our children. You are incredible. Getting to know you was the best thing that ever happened to me, and I will always love you. I will also take the chance to thank my father, Bernardino, for teaching me everything I know except coding, as well as my mother, Antonella, and my sister, Silvia, for always believing in me.

Next, I would like to acknowledge the people at Manning who helped me along the journey that ultimately allowed this book to hit the stores: Doug Rudder, my development editor, for assisting me from the book's start to its completion, and for great suggestions that had a huge effect on me regarding how to write a book properly; Brian Sawyer, my acquisitions editor, for being bold enough to think that the initial plan we had could eventually become a book; and also Heather Tucker, Rebecca Rinehart, Rejhana Markanovic, Melissa Ice, Branko Latincic, Aira Dučić, Charlotte Harborne, and Ana Romac for the roles they played. I'd also like to thank Mwiza Kumwenda (technical editor) and Emanuele Origgi (technical proofreader) for their incredible work; their countless suggestions and insights added value to the book. Also, plenty of thanks go to the behind-the-scenes Manning staff who produced this book.

Last but definitely not least, I'd like to thank all the reviewers who spent their valuable time reading the individual chapters during the writing process, providing a huge amount of invaluable feedback: Al Pezewski, Ben McNamara, Bruno Sonnino,

Chriss Jack Barnard, Daniel Vásquez, Darren Gillis, Édgar Sánchez, Emanuele Origgi, Emmanouil Chardalas, Foster Haines, George Onofrei, Gustavo Gomes, Jason Hales, Jeff Smith, Joel Kotarski, Karl van Heijster, Lakshminarayanan A. S., Milorad Imbra, Mitchell Fox, Paul Brown, Pedro Seromenho, Raushan Jha, Reza Zeinali, Ron Lease, Rui Ribeiro, Samuel Bosch, Sebastian Felling, Stephen Byrne, Tanya Wilke, Vipin Mehta, Werner Nindl, and Will Hampton. Your suggestions helped make this book better.

about this book

Who should read this book

This book illustrates how to use ASP.NET Core to create a fully featured web API project (from the data model to the JSON output, including unit testing) using REST, GraphQL, and gRPC standards. If you're looking for an efficient and structured way to create stable, secure, and reliable web API projects for enterprise markets, I'm confident that you won't be disappointed by what you've got.

How this book is organized: A road map

The book is made up of 12 chapters, split into four parts. Part 1 is an introductory section that explains to the reader what we'll be talking about. The purpose of this part is to ensure that the reader is fully able to understand the book's main topics while teaching several fundamental concepts of REST and ASP.NET Core.

- Chapter 1 introduces the concept of web APIs and provides a brief overview of the main architectures and message protocols available today (REST, SOAP, and GraphQL). It also describes the overall architecture of the ASP.NET Core framework and the reasons to use it.
- Chapter 2 explains how to set up the developer environment: installing the required software, choosing a suitable IDE, creating a first project, and inspecting the preassembled templates to understand the typical structure of an ASP.NET Core application.
- Chapter 3 is a journey through the RESTful principles and guidelines. Each one of them is explained with real-world examples, practical use-case scenarios,

and implementation guidelines using ASP.NET Core. It's the first approach to most of the concepts that will be explained in the following chapters.

Part 2 is dedicated to understanding and implementing the main development concepts related to the web API. After completing this part, you'll be able to create simple yet fully working web APIs.

- Chapter 4 introduces the concepts of data source and data model, explaining how to choose the most suitable database for any given scenario. It also contains a comprehensive guide to installing and configuring a SQL Server instance, which will be used as the web API's main data source through the rest of the book, and an object-relational mapper (ORM) such as Entity Framework Core (EF Core) to deal with it in a structured, standardized, and strongly typed fashion.
- Chapter 5 explains how to perform SELECT, INSERT, UPDATE, and DELETE queries with EF Core, as well as handle different requests using HTTP GET, POST, PUT, and DELETE methods. You'll learn to implement paging, sorting, and filtering with EF Core and use data-transfer objects (DTOs) to exchange JSON data with the client.
- Chapter 6 is dedicated to data validation and illustrates several ASP.NET Core features that can be used to implement it properly: model binding, validation attributes, and ModelState. It also contains an in-depth section on error and exception handling, illustrating some built-in and custom implementation techniques.

Part 3 follows a modular approach. Each chapter provides a comprehensive overview of a specific topic that the reader may want to implement, adding it to the sample web API project created during part 2, depending on the scenario.

- Chapter 7 introduces the concept of application logging, from its historical roots to the exponential growth of its importance gained in recent years. It also explains the differences between structured and unstructured logging and shows how to implement structured logging in ASP.NET Core by using the built-in ILogger interface or a third-party logging framework such as Serilog.
- Chapter 8 explains how to cache data on the server, on the client, and/or at an intermediate level by using a set of techniques made available by ASP.NET Core, such as HTTP response caching, in-memory caching, and distributed caching (using SQL Server or Redis).
- Chapter 9 features a comprehensive journey through authentication and authorization, from their abstract, high-level meaning to the concrete, practical programming tasks required to implement them. You'll learn to implement a full-featured authentication process based on user accounts and JSON Web Tokens (JWT), as well as a Role-Based Access Control (RBAC) authorization strategy using the AuthorizeAttribute and IAuthorizationFilter provided by the framework.
- Chapter 10 presents several notable API technologies that can be used as an alternative to REST and extensively explains how to implement two of them:

GraphQL, a query language for APIs developed by Facebook, and gRPC, a language-agnostic Remote Procedure Call architecture designed by Google.

Part 4 explains the concepts and activities necessary to publish the web API projects on the web: setting up the documentation, adopting a suitable security approach, choosing the cloud provider, and (most important) dealing with the ASP.NET Core release and deployment aspects.

- Chapter 11 emphasizes the importance that good API documentation could have for the potential audience of a web API. It also illustrates API documentation best practices and how to implement them by using Swagger/OpenAPI and the Swashbuckle set of libraries for ASP.NET Core, with several source-code examples.
- Chapter 12 is all about getting the web API ready to be released into production. It starts by explaining how to adopt a consistent deployment plan built around a secure, risk-based approach, and proceeds to show how to implement it properly, providing step-by-step guidance through all the relevant phases: setting up a content-delivery network (CDN), creating a Windows Server virtual machine in Microsoft Azure, installing and configuring Internet Information Services, and deploying the web API to Windows Server using Visual Studio.

About the code

This book contains many examples of source code, both in numbered listings and inline with normal text. In both cases, source code is formatted in a `fixed-width font` `like this` to separate it from ordinary text. Sometimes, code is also **in bold** to highlight code that has changed from previous steps in the chapter, such as when a new feature adds to an existing line of code.

In many cases, the original source code has been reformatted; we've added line breaks and reworked indentation to accommodate the available page space in the book. In rare cases, even this was not enough, and listings include line-continuation markers (➡). Additionally, comments in the source code have often been removed from the listings when the code is described in the text. Code annotations accompany many of the listings, highlighting important concepts.

You can get executable snippets of code from the liveBook (online) version of this book at https://livebook.manning.com/book/building-web-apis-with-asp-net-core. The complete code for the examples in the book is available for download from the Manning website at https://www.manning.com/books/building-web-apis-with-asp-net-core, and from the author's Github repository at https://github.com/Darkseal/ASP.NET-Core -Web-API.

liveBook discussion forum

Purchase of *Building Web APIs with ASP.NET Core* includes free access to liveBook, Manning's online reading platform. Using liveBook's exclusive discussion features, you can attach comments to the book globally or to specific sections or paragraphs. It's a snap to make notes for yourself, ask and answer technical questions, and receive help from the author and other users. To access the forum, go to https://livebook.manning .com/book/building-web-apis-with-asp-net-core/discussion. You can also learn more about Manning's forums and the rules of conduct at https://livebook.manning.com/ discussion.

Manning's commitment to our readers is to provide a venue where a meaningful dialogue between individual readers and between readers and the author can take place. It is not a commitment to any specific amount of participation on the part of the author, whose contribution to the forum remains voluntary (and unpaid). We suggest that you try asking the author some challenging questions lest his interest stray! The forum and the archives of previous discussions will be accessible on the publisher's website as long as the book is in print.

about the author

VALERIO DE SANCTIS is a skilled IT professional with 25 years of experience in lead programming, web-based development, and project management using ASP.NET, PHP, and Java. He has held senior positions at a range of financial and insurance companies, most recently serving as chief technology officer, chief security officer, and chief operating officer at a leading after-sales and IT service provider for multiple top-tier life and non-life insurance groups. He's also a Microsoft Most Valuable Professional (MVP) for Developer Technologies and Cloud and Datacenter Management.

Since 2014, he has operated an IT-oriented, web-focused blog at www.ryadel.com, featuring news, reviews, code samples, and guides designed to help developers and tech enthusiasts around the world. He has written several books on web development, many of which have become best sellers on Amazon, with tens of thousands of copies sold worldwide. You can reach him on LinkedIn at https://www.linkedin.com/in/darkseal.

The technical editor for this book, MWIZA KUMWENDA, develops software by profession and writes online articles on Linux and software development practices. He has a master's degree in information systems and is a certified C# developer. His interests include history, economics, and enterprise architecture.

about the cover illustration

The figure on the cover of *Building Web APIs with ASP.NET Core* is "Tattare de Kazan," or "Tatar from Kazan," taken from a collection by Jacques Grasset de Saint-Sauveur, published in 1788. Each illustration is finely drawn and colored by hand.

In those days, it was easy to identify where people lived and what their trade or station in life was just by their dress. Manning celebrates the inventiveness and initiative of the computer business with book covers based on the rich diversity of regional culture centuries ago, brought back to life by pictures from collections such as this one.

Part 1

Getting started

This part is an introductory section explaining the main topics of the book and showing how to deal with them properly. The main goals here are to understand a web API and the fundamental concepts of representational state transfer (REST) and to see how we can use ASP.NET Core to implement what we need.

In chapter 1, we'll define and introduce the most important characteristics of a web API, as well as present an overview of the main architectures and message protocols available today (REST, SOAP, and GraphQL). Then we'll take a look at the overall architecture of the ASP.NET Core framework and discuss the reasons to use it.

Using ASP.NET Core requires setting up an integrated development environment (IDE), which is the topic of chapter 2. We'll determine the required software and installation prerequisites; choose a suitable IDE, such as Visual Studio; and eventually create our first project. Right after that, we'll extensively inspect the preassembled templates to understand the structure, conventions, and standards of a typical ASP.NET Core application.

Chapter 3 is dedicated to RESTful principles and guidelines. We'll review these principles to understand how they work and why they're important, using real-world examples and practical use scenarios. Eventually, we'll learn how to implement them within our new ASP.NET Core application.

At the end of this part, we'll have a rough, yet working, ASP.NET Core web API application incorporating the concepts, topics, and good practices covered in these introductory chapters. The tree isn't yet able to stand on its own, but its roots are strong enough to bear the weight of the following parts, in which we'll further examine the topics discussed in these chapters and explore other topics.

Web APIs at a glance

This chapter covers

- Web API overview and real-world case samples
- Types of web APIs and their pros and cons
- ASP.NET Core overview
- Main ASP.NET Core architectural principles

Almost all applications need data, especially web-based applications, in which large numbers of clients interact with a centralized entity—typically, an HTTP-based service—to access information and possibly update or manipulate them. In this book, we'll learn how to design and develop a specific type of HTTP-based service that has the sole purpose of providing data to these clients, allowing them to interact with the information they require in a uniform, structured, and standardized way: a *web API*.

In the first section of this chapter, we'll see the distinctive characteristics of a web API and learn how it can be applied to several real-world scenarios. In the second section, we'll get familiar with ASP.NET Core, the web framework we'll be using to create web APIs throughout this book.

1.1 Web APIs

An *application programming interface (API)* is a type of software interface that exposes tools and services that computer programs use to interact with each other and exchange information. The connection required to perform such exchanges is established by means of common communication standards (*protocols*), given sets of available operations (*specifications*), and data exchange formats (JSON, XML, and the like).

From that definition, we can easily see that the main purpose of an API is to allow parties to communicate by using a common syntax (or *abstraction*) that simplifies and standardizes what happens under each hood. The overall concept is similar to that of real-world interfaces, which also provide a common "syntax" to allow different parties to operate. A perfect example is the plug socket, an abstraction used by all national electrical systems to allow household appliances and electronic devices to interact with the power supply through given voltage, frequency, and plug type standards.

Figure 1.1 shows the main components that form an electrical grid: an interconnected network for generating, transmitting, and delivering electricity from producers to residential consumers. As we can see, each component handles electricity in a

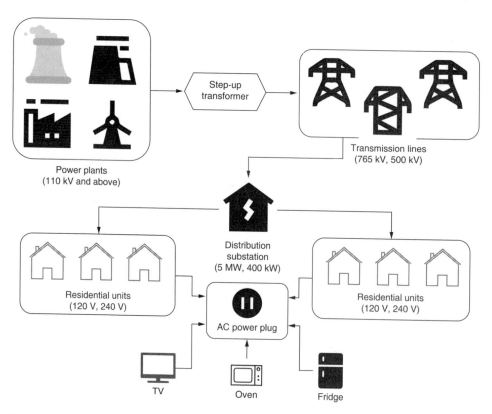

Figure 1.1 A common example of an interface: the AC power plug socket

different way and communicates with the others by using various "protocols" and "adapters" (cable lines, transformers, and so on) with the ultimate goal of bringing it to people's houses. When the residential units are connected to the grid, the electricity can be used by home appliances (TV sets, ovens, refrigerators, and so on) through a secure, protected, easy-to-use interface: the AC power plug. If we think about how these sockets work, we can easily understand how much they simplify the technical aspects of the underlying power grid. Home appliances don't have to know how such a system works as long as they can deal with the interface.

A web API is the same concept brought to the World Wide Web: an interface accessible through the web that exposes one or more plugs (the endpoints), which other parties (the clients) can use to interact with the power supply (the data) by using common communication protocols (HTTP) and standards (JSON/XML formats).

NOTE Throughout this book, the term *web API* will be used interchangeably to mean both the interface and the actual web application.

1.1.1 Overview

Figure 1.2 illustrates the purpose of a web API within a typical *service-oriented architecture* (SOA) environment. SOA is an architectural style built around the separation of responsibility of various independent services that communicate over a network.

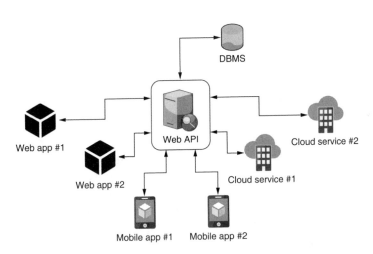

Figure 1.2   The role of a web API in a typical SOA-based environment

As we can see, the web API plays a key role because it is responsible for retrieving the data from the underlying database management system (DBMS) and making it available to the services:

- *Web app 1* (such as a React informative website), which fetches data from the web API to display it to end users through HTML pages and components

- *Mobile app 1* (such as an Android app) and *mobile app 2* (which can be the iOS port of the same app), which also fetches data and show them to end users through their native user interfaces (UIs)
- *Web app 2* (such as a PHP management website), which accesses the web API to allow administrators to interact with and possibly modify the data
- *Cloud service 1* (such as a data warehouse), which periodically pulls data from the web API to feed its internal repository (to persist some access logs, for example)
- *Cloud service 2* (such as machine learning software), which periodically retrieves some test data from the web API and uses it to perform predictions and provide useful insights

What we've just described is an interesting scenario that can help us understand the role of a web API within a rather common service-based ecosystem. But we're still discussing an impersonal, theoretical approach. Let's see how we can adapt the same architecture to a specific real-world scenario.

1.1.2 *Real-world example*

In this section, we instantiate the abstract concept depicted in figure 1.1 into a concrete, credible, and realistic scenario. Everyone knows what a board game is, right? We're talking about tabletop games with dice, cards, playing pieces, and stuff like that. Suppose that we work in the IT department of a board-gaming club. The club has a database of board games that includes gaming info such as Name, Publication Year, Min-Max players, Play Time, Minimum Age, Complexity, and Mechanics, as well as some ranking stats (number of ratings and average rating) given by club members, guests, and other players over time. Let's also assume that the club wants to use this database to feed some web-based services and applications, such as the following:

- *An end-user website*—Accessible to everyone, to showcase the board games and their ratings, as well as provide some additional features to registered users (such as the ability to create lists)
- *A mobile app*—Also publicly accessible, with the same features as the website and an optimized UI/UX (user experience) interface for smartphones and tablets
- *A management portal*—Available to a restricted list of authorized users, that allows those users to perform Create, Read, Update, and Delete (CRUD) operations in the database and carry out other administration-based tasks
- *A data analysis service*—Hosted on a third-party platform

As we can easily guess, a great way to fulfill such requirements would be to implement a dedicated web API. This approach allows us to feed all these services without exposing the database server—and its underlying data model—to any of them. Figure 1.3 shows the architecture.

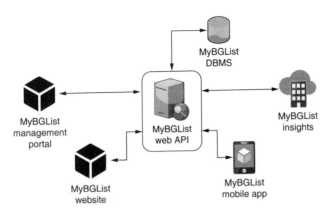

Figure 1.3   Several board-game-related web applications and services fed by a single `MyBGList` web API

Again, the web API is the playmaker, fetching the data source containing all the relevant data (`MyBGList` DBMS) and making it available to the other services:

- `MyBGList` *website*—A ReactJS website entirely hosted on a content-delivery network (following the Jamstack approach) where users can browse the board-game catalog and add games to a set of predefined lists (Own, Want to Try, Want to Buy, and so on), as well as add their own custom lists
- `MyBGList` *mobile app*—A React Native app available for Android and iOS that allows users to perform the same actions that are available on the `MyBGList` website (browse and add to lists)
- `MyBGList` *management portal*—An ASP.NET web application hosted on a dedicated virtual machine (VM) server within a secure private cloud that system administrators can access to add, update, and delete board games, as well as perform maintenance-based tasks
- `MyBGList` *insights*—A Software as a Service (SaaS) service that periodically pulls data from the web API to feed its internal repository and to perform logging, monitoring, performance analysis, and business intelligence tasks

This web API is the one we'll be working with throughout the following chapters.

What is Jamstack?

Jamstack (JavaScript, API, and Markup) is a modern architecture pattern based on prerendering the website as static HTML pages and loading the content using JavaScript and web APIs. For further information regarding the Jamstack approach, see https://jamstack.org. For a comprehensive guide to developing standards-based static websites using the Jamstack approach, check out *The Jamstack Book: Beyond Static Sites with JavaScript, APIs, and Markup*, by Raymond Camden and Brian Rinaldi (https://www.manning.com/books/the-jamstack-book).

1.1.3   *Types of web APIs*

Now that we know the general picture, we can spend some time exploring the various architectures and messaging protocols available to web API developers nowadays. As we'll be able to see, each type has characteristics, pros, and cons that make it suitable for different applications and businesses.

> **What you won't find in this book**
>
> For reasons of space, I've intentionally restricted this book's topics to HTTP web APIs, skipping other Application-layer protocols such as Advanced Message Queuing Protocol (AMQP). If you're interested in knowing more about message-based applications through AMQP, I suggest reading *RabbitMQ in Depth*, by Gavin M. Roy (https://www.manning.com/books/rabbitmq-in-depth).

Before looking at the various architectures, let's briefly summarize the four main scopes of use in which each web API commonly falls:

- *Public APIs*—Public APIs are also called *open APIs* (not to be confused with the OpenAPI specification). As the name suggests, this term refers to APIs that are meant to be available for use by any third party, often without access limitations. These APIs typically involve no authentication and authorization (if they're free to use), or they employ a key or token authentication mechanism if they need to identify the caller for various reasons (such as applying per-call costs). Furthermore, because their endpoints are usually accessible from the World Wide Web, public APIs often use various throttling, queueing, and security techniques to avoid being crippled by a massive number of simultaneous requests, as well as denial of service (DoS) attacks.

- *Partner APIs*—The APIs that fall into this category are meant to be available only to specifically selected and authorized partners, such as external developers, system integrator companies, whitelisted external internet protocols (IPs), and the like. Partner APIs are used mostly to facilitate business-to-business (B2B) activities. An example would be an e-commerce website that wants to share its customer data with a third-party business partner that needs to feed its own customer relationship management (CRM) and marketing automation systems. These APIs typically implement strong authentication mechanisms and IP restriction techniques to prevent them from being accessed by unauthorized users; they're definitely not meant to be consumed by end users or "public" clients such as standard websites.

- *Internal APIs*—Also known as *private APIs*, these APIs are meant for internal use only, such as to connect different services owned by the same organization, and are often hosted within the same virtual private network, web farm, or private cloud. An internal API, for example, can be used by the internal enterprise resource planning software to retrieve data from various internal business sources (payroll, asset management, project management, procurement, and so on), as well as create high-level reports and data visualizations. Because these APIs are not exposed to the outside, they often implement mild authentication techniques, depending on the organization's internal security model and its performance and load-balancing tweaks.

- *Composite APIs*—Sometimes referred to as *API gateways*, these APIs combine multiple APIs to execute a sequence of related or interdependent operations with a single call. In a nutshell, they allow developers to access several endpoints at the same time. Such an approach is used mostly in microservice architecture patterns, in which executing a complex task can require the completion of a chain of subtasks handled by several services in a synchronous or asynchronous way. A composite API acts mostly as an API orchestrator, ensuring that the various subtasks required to perform the main call are successful and capable of returning a valid result (or invalidating the whole process if they aren't). A common use scenario ensures that multiple third-party services fulfill their respective jobs, such as when we need to delete a user record (and all its personal info) permanently in our internal database *and* in several external data sources without creating atomicity problems, such as leaving potentially sensitive data somewhere. Because the orchestrated calls can be of multiple types (public, partner, and/or internal), composite APIs often end up being hybrids, which is why they're generally considered to represent a different API type.

1.1.4 Architectures and message protocols

To fulfill its role of enabling data exchange among parties, a web API needs to define a clear, unambiguous set of rules, constraints, and formats. This book deals with the four most-used web API architectural styles and message protocols: REST, RPC, SOAP, and GraphQL. Each has distinctive characteristics, trade-offs, and supported data interchange formats that make it viable for different purposes.

REST

Representational state transfer (REST) is an architectural style specifically designed for network-based applications that use standard HTTP GET, POST, PATCH, PUT, and DELETE request methods (first defined in the now-superseded RFC 2616, https://www.w3.org/Protocols/rfc2616/rfc2616.html) to access and manipulate data. More specifically, GET is used to read data, POST to create a new resource or perform a state change, PATCH to update an existing resource, PUT to replace an existing resource with a new one (or create it if it doesn't exist), and DELETE to erase the resource permanently. This approach does not require additional conventions to allow the parties to communicate, which makes it easy to adopt and fast to implement.

REST is much more, however. Its architectural paradigm relies on six guiding constraints that, if implemented correctly, can greatly benefit several web API properties:

- *Client-server approach*—RESTful APIs should enforce the *Separation of Concerns* principle by keeping the UI and data storage concerns apart. This approach is particularly suitable for the World Wide Web, where clients (such as browsers) have a separate role from web applications and don't know anything about how they were implemented. It's important to understand that separating these concerns not only improves their *portability*, but also keeps them simpler to implement and maintain, thus improving the *simplicity, scalability,* and *modifiability* of the whole system.

- *Statelessness*—The server should handle all communications between clients without keeping, storing, or retaining data from previous calls (such as session info). Also, the client should include any context-related info, such as authentication keys, in each call. This approach reduces the overhead of each request on the server, which can significantly improve the *performance* and *scalability* properties of the web API, especially under heavy load.

- *Cacheability*—The data exchanged between the client and the server should use the caching capabilities provided by the HTTP protocol. More specifically, all HTTP responses must contain the appropriate caching (or noncaching) info within their headers to optimize client workload while preventing them from serving stale or outdated content by mistake. A good caching strategy can have a huge affect on the *scalability* and *performance* properties of most web APIs.

- *Layered system*—Putting the server behind one or more intermediary HTTP services or filters—such as forwarders, reverse proxies, and load balancers—can greatly improve the overall security aspects of a web API, as well as its *performance* and *scalability* properties.

- *Code on demand (COD)*—COD is the only optional REST constraint. It allows the server to provide executable code or scripts that clients can use to adopt custom behavior. Examples of COD include distributed computing and remote evaluation techniques, in which the server delegates part of its job to clients or needs them to perform certain checks locally by using complex or custom tasks, such as verifying whether some applications or drivers are installed. In a broader sense, such a constraint also refers to the capability—rare in the early days of REST yet common in most recent JavaScript-powered web apps—to fetch from the server the source code required to build and load the application, as well as problem further REST calls. COD can improve the performance and scalability of a web API, but at the same time, it reduces overall visibility and poses nontrivial security risks, which is why it is flagged as optional.

- *Uniform interface*—The last REST constraint is the most important one. It defines the four fundamental features that a RESTful interface must have to enable clients to communicate with the server without the server knowing anything about how they work, keeping them decoupled from the underlying implementation of the web API. These features are

  – *Identification of resources*—Each resource must be univocally identified through its dedicated, unique universal resource identifier (URI). The URI `https:// mybglist.com/api/games/11`, for example, identifies a single board game.

- *Manipulation of resources through representations*—Clients must be able to perform basic operations on resources by using the resource URI and the corresponding HTTP method, without the need for additional info. To read board game 11's data, for example, a client should make a `GET` request to `https://mybglist.com/api/games/11`. If the client wants to delete that data, it should make a `DELETE` request to that same URI, and so on.
- *Self-descriptive messages*—Each sender's message must include all the information the recipient requires to understand and process it properly. This requirement is valid for the client and server and is quite easy to implement by means of the HTTP protocol. Both requests and responses are designed to include a set of HTTP headers that describe the protocol version, method, content type, default language, and other relevant metadata. The web API and connecting clients need only ensure that the headers are set properly.
- *HATEOAS (Hypermedia as the Engine of Application State)*—The server should provide useful information to clients, but only through hyperlinks and URIs (or URI templates). This requirement decouples the server from its clients because clients require little to no knowledge of how to interact with the server beyond a generic understanding of hypermedia. Furthermore, server functionality can evolve independently without creating backward-compatibility problems.

A web API that implements all these constraints can be described as *RESTful*.

Introducing Roy Fielding, the undisputed father of REST
The six REST constraints are described by Roy Fielding, one of the principal authors of the HTTP specification and widely considered to be the father of REST, in his dissertation *Architectural Styles and the Design of Network-based Software Architectures*, which earned him a doctorate in computer science in 2000. The original text of Fielding's dissertation is available in the University of California publications archive at http://mng.bz/19ln.

The widely accepted rules and guidelines, the proven reliability of the HTTP protocol, and the overall simplicity of implementation and development make REST the most popular web API architecture used nowadays. For that reason, most of the web API projects we'll develop throughout this book use the REST architectural style and follow the RESTful approach with the six constraints introduced in this section.

SOAP

Simple Object Access Protocol (SOAP) is a messaging protocol specification for exchanging structured information across networks by means of Extensible Markup Language (XML). Most SOAP web services are implemented by using HTTP for message negotiation and transmission, but other Application-layer protocols, such as Simple Mail Transfer Protocol (SMTP), can be used as well.

The SOAP specification was released by Microsoft in September 1999, but it didn't become a web standard until June 24, 2003, when it finally achieved W3C Recommendation status (SOAP v1.2, https://www.w3.org/TR/soap12). The accepted specification defines the SOAP messaging framework, consisting of the following:

- *SOAP Processing Model*—Which defines the rules for processing a SOAP message
- *SOAP Extensibility Model*—Which introduces SOAP features and SOAP modules
- *SOAP Underlying Protocol binding framework*—Which describes the rules for creating bindings with an underlying protocol that can be used for exchanging SOAP messages between SOAP nodes

The main advantage of SOAP is its extensibility model, which allows developers to expand the base protocol with other official message-level standards—WS-Policy, WS-Security, WS-Federation, and the like—to perform specific tasks, as well as create their own extensions. The resulting web service can be documented in Web Services Description Language (WSDL), an XML file that describes the operations and messages supported by the various endpoints.

This approach is also a flaw, however, because the XML used to make requests and receive responses can become extremely complex and difficult to read, understand, and maintain. This problem has been mitigated over the years by many development frameworks and IDEs, including ASP.NET and Visual Studio, which started to provide shortcuts and abstractions to ease the development experience and generate the required XML code automatically. Even so, the protocol has several disadvantages compared with REST:

- *Fewer data formats*—SOAP supports only XML, whereas REST supports a greater variety of formats, including JavaScript Object Notation (JSON), which offers faster parsing and is definitely easier to work with, and comma-separated values (CSV), a great JSON alternative for huge data sets in which bandwidth optimization is a major concern.
- *Worse client support*—Both modern browsers and frontend frameworks have been optimized to consume REST web services, which typically provide better compatibility.
- *Performance and caching problems*—SOAP messages are typically sent via HTTP POST requests. Because the HTTP POST method is nonidempotent, it's not cached at the HTTP level, which makes its requests much harder to cache than those of RESTful counterparts.
- *Slower and harder to implement*—A SOAP web service is generally harder to develop, especially if it must be integrated with an existing website or service. Conversely, REST typically can be implemented as a drop-in functionality of the existing code without the need to refactor the whole client-server infrastructure.

For all these reasons, the general consensus today when it comes to the REST-versus-SOAP debate is that REST web APIs are the preferred way to go unless there are specific reasons to use SOAP. These reasons might include hardware, software, or infrastructure limitations, as well as requirements of existing implementations, which is why we won't be using SOAP within this book.

GraphQL

The supremacy of REST was questioned in 2015 with the public release of GraphQL, an open source data query and manipulation language for APIs developed by Facebook. The main differences between the two approaches are related not to the architectural styles, but to their different ways of sending and retrieving data.

As a matter of fact, GraphQL follows most of the RESTful constraints, relies on the same Application-layer protocol (HTTP), and adopts the same data format (JSON). But instead of using different endpoints to fetch different data objects, it allows the client to perform dynamic queries and ask for the concrete data requirements of a single endpoint.

I'll try to explain this concept with an actual example taken from the board-game web API scenario. Suppose that we want to retrieve the names and unique IDs of all the users who gave positive feedback on the Citadels board game. When we're dealing with typical REST APIs, fulfilling such a task would require the following operations:

1 *A web API request to the full-text search endpoint*—To retrieve a list of board games with a name equal to `"Citadels"`. To keep things simple, let's assume that such a call returns a single result, allowing us to get our target board game's info, including its unique ID, which is what we're looking for.

2 *Another web API request to the feedback endpoint*—To retrieve all the feedback received from that user's unique ID. Again, let's assume that the feedback ranges from 1 ("worst gaming experience I've ever had") to 10 ("best game ever").

3 *A client-side iteration* (such as a `foreach` loop)—To cycle through all the retrieved feedback and retrieve the user ID of those with a rating equal to or greater than 6.

4 *A third web API request to the user endpoint*—To retrieve the users who correspond to those unique IDs.

The complete request/response cycle is represented graphically in figure 1.4.

That plan is feasible, yet it undeniably involves a huge amount of work. Specifically, we would have to perform multiple round-trips (three HTTP requests) and a lot of over-fetching—the Citadels game info, the data of all feedback, and the data of all users who gave a positive rating—to get some names. The only workaround would be to implement additional API endpoints to return what we need or to ease some of the intermediate work. We could add an endpoint to fetch the positive feedback for a given board game ID or maybe even for a given board game name, including the full-text query in the underlying implementation. If we're up for it, we could even implement a dedicated endpoint, such as `api/positiveFeedbacksByName`, to perform the whole task.

This approach, however, would undeniably affect backend development time and add complexity to our API, and wouldn't be versatile enough to help in similar,

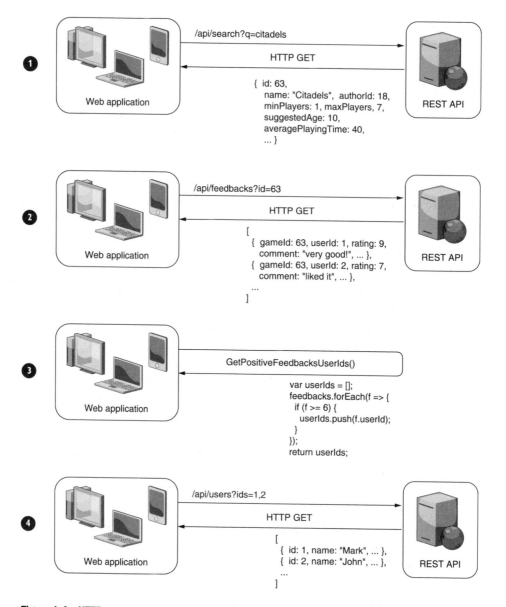

Figure 1.4 HTTP request-response cycle in REST

nonidentical cases. What if we want to retrieve negative feedback instead or positive feedback for multiple games or for all the games created by a given author? As we can easily understand, overcoming such problems may not be simple, especially if we need a high level of versatility in terms of client-side data fetching requirements.

Now let's see what happens with GraphQL. When we take this approach, instead of thinking in terms of existing (or additional) endpoints, we focus on the query we need to send to the server to request what we need, as we do with a DBMS. When we're done, we send that query to the (single) GraphQL endpoint and get back precisely the data we asked for, within a single HTTP call and without fetching any field we don't need. Figure 1.5 shows a GraphQL client-to-server round trip.

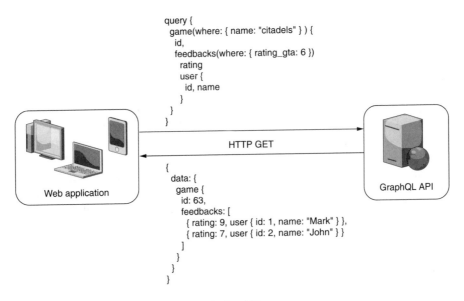

Figure 1.5   HTTP request-response cycle in GraphQL

As we can see, the performance optimizations aren't limited to the web API. The GraphQL approach doesn't require client-side iteration, because the server already returns the precise result we're looking for.

The GraphQL specification is available at https://spec.graphql.org. I talk extensively about GraphQL in chapter 10, showing you how to use it alongside REST to achieve specific query-oriented goals.

1.2 ASP.NET Core

Now that we've seen what web APIs are and how we can use them to exchange data within web applications and services across a network, it's time to introduce the framework that we'll use to create them throughout this book. That framework is *ASP.NET Core,* a high-performance, cross-platform, open source web development framework introduced by Microsoft in 2016 as the successor to ASP.NET.

In the following sections, I briefly cover its most distinctive aspects: the overall architecture, the request/response pipeline management, the asynchronous programming pattern, the routing system, and so on.

> **NOTE** In this book, we're going to use .NET 6.0 and the ASP.NET Core Runtime 6.0.11, the latest generally available version at this writing and the ninth

installment released so far, following .NET Core 1.0, 1.1, 2.0, 2.1, 2.2, 3.0, 3.1, and .NET 5.0. Each version introduced several updates, improvements, and additional features, but for the sake of simplicity, I'll review the resulting characteristics shipped with the latest version. Furthermore, starting with .NET 5, all even-numbered .NET releases, including .NET 6, are granted with long-term support (LTS) status, meaning that they'll be supported for many years to come, as opposed to odd-numbered versions, which have shorter time frames. Currently, the support period is three years for even-numbered versions and 18 months for odd-numbered versions (http://mng.bz/JVpa).

1.2.1   *Architecture*

I've chosen to use ASP.NET Core for our web API projects because the new Microsoft Framework enforces several modern architectural principles and best practices that allow us to build lightweight, highly modular apps with a high level of testability and maintainability of the source code. Such an approach naturally guides developers to build (or adopt) applications composed of discrete and reusable components that perform specific tasks and communicate through a series of interfaces made available by the framework. These components are called *services* and *middleware,* and they're registered and configured in the web application's `Program.cs` file, which is the app's entry point.

> **NOTE**   If you're coming from an older ASP.NET Core version, such as 3.1 or 5.0, you may wonder what happened to the `Startup` class (and its corresponding `Startup.cs` file), which used to contain the services and middleware configuration settings. This class was removed from the minimal hosting model introduced with .NET 6, which merged the `Program` and `Startup` classes into a single `Program.cs` file.

SERVICES

Services are components that an application requires to provide its functionalities. We can think of them as app *dependencies*, because our app depends on their availability to work as expected. I use the term *dependencies* here for a reason: ASP.NET Core supports the Dependency Injection (DI) software design pattern, an architectural technique that allows us to achieve inversion of control between a class and its dependencies. Here's how the whole services implementation, registration/configuration, and injection process works in ASP.NET Core:

- *Implementation*—Each service is implemented by means of a dedicated interface (or base class) to abstract the implementation. Both the interface and the implementation can be provided by the framework, created by the developer, or acquired from a third party (GitHub, NuGet packages, and the like).
- *Registration and configuration*—All services used by the app are configured and registered (using their interfaces) in the built-in `IServiceProvider` class, which is a service container. The actual registration and configuration process happens within the `Program.cs` file, where the developer can also choose a suitable lifetime (`Transient`, `Scoped`, or `Singleton`).

- *Dependency injection*—Each service can be injected into the constructor of the class where it's meant to be used. The framework, through the `IServiceProvider` container class, automatically makes available an instance of the dependency, creating a new one or possibly reusing an existing one, depending on the configured service's lifetime, as well as disposing of it when it's no longer needed.

Typical examples of service interfaces provided by the framework include `IAuthorizationService`, which can be used to implement policy-based permissions, and `IEmailService`, which can be used to send email messages.

MIDDLEWARE

Middleware is a set of components that operates at the HTTP level and can be used to handle the whole HTTP request processing pipeline. If you remember the `HttpModules` and `HttpHandlers` used by ASP.NET before the advent of ASP.NET Core, you can easily see how middleware plays a similar role and performs the same tasks. Typical examples of middleware used in ASP.NET Core web applications include `Https-RedirectionMiddleware`, which redirects non-HTTPS requests to an HTTPS URL, and `AuthorizationMiddleware`, which use the authorization service internally to handle all authorization tasks at the HTTP level.

Each type of middleware can pass the HTTP request to the next component in the pipeline or provide an HTTP response, thus short-circuiting the pipeline itself and preventing further middleware from processing the request. This type of request-blocking middleware is called *terminal middleware* and usually is in charge of processing the main business logic tasks of the various app's endpoints.

> **WARNING** It's worth noting that middleware is processed in registration order (first in, first out). Always add terminal middleware after nonterminal middleware in the `Program.cs` file; otherwise, the file won't work.

A good example of terminal middleware is `StaticFileMiddleware`, which ultimately handles the endpoint URLs pointing to static files, as long as they are accessible. When such a condition happens, it sends the requested file to the caller with an appropriate HTTP response, thus terminating the request pipeline. The `HttpsRedirection-Middleware` that I mentioned briefly earlier is also terminal middleware, because it ultimately responds with an HTTP-to-HTTPS redirect to all non-HTTPS requests.

> **NOTE** Both `StaticFileMiddleware` and `HttpsRedirectionMiddleware` will terminate the HTTP request only when certain circumstances are met. If the requested endpoint doesn't match their activation rules (such as a URL pointing to a nonpresent static file for the former or already in HTTPS for the latter), they pass it to the next middleware present in the pipeline without taking action. For this reason, we could say that they are potentially terminal middleware to distinguish them from middleware that always ends the request pipeline when the HTTP request reaches it.

1.2.2   *Program.cs*

Now that I've introduced services and middleware, we can finally take a look at the `Program.cs` file, which is executed at the start of the application:

```
var builder = WebApplication.CreateBuilder(args);          ◁─┐  Creates the
                                                              │  WebApplicationBuilder
// Add services to the container.                             │  factory class

builder.Services.AddControllers();                        ─┐
// Learn more about configuring Swagger/OpenAPI             │  Registers and
// at https://aka.ms/aspnetcore/swashbuckle                 │  configures services
builder.Services.AddEndpointsApiExplorer();                │
builder.Services.AddSwaggerGen();                         ─┘

var app = builder.Build();                    ◁─┐  Builds the
                                                 │  WebApplication
// Configure the HTTP request pipeline.          │  object
if (app.Environment.IsDevelopment())
{
    app.UseSwagger();                        ─┐
    app.UseSwaggerUI();                       │
}                                             │  Registers and configures
                                              │  nonterminal and
app.UseHttpsRedirection();                    │  potentially terminal
                                              │  middleware
app.UseAuthorization();                      ─┘

app.MapControllers();

app.Run();          ◁─┐  Registers and configures
                       │  terminal middleware
```

By analyzing this code, we can easily see that the file is responsible for the following initialization tasks:

- Instantiating the web application
- Registering and configuring the services
- Registering and configuring the middleware

More precisely, the web application is instantiated by the `WebApplicationBuilder` factory class, creating a `WebApplication` object. This instance is stored in the app local variable, which is used to register and configure the required services and middleware.

> **NOTE** Both services and middleware are registered and configured by dedicated extension methods, a convenient way to shortcut the setup process and keep the `Program.cs` file as concise as possible. Under ASP.NET Core naming conventions, services are configured mostly by using extension methods with the `Add` prefix; middleware prefixes are `Use`, `Map`, and `Run`. The only difference that concerns us, at least for now, is that the `Run` delegate is always 100% terminal and the last one to be processed. We'll talk more about these conventions and their meaning when we experiment with Minimal APIs later.

For the sake of simplicity, I split middleware into two categories: potentially terminal and terminal. The difference should be clear at this point. Potentially terminal middleware ends the HTTP request pipeline only if it matches certain rules, whereas terminal middleware always does (so no wonder it's the last of the pile).

1.2.3 *Controllers*

In ASP.NET Core, a *controller* is a class used to group a set of *action methods* (also called *actions*) that handle similar HTTP requests. From such a perspective, we could say that controllers are containers that can be used to aggregate action methods that have something in common: routing rules and prefixes, services, instances, authorization requirements, caching strategies, HTTP-level filters, and so on. These common requirements can be defined directly on the controller class, thus avoiding the need to specify them for each action. This approach, enforced by some powerful built-in naming and coding conventions, helps to keep the code DRY and simplifies the app's architecture.

> **NOTE** *DRY* is an acronym for *Don't Repeat Yourself,* a well-known principle of software development that helps us remember to avoid redundancy, pattern repetition, and anything else that could result in a code smell. It's the opposite of *WET* (*Write Everything Twice* or *Write Every Time*).

Starting with ASP.NET Core, controllers can inherit from two built-in base classes:

- `ControllerBase`, a minimal implementation without support for views
- `Controller`, a more powerful implementation that inherits from `Controller-Base` and adds full support for views

As we can easily understand, the `Controller` base class is meant to be used in web applications that adopt the Model-View-Controller (MVC) pattern, where they're meant to return the data coming from business logic (typically handled by dependency-injected services). In a typical ASP.NET Core web application, the resulting data is returned to the client through the views, which handle the app's data Presentation layer by using client-side markup and scripting languages such as HTML, CSS, JavaScript, and the like (or server-side rendered syntaxes such as Razor). When dealing with web APIs, we generally don't use views because we want to return JSON or XML data (no HTML) directly from the `Controller`. Given such a scenario, inheriting from the `ControllerBase` base class is the recommended approach in our specific case. Here's a sample web API `Controller` that handles two types of HTTP requests:

- A `GET` request to `/api/Sample/` to receive a list of items
- A `GET` request to `/api/Sample/{id}` to receive a single item with the specified `{id}`, assuming that it's a unique integer value acting as a primary key
- A `DELETE` request to `/api/Sample/{id}` to delete the single item with the specified `{id}`

```
        [ApiController]
        [Route("api/[controller]")]                    ⟵    Default
        public class SampleController : ControllerBase       routing
        {                                                    rules
Adds        public SampleController()
API-specific    {
behaviors       }                          Action to handle
                                           HTTP GET to
            [HttpGet]           ⟵         /api/Sample/
            public string Get()
            {
                return "TODO: return all items";
            }
                                        Action to handle
            [HttpGet("{id}")]     ⟵      HTTP GET to
            public string Get(int id)     /api/Sample/{id}
            {
                return $"TODO: return the item with id #{id}";
            }
                                          Action to handle
            [HttpDelete("{id}")]   ⟵      HTTP DELETE to
            public string Delete(int id)  /api/Sample/{id}
            {
                return $"TODO: delete the item with id #{id}";
            }
        }
```

As we can see by looking at this code, we were able to fulfill our given tasks with few lines of code by taking advantage of some useful built-in conventions:

- A centralized /api/Sample/ routing prefix valid for all action methods, thanks to the [Route("api/[controller]")] attribute applied at the controller level
- Automatic routing rules for all the implemented HTTP verbs (including the required parameters) thanks to the [HttpGet] and [HttpDelete] attributes applied to the corresponding action methods
- Automatic routing mapping using the ControllerMiddleware's default rules, because we applied the Controller suffix to the class name, as long as the app.MapControllers() extension method is present in the Program.cs file

NOTE Furthermore, because we've used the [ApiController] attribute, we also need some additional conventions specific to web APIs that automatically return certain HTTP status codes, depending on the action type and result. We'll talk more about them in chapter 6, when we delve into error handling.

1.2.4   Minimal APIs

Controllers with built-in conventions are great ways to implement web API business logic with few lines of code. In ASP.NET Core 6, however, the framework introduced a minimal paradigm that allows us to build web APIs with even less ceremony. This feature is called *minimal APIs,* and despite its young age, it's getting a lot of attention from new and seasoned ASP.NET developers because it often allows for a much smaller and more readable codebase.

The best way to explain what Minimal API is about is to perform a quick code comparison between a controller-based approach and the new kid on the block. Here's how the same HTTP requests that we handled with the `SampleController` can be handled by Minimal APIs with some minor updates to the `Program.cs` file:

Adds these lines instead

```
// app.MapControllers();          ←──  Removes this line (and the
app.MapGet("/api/Sample",              SampleController class)
    () => "TODO: return all items");
app.MapGet("/api/Sample/{id}",
    (int id) => $"TODO: return the item with id #{id}");
app.MapDelete("/api/Sample/{id}",
    (int id) => $"TODO: delete the item with id #{id}");
```

As we can see, all the implementation is transferred to the `Program.cs` file without the need for a separate `Controller` class. Also, the code can be further simplified (or DRYfied), such as by adding a `prefix` variable that eliminates the need to repeat `"/api/Sample"` multiple times. The advantage is visible in terms of code readability, simplicity, and overhead reduction.

> **TIP** The business logic of any Minimal API method can be put outside the `Program.cs` file; only the `Map` methods are required to go there. As a matter of fact, moving the actual implementation to other classes is almost always good practice unless we're dealing with one-liners.

The Minimal APIs paradigm isn't likely to replace controllers, but it will definitely ease the coding experience of most small web API projects (such as microservices) and attract most developers who are looking for sleek approaches and shallow learning curves. For all these reasons, we'll often use it alongside controllers throughout this book.

1.2.5 *Task-based asynchronous pattern*

Most performance problems that affect web applications are due to the fact that a limited number of threads needs to handle a potentially unlimited volume of concurrent HTTP requests. This is especially true when, before responding to these requests, these threads must perform some resource-intensive (and often noncacheable) tasks, being blocked until they eventually receive the result. Typical examples include reading or writing data from a DBMS through SQL queries, accessing a third-party service (such as an external website or web API), and performing any other task that requires a considerable amount of execution time.

When a web application is forced to deal with a lot of these requests simultaneously, the number of available threads quickly decreases, leading to degraded response times and, eventually, to service unavailability (HTTP 503 and the like).

NOTE This scenario is the main goal of most HTTP-based denial-of-service (DoS) attacks, in which the web application is flooded by requests to make the whole server unavailable. Thread-blocking, noncached HTTP requests are goldmines for DoS attackers because they have a great chance of starving the thread pool quickly.

A general rule of thumb in dealing with resource-intensive tasks is to cache the resulting HTTP response aggressively, as stated by REST constraint 3 (cacheability). In several scenarios, however, caching is not an option, such as when we need to write into a DBMS (HTTP POST) or read mutable or highly customizable data (HTTP GET with a lot of parameters). What do we do in those cases?

The ASP.NET Core framework allows developers to deal with this problem efficiently by implementing the C# language-level asynchronous model, better known as the *Task-based Asynchronous Pattern (TAP)*. The best way to understand how TAP works is to see it in action. Take a look at the following source code:

```
[HttpGet]
public async Task<string> Get()        ⊲—┘  async
{
    return await Task.Run(() => {      ⊲—┘  await
        return "TODO: return all items";
    });
}
```

As we can see, we applied some minor updates to the first action method of the Sample-Controller that we worked with earlier to implement TAP. The new pattern relies on using the async and await keywords to handle a Task in a nonblocking way:

- The async keyword defines the methods returning a Task.
- The await keyword allows the calling thread to start the newly implemented Task *in a nonblocking way*. When the Task is completed, the thread continues the code execution, thus returning the resulting comma-separated string.

It's worth noting that because we used the await keyword inside the Get() action method, we had to mark that method async as well. That's perfectly fine; it means that the method will be awaited by the calling thread instead of blocking it, which is what we want.

Our minimal implementation won't have any benefit in terms of performance. We definitely don't need to await for something as trivial as a literal TODO string. But it should give us an idea of the benefits that the async/await pattern will bring the web application when that sample Task.Run is replaced by something that requires the server to perform some actual work, such as retrieving real data from a DBMS. I'll talk extensively about asynchronous data retrieval tasks in chapter 4, which introduces Microsoft's most popular data access technology for .NET: Entity Framework Core.

Summary

- Web APIs are HTTP-based services that any software application can use to access and possibly manipulate data.
- Web APIs are designed to work by using common communication standards (protocols), given sets of available operations (specifications), and data exchange formats (JSON, XML, and the like).
- Web APIs are commonly split among four possible scopes of use:
  - *Public* or *open*—When anyone has (or can acquire) access
  - *Partner*—When access is restricted to business associates
  - *Internal* or *private*—When access is limited to the organization's network
  - *Composite*—When they orchestrate multiple *public, partner,* and/or *internal* API calls
- To fulfill their role, web APIs require a uniform set of rules, constraints, and formats that depend on the chosen architectural style or messaging protocol. The most-used standards nowadays are REST, SOAP, gRPC, and GraphQL:
  - Each of which has distinctive characteristics, tradeoffs, and supported formats.
  - This book focuses mostly on REST, but chapter 10 is dedicated to GraphQL.
- ASP.NET Core is the high-performance, cross-platform, open source web development framework that we will use to design and develop web APIs throughout this book:
  - ASP.NET Core's modern architectural principles allow developers to build lightweight, highly modular apps with a great level of testability and maintainability.
- ASP.NET Core architecture allows developers to customize the app's capabilities and workloads by using discrete and reusable components to perform specific tasks. These components fall into two main categories, both of which are registered and configured in the app's entry point (the `Program.cs` file):
  - *Services*—Required to provide functionalities and instantiated through dependency injection
  - *Middleware*—Responsible for handling the HTTP request pipeline
- ASP.NET Core supports two paradigms for building web APIs: controllers, which offer great versatility and a full set of supported features, and minimal APIs, a simplified approach that allows us to write less code while reducing overhead:
  - The minimal API approach, introduced in .NET 6, can be a great way to build simple web APIs in a time-efficient fashion and is great for developers who are looking for a sleek, modern programming approach.
- ASP.NET Core web apps can overcome most performance problems due to resource-intensive, thread-blocking calls by using TAP, an asynchronous programming model that allows the main thread to start tasks in a nonblocking way and resume execution upon their completion.

Our first web API project

In this chapter, we'll create the MyBGList web API, the cornerstone of the service-oriented architecture concrete scenario that we introduced in chapter 1. More specifically, we'll put on the shoes of the software development team in charge of creating and setting up the project. We'll have to make some high-level decisions, such as choosing the integrated development environment (IDE) to adopt and then switch to a more practical approach, such as getting our hands on the source code for the first time, as well as debugging and testing it to ensure that it works as expected.

By the end of the chapter, you'll be able to test your knowledge by solving some wrap-up exercises on the topics and concepts covered. The main goal is to create a working ASP.NET web API project, which you'll expand and improve in the following chapters.

2.1 System requirements

Because we've already chosen to develop our web API with ASP.NET Core, it could be useful to recap the system requirements—what we need to install to start our development journey.

2.1.1 .NET SDK

The most important tool to obtain is the .NET software development kit (better known as .NET SDK), which contains the .NET command-line interface (.NET CLI), the .NET libraries, and the three available runtimes:

- ASP.NET Core runtime, required to run ASP.NET Core apps
- Desktop runtime, required to run WPF and Windows Forms apps
- .NET runtime, which hosts a set of low-level libraries and interfaces required by the preceding two runtimes

NOTE The .NET SDK is available as a standalone package for Windows, Linux, and macOS at the following URL: https://dotnet.microsoft.com/download.

2.1.2 Integrated development environment

From a strict point of view, installing the .NET SDK is all we need to do to start building any kind of .NET app, including our ASP.NET Core web API. But writing source code using the built-in tools available in Windows, Linux, or macOS—such as the default text editor and the command-line terminal—is far from ideal. The days when an experienced developer could proudly say that they could do anything by using Notepad, Emacs, or vim are long gone. As a matter of fact, modern IDEs are packed with a ton of useful features that will undeniably boost the productivity of any software developer who's willing to learn how to take advantage of them productively. I'm not talking only about syntax highlighting, code completion, and other "cosmetic" features. What makes modern IDEs great is their ability to provide tools and extensions that allow the development team to standardize and automate some processes, thus favoring a DevOps-oriented approach: task runners, package managers, code inspectors, integrated source control, automatic deployment system, secure credentials storage, syntax highlighting, and much more.

For all these reasons, because we want to put ourselves in the shoes of the MyBG-List software development team, we're going to build our web API using an IDE (or a code editor with advanced features). Microsoft provides two alternatives:

- *Visual Studio*—Visual Studio is a comprehensive .NET development solution for Windows and macOS that includes compilers, code completion tools, graphical designers, and a lot of useful features to enhance the software development experience and productivity.

- *Visual Studio Code*—Visual Studio Code is a lightweight open source code editor for Windows, Linux, and macOS. Unlike Visual Studio, which focuses strongly on .NET development, this product embraces a framework-neutral, language-agnostic approach. But it provides a rich ecosystem of extensions to add support for most development frameworks and programming languages, including ASP.NET Core and C#.

> **NOTE** A lot of non-Microsoft alternatives are worth mentioning, such as Rider by JetBrains and Brackets by Adobe. For the sake of simplicity, however, we'll restrict our analysis to the Microsoft development tools.

Both Visual Studio and Visual Studio Code are viable for creating, configuring, and maintaining an ASP.NET web API project. Because we want to explore the .NET and ASP.NET Core frameworks to their full extent while we work on our task, however, we're going to choose Visual Studio. Specifically, we'll be using Visual Studio 2022, which is the latest version available at the time of this writing.

> **NOTE** If you want to use Visual Studio Code or another editor, don't worry. All the code samples in this book, as well as all the content available in the GitHub repository, will work in those editors too.

2.2   *Installing Visual Studio*

Visual Studio 2022 is available in three editions, each with a specific set of supported features:

- Community Edition has all the required features to create, develop, debug, test, and publish all kinds of .NET apps. This edition is free to use, but it can be used only for open source projects, academic research, and classroom learning, as well as by nonenterprise organizations with no more than five developers.
- Professional Edition has all the features of Community Edition and has less restrictive paid licensing.
- Enterprise Edition has all the features of the other two editions, plus some advanced architectural-level design, validation, analysis, and testing tools.

> **NOTE** For the purposes of this book, you're entitled to download and install Community Edition at the following URL: https://visualstudio.microsoft.com.

The Visual Studio installation process is divided into three phases:

1 Download and install the Visual Studio Installer, which acts as an installation and update-management tool for the whole Visual Studio family.
2 Choose the workloads, individual components, and language packs. Each workload contains a group of components required for the framework, programming language, and platform we want to use. In our scenario, because we want

to develop an ASP.NET Core web API, we need to install only the ASP.NET and web development workload (see figure 2.1) without additional individual components—at least for the time being. The language pack depends on how we want to set the language used by the graphical user interface (GUI).

3   Install Visual Studio 2022, along with the selected workloads, components, and language packs.

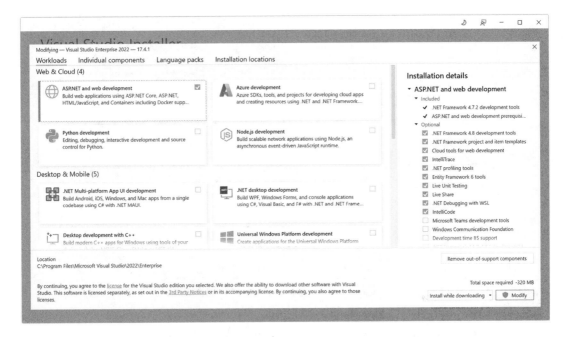

Figure 2.1   Adding the ASP.NET and web development workload to the Visual Studio installation

NOTE   If you're reading this book for the first time, installing the English language pack might be a good choice so that the IDE commands always match the samples and screenshots.

2.3   *Creating the web API project*

When we have the .NET SDK and Visual Studio 2022 installed on our system, we can start creating our first web API project. Perform the following steps:

1   Launch Visual Studio 2022.
2   Select the Create a New Project option.
3   Use the search box to find the ASP.NET Core web API project template, as shown in figure 2.2.

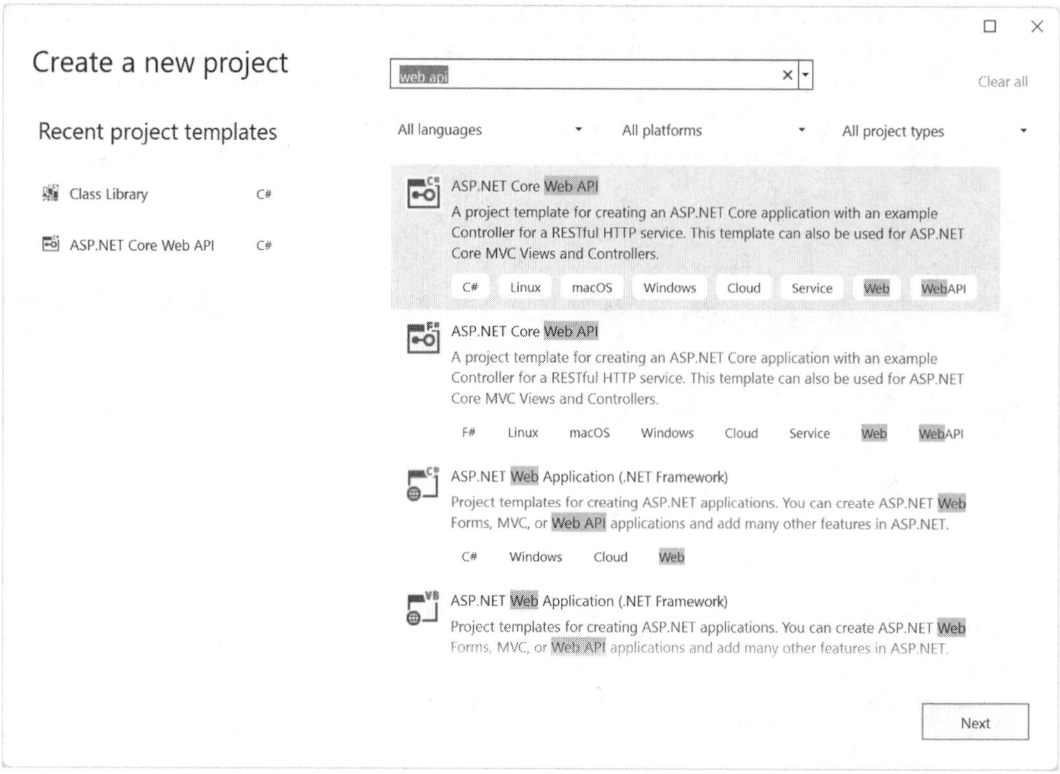

Figure 2.2   Finding the ASP.NET Core web API project template in Visual Studio

Configuring the template is rather easy. We give our project a name—MyBGList, in our scenario—and accept the other default settings, as shown in figure 2.3. Be sure to select the .NET 6.0 framework, which is the latest version available at the time of this writing.

> **WARNING**   If you want to use a different .NET version, you're free to do that. Keep in mind, however, that some of the source code samples in this book might require some changes to work with framework updates and/or breaking changes.

As soon as you click the Create button, Visual Studio generates the source code for our new MyBGList project, adds it to a solution with the same name, and opens it in the IDE. We're all set!

Before continuing, let's quickly check that everything works. Press the F5 key (or click the Run button in the topmost toolbar) to launch the project in Debug mode. If we did everything correctly, Visual Studio should start our default browser automatically, pointing to https://localhost:<someRandomPort> and showing the page displayed in figure 2.4.

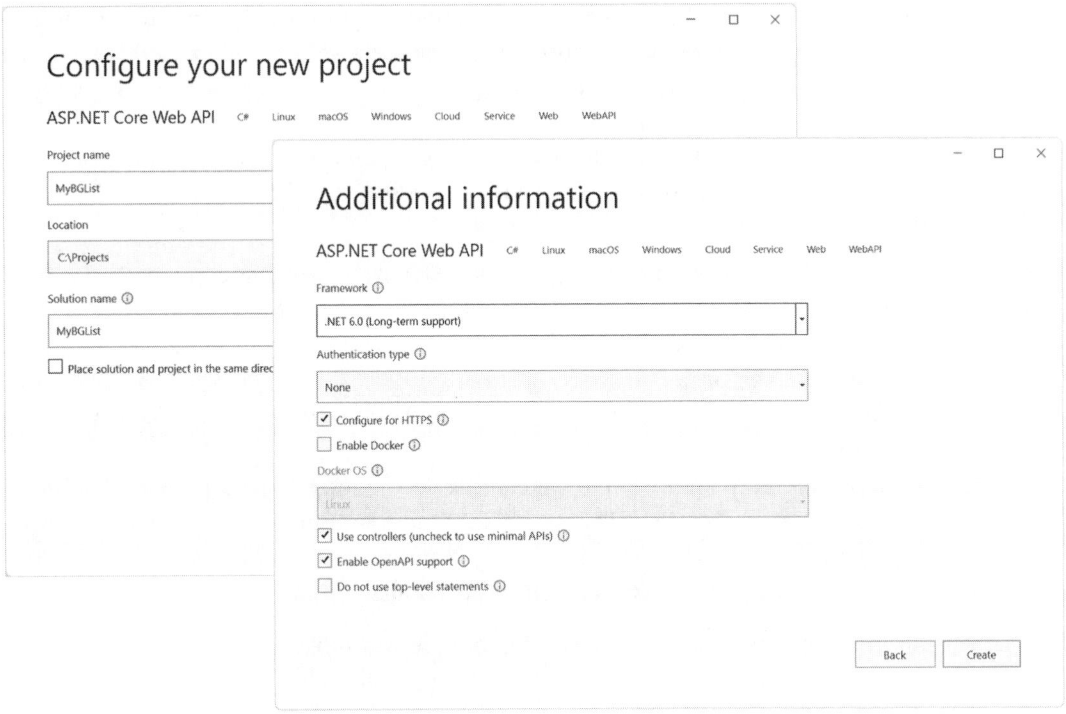

Figure 2.3   Configuring the ASP.NET Core web API project

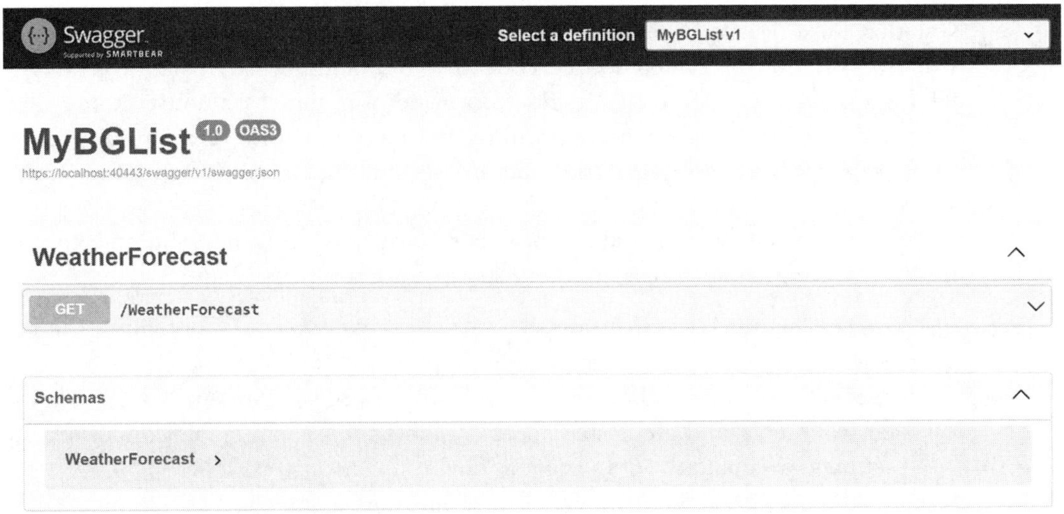

Figure 2.4   MyBGList project first run

As we can see, the Visual Studio web API template that we used to create our project provides a neat start page that mentions Swagger, a convenient tool that describes the structure of our API. I'll introduce Swagger later in this chapter. Now we're ready to take a better look at our project.

Before we start coding, it might be worth discussing projects and solutions and the roles they're meant to play within the Visual Studio ecosystem. In a nutshell, we can say that

- A *project* is a group of source-code files that are typically compiled into an executable, library, or website together with some (required) configuration files and a bunch of (optional) content files such as icons, images, and data files. The MyBGList project includes a small set of .cs and .json files generated by Visual Studio to create our ASP.NET web API, using the configuration settings that we choose.
- A *solution* is a container that we can use to organize one or more related projects. When we open a solution, Visual Studio automatically opens all the projects that the solution contains. In our scenario, the solution contains only our MyBGList web API project and shares its name.

In the following chapters, we'll add other projects to our solution. Specifically, we'll create some class libraries that we'll want to keep separate from the web API project so we can use them elsewhere. Such an approach increases the reusability of our code while granting us the chance to keep our projects logically grouped and accessible within the same IDE window.

2.4   *MyBGList project overview*

Now that we've learned the basics of Visual Studio, let's spend some valuable time reviewing the autogenerated source code of our brand-new web API project. The default ASP.NET Core web API template provides a minimal yet convenient boilerplate that can be useful for understanding the basic structure of a typical project, which is precisely what we need to do before we start coding our board-game-related web API.

Let's start by taking a look at the project's file structure. In the Solution Explorer window, we see that our project contains some important files:

- launchSettings.json (inside the /Properties/ folder)—Containing the settings for launching the project in development mode
- appsettings.json—Containing the app's configuration settings for all the environments, and the nested appsettings.Development.json, containing the settings specific to the development environment only
- Program.cs—The bootstrap class introduced in chapter 1
- WeatherForecastController.cs—A sample controller showing how to serve some dummy weather-forecast data

- WeatherForecast.cs—A minimal data-transfer object (DTO) class that the controller uses to serve the sample weather forecast JavaScript Object Notation (JSON) data, using a strongly typed approach

In the following section, we'll briefly review all these files to understand their purposes and the roles they play within the boilerplate. While we perform code review, we'll also make some small yet significant updates of some of the default behaviors to better suit our needs. Eventually, we'll replace the boilerplate files related to weather forecasts with our own board-game-themed classes.

2.4.1 Reviewing launchSettings.json

The first file to look at is launchSettings.json, located in the /Properties/ folder. As the name suggests, this file contains some configuration settings related to how our project should be launched. It's important to understand, however, that this file—along with all the settings included—will be used only within the local development machine. In other words, it won't be deployed with our app when we publish our project on a production server. As we can see by opening it, the configuration settings are split into three main sections (or JSON keys):

- "$schema"—Pointing to a URL that describes the schema used by the file
- "iisSettings"—Containing some base configuration settings for the IIS Express web server
- "profiles"—Which is split into two subsections:
  - "IIS Express"—Containing other settings for the IIS Express web server
  - "MyBGList"—Containing settings specific to the Kestrel web server

If you don't know what IIS Express and Kestrel are, let's quickly recap the backstory. ASP.NET Core provides built-in support for two web servers that can be used for local development purposes:

- IIS Express—A lightweight version of the Internet Information Services (IIS) Web Server, available since Windows XP and Visual Studio 2012
- Kestrel—An open source, cross-platform, event-driven, asynchronous HTTP server implementation, introduced with the first version of ASP.NET Core

NOTE In Visual Studio 2010 and earlier, the default web server for development purposes was the ASP.NET Development Server, better known as Cassini.

We can choose the web server to use when running our app in Visual Studio by clicking the arrow handler to the right of the Start button. This handler is the button with the green arrow on the Visual Studio top-level toolbar, as shown in figure 2.5.

The option with the app's name—MyBGList in our scenario—corresponds to Kestrel. As we can see, we can also choose the web browser to use, as well as some other options that we can skip for now.

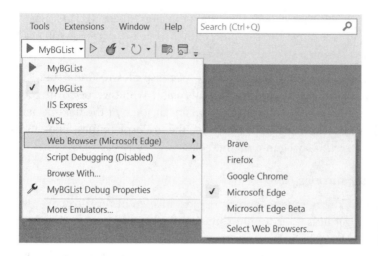

Figure 2.5   The Visual Studio Start button

The `iisSettings` and `profiles` sections of the `launchSettings.json` file contain the configuration settings for IIS Express and Kestrel. For each server, we can choose the HTTP and HTTPS port to use, the launch URL, the environment variables to set before launching the app, and so on.

As figure 2.5 shows, if we click the Start button (or choose Debug > Start Debugging or press F5) now, we'll see the SwaggerUI page, which handles the `swagger` endpoint, configured in the `launchUrl` option for both browsers. Notice that the SwaggerUI page shown in figure 2.4 appears regardless of the web server we choose because the browsers have been configured to use that endpoint. The only things that visibly change are the local TCP ports used to establish the HTTPS connection because Visual Studio randomly determines them when creating the project. Let's take the chance to normalize those ports.

> **NOTE**   We'll use the SwaggerUI page and its contents extensively in later chapters while implementing our sample web API. Also, chapter 11 discusses Swagger in depth.

Open the `launchSettings.json` file, and change its contents as shown in the following listing. The updated lines and values are boldfaced.

Listing 2.1   Modified `launchSettings.json` file

```
{
  "$schema": "https://json.schemastore.org/launchsettings.json",
  "iisSettings": {
    "windowsAuthentication": false,
    "anonymousAuthentication": true,
    "iisExpress": {
      "applicationUrl": "http://localhost:40080",
      "sslPort": 40443
    }
```

IIS Express local URLs and TCP ports to use for HTTP and HTTPS

```
    },
    "profiles": {
      "MyBGList": {
        "commandName": "Project",
        "dotnetRunMessages": true,
        "launchBrowser": true,
        "launchUrl": "swagger",
        "applicationUrl": "https://localhost:40443;http://localhost:40080",
        "environmentVariables": {
          "ASPNETCORE_ENVIRONMENT": "Development"
        }
      },
      "IIS Express": {
        "commandName": "IISExpress",
        "launchBrowser": true,
        "launchUrl": "swagger",
        "environmentVariables": {
          "ASPNETCORE_ENVIRONMENT": "Development"
        }
      }
    }
  }
}
```

Kestrel local URLs and TCP ports to use for HTTP and HTTPS

Kestrel starting page

Kestrel environment variables

IIS Express environment variables

IIS Express starting page

As we can see, we've set the 40080 (HTTP) and 40443 (HTTPS) TCP ports for both IIS Express and Kestrel. This simple tweak ensures that the URLs referenced in this book will work properly within our local codebase, regardless of the web server we want to use.

The rest of the settings specified in the built-in launchSettings.json file are good enough for the time being, so we can leave them as they are. Before closing the file, however, let's take a good look at the "environmentVariables" sections, which contain a single ASPNETCORE_ENVIRONMENT environment variable for both IIS Express and Kestrel.

2.4.2 Configuring the appsettings.json

Let's move to the appsettings.json files, which store the application configuration settings in JSON key-value pairs. If we look at the autogenerated code of our MyBGList web API project, we can see that Visual Studio created two instances of the file:

- appsettings.json
- appsettings.Development.json

Before seeing how these files are meant to work, it could be useful to explore the concept of runtime environments in ASP.NET Core.

RUNTIME ENVIRONMENTS

Web application development typically involves at least three main phases:

- Development, in which software developers perform their debug sessions
- Staging, in which a selected group of users (or testers) performs internal and/or external tests
- Production, in which the app is made available to end users

These phases, by .NET conventions, are called *environments*, and they can be set using the DOTNET_ENVIRONMENT and/or ASPNETCORE_ENVIRONMENT environment variables in the app's execution context. Whenever we launch our application, we can choose which runtime environment to target by setting that environment variable accordingly.

> **TIP** If we remember the "environmentVariables" section of the launch-Settings.json file, we already know how the ASPNETCORE_ENVIRONMENT variable can be set in our local development machine. We'll learn how to do that in a production server in chapter 12, when we deploy our web API.

THE APPSETTINGS FILES

Now that we know all that, we can easily understand the purpose of those two app-settings files:

- appsettings.json is meant to store configuration settings that will be used by all the runtime environments unless they're overridden—or complemented by—specific environment-specific files.
- appsettings.Development.json is one of those files. The settings put there will be used by the development environment only (and ignored by any other environment), overriding and/or integrating the settings present in the appsettings .json "generic" file.

> **WARNING** The environment-specific file will be read *after* the generic version, thus overriding any key-value pair present there. In other words, if we run our app using the development environment, every key-value pair present in the appsettings.Development.json will be added to the key-value pairs present in the appsettings.json files, replacing them if they're already set.

If we look inside those two appsettings files, we'll see a bunch of log-related settings (within the Logging JSON key), which we can ignore for now. We'll have the chance to play with them in chapter 7 when we talk about logging techniques. What we can do now instead is add a new key/value pair that can help us later. Open the appsettings.json file, and add the following line (in bold) to the existing JSON:

```
{
  "Logging": {
    "LogLevel": {
      "Default": "Information",
      "Microsoft.AspNetCore": "Warning"
    }
  },
  "AllowedHosts": "*",
  "UseDeveloperExceptionPage": false
}
```

This new configuration setting will give us some practice with the appsettings file(s) and also allow us to switch between implementation techniques that we'll put in place in a short while.

2.4.3 *Playing with the Program.cs file*

Let's move to the Program.cs file, which we saw briefly in chapter 1. We already know that this file is executed at the start of the application to register and configure the required services and middleware to handle the HTTP request-and-response pipeline.

As a matter of fact, the default Program.cs file created by the ASP.NET web API template is identical to what we saw in chapter 1, so we won't find anything new there. By briefly reviewing it, we clearly see the services and middleware that our web API is meant to use, as shown in the following listing.

Listing 2.2 Program.cs file

```
var builder = WebApplication.CreateBuilder(args);

// Add services to the container.

builder.Services.AddControllers();                    Controllersservice
                                                      and middleware
// Learn more about configuring Swagger/OpenAPI at https://aka.ms/
    aspnetcore/swashbuckle
builder.Services.AddEndpointsApiExplorer();
builder.Services.AddSwaggerGen();

var app = builder.Build();                             Swagger
                                                      services and
// Configure the HTTP request pipeline.               middleware
if (app.Environment.IsDevelopment())
{
    app.UseSwagger();
    app.UseSwaggerUI();
}

app.UseHttpsRedirection();                    HTTP to HTTPS
                                              redirection middleware

app.UseAuthorization();                       ASP.NET Core
                                              authorization middleware

app.MapControllers();                         Controllersservice
                                              and middleware
app.Run();
```

While we're here, let's take the chance to add some useful middleware that will help us handle errors and exceptions better.

EXCEPTION HANDLING

Locate the following code within the Program.cs file:

```
if (app.Environment.IsDevelopment())
{
    app.UseSwagger();
    app.UseSwaggerUI();
}
```

Replace it with the following (changes marked in bold):

```
if (app.Environment.IsDevelopment())
{
    app.UseSwagger();
    app.UseSwaggerUI();
    app.UseDeveloperExceptionPage();
}
else
{
    app.UseExceptionHandler("/error");
}
```

As we can see, we've added new middleware to the HTTP pipeline. The first addition will be included only if the app is run in the development environment; the second addition will be present in only the staging and production environments. Here's what this middleware does in detail:

- DeveloperExceptionPageMiddleware—As its name implies, this middleware captures synchronous and asynchronous exceptions from the HTTP pipeline and generates an HTML error page (the developer exception page), which contains useful information regarding the exception, such as stack trace, query string parameters, cookies, and headers. This information might expose configuration settings or vulnerabilities to a potential attacker. For that reason, we're using it only in the development environment, so that this useful, yet potentially harmful information will be available for the developer's eyes only.
- ExceptionHandlingMiddleware—This middleware also handles HTTP-level exceptions but is better suited to nondevelopment environments, because it sends all the relevant error info to a customizable handler instead of generating a detailed error response and automatically presenting it to the end user.

Now, although the DeveloperExceptionPageMiddleware works straight out of the box and doesn't require any additional work, the ExceptionHandlingMiddleware requires us to implement a dedicated handler. As we can see by looking at our code, we've passed the /error string parameter, meaning that we want to handle these errors with a dedicated HTTP route, which we need to implement.

As we already know from chapter 1, we have two ways to do that: with a Controller or with the Minimal API. Let's see both of them and then pick the most effective one.

USING A CONTROLLER

Let's start with the Controller-based approach. From Visual Studio's Solution Explorer, perform the following steps:

1 Right-click the Controllers folder of our MyBGList project, and choose Add > Controller. A pop-up window opens, asking us to select the controller we want to add.

2 Navigate to the Common > API node in the tree view on the left, select the API Controller - Empty option, and click the Add button.

3 Name the new controller ErrorController.cs, and click OK to create it.

We'll see our new ErrorController.cs file's content: an empty class that we can use to add our action methods—specifically, the action method that we need to handle the /error/ route where our ExceptionHandlingMiddleware will forward the HTTP errors. Here's a minimal implementation of the action method we need:

```
using Microsoft.AspNetCore.Mvc;

namespace MyBGList.Controllers
{
    [ApiController]
    public class ErrorController : ControllerBase
    {
        [Route("/error")]        ⟵——| The HTTP route
        [HttpGet]                     | to handle
        public IActionResult Error()
        {
            return Problem();    ⟵——| The HTTP response
        }                             | to return to the
    }                                 | caller
}
```

The HTTP method to handle ┌⤑ (points to `[HttpGet] public IActionResult Error()`)

The Problem() method that we're returning is a method of the ControllerBase class (which our ErrorController extends) that produces a ProblemDetail response—a machine-readable standardized format for specifying errors in HTTP API responses based on RFC 7807 (https://tools.ietf.org/html/rfc7807). In a nutshell, it's a JSON file containing some useful info regarding the error: title, detail, status, and so on. Because we're calling the Problem() method without specifying any parameter, however, these values will be set automatically by ASP.NET Core, using default values taken from the exception that has been thrown.

USING MINIMAL API

Let's see how we can pull off the same outcome by using Minimal APIs. In Visual Studio's Solution Explorer, open the Program.cs file, and add the following code right before the app.MapControllers() method:

```
app.MapGet("/error", () => Results.Problem());
```

That's it. As a matter of fact, Minimal API seems to be the clear winner of this match, because it allows us to achieve the same result as our ErrorController with a one-liner without having to create a dedicated file. This outcome shouldn't be a surprise: This scenario is a perfect example of the dead-simple routing actions in which Minimal API shines, whereas Controllers are better suited to complex tasks.

In the following chapters, we'll see a lot of scenarios in which the Controller-based approach will take its revenge. For the time being, we may as well delete the

ErrorController.cs file and keep the Minimal API one-liner in the Program.cs file. First, though, let's spend a couple of minutes discussing what might happen if we keep ErrorController.cs in place.

ROUTING CONFLICTS

Controllers and Minimal API can exist in the same project without problems, so the developer can get the best of both worlds. But they should be configured to handle different routes. What happens if they share an endpoint?

If we remember what we learned in chapter 1, we already know the answer: the middleware that comes first in the Program.cs file handles the HTTP request first and likely terminates it, thus preventing the other from coming into play. Such behavior is perfectly fine and won't cause any significant problem in the HTTP lifecycle, aside from the waste of having a useless implementation within our project's codebase.

In our current scenario, because we put the Minimal API's app.MapGet() method right before the app.MapControllers() method, the "dead code" victim would be our ErrorController.cs file. If everything is fine, why should we delete that controller? Can't we just leave it there?

The best way to answer that question is to press F5 again and execute our app before deleting the ErrorController.cs file. Figure 2.6 shows what we should get.

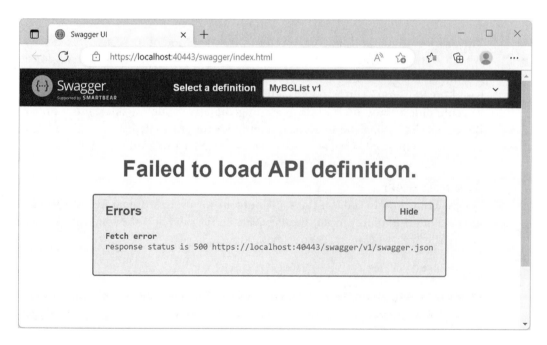

Figure 2.6   SwaggerUI error 500 (due to routing conflicts)

As we can see, the previously working SwaggerUI page displays a fetch error, due to the fact that its data source (the autogenerated swagger.json file used internally to build the UI) is returning an HTTP 500 error. If we copy that URL (https://localhost:40443/swagger/v1/swagger.json) and paste it in our web browser's address bar, we can see the actual error:

```
SwaggerGeneratorException: Conflicting method/path combination "GET error"
for actions - MyBGList.Controllers.ErrorController.Error (MyBGList),HTTP:
GET /error. Actions require a unique method/path combination for
Swagger/OpenAPI 3.0. Use ConflictingActionsResolver as a workaround.
```

This error message brings us to the root of the problem: we have two handlers for the same method/path combination (GET /error), which prevents Swagger from working properly. To fix the problem, we can do one of two things:

- Remove one of the "duplicate" handlers (the Controller's Error() action or the Minimal API's MapGet() method).
- Set up a ConflictingActionsResolver to instruct Swagger how to handle duplicate handlers.

In this scenario, deleting the ErrorController.cs file or removing it from the project is the better thing to do, because we don't want to keep redundant code anyway. But in case we wanted to keep it for some reason, we could instruct Swagger to deal with the situation by changing the SwaggerGeneratorMiddleware configuration within the Program.cs file in the following way (updated code marked in bold):

```
builder.Services.AddSwaggerGen(opts =>
    opts.ResolveConflictingActions(apiDesc => apiDesc.First())
    );
```

We're telling Swagger to resolve all conflicts related to duplicate routing handlers by always taking the first one found and ignoring the others. This approach is highly discouraged, however, because it can hide potential routing problems and lead to unexpected results. No wonder the error message calls it a workaround!

> **WARNING** In more general terms, always address routing conflicts by removing the redundant (or wrong) action handler. Setting up the framework (or the middleware) to automatically "resolve" conflicts is almost always bad practice unless the developers are experienced enough to know what they're doing.

For that reason, the best thing we can do before proceeding is delete the Error-Controller.cs file or exclude it from the project (right-click it and then choose Exclude from Project from the contextual menu in Solution Explorer) so that Swagger won't have the chance to find any dupes.

TESTING IT
Now that we've configured the developer exception page for the development environment and the Error() action for the production environment, we need to emulate an actual error. The quickest way is to add another action method (or Minimal

API) that throws an exception. If we still had our `ErrorController`, we could implement the action method in the following way:

```
[Route("/error/test")]
[HttpGet]
public IActionResult Test()
{
    throw new Exception("test");
}
```

Because we chose to delete or exclude the `ErrorController` from the project, however, we can put the following Minimal API one-liner in the `Program.cs` file right below the other `MapGet()` method that we added:

```
app.MapGet("/error/test", () => { throw new Exception("test"); });
```

Then click the Start button (or press the F5 key) and point the web browser to https://localhost:40443/error/test. If we did everything correctly, we should see the developer exception page generated by `DeveloperExceptionPageMiddleware`, as shown in figure 2.7.

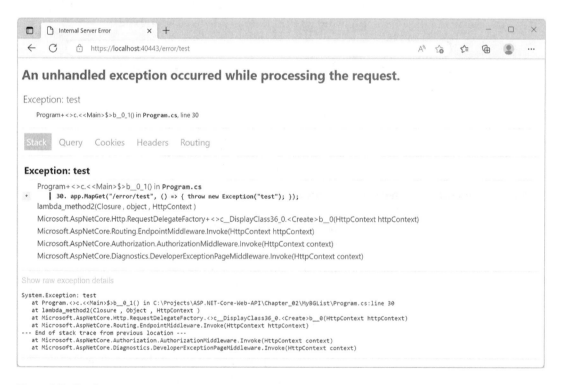

Figure 2.7   Testing `DeveloperExceptionPageMiddleware`

This outcome is expected because we're executing our app in the *development* environment, as specified by the ASPNETCORE_ENVIRONMENT variable in the launchSettings .json file. If we want to test ExceptionHandlerMiddleware, all we need to do is to change the value of the variable from Development to Production.

Alternatively, we can make good use of the UseDeveloperExceptionPage key that we added to our appsettings.json file. Implementing this setting will allow us to switch between the developer exception page and the ExceptionHandler without having to change the runtime environment of our app. Open the Program.cs file, and replace the code

```
if (app.Environment.IsDevelopment())
{
    app.UseSwagger();
    app.UseSwaggerUI();
    app.UseDeveloperExceptionPage();
}
else
{
    app.UseExceptionHandler("/error");
}
```

with this code:

```
if (app.Environment.IsDevelopment())
{
    app.UseSwagger();
    app.UseSwaggerUI();
}

if (app.Configuration.GetValue<bool>("UseDeveloperExceptionPage"))
    app.UseDeveloperExceptionPage();
else
    app.UseExceptionHandler("/error");
```

Retrieves that literal value from the appsettings.json file(s)

If TRUE, uses the DeveloperExceptionPageMiddleware

If FALSE, uses the ExceptionHandlerMiddleware instead

Now ExceptionHandlerMiddleware will be used instead of DeveloperExceptionPage-Middleware, because the value of the UseDeveloperExceptionPage key was set to false in the appsetting.json file. We can immediately press F5, navigate to the https://localhost:40443/error/test URL, and receive the ProblemDetail JSON response in all its glory:

```
{
  "type":"https://tools.ietf.org/html/rfc7231#section-6.6.1",
  "title":"An error occurred while processing your request.",
  "status":500
}
```

NOTE This JSON output is viable enough in our scenario (for now) because it doesn't expose potentially exploitable info regarding our app. We can further customize the output. We could replace the generic "an error occurred" title with the actual `Exception` message, provide different status codes for different kinds of errors, and so on, using the optional parameters supported by the method's overloads.

Now that we've completed this series of tests, we should reenable `DeveloperException-PageMiddleware` for the development environment. We could open the `appsettings .json` file and change the `UseDeveloperExceptionPage` value from `false` to `true`, but that wouldn't be the right thing to do. We want to be sure that such a potentially insecure page could be seen only by developers, remember? For that reason, the proper way to reenable it is to perform the following steps:

1 Open the `appsettings.Development.json` file.
2 Add a `UseDeveloperExceptionPage` key (which doesn't exist in this file).
3 Set the key's value to `true`.

Here's what the updated file will look like (new line in bold):

```
{
  "Logging": {
    "LogLevel": {
      "Default": "Information",
      "Microsoft.AspNetCore": "Warning"
    }
  },
  "UseDeveloperExceptionPage": true
}
```

Now the value we put in the `appsettings.Development.json` file will `overwrite` the value in the `appsettings.json` file whenever our app is launched in the development runtime environment—which is precisely what we want.

2.4.4   *Inspecting the WeatherForecastController*

The next file to look at is `WeatherForecastController.cs`, which we can find in the `/Controllers/` folder.

> **NOTE**   By ASP.NET convention, all controller classes must reside in the project's root-level `/Controllers/` folder and inherit from the `Microsoft.Asp-NetCore.Mvc.Controller` base class.

Controllers, as we know from chapter 1, are used in ASP.NET Core to define and group actions that handle HTTP requests (mapped through routing) and return HTTP responses accordingly. If we look at the source code of the `WeatherForecast-Controller`, we can see that it makes no exception. This sample Controller is meant to handle an HTTP `GET` request to the `/WeatherForecast` route and return an HTTP response containing an array of five JSON objects containing some randomly generated `Date`, `TemperatureC`, and `Summary` property values:

```csharp
using Microsoft.AspNetCore.Mvc;

namespace MyBGList.Controllers
{
    [ApiController]
    [Route("[controller]")]
    public class WeatherForecastController : ControllerBase
    {
        private static readonly string[] Summaries = new[] {
            "Freezing", "Bracing", "Chilly", "Cool",
            "Mild", "Warm", "Balmy", "Hot", "Sweltering", "Scorching"
        };

        private readonly ILogger<WeatherForecastController> _logger;

        public WeatherForecastController
            (ILogger<WeatherForecastController> logger)
        {
            _logger = logger;
        }

        [HttpGet(Name = "GetWeatherForecast")]
        public IEnumerable<WeatherForecast> Get()
        {
            return Enumerable.Range(1, 5)
                .Select(index => new WeatherForecast
            {
                Date = DateTime.Now.AddDays(index),
                TemperatureC = Random.Shared.Next(-20, 55),
                Summary = Summaries[Random.Shared.Next(Summaries.Length)]
            })
            .ToArray();
        }
    }
}
```

Default routing rules → `[Route("[controller]")]`

Adds API-specific behaviors → `[ApiController]`

ILogger instance (instantiated through Dependency Injection)

Action to handle HTTP GET to /WeatherForecast

Here's what we get if we try to execute this code:

```
[{
  date: "2021-12-03T02:04:31.5766653+01:00",
  temperatureC: 0,
  temperatureF: 32,
  summary: "Warm"
},
{
  date: "2021-12-04T02:04:31.5770138+01:00",
  temperatureC: 23,
  temperatureF: 73,
  summary: "Freezing"
},
{
  date: "2021-12-05T02:04:31.5770175+01:00",
  temperatureC: 40,
```

```
  temperatureF: 103,
  summary: "Freezing"
},
{
  date: "2021-12-06T02:04:31.5770178+01:00",
  temperatureC: 47,
  temperatureF: 116,
  summary: "Cool"
},
{
  date: "2021-12-07T02:04:31.577018+01:00",
  temperatureC: 36,
  temperatureF: 96,
  summary: "Mild"
}]
```

The returned object is a JSON representation of the C# `WeatherForecast` class, defined in the `WeatherForecast.cs` file in our project's root folder. As we can see by looking at its source code, it's a POCO class containing some properties that can easily be serialized into JSON output:

```
namespace MyBGList
{
    public class WeatherForecast
    {
        public DateTime Date { get; set; }

        public int TemperatureC { get; set; }

        public int TemperatureF => 32 + (int)(TemperatureC / 0.5556);

        public string? Summary { get; set; }
    }
}
```

> **NOTE**   *POCO* stands for *Plain Old CLR Object*—in other words, a normal class without dependencies, attributes, infrastructure concerns, special types, or other responsibilities.

The `WeatherForecastController` and `WeatherForecast` sample classes can be useful for understanding how an ASP.NET controller works, but they don't fit well in our concrete scenario. We don't need to know anything about temperatures or forecasts when dealing with a board-game-related API. For that reason, we're going to delete those files or exclude them from the project, as we did with the `ErrorController.cs` file earlier, and replace them with a more pertinent sample.

2.4.5 Adding the BoardGameController

Let's start with the POCO class that will take the place of the previous `WeatherForecast`. In Visual Studio's Solution Explorer, perform the following steps (listing 2.3):

1 Delete the existing `WeatherForecast.cs` file.
2 Right-click the `MyBGList` project's root folder, choose Add > New Item from the contextual menu, and create a new `BoardGame.cs` class file.
3 Fill the new file with a POCO class hosting some board-game data.

Listing 2.3 `BoardGame.cs file`

```
namespace MyBGList
{
    public class BoardGame
    {
        public int Id { get; set; }

        public string? Name { get; set; }

        public int? Year { get; set; }
    }
}
```

This new class is still a sample, yet it's more consistent with our chosen scenario! Let's do the same with the controller. In Visual Studio's Solution Explorer, perform the following steps (listing 2.4):

1 Navigate to the `/Controllers/` folder, and delete the existing `WeatherForecast-Controller.cs` file.
2 Right-click the `/Controllers/` folder, choose Add > Controller from the contextual menu, create a new API `Controller - Empty`, and name the new file `BoardGamesController.cs`.
3 Remove the `/api/` prefix, because we don't need it.
4 Add a new action method to return an array of board-game data, using the `BoardGame` POCO class we created.

Listing 2.4 `BoardGamesController.cs file`

```
using Microsoft.AspNetCore.Mvc;

namespace MyBGList.Controllers
{
    [Route("[controller]")]      <── Updated Route pattern
    [ApiController]
    public class BoardGamesController : ControllerBase
    {
        private readonly ILogger<BoardGamesController> _logger;
```

```
public BoardGamesController(ILogger<BoardGamesController> logger)
{
    _logger = logger;
}

[HttpGet(Name = "GetBoardGames")]              ◁──┐  New Get
public IEnumerable<BoardGame> Get()                │  method
{
    return new[] {
        new BoardGame() {
            Id = 1,
            Name = "Axis & Allies",
            Year = 1981
        },
        new BoardGame() {
            Id = 2,
            Name = "Citadels",
            Year = 2000
        },
        new BoardGame() {
            Id = 3,

            Name = "Terraforming Mars",
            Year = 2016
        }
    };
}
}
}
```

That's it. Our new BoardGamesController will handle the /BoardGames route and respond with a JSON array containing some relevant sample info on three highly acclaimed board games released in the past 45 years or so.

The minimal behavior of our BoardGamesController could be easily handled by Minimal API with a few lines of code. Here's a code snippet that we can put in the Program.cs file to obtain the same output from the Get() action method:

```
app.MapGet("/BoardGames", () => new[] {
    new BoardGame() {
        Id = 1,
        Name = "Axis & Allies",
        Year = 1981
    },
    new BoardGame() {
        Id = 2,
        Name = "Citadels",
        Year = 2000
    },
    new BoardGame() {
        Id = 3,
        Name = "Terraforming Mars",
        Year = 2016
    }
});
```

This example is only a sample JSON response that mimics more complex behavior, which often includes nontrivial data retrieval. In the following chapters, we're going to get the board-game data from a database management system (DBMS) using Entity Framework Core and possibly even update it for users. When we're dealing with these kinds of actions, the controller-based approach becomes convenient, possibly even more convenient than Minimal API. For that reason, this time we're going to keep the controller instead of replacing it.

2.5 Exercises

The best way to build confidence with ASP.NET and Visual Studio is to practice using various tools as soon as we learn how they work. This section provides some useful exercises that allow us to further customize our first web API project, using the skills we learned in this chapter. Each exercise is meant to modify a single file, but by completing all the exercises, we will be able to achieve a consistent overall goal.

Suppose that we need to configure our new `MyBGList` web API for a selected group of internal testers, which will be able to access our development machine through a given set of TCP ports. Here's the full backlog of the specifics we need to ensure:

1 Testers can use only the 55221 and 55222 TCP ports.
2 Testers can only use the Kestrel web server.
3 The web browser used to test the app should start with the JSON list of the `BoardGames` returned by the `BoardGamesController`'s `Get()` action method.
4 Testers, like developers, must be allowed to access the SwaggerUI page but not the developer exception page, which should be unavailable to them.
5 Testers need to retrieve two additional fields for each board game: `MinPlayers` and `MaxPlayers`. These fields should contain the number of minimum and maximum players supported by the board game.

TIP If you're feeling bold, stop reading here, and start the exercise without further help (hard mode). If you're less confident about what you've learned so far, you can read the following sections, which provide general guidance on all the relevant steps without giving the solution away (relaxed mode). The solutions to all the given exercises are available on GitHub in the /Chapter_02/Exercises/ folder. To test them, replace the relevant files in your `MyBGList` project with those in that folder, and run the app.

2.5.1 launchSettings.json

The first thing we need to do is ensure that testers will be able to access the local machine through the given TCP ports. It would be wise to set up a dedicated runtime environment for them to use. The staging environment seems to be the perfect choice because it allows us to define some specific configuration settings without altering the configuration for the production and development environments, which we're likely going to need. We can perform these tasks by updating the `launchSettings.json` file and configuring the Kestrel launch settings for the `MyBGList` project in the following way:

1   Use TCP port 55221 for HTTP and 55222 for HTTPS.
2   Set the runtime environment to Staging.
3   Set the starting endpoint URL to the route handled by the `BoardGames-Controller`'s `Get()` action method so that the web browser will automatically show that page when the app starts.

We don't need to change the settings for IIS Express because testers won't be using it. These tasks fulfill items 1, 2, and 3 in our backlog.

2.5.2   *appsettings.json*

The next things to do are to create the settings file for the staging runtime environment and define some default behaviors, valid for all the environments, that we can override conditionally whenever we need to. Here's how we can pull off all those tasks:

1   Add a new `UseSwagger` configuration setting to the `MyBGList` app settings, valid for all the runtime environments, with the value of `False`.
2   Add that same `UseSwagger` configuration setting in the existing configuration file to the development environment, with the value of `True`.
3   Create a new configuration file for the staging environment, and override the settings as follows:
    – `UseDeveloperExceptionPage: false`
    – `UseSwagger: true`

These tasks won't affect anything yet, but they fulfill item 4 of our specifications.

> **TIP**   Setting the `UseDeveloperExceptionPage` to `false` for the staging environment could be redundant because that value is already set in the generic `appsettings.json` file. Because we're talking about a page containing potentially confidential information, however, explicitly denying access in a given environment won't hurt.

2.5.3   *Program.cs*

Now that we have the proper app setting variables, we can use them to conditionally add (or skip) the relevant middleware, depending on the app's runtime environment. We need to open the `Program.cs` file and change the current initialization strategy of `SwaggerMiddleware` and `SwaggerUIMiddleware` to ensure that they'll be used only if `UseSwagger` is set to `True`. By doing that, we fulfill item 4 of our backlog.

2.5.4   *BoardGame.cs*

To implement item 5 of our backlog, we need to add two new properties to the existing `BoardGame` POCO class. As for the type to use, the most suitable choice is a nullable `int`, as we used for the `Year` property; we can't be sure that such info will always be available for all board games.

2.5.5   *BoardGameControllers.cs*

Adding these properties to the `BoardGame` class won't be enough to show them properly in the JSON file unless we want them always to be `null`. Because we're currently dealing with sample data, the only thing we can do is update our `BoardGameController`'s `Get()` method and set fixed values manually. This task is enough to fulfill item 5 of our backlog and complete the exercise.

All we have left to do is select Kestrel as the startup web server, click the Start button (or press F5) to launch our web API project, and see what happens. If we did everything correctly, our web browser should automatically call the https://localhost :55221/boardgames endpoint and show the following JSON response:

```
[{
  "id":1,
  "name":"Axis & Allies",
  "year":1981,
  "minPlayers":2,
  "maxPlayers":5
},
{
  "id":2,
  "name":"Citadels",
  "year":2000,
  "minPlayers":2,
  "maxPlayers":8
},
{
  "id":3,
  "name":"Terraforming Mars",
  "year":2016,
  "minPlayers":1,
  "maxPlayers":5
}]
```

If we achieved that result, we're ready to move on.

Summary

- To create ASP.NET Core apps, we need to download and install the .NET Core SDK, the .NET Core runtime, and the ASP.NET Core runtime (unless you chose an IDE that automatically does those things, such as Visual Studio).
- We should also provide ourselves with a suitable IDE such as Visual Studio: a comprehensive .NET development solution for Windows and macOS that we'll use throughout this book. Visual Studio can dramatically boost our productivity and help us standardize our development processes thanks to built-in features such as task runners, package managers, integrated source control, and syntax highlighting.
- Visual Studio includes a lot of useful templates that we can use as boilerplate for creating our apps, including the ASP.NET Core web API template, which is the perfect choice to start our `MyBGList` web API project.

- Visual Studio's ASP.NET Core web API template comes with a small group of autogenerated files:
  - A startup file to set up services and middleware (`Program.cs`)
  - A settings file to launch the app with the development web server (`launch-Settings.json`)
  - A set of configuration files that store the app's environment-specific settings (`appsettings.json`)
  - A POCO class to emulate a data object (`WeatherForecast.cs`)
  - A `Controller` class that can respond to simple HTTP requests with some sample JSON data (`WeatherForecastController.cs`)
- After a brief review of the template files and some minor code changes to understand how each of them works, we can start replacing the built-in weather forecast sample classes with some board-game-related classes.
- Before going further, it may be useful to test our acquired knowledge with some exercises, simulating a series of requests (backlog items) from the client.
  - Depending on our confidence, we can try to fulfill them without any suggestions or follow some high-level guidance.
  - Regardless of the chosen complexity level, performing such exercises is a great way to test our current skills and prepare for the topics yet to come.

RESTful principles and guidelines

This chapter covers

- Reviewing the six REST guiding constraints
- Setting up and configuring CORS and caching techniques in ASP.NET Core
- Understanding the role of reverse proxies and CDN services
- Implementing code on demand with a use-case example
- Adopting a uniform interface with HATEOAS capabilities
- Adding API documentation and versioning with Swagger/OpenAPI

Now that we have a minimal web API boilerplate up and running, we're ready to review the representational state transfer (REST) properties and constraints briefly introduced in chapter 1 and see how they can be implemented in ASP.NET Core. Specifically, we'll add some built-in and third-party services and middleware to our existing MyBGList project to achieve true RESTful status. The chapter introduces concepts such as separation of concerns, state management, caching, idempotency,

51

API versioning, Hypermedia as the Engine of Application State (HATEOAS), and Cross-Origin Resource Sharing (CORS). Rest assured that we won't dwell too much on theory. This chapter shows how to put these topics into practice in ASP.NET Core.

By the end of the chapter, you'll be able to test your knowledge by solving some wrap-up exercises on the concepts and programming techniques discussed here. The main goal is to understand the differences between a REST-based web application and a true RESTful web API, paving the way for what comes next.

3.1   REST guiding constraints

Let's start by revisiting the six REST guiding constraints. For the sake of simplicity, we'll follow the same order used in chapter 1.

3.1.1   Client-server approach

To enforce this constraint, we must separate the concerns of the server from those of the clients. In practical terms, our web API

- Can respond only to requests initiated by the clients, thus being unable to make requests on its own
- Has no constraints or dependencies on the location, environment, technology, architecture, and underlying implementation of the individual clients, thus is able to grow, evolve, experience change, and even be rebuilt from scratch without knowing anything

If we look at our existing web API project, we can see that this approach is mostly already in place. Controllers and Minimal APIs are meant only to return standard HTTP responses; they don't need to know anything about the requesting client. The default ASP.NET Core settings, however, enforce an HTTP security mechanism that might restrict some clients' locations and/or technologies. This mechanism is a fundamental topic for any web developer.

CROSS-ORIGIN RESOURCE SHARING

CORS is an HTTP header-based mechanism proposed in 2004 to allow safe cross-origin data requests by VoiceXML browsers. Later, it was formalized as a working draft by the WebApps Working Group of the World Wide Web Consortium (W3C), with participation by the major browser vendors, which started to implement it around 2009; then the draft was accepted as a W3C recommendation in January 2014. The current CORS specification, implemented in all major browsers, is included in the Fetch Living Standard of the Web Hypertext Technology Working Group (WHATWG).

> **DEFINITION**   WHATWG is a community of people who are interested in evolving HTML and related technologies. The working group was founded in 2004 by representatives of Apple Inc., the Mozilla Foundation, and Opera Software.

The purpose of CORS is to allow browsers to access resources by using HTTP requests initiated from scripts (such as XMLHttpRequest and Fetch API) when those resources are located in domains other than the one hosting the script. In the absence of such a mechanism, browsers would block these "external" requests because they would break the *same-origin* policy, which allows them only when the protocol, port (if specified), and host values are the same for both the page hosting the script and the requested resource.

TIP For additional info regarding the same-origin policy, check out http:// mng.bz/gJaG.

To understand the concept, let's create a practical example using our current web API scenario. Suppose that we want to use our `MyBGList` web API, which we previously published to the `mybglist-api.com` domain, to feed a board-gaming web app created with a JavaScript framework such as Angular and located in a different domain (such as `webapp.com`). The client's implementation relies on the following assumptions:

- The browser client performs an initial HTTP `GET` request to the `webapp.com/index.html` page, which loads the Angular app.
- The `webapp.com/index.html` page returns an HTTP `200 - OK` response containing the HTML content, which includes two additional references:
  - A `<script>` element pointing to a `/app.js` file, which contains the web app's Angular JavaScript code.
  - A `<link>` element pointing to a `/style.css` file, which contains the web app's UI styles.
- When retrieved, the `/app.js` file autostarts the Angular app, which performs an `XMLHttpRequest` to the `mybglist-api.com/BoardGames` endpoint, handled by our `MyBGList` web API's `BoardGamesController`, to retrieve a list of board games to display.

Figure 3.1 shows these requests.

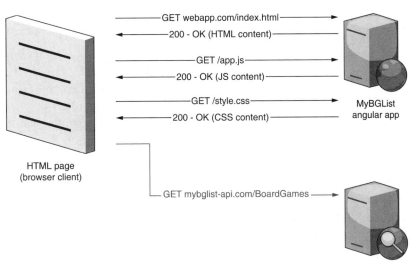

Figure 3.1 Same-origin and cross-origin client-server interactions

As we can see, the first HTTP request—the `webapp.com/index.html` page—points to the `webapp.com` domain. This initial request defines the *origin*. The subsequent two requests—`/app.js` and `/style.css`—are sent to the same origin as the first one, so they are *same-origin* requests. But the last HTTP request—`mybglist-api.com/BoardGames`—points to a different domain, violating the same-origin policy. If we want the browser to perform that call, we can use CORS to instruct it to relax the policy and allow HTTP requests from external origins.

> **NOTE** It's important to understand that the same-origin policy is a security mechanism controlled by the browser, not by the server. In other words, it's not an HTTP response error sent by the server because the client is not authorized; it's a block applied by the client after completing an HTTP request, receiving the response, and checking the headers returned with it to determine what to do. Starting from this assumption, we can easily understand that the CORS settings sent by the server have the function of telling the client what to block and what not to block.

All modern browsers use two main techniques to check for CORS settings and apply them: *simple mode,* which uses the same HTTP request/response used to fetch the accessed resource, and *preflight mode,* which involves an additional HTTP `OPTIONS` request. The next section briefly explains the differences between these approaches.

A practical guide to CORS

For additional info about CORS from both the server and client perspectives, check out *CORS in Action: Creating and Consuming Cross-Origin APIs*, by Monsur Hossain (https://www.manning.com/books/cors-in-action).

SIMPLE REQUESTS VS. PREFLIGHT REQUESTS

Whenever a client-side script initiates an HTTP request, the browser checks whether it meets a certain set of requirements—such as using standard HTTP methods, headers, and content—that can be used to define it as simple. If all these requirements are met, the HTTP request is processed as normal. CORS is handled by checking the `Access-Control-Allow-Origin` header and ensuring that it complies with the origin of the script that issued the call. This approach is a simple request.

> **NOTE** The requirements that define a simple request are documented at http://mng.bz/wyKa.

In case the HTTP request doesn't meet any of the requirements, the browser puts it on hold and automatically issues a preemptive HTTP `OPTIONS` request before it. The browser uses this preflight request to determine the exact CORS capabilities of the server and act accordingly.

As we can easily understand, an important difference between a simple request and a preflight request is that the former directly asks for (and receives) the content we want to fetch, whereas the latter asks the server for permission before issuing the request.

Preflight requests provide an additional security layer because CORS settings are checked and applied beforehand. A preflight request uses three headers to make the server aware of the characteristics of the subsequent request:

- `Access-Control-Request-Method`—The HTTP method of the request
- `Access-Control-Request-Headers`—A list of custom headers that will be sent with the request
- `Origin`—The origin of the script initiating the call

The server, if configured to handle this kind of request, will answer with the following HTTP response headers to indicate whether the subsequent HTTP request will be allowed:

- `Access-Control-Allow-Origin`—The origin allowed to make the request (or the * wildcard if any origin is allowed). This is the same header used by simple requests.
- `Access-Control-Allow-Headers`—A comma-separated list of allowed HTTP headers.
- `Access-Control-Allow-Methods`—A comma-separated list of allowed HTTP methods.
- `Access-Control-Max-Age`—How long the results of this preflight request can be cached (in seconds).

The browser checks the preflight request's response values to determine whether to issue the subsequent HTTP request.

> **NOTE** When implementing a web app by using a client-side framework such as Angular or ReactJS, software developers typically don't need to delve into the technical details of CORS; the browser transparently takes care of all that and communicates with the server in the appropriate way. Because we're dealing with the server-side part of the story, however, we need to know what to allow and what not to allow.

That's enough theory. Let's see how we can implement CORS in our web API project.

IMPLEMENTING CORS

In ASP.NET Core, CORS can be set up via a dedicated service, which gives us the chance to define a default policy and/or various named policies. As always, such a service must be added in the service container in the `Program.cs` file.

We can use different policies to allow CORS for specific origins, HTTP headers (for preflight requests, explained earlier) and/or methods. If we want to allow cross-origin requests for all origins, headers, and methods, we could add the service by using the following settings:

```
builder.Services.AddCors(options =>
    options.AddDefaultPolicy(cfg => {
        cfg.AllowAnyOrigin();
        cfg.AllowAnyHeader();
        cfg.AllowAnyMethod();
    }));
```

Configuring CORS this way, however, means disabling the same-origin policy for all the endpoints that will adopt the default policy, thus posing nontrivial security problems. For that reason, it would be safer to define a more restrictive default policy, leaving the relaxed settings for a named policy. The following code shows how we can achieve that goal by defining two policies:

- A default policy that accepts every HTTP header and method from a restricted set of known origins, which we can safely set whenever we need to
- An "AnyOrigin" named policy that accepts everything from everyone, which we can use situationally for a limited set of endpoints that we want to make available for any client, including a client we are not aware of

Here's how we can improve the snippet in the Program.cs file:

```
builder.Services.AddCors(options => {
    options.AddDefaultPolicy(cfg => {
        cfg.WithOrigins(builder.Configuration["AllowedOrigins"]);
        cfg.AllowAnyHeader();
        cfg.AllowAnyMethod();
    });
    options.AddPolicy(name: "AnyOrigin",
        cfg => {
            cfg.AllowAnyOrigin();
            cfg.AllowAnyHeader();
            cfg.AllowAnyMethod();
        });
});
```

The value that we pass to the WithOrigins() method will be returned by the server within the Access-Control-Allow-Origin header, which indicates to the client which origin(s) should be considered valid. Because we used a configuration setting to define the origins to allow for the default policy, we need to set them up. Open the appSettings.json file, and add a new "AllowedOrigins" key, as shown in the following listing.

Listing 3.1   `appSettings.json` file

```
{
  "Logging": {
    "LogLevel": {
```

```
      "Default": "Information",
      "Microsoft.AspNetCore": "Warning"
    }
  },
  "AllowedHosts": "*",
  "AllowedOrigins": "*",
  "UseDeveloperExceptionPage": false
}
```

In this example, we used a literal value of `"*"`—a value that can be used as a wildcard to allow any origin to access the resource when the request has no credentials. If the request is set to allow credentials such as cookies, authorization headers, or TLS client certificates, the `"*"` wildcard can't be used and would result in an error.

> **WARNING** Such behavior, which requires both the server and the client to acknowledge that it's OK to include credentials in requests and to specify a specific origin, is enforced to reduce the chance of Cross-Site Request Forgery (CSRF) vulnerabilities in CORS. The reason is simple: requests with credentials are likely used to read restricted data and/or perform data updates, so they require additional security measures.

Now that we've defined our CORS policies, we need to learn how to apply them.

APPLYING CORS

ASP.NET Core gives us three ways to enable CORS:

- The CORS middleware
- Endpoint routing
- The [EnableCors] attribute

CORS middleware is the simplest technique to use, as it applies the selected CORS policy to all the app's endpoints (Controllers, Minimal APIs, and the like). In our scenario, it can be useful to globally set the default policy that we defined earlier. Set it up by adding the following line of code to our `Program.cs` file right before the `Authorization` middleware:

```
// ...

app.UseCors();

app.UseAuthorization();

// ...
```

We have to put that code there for a reason: the order in which middleware components are added to the `Program.cs` file defines the order in which they are invoked. If we want the CORS middleware to be applied to the endpoints handled by our controllers and Minimal APIs, as well as taken into account by our global authorization settings, we need to add it before any of those endpoints.

NOTE   For additional info on middleware order and best practices, read the following page of the ASP.NET Core official documentation: http://mng.bz/qop6.

In case we want to apply the `"AnyOrigin"` named policy to all our endpoints instead of the default policy, we could add the CORS middleware by specifying the policy name in the following way:

```
// ...

app.UseCors("AnyOrigin");

// ...
```

This approach would make no sense, however, because that named policy is clearly meant to be applied only in some edge-case scenarios when we want to relax the same-origin policy for all origins. That's definitely not the case for our `BoardGames-Controller`'s action methods unless we're OK with letting any web app consume it without restrictions. But this approach might be acceptable for the /error and /error/test routes, currently handled by Minimal APIs. Let's apply the `"AnyOrigin"` named policy to them by using the endpoint routing method:

```
// ...

// Minimal API
app.MapGet("/error", () => Results.Problem())
    .RequireCors("AnyOrigin");
app.MapGet("/error/test", () => { throw new Exception("test"); })
    .RequireCors("AnyOrigin");

// ...
```

As we can see, endpoint routing allows us to enable CORS on a per-endpoint basis by using the `RequireCors()` extension method. This approach is good for nondefault named policies because it gives us better control in choosing the endpoints that support them. If we want to use it for controllers instead of Minimal API methods, however, we won't have the same level of granularity, because it could be applied only globally (to all controllers):

```
// ...

app.MapControllers()
    .RequireCors("AnyOrigin");

// ...
```

Furthermore, enabling CORS by using the `RequireCors()` extension method currently doesn't support automatic preflight requests, for the reason explained at https://github .com/dotnet/aspnetcore/issues/20709.

For all these reasons, endpoint routing currently isn't the suggested approach. Luckily, the same granularity is granted by the third and last technique allowed by ASP.NET Core: the [EnableCors] attribute, which is also the Microsoft-recommended way to implement CORS on a per-endpoint basis. Here's how we can implement it in our Minimal API method, replacing the previous endpoint routing technique based on the RequireCors() extension method:

```
// ...

// Minimal API
app.MapGet("/error", [EnableCors("AnyOrigin")] () =>
    Results.Problem());
app.MapGet("/error/test", [EnableCors("AnyOrigin")] () =>
    { throw new Exception("test"); });

// ...
```

To use the attribute, we also need to add a reference to the Microsoft.AspNetCore .Cors namespace at the start of the Program.cs file in the following way:

```
using Microsoft.AspNetCore.Cors;
```

A big advantage of the [EnableCors] attribute is that it can be assigned to any controller and/or action method, allowing us to implement our CORS named policies in a simple, effective way.

> **NOTE** Using the [EnableCors] attribute without specifying a named policy as a parameter will apply the default policy, which would be redundant in our scenario because we've already added it on a global basis by using CORS middleware. Later, we'll use such an attribute to override the default policy with a named policy whenever we need to.

3.1.2 Statelessness

The statelessness constraint is particularly important in RESTful API development because it prevents our web API from doing something that most web applications do: store some of the client's info on the server and retrieve it on subsequent calls (using a session cookie or a similar technique). In more general terms, enforcing a statelessness approach means that we have to restrain ourselves from using convenient ASP.NET Core features such as session state and application state management, as well as load-balancing techniques such as session affinity and sticky sessions. All the session-related info must be kept entirely on the client, which is responsible for storing and handling them on its own side. This capability is typically handled by frontend state management libraries such as Redux, Akita, ngrx, and Elf.

In our current scenario, because we used a minimal ASP.NET Core web API template without authentication support, we can say that we're already compliant. Our current project doesn't have the required services and middleware (available mostly through the built-in `Microsoft.AspNetCore.Session` namespace) to enable session state. This fact also means that we won't be able to benefit from these convenient techniques if we need to authenticate specific calls and/or restrict some endpoints to authorized clients, such as adding, updating, or deleting board games or reading some reserved data. Whenever we want to do those things, we have to provide the client with all the required information to create and maintain a session state on its side. We'll learn how to do that in chapter 9, which introduces JSON Web Token (JWT), token-based authentication, and other RESTful techniques.

Session state and application state, as well as any data stored by the server to identify requests, interactions, and context information related to clients, has nothing to do with resource state or any other states related to the response returned by the server. These types of states are not only allowed within a RESTful API but also constitute a required constraint, as discussed in the next section.

3.1.3 *Cacheability*

The term *cache*, when used in an IT-related context, refers to a system, component, or module meant to store data to make it available for further requests with less effort. When dealing with HTTP-based web applications, caching is typically intended to store frequently accessed (requested) content in various places within the request-response lifecycle. Within this context, most available caching techniques and mechanisms can be divided into three main groups:

- *Server-side caching* (also known as *application caching*)—A caching system that saves data to key/value stores by using either a built-in service or a third-party provider such as Memcached, Redis, Couchbase, managed abstraction layers such as Amazon ElastiCache, or a standard database management system (DBMS)
- *Client-side caching* (also known as *browser caching* or *response caching*)—A caching mechanism defined in the HTTP specifications that relies on several HTTP response headers (including `Expires`, `Cache-Control`, `Last-Modified`, and `ETag`) that can be set from the server to control the caching behavior of the clients
- *Intermediate caching* (also known as *proxy caching, reverse-proxy caching*, or *content-delivery network [CDN] caching*)—A response-caching technique that stores cached data by using dedicated services (proxies) and/or relies on third-party services optimized for accelerated and geographically distributed content distribution (CDN providers), following the same HTTP header-based rules as client-side caching

In the following sections, we'll set up and configure these caching methods by using some convenient ASP.NET Core features. We'll also explore most of them in chapter 8.

SERVER-SIDE CACHING

Being able to store frequently accessed data in high-performance storage (such as system memory) is traditionally considered to be a valid implementation technique for a web application, because it allows us to preserve a data provider—a DBMS, a network resource, or the filesystem—from being stressed by a high number of simultaneous requests. But because most of these data sources now come with their own caching features and mechanisms, the idea of building a centralized, application-level cache is less and less attractive, especially when dealing with highly decentralized architectural styles such as service-oriented architecture (SOA) and microservices. In general terms, we can say that using several caching methods provided by different services is preferable, because it allows us to fine-tune the caching requirements for each data source, often leading to better overall performances.

That said, there are several scenarios in which server-side caching might be a viable option. Because we plan to store our board-game data in a dedicated DBMS, we could think about caching the results of some frequently used performance-heavy database queries, assuming that the retrieved data doesn't change too often over time. We'll talk more about that topic in chapter 8, which introduces some database optimization strategies based on the `Microsoft.Extensions.Caching.Memory` NuGet package; until then, we'll focus on client-side caching.

CLIENT-SIDE CACHING

Unlike server-side caching, which is used mostly to store data retrieved from backend services and DBMS queries, client-side caching focuses on the content served by web applications: HTML pages, JSON outputs, JavaScript, CSS, images, and multimedia files. That kind of content is often called static because it's typically stored in the filesystem using standard text or binary files. This definition isn't always formally correct, however, because most HTML and JSON content is retrieved dynamically and then rendered on the fly by the server right before being sent along with the HTML response. That's the case with the JSON data sent by our web API.

A major advantage of client-side caching is that, as its name implies, it requires no server-side activity because it fully satisfies the HTTP request to which it applies. This behavior can lead to tremendous advantages in terms of performance, latency, and bandwidth optimization and greatly reduces the server-side load. These benefits are clearly stated in the HTTP/1.1 specifications (RFC 2616 Section 13, "Caching in HTTP," https://www.rfc-editor.org/rfc/rfc2616#section-13):

> *The goal of caching in HTTP/1.1 is to eliminate the need to send requests in many cases and to eliminate the need to send full responses in many other cases. The former reduces the number of network round-trips required for many operations; [...] The latter reduces network bandwidth requirements; [...]*

For all these reasons, we can say that client-side caching is the most important caching technique to implement when we work with any HTTP-based application, especially if we're dealing with a RESTful interface.

RESPONSE CACHING

As we already know, response caching is controlled by HTTP headers that specify how we want the client—as well as any intermediate proxy, CDN, or another service—to cache each HTTP response. The most relevant is `Cache-Control`, which can be used to specify several caching directives explaining who can cache the response (public, private, no-cache, no-store), the cache duration (max-age), stale-related info (max-stale, must-revalidate) and other settings. Ideally, such directives are honored by all the caching systems and services along the request/response chain.

ASP.NET Core gives us the chance to configure these headers (and their directives) by using the [ResponseCache] attribute, which can be applied to any controller or Minimal API method. The [ResponseCache] attribute can be configured by using the following properties:

- Duration—Determines the max-age value of the Cache-Control header, which controls the duration (in seconds) for which the response is cached.
- Location—Determines who can cache the response: Any if both clients and proxies are allowed to, Private to allow clients only, or None to disable it. These values respectively set the public, private, or no-cache directive in the Cache-Control header.
- NoStore—When set to true, sets the Cache-Control header value to no-store, thus disabling the cache. This configuring is typically used for error pages because they typically contain unique info for the specific request that raised the error—info that would make no sense to cache.

TIP The [ResponseCache] attribute is part of the Microsoft.AspNet-Core.Mvc namespace. For that reason, we need to add a reference in the Program.cs file (for Minimal APIs) and/or in the controller files where we want to use it.

Let's see how we can implement this attribute in our existing method, starting with the Minimal API error handlers in the Program.cs file. Because we're dealing with error response messages, we can use this opportunity to use the NoStore property to prevent anyone from caching them in the following way:

```
// ...

app.MapGet("/error",
    [EnableCors("AnyOrigin")]
    [ResponseCache(NoStore = true)] () =>
    Results.Problem());
app.MapGet("/error/test",
    [EnableCors("AnyOrigin")]
    [ResponseCache(NoStore = true)] () =>
    { throw new Exception("test"); });

// ...
```

We can use a different approach with our BoardGamesController because it's meant to return a list of board games that we may want to cache for a reasonable amount of time. Here's how we can set up a public cache with a max-age of 60 seconds for that response:

```
// ...

[HttpGet(Name = "GetBoardGames")]
[ResponseCache(Location = ResponseCacheLocation.Any, Duration = 60)]
public IEnumerable<BoardGame> Get()

// ...
```

That's enough for now. We'll define further response-caching rules whenever we add other action methods.

INTERMEDIATE CACHING

From a web development perspective, intermediate caching is similar to client-side caching, because both techniques store data outside the server following the rules specified in the HTTP response headers. For that reason, the implementation that we've pulled off will work seamlessly for both of them, assuming that we set the `Location` property to `Public`, as explained earlier.

The main differences between the two caching methods are set on the architectural level. The term *intermediate* means that cached resources are stored in a server (or services) located between the client and the server instead of on the former's local drive. This approach involves three important concepts:

- Each cached resource can be used to serve multiple clients. The intermediate cache is also a shared cache, because the same cached response can be issued by several HTTP requests coming from different peers.
- The intermediate caching server must sit between the client and the server so that it can answer each incoming call by serving a cached response (without calling the server) or forwarding it to the server (and possibly caching it for further requests).
- The whole caching mechanism is not visible to clients, to the point that they're mostly unable to tell whether the response comes from the original server or from the cache (unless the owner wants to explicitly make them aware).

Figure 3.2 shows how intermediate caching is intended to work and how it can "stack" with client caching. These concepts are true for proxies, reverse proxies, and CDN services, regardless of where they're physically (or logically) located.

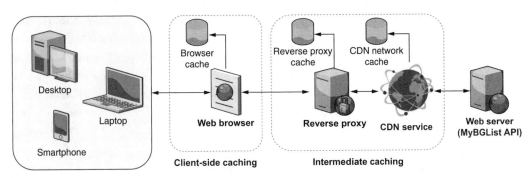

Figure 3.2 Client-side caching and intermediate caching at a glance

From a technical point of view, we can see that the intermediate caching service works like the browser's local cache, sitting between requests and responses, and acting according to the HTTP headers. The scalability performance gains are considerably higher, however, especially when we're dealing with multiple simultaneous requests for the same content. Such benefits are of utmost importance for most web applications and deserve the added complexity of setting up and configuring a dedicated server or service.

> **WARNING** When implementing intermediate caching, we are basically creating "cached copies" of some URL-related content (HTML pages, JSON data, binary files, and so on) that typically become accessible regardless of any authentication and authorization logic used by the server to render that content in the first request/response cycle. As a general rule, intermediate caching services should be used to cache only publicly available content and resources, leaving restricted and personal data to private caching approaches (or no-cache) to prevent potentially critical data security problems.

3.1.4 *Layered system*

This constraint further employs the separation-of-concerns principle already enforced by the client-server approach by applying it to various server components. A RESTful architecture can benefit greatly from a service-distributed approach, in which several (micro)services work together to create a scalable and modular system. We've embraced such a pattern in our concrete scenario, because our board-game API is part of a wider SOA ecosystem with at least two server-side components: the web API itself, which handles the incoming HTTP requests and the whole data exchange process with the third parties, and the DBMS, which provides the data securely. Ideally, the web API and the DBMS can be deployed on different servers located within the same web farm or even different server farms.

Starting from that setting, we can further expand the layered system concept by adding two additional, decentralized architectural components: a reverse-proxy server, which will be installed in a virtual machine under our control, and a CDN service hosted by a third-party provider such as Cloudflare. Figure 3.3 shows the updated architectural SOA diagram with the new components.

The web API still plays the same pivotal role, but we've put two additional layers between the API server and the clients, which will definitely increase the overall performance and availability of our system under heavy load:

- The reverse proxy will allow us to implement an efficient intermediate caching mechanism, as well as pave the way for several load balancing techniques (such as the edge-origin pattern) to improve the horizontal scalability of our app.
- The CDN service will add an intermediate caching layer, lower network latency for most countries and regions, and contribute to cost savings by reducing the server's bandwidth use.

We'll actively implement this plan in chapter 12 when we deploy our app in production.

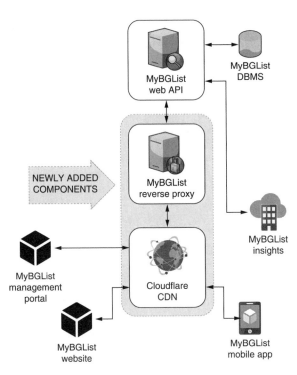

Figure 3.3   Updated MyBGList SOA using CDN and reverse proxy

3.1.5   *Code on demand*

When Roy Fielding wrote his dissertation on REST, JavaScript was still in its early days, the AJAX acronym didn't exist, and the XMLHttpRequest model was unknown to most developers. It wasn't easy to imagine that over the next few years, we would witness a real revolution following the advent of thousands of JavaScript-powered libraries (JQuery) and web frameworks (Angular, React, Vue.js, and more).

The code on demand (COD) optional constraint is easier to understand now than it was before. In a nutshell, we can describe it as the ability of a RESTful API to return executable code, such as JavaScript, to provide the client with additional capabilities. It's precisely what happens when we use a `<script>` element within an HTML page to retrieve a combined JavaScript file containing, say, an Angular app. As soon as the file is downloaded and executed, the browser loads an app that can render UI components, interact with the user, and even perform further HTTP requests to get additional content (or code).

In our given scenario, we'll hardly have the chance to adhere to this optional constraint, because we'll want to return mostly JSON data. Before putting this topic aside, however, I'll show how we can implement COD by using ASP.NET Core and Minimal APIs with only a few lines of source code.

Suppose that our development team has been asked to provide an endpoint that can be used to check whether the calling client supports JavaScript and provide visual proof of the result. That scenario is a perfect chance to develop an endpoint that can return some JavaScript COD.

We'll set up a `/cod/test/` route that will respond with some HTML containing a `<script>` element, with the JavaScript code to render a visual alert in case of success and a `<noscript>` tag to render a text-only message in case of failure. Here's a Minimal API method that we can add to our `Program.cs` file right below the other `MapGet` methods that we've added:

```
app.MapGet("/cod/test",
    [EnableCors("AnyOrigin")]
    [ResponseCache(NoStore = true)] () =>
    Results.Text("<script>" +
        "window.alert('Your client supports JavaScript!" +
        "\\r\\n\\r\\n" +
        $"Server time (UTC): {DateTime.UtcNow.ToString("o")}" +
        "\\r\\n" +
        "Client time (UTC): ' + new Date().toISOString());" +
        "</script>" +
        "<noscript>Your client does not support JavaScript</noscript>",
        "text/html"));
```

As we can see, we also used the `[EnableCors]` and `[ResponseCache]` attributes to set up some CORS and caching rules. We want to enable CORS (because we used the `"AnyOrigin"` named policy), but we don't want the HTTP response to be cached by clients or proxies.

> **TIP** The `[ResponseCache]` attribute requires adding the following reference at the top of the `Program.cs` file: using `Microsoft.AspNetCore.Mvc`.

To test what we did, launch the project in Debug mode and navigate to the following URL, which corresponds to our newly added endpoint: https://localhost:40443/cod/test. If we did everything properly, and if our browser supports JavaScript, we should get the "visual" result shown in figure 3.4.

The alert window rendered by the sample JavaScript code we sent to the client is a good demonstration of COD because it shows both server-computed and client-computed data. While we're here, we might as well test the `<noscript>` outcome as well. Press Ctrl+Shift+I (or F12) to access the browser's developer console; then click the cog icon to access the Settings page, and select the Disable JavaScript check box (figure 3.5).

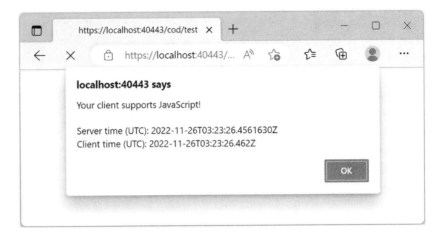

Figure 3.4 COD testing with JavaScript enabled

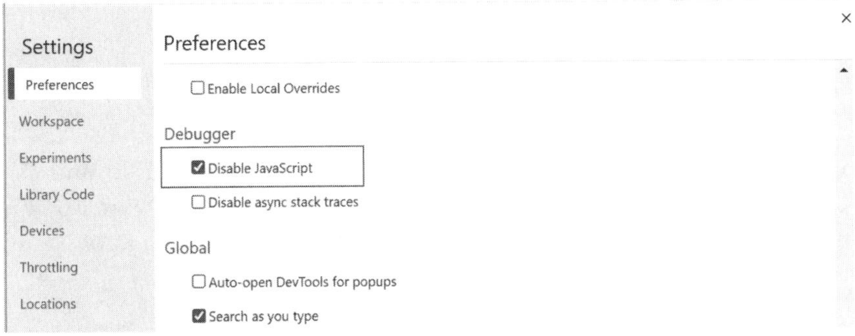

Figure 3.5 Disabling JavaScript in Microsoft Edge

> **WARNING** These commands assume that we're using a Chromium-based browser, such as Microsoft Edge or Google Chrome. Different browsers/engines require different methods. In Mozilla Firefox, for example, we can turn off JavaScript by typing `about:config` in the search bar, accepting the disclaimer, and changing the `javascript.enabled` toggle value from true to false.

Right after that, without closing the Settings window, press F5 to issue a reload of the `/cod/test/` endpoint. Because JavaScript is now disabled (temporarily), we should see the negative outcome shown in figure 3.6.

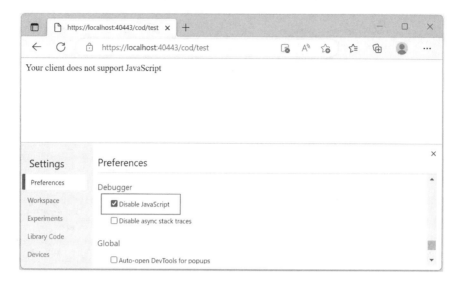

Figure 3.6   COD testing with JavaScript disabled

3.1.6   *Uniform interface*

The RESTful constraint I've left for last is also the one that often takes the longest to implement properly, as well as being arguably the most difficult to understand. Not surprisingly, the best definition of a uniform interface is given by Roy Fielding in section 5.1.5 of his dissertation "Architectural Styles and the Design of Network-based Software Architectures" (http://mng.bz/eJyq), in which he states

> *The central feature that distinguishes the REST architectural style from other network-based styles is its emphasis on a uniform interface between components. By applying the software engineering principle of generality to the component interface, the overall system architecture is simplified and the visibility of interactions is improved. Implementations are decoupled from the services they provide, which encourages independent evolvability.*

This statement implies that a RESTful web API, along with the data, should provide the clients with all the actions and resources they need to retrieve related objects, even without knowing them in advance. In other words, the API must not only return the requested data, but also make the client aware of how it works and how it can be used to request further data. But how can we make the client understand what to do?

Adopting a uniform interface is what we can do. We can think of a uniform interface as being standardized, structured, machine-friendly self-documentation included with any HTTP response, explaining what has been retrieved and (most important) what to do next.

NOTE Fielding's statement and the whole uniform interface concept have long been misunderstood and underestimated by many web developers, who preferred to focus on the other REST constraints. Such behavior started to become common in the 2000s, eventually pushing Fielding to revamp the subject in a famous 2008 post on his personal blog (http://mng.bz/7ZA7).

REST specifications don't force developers to adopt a specific interface. But they do provide four guiding principles that we should follow to implement a viable uniform interface approach:

- *Identification of resources*—Each individual resource must be univocally identified, such as by using universal resource identifiers (URIs) and represented by a standard format (such as JSON).
- *Manipulation through representations*—The representation sent to the client should contain enough info to modify or delete the resource, as well as add further resources of the same kind if the client has permission to do so.
- *Self-descriptive messages*—The representation sent to the client should contain all the required info to process the received data. We can do this by adding relevant info with JSON (which HTTP method to use, which MIME type to expect, and so on), as well as using HTTP headers and metadata (for caching info, character sets, and the like).
- *HATEOAS*—Clients should be able to interact with the application without any specific knowledge beyond a generic understanding of hypermedia. In other words, manipulation through representation should be handled (and documented) only by means of standard descriptive links.

To understand these concepts better, let's adapt them to our current scenario. Our `BoardGamesController` currently returns the following JSON structure:

```
[
  {
    "id": <int>,
    "name": <string>,
    "year": <int>
  }
]
```

This structure means that whenever our clients request a list of board games, our web API responds with the objects they're looking for . . . and nothing more. What it should do instead—assuming that we want to adopt the uniform interface REST constraint—is to return those objects as well as some descriptive links to inform the clients how they can alter those resources and request further resources of the same kind.

IMPLEMENTING HATEOAS

Our current `BoardGamesController`'s `Get()` action method currently returns a dynamic object containing an array of objects created with the `BoardGame` Plain Old CLR Object (POCO) class (the `BoardGame.cs` file). We made that choice in chapter 2, using a handy C# feature (anonymous types) to serve data quickly and effectively with our ASP.NET Core web API. If we want to adopt a uniform interface to return data and descriptive links, however, we need to switch to a more structured approach.

NOTE   For more info regarding C# anonymous types, see the official docs at http://mng.bz/m2MW.

We want to replace the current anonymous type with a base data-transfer object (DTO) class that can contain one or more records of a generic type, as well as the descriptive links that we want to provide the client. A *generic type* is a placeholder for a specific type that can be defined whenever an instance of that object is declared and instantiated. A perfect example is the built-in `List<T>` type, which we can use in C# to declare and instantiate a constructed type list by specifying a specific type argument inside the angle brackets:

```
var intList = new List<int>();
var stringList = new List<string>();
var bgList = new List<BoardGame>();
```

This snippet creates three separate type-safe objects with a single class definition, thanks to the fact that the class accepts a generic type. That's precisely why we need to create our uniform interface DTO.

DEFINITION   DTOs should be familiar to most web developers. In a nutshell, DTOs are POCO classes that can be used to expose relevant info about that object only to the requesting client. The basic idea is to decouple the response data from the data returned by the Data Access layer. I talk more about this concept in chapter 4 when we replace our code sample with an actual data provider powered by SQL Server and Entity Framework Core.

Create a new /DTO/ folder in the project's root. We'll put all the DTOs in that folder from now on. Then use Visual Studio's Solution Explorer to add two new files:

- `LinkDTO.cs`—The class that will host our descriptive links
- `RestDTO.cs`—The class containing the data and the links that will be sent to the client

Both classes have a simple structure. The `RestDTO` class is a container for the `<T>` *generic type*, which will host the actual data, and the `LinkDTO` class will contain the descriptive links. The following listing shows the code for the `LinkDTO` class.

Listing 3.2   `LinkDTO.cs` file

```
namespace MyBGList.DTO
{
    public class LinkDTO
    {
        public LinkDTO(string href, string rel, string type)
        {
            Href = href;
            Rel = rel;
```

```
            Type = type;
        }

        public string Href { get; private set; }

        public string Rel { get; private set; }

        public string Type { get; private set; }
    }
}
```

Listing 3.3 shows the code for the RestDTO class.

Listing 3.3   RestDTO.cs file

```
namespace MyBGList.DTO
{
    public class RestDTO<T>
    {
        public List<LinkDTO> Links { get; set; } = new List<LinkDTO>();

        public T Data { get; set; } = default!;
    }
}
```

C generic classes, methods, and type parameters

For additional info regarding C# generic classes, methods, and type parameters, see the following official docs:

- http://mng.bz/5mV8
- http://mng.bz/69xp

Now that we have these two classes, we can refactor our BoardGamesController's Get() action method to use them, replacing our existing implementation. We want to change the existing anonymous type with the RestDTO class and use the LinkDTO class to add the descriptive links in a structured way. Open the BoardGamesController.cs file, and perform these updates in the following way:

```
public RestDTO<BoardGame[]> Get()                    ◁——┐ Changes the
{                                                        │ return value
    return new RestDTO<BoardGame[]>()          ◁——┘
    {                                                    Changes the
        Data = new BoardGame[] {                         anonymous type
            new BoardGame() {                            with RestDTO
                Id = 1,
                Name = "Axis & Allies",
                Year = 1981
            },
            new BoardGame() {
                Id = 2,
```

```
                    Name = "Citadels",
                    Year = 2000
                },
                new BoardGame() {
                    Id = 3,
                    Name = "Terraforming Mars",
                    Year = 2016
                }
            },                              ┌── Adds the
            Links = new List<LinkDTO> {    <─┘   descriptive links
                new LinkDTO(
                    Url.Action(null, "BoardGames", null, Request.Scheme)!,
                    "self",
                    "GET"),
            }
        };
}
```

We've made three main changes:

- Replaced the previous IEnumerable<BoardGame> return value with a new Rest-
  DTO<BoardGame[]> return value, which is what we're going to return now.
- Replaced the previous anonymous type, which contained only the data, with the
  new RestDTO type, which contains the data and the descriptive links.
- Added the HATEOAS descriptive links. For the time being, we support a single
  board-game-related endpoint; therefore, we've added it by using the "self"
  relationship reference.

NOTE This HATEOAS implementation requires us to add our descriptive
links manually to each action method. We did that for the sake of simplicity,
because it's a great way to understand the logic of what we've done so far. But
if we adopt a common development standard throughout all our controllers
and action methods, we could automatically fill the RestDTO.Links property
by using a helper or factory method and a bunch of parameters.

If we run our project now and call the /BoardGames/ endpoint, here's what we'll get:

```
{
    "data": [
        {
            "id": 1,
            "name": "Axis & Allies",
            "year": 1981
        },
        {
            "id": 2,
            "name": "Citadels",
            "year": 2000
        },
        {
            "id": 3,
            "name": "Terraforming Mars",
```

```
            "year": 2016
        }
    ],
    "links": [
        {
            "href": "https://localhost:40443/BoardGames",
            "rel": "self",
            "type": "GET"
        }
    ]
}
```

Our uniform interface is up and running. We need to adhere to it from now on, improving and extending it as necessary so that the client always knows what to do with our given data.

> **NOTE** For the sake of simplicity, we won't refactor our existing Minimal API methods to use the RestDTO type, as those methods are meant only for testing purposes. We'll remove them from our codebase as soon as we learn how to handle actual errors properly.

CLASSES OR RECORDS?

Instead of creating our DTOs by using the standard C# class type, we could have used the relatively new C# record type (introduced in C# 9). The main difference between these two class types is that records use value-based equality, meaning that two record variables are considered to be equal if all their field values are equal. Conversely, two class variables are considered to be equal only if they have the same type and refer to the same object.

C# record types can be a great replacement of standard class types for defining DTOs, because value-based equality can be useful for dealing with object instances representing JSON data. Because we won't need such a feature in our scenario, we created our first DTOs by using "good old" class types.

> **TIP** For further information on C# record types, I strongly suggest checking out the following Microsoft Docs tutorial: http://mng.bz/GRYD.

This section concludes our journey through the REST constraints. Now we've got all the required knowledge to stick to these best practices throughout the rest of the book. The following sections introduce a couple of topics that aren't strictly related to any of the REST constraints but can be useful for improving the overall usability and readability of our web API:

- API documentation, intended to expose the use of our API in a human-readable way for developers and nondevelopers
- API versioning, which keeps a history of the various releases and performs breaking changes without disrupting existing integrations with the clients

These two features, when implemented correctly, can greatly improve the effectiveness of a web API because they directly affect development and consumption time, increasing customer satisfaction and reducing overall cost. Implementing each feature requires a different set of efforts and tasks, which I cover in the following sections.

3.2   *API documentation*

Web-based products tend to evolve quickly, not only during the development phase, but also between subsequent deployment cycles after the product is released. Continuous (and inevitable) improvement is a proven, intrinsic, almost ontological characteristic of technology, and the main reason why Agile methodologies are frequently used to deal with it. Fixing bugs, adding new features, introducing security requirements, and dealing with performance and stability problems are tasks that any web project will have to deal with to succeed.

Web APIs are no exception. Unlike standard websites or services, however, they don't have a user interface that can show changes and make users aware of them. If a WordPress blog adds a comments section to posts, for example, there's a high chance that visitors will see the new feature, learn how it works, and start using it right away. If we do the same with our web API, maybe adding a brand-new `CommentsController` with a set of endpoints, that's not likely going to happen. Chances are low that the various developers who work with the clients and services that interact with our data will notice the new feature. The same would happen if we make some changes or improvements to an existing feature. If that blog chooses to allow visitors to alter their comments after they've been sent, a new Edit button will be enough. If we add an `Edit()` action method to a controller, however, no one will know unless we find a way to make the interested parties aware of the fact. That's why we should find a way to document our API.

In an ever-changing environment, this activity comes with a cost. Maintaining and updating this documentation for our development team, as well as any external third party that expects to consume our API and/or integrate with it, can become difficult and expensive unless we find a way to do the work automatically, with minimal effort. That task is precisely what OpenAPI (previously known as Swagger) can do.

3.2.1   *Introducing OpenAPI*

The OpenAPI specification is a JSON-based interface description language for documenting, consuming, and visualizing RESTful web services and APIs. It was known as Swagger until 2015, when it was donated to the OpenAPI initiative by the Swagger team. OpenAPI has become the most used, most widely acknowledged documentation standard for RESTful APIs.

> **NOTE** For additional info about Swagger and OpenAPI, check out *Designing APIs with Swagger and OpenAPI*, by Joshua S. Ponelat and Lukas L. Rosenstock (http://mng.bz/neaV).

The main purpose of OAS is to define a standardized contract between the server and the client, allowing the latter to understand how the former works and to interact with its available endpoints without accessing the source code. Furthermore, such a "contract" is intended to be language agnostic and human readable, allowing both machines and humans to understand what the API is supposed to do. From this perspective, OpenAPI is closely related to uniform interface and HATEOAS, discussed earlier in this chapter. Because it can be used to serve many purposes, it's advisable to treat it as a separate topic.

3.2.2 ASP.NET Core components

The .NET framework provides two OpenAPI implementations that can be used in any ASP.NET Core web application: Swashbuckle and NSwag. For the sake of simplicity, we'll use Swashbuckle, which is shipped with the Visual Studio ASP.NET Core web API template that we used to create our `MyBGList` project.

In chapter 2, when we created the web API project with Visual Studio, we chose to keep the Enable OpenAPI support check box selected. That choice allowed us to get the Swashbuckle services and middleware up and running. Check it out by opening the `Program.cs` file and looking at the following lines of code:

```
// ...

builder.Services.AddSwaggerGen();          ⟵——  Swagger JSON
                                                 generator service
// ...

if (app.Environment.IsDevelopment())
{
    app.UseSwagger();          ⟵——┐  Swagger middleware to
    app.UseSwaggerUI();        ⟵——┘  serve the generated JSON
}
      Swagger middleware to
      enable the user interface
```

The Swagger generator service creates a `swagger.json` file that describes all the endpoints available within our web API using the OpenAPI specification. The first middleware exposes such a JSON file by using a configurable endpoint (the default is `/swagger/v1/swagger.json`), and the second enables a handy user interface that allows users to see and browse the documentation. To see the `swagger.json` file, launch the app in Debug mode and navigate to https://localhost:40443/swagger/v1/swagger.json. To access the SwaggerUI (which uses the JSON file as a documentation source), navigate to https://localhost:40443/swagger.

As we can see by looking at the UI main page, the JSON file was created with OAS version 3.0 (per the Swagger Generator default settings) and takes for granted that we're dealing with version 1.0 of our API. Most of the default settings, including the URL of the endpoint serving the `swagger.json` file, can be changed by using the service and middleware options. We can switch from OAS 3.0 to 2.0, add `swagger.json` files, include custom stylesheet files in the `index.html` page, and so on.

> ### A few words about Swashbuckle
>
> For the sake of simplicity, I won't dive into Swashbuckle's configuration settings for now. I'll talk more about them in chapter 11. For additional info, I suggest looking at the official docs:
>
> - http://mng.bz/vX0m
> - http://mng.bz/49r5

In our current scenario, the default settings are good enough, at least for the time being. As we can see by looking at figure 3.7, the SwaggerUI already includes all the endpoints (and return types) that we've added since we started to work with our project—and will automatically keep doing that for those we'll add throughout the rest of the book.

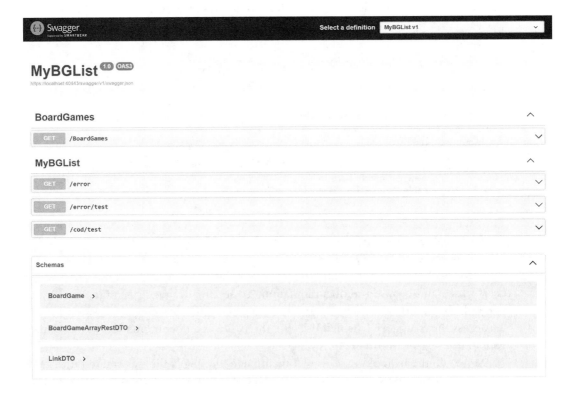

Figure 3.7   SwaggerUI main page for the MyBGList web API project

The SwaggerUI already includes all the controller and Minimal API endpoints that we've added since we started to work with our project—as well as their DTO return types—and will keep doing that for everything we'll add throughout the rest of the book.

Each endpoint and schema type shown by the UI can be expanded; use the right handle to see the full documentation info. The detail level is incredibly high, which is why the middleware that exposes the info was set up in the `Program.cs` file within a conditional block that makes it available only in a development environment. The Visual Studio template is acting conservatively here because it doesn't know whether we want to share such info publicly. That way, we'll be able to benefit from the SwaggerUI during the whole development phase without the risk of sharing our whole endpoint structure in case of a "reckless" deploy. We have no reason to change this convenient behavior for the time being, because we don't plan to publish our app any time soon. All of Swashbuckle's goodies are already set up, and we don't need to do anything.

3.3   API versioning

If we take another look at the SwaggerUI, we can notice the Select a Definition drop-down list in the top-right corner of the screen (figure 3.8).

Figure 3.8   SwaggerUI's API version selector

We can use this list to switch between the Swagger documentation files with which we're feeding the UI. Because we're using only the default file, which has the project's name and is version 1.0 by default, this list contains a single `MyBGList v1` entry. We can generate (and add) multiple `swagger.json` files and feed them all to the UI so that we'll be able to handle and document different versions at the same time. Before I explain how to achieve this result, it could be wise to spend a couple of minutes explaining what API versioning is and, most important, why we should consider it.

3.3.1   Understanding versioning

In software development, *versioning* a product means assigning a unique version number to each release. That's a common practice for software bundles as well as middleware packages and libraries, as it allows developers and users to track each version of the product. Applying this concept to web applications could be considered to be odd, because apps are typically published to a single static URI (a hostname, domain, or folder), and any new version overrides the previous one.

As mentioned earlier, web applications, including web APIs, are meant to evolve throughout their whole lifecycle. Each time we apply a change and deploy it in production, there's a risk that a feature that worked correctly will stop working. Regression bugs, interface modifications, type mismatches, and other backward-incompatibility problems can result in a breaking change. The word *breaking* isn't metaphorical, because there's a high chance that the existing system integrations with the clients, as well as with any third party that consumes the API, will break.

Adopting a versioning system and applying it to our APIs can reduce the risk. Instead of applying the updates directly to the API, forcing all clients to use it immediately, we can publish the new version in a new location, accessible by means of various techniques (such as URIs or headers) without removing or replacing the old version(s). As a result, the latest version and the old version(s) are online simultaneously, giving clients the choice to adopt the new version immediately or stick with the previous one until they're ready to embrace the change.

That scenario sounds great, right? Unfortunately, it's not so simple.

3.3.2 *Should we really use versions?*

API versioning can help us and our clients mitigate the effect of breaking changes, but it also adds complexity and cost. Here's a brief list of the most significant drawbacks:

- *Increased complexity*—The whole point of adopting a versioning strategy is to keep multiple versions of the same API online in a production environment at the same time. This strategy will likely lead to a massive increase in the number of available endpoints, which means having to deal with a lot of additional source code.

- *Conflict with DRY*—Chapter 1 introduced the Don't Repeat Yourself (DRY) principle. If we want to adhere to this principle, we should have a single, unambiguous, and authoritative representation for each component of our code. API versioning often points in the opposite direction, which is known as Write Everything Twice or Write Every Time (WET).

- *Security and stability problems*—Adding features isn't the only reason to update a web API. Sometimes, we're forced to do that to fix bugs, performance problems, or security flaws that could negatively affect our system or to adopt new standards that are known to be more stable and secure. If we do that while keeping the old versions available, we leave the door open to these kinds of troubles. In the worst-case scenario, a malicious third party could exploit our web API by using a bug that we fixed years ago because a vulnerable endpoint is still available.

- *Wrong mindset*—This drawback is more subtle than the previous ones, yet relevant. Relying on API versioning could affect the way that we think about and evolve our app. We might be tempted to refactor our system in backward-compatible ways so that old versions will still be able to use it or be compatible with it. This practice could easily affect not only our approach to the source code, but also other architectural layers of our project: database schemas, design patterns, business logic, data retrieval strategies, DTOs structure, and so on. We could give up adopting the new version of a third-party library because its new interface would be incompatible with an older version of our API that we want to keep online because some clients are still actively using it—and they're doing that because we allow them to.

Most of these drawbacks and others were pointed out by Roy Fielding on a couple of occasions. In August 2013, during a talk at the Adobe Evolve conference, he offered some advice on how to approach API versioning in RESTful web service (figure 3.9) by using a single word: *don't.*

**What is
the best practice for
versioning
a REST API?**

DON'T

Versioning an interface
is just a "polite" way
to kill deployed applications.

Ɛ | VOLVE '13   22

Figure 3.9   Advice on API versioning

> **Roy Fielding's thoughts on API versioning**
> The 46 slides Roy Fielding used throughout his talk can be downloaded at http://mng.bz/Qn91. A year later, he gave a more verbose explanation of that concept in a long interview with InfoQ, available at http://mng.bz/Xall.

I'm not saying that API versioning is always bad practice. In some scenarios, the risk of losing backward compatibility is so high that these drawbacks are more than acceptable. Suppose that we need to perform major updates on a web API that handles online payments—an API that's actively used by millions of websites, services, and users worldwide. We definitely wouldn't want to force breaking changes on the existing interface without giving users a sort of grace period to adapt. In this case, API versioning might come to the rescue (and save a lot of money).

That example doesn't apply to our `MyBGList` web API, however. Our RESTful API is meant to evolve, and we want our clients to embrace that same path, so we won't give them any excuse to be stuck in the past. For this reason, I'll explain how to implement a new version of our existing API and then follow a different path.

3.3.3   *Implementing versioning*

Suppose that our development team has been asked to introduce a simple yet breaking change to our existing `BoardGamesController` for a new board-games-related mobile app, such as renaming the `Data` property of our `RestDTO` type to `Items`. From a code-complexity perspective, implementing this requirement would be a no-brainer; we're talking about a single line of updated code. But some websites use the current API, and we don't want to jeopardize the system integration that they've struggled so much to pull off. Given this scenario, the best thing we can do is set up and release a new version of our API while keeping the current one available.

API VERSIONING TECHNIQUES

REST doesn't provide any specifications, guidelines, or best practices for API versioning. The most common approaches rely on the following techniques:

- *URI versioning*—Using a different domain or URL segment for each version, such as api.example.com/v1/methodName
- *QueryString versioning*—A variant of URI versioning, using a `GET` parameter instead, such as api.example.com/methodName?api-version=1.0
- *Route versioning*—Another variant of URI versioning, using a different route, such as api.example.com/methodName-v1
- *Media Type versioning*—Using the standard `Accept` HTTP header to indicate the version, such as `Accept: application/json;api-version=2.0`
- *Header versioning*—Using a custom HTTP header to indicate the version, such as `Accept-Version: 2.0`

Segment-based URI versioning, which separates the various versions by using unique URL segments (also known as path segments) representing the version ID, is by far the most common approach. Here's an example taken from the PayPal APIs:

- https://api-m.paypal.com/v1/catalogs/products
- https://api-m.paypal.com/v2/checkout/orders

> **WARNING**   These URLs aren't publicly accessible and won't load unless you have a valid access token; they're provided for reference purposes only.

These URLs were taken from https://developer.paypal.com, which contains the up-to-date API documentation and recommended endpoints for the various services. As we can see, the Orders API currently uses version 2, and the Catalog Products API (at this writing) is still stuck on version 1. As I said earlier, API versioning can help us deal with breaking changes gracefully, even on an endpoint basis, because all the versions that we choose to keep online can be used simultaneously and are (or should be) guaranteed to work. At the same time, the increase in complexity is evident. We're going to adopt that same segment-based URI versioning approach to fulfill our assigned task.

FORMATS AND CONVENTIONS

The most widely used versioning format for many years was semantic versioning, also known as SemVer, which can be summarized in the following way: MAJOR.MINOR.PATCH. The most recent SemVer version (which, not surprisingly, adopts its own conventions) is 2.0.0. These numbers must be changed according to the following rules:

- MAJOR—When we make backward-incompatible API changes
- MINOR—When we add functionality in a backward-compatible manner
- PATCH—When we make backward-compatible bug fixes

The SemVer specification also allows the use of prerelease labels, metadata, and other extensions. For simplicity, we'll stick to the basics, which are more than enough for our current needs. For additional info, see the official specification at http://mng .bz/yaj7.

ASP.NET CORE API VERSIONING

Now that we know what we want to do, we can finally move to the implementation part. But because we don't want to be stuck to the versioning system we're going to implement for the rest of the book, we're going to create a separate project and put everything there. Here's what we need to do to create such a clone:

1 In Visual Studio's Solution Explorer, right-click the MyBGList solution and choose Add > New Project from the contextual menu.
2 Select the same ASP.NET Core web API template that we used in chapter 2, with the same settings.
3 Give the new project a distinctive name, such as MyBGList_ApiVersion.
4 Delete the /Controller/ folder and the root files of the new project.
5 Copy the /Controller/ folder, the /DTO/ folder, and the root files of the MyBG-List project—the one we've been working with up to now—to the new project.

Now we have a clean copy of our project that we can use to play with API versioning without messing with the other codebase.

> **TIP** Rest assured that there are several alternatives—and arguably better— ways to do the same thing. If we're using a version-control system such as Git, for example, we could create an ApiVersioning branch of the existing project instead of adding a new one. Because this exercise is for demonstrative purposes only, however, we want to have both codebases accessible at the same time. For further references, you can find the MyBGList_ApiVersion project in the book's GitHub repository for chapter 2.

SETTING UP THE VERSIONING SERVICES

The most effective way to implement a SemVer-based API versioning system in ASP.NET Core relies on installing the following NuGet packages:

- Microsoft.AspNetCore.Mvc.Versioning
- Microsoft.AspNetCore.Mvc.Versioning.ApiExplorer

To install them, right-click the `MyBGList` project's root node, and choose Manage NuGet Packages from the contextual menu. Then use the search box to find these packages and install them. Alternatively, open the Visual Studio's Package Manager console, and type the following command:

```
PM> Install-Package Microsoft.AspNetCore.Mvc.Versioning -Version 5.0.0
PM> Install-Package Microsoft.AspNetCore.Mvc.Versioning.ApiExplorer -
➡ Version 5.0.0
```

In case you prefer to use the dotnet command-line interface, here's the command to issue from the project's root folder:

```
> dotnet add package Microsoft.AspNetCore.Mvc.Versioning --version 5.0.0
> dotnet add package Microsoft.AspNetCore.Mvc.Versioning.ApiExplorer --
➡ version 5.0.0
```

> **NOTE**   At the time of this writing, version 5.0.0, which was released in February 2021 for .NET 5, is the latest for both packages. This version is mostly compatible with .NET 6, with some minor pitfalls in Minimal API support (as we'll see later).

The `Microsoft.AspNetCore.Mvc.Versioning` namespace includes a lot of useful features that implement versioning with a few lines of code. These features include the `[ApiVersion]` attribute, which we can use to assign one or more versions to any controller or Minimal API method, and the `[MapToApiVersion]` attribute, which allows us to do the same for the controller's action methods. Before using these features, however, we need to set up a couple of required versioning services. Furthermore, because we're using OpenAPI, we'll need to alter the configuration of the existing middleware so that Swashbuckle can recognize and work with the versioned routes. As always, all these tasks need to be done in the `Program.cs` file. Open that file, and add the following lines below the CORS service configuration:

```
// ...

builder.Services.AddApiVersioning(options => {              Enables URI
    options.ApiVersionReader = new UrlSegmentApiVersionReader();   ⟵  versioning
    options.AssumeDefaultVersionWhenUnspecified = true;
    options.DefaultApiVersion = new ApiVersion(1, 0);
});
                                                           Sets the API
builder.Services.AddVersionedApiExplorer(options => {      versioning
    options.GroupNameFormat = "'v'VVV";              ⟵     format
    options.SubstituteApiVersionInUrl = true;    ⟵    Replaces the {apiVersion}
});                                                    placeholder with version
                                                       number
// ...
```

The new code also requires the following namespace reference, which can be added to the top of the file:

```
using Microsoft.AspNetCore.Mvc.Versioning;
using Microsoft.OpenApi.Models;
```

The two services that we've added, as well as their configuration settings, give our web API the necessary info to set up URI versioning. In a nutshell, we're telling the service that we want to use URI versioning, define the versioning format to use, and replace the {version:apiVersion} placeholder with the actual version number. This convenient feature allows us to set up the "versioned" routes for our controllers and Minimal API methods dynamically, as we'll see in a short while.

> **TIP** In case we want to use an alternative versioning technique, such as QueryString or HTTP headers, we can replace the UrlSegmentApiVersionReader or combine it with one of the other version readers: QueryStringApiVersionReader, HeaderApiVersionReader, and/or MediaTypeApiVersionReader.

UPDATING THE SWAGGER CONFIGURATION

Now we need to configure the Swagger Generator service to create a JSON documentation file for each version we want to support. Suppose that we require version 1.0 (the existing one) and version 2.0 (the new one), which we want to configure to use the /v1/ and /v2/ URL fragments, respectively:

```
builder.Services.AddSwaggerGen(options => {
    options.SwaggerDoc(
        "v1",
        new OpenApiInfo { Title = "MyBGList", Version = "v1.0" });
    options.SwaggerDoc(
        "v2",
        new OpenApiInfo { Title = "MyBGList", Version = "v2.0" });
});
```

This code requires the following namespace reference:

```
using Microsoft.OpenApi.Models;
```

Right after that, we need to make sure that the SwaggerUI will load the swagger.json files. Scroll down to the SwaggerUI middleware, and add the following configuration settings:

```
app.UseSwaggerUI(options => {
    options.SwaggerEndpoint(
        $"/swagger/v1/swagger.json",
        $"MyBGList v1");
    options.SwaggerEndpoint(
        $"/swagger/v2/swagger.json",
        $"MyBGList v2");
});
```

Last but not least, because we've chosen URI versioning, we need to alter the existing routes for our controllers and Minimal APIs to support the /v1/ and /v2/ URL fragments properly. To do that, we can take advantage of the {version:ApiVersion} placeholder made available by the versioning services, which will be replaced by the actual version number used in the HTTP request, because we've set the Substitute-ApiVersionInUrl option to true in the Program.cs file.

ADDING VERSIONING TO MINIMAL API

Let's apply versioning plan to the Minimal APIs, because they're in the Program.cs file. Scroll down to them, and update the existing code in the following way:

```
app.MapGet("/v{version:ApiVersion}/error",
    [ApiVersion("1.0")]
    [ApiVersion("2.0")]
    [EnableCors("AnyOrigin")]
    [ResponseCache(NoStore = true)] () =>
    Results.Problem());

app.MapGet("/v{version:ApiVersion}/error/test",
    [ApiVersion("1.0")]
    [ApiVersion("2.0")]
    [EnableCors("AnyOrigin")]
    [ResponseCache(NoStore = true)] () =>
    { throw new Exception("test"); });

app.MapGet("/v{version:ApiVersion}/cod/test",
    [ApiVersion("1.0")]
    [ApiVersion("2.0")]
    [EnableCors("AnyOrigin")]
    [ResponseCache(NoStore = true)] () =>
    Results.Text("<script>" +
        "window.alert('Your client supports JavaScript!" +
        "\\r\\n\\r\\n" +
        $"Server time (UTC): {DateTime.UtcNow.ToString("o")}" +
        "\\r\\n" +
        "Client time (UTC): ' + new Date().toISOString());" +
        "</script>" +
        "<noscript>Your client does not support JavaScript</noscript>",
        "text/html"));
```

As we can see, we're using the [ApiVersion] attribute to assign one or more version numbers to each method. Furthermore, we're changing the existing route to prepend the version number by using the {version:ApiVersion} placeholder. The placeholder will be replaced by the actual version number specified by the URL fragment included in the HTTP request: /v1/ or /v2/, depending on which version the client wants to use.

> **NOTE** Because our task assignment doesn't require these Minimal API methods to behave differently in versions 1.0 and 2.0, the best thing we can do to optimize our source code and keep it as DRY as possible is to configure them to handle both versions. Doing that will ensure that all these methods will be

executed regardless of the URL fragment used by the client, without our having to duplicate them.

FOLDER AND NAMESPACE VERSIONING

Now that we've adapted the Minimal API methods to our new versioned approach, we can switch to our `BoardGamesController`. This time, we'll be forced to duplicate our source code to a certain extent; our task assignment requires such a controller (and its action method) to behave differently in version 1 and version 2, because it's expected to return a different DTO. Here's what we need to do:

1 In the `/Controllers/` root directory, create two new `/v1/` and `/v2/` folders.

2 Move the `BoardGamesController.cs` file to the `/v1/` folder, and put an additional copy of that same file in the `/v2/` folder. This action immediately raises a compiler error in Visual Studio, because now we have a duplicate class name.

3 To fix the error, change the namespace of the two controllers from `MyBGList.Controllers` to `MyBGList.Controllers.v1` and `MyBGList.Controllers.v2`, respectively.

4 In the `/DTO/` root directory, create two new `/v1/` and `/v2/` folders.

5 Move the `LinkDTO.cs` and `RestDTO.cs` files to the `/v1/` folder, and put an additional copy of the `RestDTO.cs` file in the `/v2/` folder. Again, this action raises a compiler error.

6 To fix the error, replace the existing namespace with `MyBGList.DTO.v1` and `MyBGList.DTO.v2`, and change the namespace of the `/v1/LinkDTO.cs` file from `MyBGList.DTO` to `MyBGList.DTO.v1`. This action raises a couple more errors in the two `BoardGamesControllers.cs` files, because both have an existing using reference to `MyBGList.DTO`: change—to `MyBGList.DTO.v1` for the v1 controller and to `MyBGList.DTO.v2` for v2. The v2 controller won't be able to find the `LinkDTO` class anymore, as we didn't create a v2 version for that class to keep our codebase as DRY as possible.

7 Fix the error by adding an explicit reference and changing the `LinkDTO` references in the v2 controller to `DTO.v1.LinkDTO`:

```
Links = new List<DTO.v1.LinkDTO> {          Adds an explicit reference
    new DTO.v1.LinkDTO(                      to the v1 namespace
        Url.Action(null, "BoardGames", null, Request.Scheme)!,
        "self",
        "GET"),
}
```

After all these file-copy and namespace-rename tasks, we should end up with the structure shown in figure 3.10.

As we can see, we created two new "instances" of the types that we need to alter in version 2: `RestDTO`, which contains the property we've been asked to rename, and `BoardGamesController`, which is the action method that will serve it. Now we have everything we need to implement the required changes.

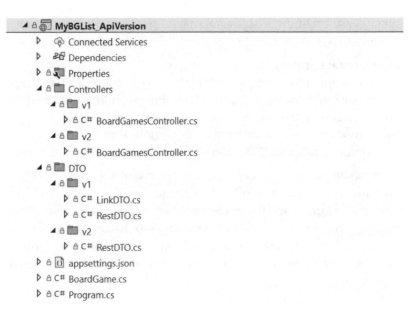

Figure 3.10 `MyBGList_ApiVersion` **project structure**

UPDATING THE V2

Let's start with the `RestDTO.cs` file. We need to change the instance that we put in the `/v2/` folder, because we want the other one to preserve its current structure and behavior. Open the `/DTO/v2/RestDTO.cs` file, and rename the `Data` property to `Items` in the following way:

```
public T Items { get; set; } = default!;
```

That's it. Now we can finally change version 2 of `BoardGamesController` to handle the new property (and route). Open the `/Controllers/v2/BoardgamesController.cs` file. Start with the breaking change that we've been asked to implement, which now boils down to updating a single line of code:

```
// ...

Items = new BoardGame[] {

// ...
```

Now we need to explicitly assign this `BoardGamesController` to version 2 and modify its route to accept the path segment that corresponds to that version. Both tasks can use the [Route] and [ApiVersion] attributes, as follows:

```
// ...
[Route("v{version:apiVersion}/[controller]")]
[ApiController]
```

```
[ApiVersion("2.0")]
public class BoardGamesController : ControllerBase

// ...
```

We have to do the same thing for the `v1` controller, which we still need to assign to version 1:

```
// ...

[Route("v{version:apiVersion}/[controller]")]
[ApiController]
[ApiVersion("1.0")]
public class BoardGamesController : ControllerBase

// ...
```

As we can see, we used the `{version:apiVersion}` placeholder here as well. We could have used a literal string, because each controller is univocally bound to a single version:

```
[Route("v1/[controller]")]
```

Using the placeholder whenever possible is definitely good practice, however, as it allows us to configure a controller to handle multiple versions, as we did with the Minimal API methods.

TESTING API VERSIONING

Now we can finally test what we've done so far. Run the `MyBGList_ApiVersion` project in Debug mode, and type `https://localhost:40443/swagger` in the browser to access the SwaggerUI. If we did everything correctly, we should see the new `/v1/BoardGame` endpoint, shown in figure 3.11.

If we look at the Select a Definition drop-down list in the top-right corner of the screen, we can see that we can switch to `MyBGList v2`, which contains the `/v2/Board-Games` endpoint. Our API versioned project is working as expected—at least, for the most part.

> **WARNING** Truth be told, something is missing from the picture. If we compare figure 3.11 with the SwaggerUI main page of our previous, nonversioned `MyBGList` project, we see that the Minimal API methods are missing from the drop-down list, and they're not listed in the `swagger.json` file. The `VersionedApiExplorer` that we're using now to locate all the app's available endpoints (part of the second NuGet package that we installed) was released in February 2021, before the introduction of .NET 6 and Minimal APIs, so it isn't able to detect their presence. Remember what I said about the lack of some .NET 6 support? That's the pitfall I was talking about. Luckily, the problem affects only Swashbuckle. Our Minimal API methods will still work as expected for both versions of our API; they're not present in the Swagger

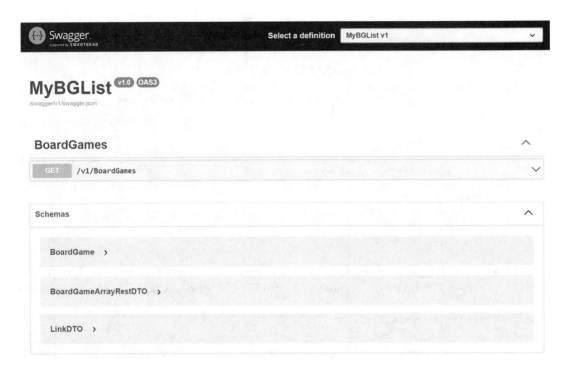

Figure 3.11   SwaggerUI with API versioning

documentation files, though, and can't be shown in the SwaggerUI. Ideally, this minor drawback will be fixed when the NuGet packages are updated to fully support all .NET 6 and Minimal API features.

3.4   Exercises

Before moving to chapter 4, spend some time testing your knowledge of the topics covered in this chapter by doing some wrap-up exercises. Each exercise emulates a task assignment given by a product owner, which we'll have to implement by playing the role of the `MyBGList` development team. The project we'll be working on is `MyBG-List_ApiVersion`, which has the greatest functionality and is the most complete.

TIP   The solutions to the exercises are available on GitHub in the `/Chapter_03/ Exercises/` folder. To test them, replace the relevant files in your `MyBGList_ ApiVersion` project with those in that folder, and run the app.

3.4.1   CORS

Create a new CORS policy that accepts only cross-origin requests performed by using the HTTP GET method (with any origin and header). Call it `"AnyOrigin_GetOnly"`, and assign it to the Minimal API method that handles the `<ApiVersion>/cod/test` route for any API version.

3.4.2 *Client-side caching*

Update the existing caching rules for the `BoardGamesController`'s `Get()` method (API version 2 only) in the following way:

- Ensure that the response will set the `Cache-Control` HTTP header to `private`.
- Change the `max-age` to 120 seconds.

Then switch to the API v1 and disable the cache by setting the `Cache-Control` HTTP header to `no-store`.

3.4.3 *COD*

Create a new `CodeOnDemandController` (version 2 only) with no constructor, without `ILogger` support, and with two action methods handling the following routes:

- `/v2/CodeOnDemand/Test`—This endpoint must return the same response as the Minimal API method that currently handles the `<apiVersion>/cod/test` route, with the same CORS and caching settings. Use the `ContentResult` return value for the action method and the `Content()` method to return the response text.
- `/v2/CodeOnDemand/Test2`—This endpoint must return the same response as the `Test()` action method, with the same CORS and caching settings. Furthermore, it needs to accept an optional `addMinutes` GET parameter of integer type. If this parameter is present, it must be added to the server time before it's sent to the client so that the `server time (UTC)` value shown in the alert window rendered by the script can be altered by the HTTP request.

Both action methods must be configured to accept only the HTTP `GET` method.

3.4.4 *API documentation and versioning*

Add a new version (version 3) to our API with the following requirements:

- No support for any existing Minimal API route/endpoint
- No support for any `BoardGameController` route/endpoint
- Support for the `/v3/CodeOnDemand/Test2` route/endpoint only (see the preceding exercise), but the `addMinutes` GET parameter must be renamed `minutesToAdd` without affecting version 2

The new version must also have its own `swagger.json` documentation file and must be shown in the SwaggerUI like the other ones.

Summary

- Understanding the REST constraints and their effect through the whole project's lifecycle, from overall architecture to low-level implementation efforts, is a required step for building HTTP APIs that can deal efficiently with the challenges posed by an ever-changing entity like the web.
- ASP.NET Core can greatly help with implementing most RESTful constraints because it comes with several built-in features, components, and tools that enforce the REST best practices and guidelines.

- CORS is an HTTP-header-based mechanism that can be used to allow a server to relax a browser security setting by allowing it to load resources from one or more external (third-party) origins.
  - CORS can be implemented in ASP.NET Core thanks to a built-in set of services and middleware, which allows us to use attributes to define default rules and custom policies for controllers and/or Minimal API methods.
- Response caching techniques can bring substantial advantages to a web API in terms of performance, latency, and bandwidth optimization.
  - Response caching can be implemented with a given set of HTTP headers that can be sent with the response to influence the client (browser cache), as well as intermediate parties such as proxy servers and/or CDN services.
  - The HTTP headers are easy to set in ASP.NET Core by using the [Response-Cache] attribute.
- Adopting a uniform interface to standardize the data sent by the web API using hypermedia can help the client become aware of what it can do next, with huge advantages in terms of evolvability.
  - Although REST doesn't provide specific guidance on how to create a uniform interface, ASP.NET Core can handle this requirement by implementing a response DTO to return not only the requested data, but also a structured set of links and metadata that the client can use to understand the overall logic and possibly request further data.
- Unlike most web applications, web APIs don't have a user interface that can make users aware of the frequent changes they'll likely experience.
  - This limitation is addressed by the introduction of standardized description languages such as OpenAPI (formerly Swagger), which can be fetched by readers and parsers to show the API documentation in human-readable fashion.
  - Swagger/OpenAPI can be implemented in ASP.NET Core by using Swashbuckle, an open source project that provides a set of services and middleware to generate Swagger documents for web APIs.
- API versioning is the process of iterating different versions of your API and keeping them available at the same time.
  - Adopting an API versioning procedure could bring some stability and reliability to our project, because it allows us to introduce breaking changes gracefully without forcing every client to adapt or cease working.
  - It also comes with some nontrivial drawbacks that could outweigh the benefits in some scenarios.
- ASP.NET Core provides a wide range of API versioning functionalities through two Microsoft-maintained NuGet packages that can help minimize the complexity that inevitably comes with this approach.

Part 2

Basic concepts

If you're reading this page, you survived part 1 and are willing to continue. Good job! In this part, we'll make good use of what we've learned so far and put it into practice to implement the main data-related development tasks required by a typical web API project. After completing this part, you'll be able to create simple yet fully working web APIs that are capable of dealing with underlying data sources efficiently.

Chapter 4 discusses the data source and data model concepts, explaining how to choose the most suitable database for any scenario. We'll learn how to install and configure the SQL Server instance that we'll use as the web API's main data source throughout the rest of the book. Last but not least, we'll introduce the object relational mapper (ORM) and learn how to use Entity Framework Core (EF Core) to deal with our data source in a structured, standardized, and strongly typed fashion.

The skills we learned in chapter 4 will come into play in chapter 5, where we'll see how to perform SELECT, INSERT, UPDATE, and DELETE queries with EF Core, as well as handle different requests by using HTTP GET, POST, PUT and DELETE methods. We'll also learn to implement typical web API features such as paging, sorting, and filtering, using data-transfer objects (DTOs) to exchange JSON data with the client.

Chapter 6 introduces data validation, illustrating several ASP.NET Core features that we can use to implement it properly in our web API project: model binding, validation attributes, and ModelState. The chapter also contains an in-depth section on error and exception handling, illustrating some built-in and custom implementation techniques.

Working with data 4

Up to this point, we have been working on our web API using sample data created on demand by a static procedure. Such an approach was certainly useful, as it allowed us to focus on the fundamental concepts of a REST architecture while keeping our source code as simple as possible. In this chapter, we're going to get rid of that "fake" data set and replace it with a proper data source managed by means of a database.

In the first section, we'll briefly review the key elements and distinctive properties of a database management system (DBMS), as well as the benefits of storing our data there. Right after that, we'll see how we can interact with that system using

93

Entity Framework Core (EF Core), a lightweight, extensible data access technology that allows us to work with most database services using .NET objects. More precisely, we'll learn how to use the two main development approaches provided by EF Core to generate a data model from an existing database schema (database-first) or create a data model manually and generate the database schema from that (code-first), providing a concrete scenario for both.

To achieve these goals, we will also need to provide ourselves with a real DBMS. For this reason, we will spend some valuable time analyzing some of the many alternatives available today: installing a database server on our development machine (on-premise) or relying on a cloud-hosted DBMS service using one of the many cloud computing providers available (such as Microsoft Azure).

As soon as we have a database up and running, we'll learn how to improve our web API project to retrieve and persist relational data by using the object-relational mapping (ORM) capabilities provided by EF Core.

> ### Database schema and data model
> Before continuing, it might be useful to clarify the meaning of some relevant terms that we'll be using throughout this book, because they are often used in a similar, sometimes interchangeable way.
>
> We'll use *database schema* for the database structure, intended to be the sum of all tables, collections, fields, relationships, views, indexes, constraints, and the like, and *data model* (or *model*) for the abstraction EF Core uses to interact with that structure. This means that the database schema is a logical representation of the database, whereas the data model is made of several C# classes working together, using a standardized set of conventions and rules. These distinctions will help us better understand the differences of the various operational contexts that we'll work with in this chapter and the following chapters.

4.1 Choosing a database

A *database management system* is a software program specifically designed for creating and managing large sets of structured data. Those data sets are generally called databases. For the sake of simplicity, I'll take for granted that you already know the main advantages of using a DBMS to manage a large quantity of information: improved efficiency; access versatility; data categorization; normalization capabilities; support for atomicity, consistency, isolation, and durability (ACID) transactions; and several undeniable benefits in terms of data security coming from the increased confidentiality, integrity, and availability that these solutions natively provide.

> **NOTE** Confidentiality, integrity, and availability are the three pillars of the CIA triad, a widely used security model that summarizes the key properties that any organization should consider before adopting a new technology, improving the existing IT infrastructure, or developing a project.

Since chapter 1, we've taken for granted the use of a database to store all our board-game-related data. The reason for that choice is quite simple: we not only want to benefit from all the advantages described earlier, but also aim to reproduce a suitable situation for developing a web API. Having to deal with a DBMS is likely to be the most common task for any backend web developer for years to come.

In our scenario, however, we are playing the role not only of software developers, but also of high-level IT infrastructure architects. We need to do something before starting to code: choose which DBMS to use for storing and delivering our data.

The following sections briefly review some alternative approaches we can follow, as well as their pros and cons. For the sake of simplicity, our analysis will be limited to the fundamental aspects of each option, as well as the reasons that will determine our decisions.

4.1.1 Comparing SQL and NoSQL

The first choice we're called on to make concerns the type of database we want to adopt. The two most popular choices today are SQL-type databases, also known as relational database management systems (RDBMS) and NoSQL-type (or nonrelational) databases.

> **DEFINITION** Conversely from what we might think when looking at the acronym, *NoSQL* doesn't stand for *No SQL*; it stands for *Not Only SQL*. Most NoSQL databases support variants of Structured Query Language (SQL), even if their data-retrieval API typically relies on different (JSON-like) syntax. Because SQL is typically used with relational databases, however, this term is conventionally adopted in reference only to relational databases, whereas NoSQL defines all non-relational approaches. For the sake of simplicity, we'll adopt these conventions throughout this book.

The main difference between SQL and NoSQL databases is their data storage model, which also affects the data-retrieval techniques and, eventually, their scaling capabilities and usage scenarios. The following sections shed some light on these aspects.

DATA STORAGE MODEL

Without delving too much into the characteristics of each individual product, we can summarize the data storage model concept as follows:

- *In SQL databases*—The data is modeled by using tables with a fixed schema of rows and columns, with each table representing a single record type: the Users table, the Roles table, the BoardGames table, the Comments table, and so on.
- *In NoSQL databases*—The data is modeled by using collections of documents with a flexible schema of key/value pairs, with each document typically representing a record type together with all its related info: the Users documents (including the roles, if any), the Boardgames documents (including the comments, if any), and so on.

We immediately see that the two approaches handle relationships between entities in different ways. In SQL databases, the relationships between table records are typically implemented by means of primary keys that univocally identify each record of any given type, which can be added in the tables that require such references and then used to retrieve them. In our concrete scenario, for example, the Comments table would likely require the BoardGameID column to reference each comment to a given unique board game. Such logic will produce a well-structured, highly normalized, and (often) rather complex database schema made of fixed tables.

In NoSQL databases, most of the parent-child relationships between entities are embedded in the parent document, resulting in fewer collections. Key-based relationships are still used to handle entities that need to be referenced in multiple documents (a typical example being the users collection), but for the most part, the database schema doesn't rely on them. This approach favors a loosely structured, denormalized, and (often) rather simple database schema made by collections of flexible documents.

The differences don't stop at the relationship level. Because we must deal with fixed tables in SQL databases, we're forced to determine and declare each table's schema before inserting data. NoSQL's collections don't have this requirement because they don't require their documents to have the same schema.

To better understand these concepts, take a look at a few figures. The first one (figure 4.1) depicts a possible data schema for our concrete scenario built with a table-oriented, relational, SQL database in mind: a BoardGames table and two related tables (Domains and Mechanics) linked to the main table by means of many-to-many relationships through two junction tables.

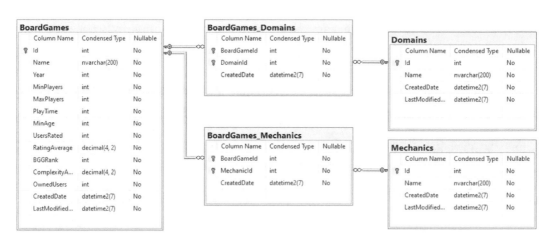

Figure 4.1   MyBGList database schema diagram for a table-oriented SQL database

Figure 4.2 shows a database schema that can host the same data by using a document-oriented, NoSQL alternative approach: a single boardGames document collection with two embedded collections of mechanic and domain documents.

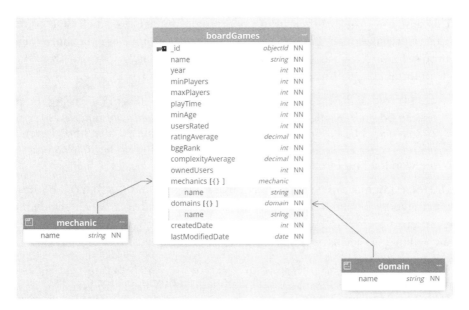

Figure 4.2 MyBGList database schema diagram for a document-oriented NoSQL database

NOTE In figure 4.2 (and its preceding text) we wrote the document and property names using camelCase because it's the preferred naming convention for most NoSQL database engines.

Both models are rather easy to understand at first glance because we're working with a simple, demonstrative data structure. But we can easily see that if we had to deal with many additional "child" entities, the complexity levels of the two models would likely rise at different paces. The SQL schema would likely require additional tables (and junction tables), as well as an increasing number of JOINs for retrieving their relevant info, thus requiring more development effort.

The overall complexity of the database schema (and data retrieval queries) is only one of the many factors that we should consider when choosing between a SQL and a NoSQL approach. Another huge factor is their scaling capabilities, as we'll see in the next section.

Scaling

In general terms, we can say that SQL databases are designed to run on a single server because they need to maintain the integrity of their tables, indexes, and constraints. They are designed to scale vertically by increasing their server's size, not to scale horizontally following a distributed computing approach; even the clustering techniques introduced to give them horizontal scaling capabilities are often subject to consistency problems, performance bottlenecks, and other drawbacks, not to mention added complexity.

Conversely, NoSQL databases are designed for scaling horizontally on distributed systems, which means having multiple servers working together and sharing the workload.

This design is probably their most important advantage over their SQL counterparts, because it makes them better suited to host huge amounts of data, more reliable, and more secure. As long as we can count on multiple NoSQL nodes, we won't have a single point of failure, thus ensuring a higher availability level.

> **DEFINITION**   *Vertical scaling*, also known as *scale-up*, refers to increasing the processing power of a single node (database server). *Horizontal scaling*, also known as *scale-out*, is based on adding nodes to form a cluster; after the cluster has been created, it can be scaled by adding or removing nodes to accommodate the workload requirements.

The huge advantage of NoSQL's horizontal scaling, however, is reduced by the advent of several modern cloud-based SQL (or hybrid) DBMS services, which greatly reduce the end-user costs of vertical scaling. Moreover, those solutions often include many clustering and redundancy techniques that effectively mitigate the risk of a single point of failure.

SUPPORT

Another important aspect to consider is the level of support for the development stack we've chosen to adopt. SQL databases have a strong edge because they have a decades-long presence in the market. Most NoSQL solutions are still behind in terms of available drivers, accessors, connectors, tooling, and cross-platform support—at least when taking the .NET ecosystem into account. Furthermore, most NoSQL databases use different APIs with no shared standards, such as the ones in relational databases (such as SQL syntax)—a fact that has slowed the widespread adoption of these technologies.

USAGE SCENARIOS

All in all, we can say that the intrinsic characteristics of SQL databases make them ideal for hosting a set of normalized data, when all the record types are supposed to have the same structure, and most of them need to be referenced several times and in multiple places. When we're dealing with this kind of data, most of the advantages of the NoSQL approach likely won't come into play.

Conversely, whenever we have a huge amount of data, or when we're forced to handle records that require a mutable structure and several parent-child relationships, the flexibility and scaling capabilities provided by a NoSQL database often make it a suitable choice (assuming that our development stack supports it).

4.1.2   *Making a choice*

Now that we have all the required info, let's put on the clothes of our `MyBGList` IT team and choose between the two approaches. Suppose that our club is handling the board-game data by using a comma-separated-values (CSV) file containing all the relevant fields (ID, name, year published, and so on), which we need to import within a DBMS to enable our web API to interact with it. We already know the data structure we're dealing with, because we saw it in the two database schema diagrams, which can be considered a couple of proofs of concept we made before making the decision. Should we go with SQL or NoSQL? Here's a list of arguments that could help us make a reasoned choice:

- By looking at the data, we can say that we are dealing—and will always have to deal—with a rather small data set. We can reasonably expect that the number of board games won't exceed a few thousand over the whole lifetime of our web API.

- Considering our overall architecture, performance won't likely be a problem. We will serve mostly small sets of data to a limited number of peers, and we'll definitely make extensive use of caching and paging techniques to reduce the server load. With such premises, horizontal scaling won't be required any time soon.

- All our record types are supposed to have the same data structure. Some of them will likely change in the future, but we will probably always want to keep it consistent between all the record types available. For example, sooner or later we might want to add additional details to the authors entities (title, job, address, and so on), but as soon as we do that we would want these new columns to be available for all authors' records, including the existing ones.

- Last but not least, we need to consider the web development stack we've chosen to adopt. As a matter of fact, ASP.NET Core provides support for both SQL and NoSQL databases. But although drivers and libraries for the most popular RDBMS software products (SQL Server, MySQL, and more) have been shipped as built-in features for decades, the NoSQL alternative is currently supported only by Azure Cosmos DB (Microsoft's proprietary NoSQL database hosted on Azure) or third-party providers (such as those for MongoDB and RavenDB). The same goes for EF Core, the most popular ASP.NET data access technology, which currently doesn't provide native NoSQL support. Even the EF Core Azure Cosmos DB provider works only with the SQL API.

For all these reasons, our final choice will eventually be the SQL (relational) database approach, which seems to be the most suitable option for our concrete scenario. This decision comes with the added value of allowing us to use EF Core (more about which later in this chapter).

Next, we need to choose a specific RDBMS product. For the sake of simplicity, we won't spend too much time comparing the various available options offered by the market. Let's start by narrowing the list to the main RDBMSes supported by EF Core, together with their respective owners and the maintainer/vendor of the most popular database provider required to support each of them (table 4.1). A comprehensive list of all the available DBMS and database providers is available at https://docs.microsoft .com/en-us/ef/core/providers.

Table 4.1 DBMS, owners, and database providers maintainers/vendors

DBMS product	Owner/developer	Database provider maintainer/vendor
SQL Server	Microsoft	EF Core Project
SQLite	Dwayne Richard Hipp	EF Core Project
Cosmos DB (SQL API)	Microsoft	EF Core Project

Table 4.1 DBMS, owners, and database providers maintainers/vendors *(continued)*

DBMS product	Owner/developer	Database provider maintainer/vendor
PostgreSQL	PostgreSQL GDG	Npgsql Development Team
MySQL	Oracle Corporation	Pomelo Foundation Project
Oracle DB	Oracle Corporation	Oracle Corporation

As we can see, each DBMS product is supported by the means of a database provider created and maintained by either the EF Core project or a third-party development team. The providers shown in table 4.1 provide a good level of support and are updated continuously by their maintainer to match the latest versions of EF Core, which makes them ideal for most production scenarios.

Taking all those factors into account, because we want to explore most of the features offered by ASP.NET Core and EF Core, a reasonable choice for demonstrative purposes would be Microsoft SQL Server, which will also allow us to experience both on-premise and cloud-based hosting models. We're going to pick that DBMS.

> **NOTE** Because EF Core provides a common interface for all those relational database engines, we'll even be able to reconsider our decision and switch to a different product during our development phase without significant problems.

4.2   *Creating the database*

Now that we've chosen our DBMS product, we can create our SQL database and populate it with our board-game data. Because we want to follow our concrete scenario, the first thing we need to do is provide ourselves with a suitable data set (such as an XML or CSV file) that we can use to emulate our initial condition: a list of board games with their most relevant info (name, year published, mechanics, domains, and so on). When we have that data set, we'll be able to perform the following tasks:

1 Install a local SQL Server instance on our development machine.
2 Create the `MyBGList` database using either a graphical user interface (GUI) tool or raw SQL queries.
3 Set up and configure EF Core to access the `MyBGList` database.
4 Use EF Core's database-first feature to create our entities.
5 Populate the database by using EF Core directly from our web API.

4.2.1   *Obtaining the CSV file*

For the sake of simplicity, instead of creating a CSV file from scratch, we're going to get one from Kaggle, an online community of data scientists that hosts several publicly accessible data sets for education and training purposes. We'll use Larxel's Board Games, a CSV file hosting a data set of approximately 20,000 board games scraped from the BoardGamesGeek website. Download the compressed data set and then unpack it to extract the `bgg_dataset.csv` file.

Larxel's board game credits and references

The dataset is published under Creative Commons Attribution 4.0 International license, which allows us to use it by giving credit to the authors.

Dataset URL: https://www.kaggle.com/andrewmvd/board-games

Maintainer: Larxel, https://www.kaggle.com/andrewmvd

Citation: Dilini Samarasinghe, July 5, 2021, "BoardGameGeek Dataset on Board Games," IEEE Dataport, doi: https://dx.doi.org/10.21227/9g61-bs59

License: CC BY 4.0, https://creativecommons.org/licenses/by/4.0

TIP Kaggle requires (free) registration to download the file: if you're not willing to register, use the `/Data/bgg_dataset.csv` file provided in the book's GitHub repository starting from chapter 4.

Before moving on to the next step, it could be useful to open the file using a text editor (or a GUI tool that can handle CSV format, such as Microsoft Excel) and take a good look at it to ensure that it contains the field we need. Figure 4.3 shows an excerpt of the first ten lines and eight columns of the file. As we can see, the file contains all the columns we need.

	A	B	C	D	E	F	G	H	I
1	ID	Name	Year Published	Min Players	Max Players	Play Time	Min Age	Users Rated	Rating Average
2	174430	Gloomhaven	2017	1	4	120	14	42055	8,79
3	161936	Pandemic Legacy: Season 1	2015	2	4	60	13	41643	8,61
4	224517	Brass: Birmingham	2018	2	4	120	14	19217	8,66
5	167791	Terraforming Mars	2016	1	5	120	12	64864	8,43
6	233078	Twilight Imperium: Fourth Edition	2017	3	6	480	14	13468	8,7
7	291457	Gloomhaven: Jaws of the Lion	2020	1	4	120	14	8392	8,87
8	182028	Through the Ages: A New Story of Civilization	2015	2	4	120	14	23061	8,43
9	220308	Gaia Project	2017	1	4	150	12	16352	8,49
10	187645	Star Wars: Rebellion	2016	2	4	240	14	23081	8,42
11	12333	Twilight Struggle	2005	2	2	180	13	40814	8,29

Figure 4.3 Excerpt of the `bgg_dataset.csv` file

NOTE The actual CSV file content may vary because it's updated frequently by its maintainer. The version used in this book is version 2.0 (the latest at this writing) and can be found in the GitHub repository for this chapter for reference purposes.

4.2.2 Installing SQL Server

We chose to install a local instance of SQL Server instead of using a cloud-based solution (such as the SQL database provided by Azure) for practical reasons:

- SQL Server provides two free editions that we can use: Developer, which comes with the full functionality of the commercial editions but can be used only for testing, educational, and teaching purposes, and Express, which has several size and performance limitations but can be used in production for small-scale applications.

- We can use SQL Server Management Studio (SSMS) to its full extent, as most of its GUI-related features—such as the visual table designer and the modeling tools—might not work when we're dealing with a cloud-hosted SQL database (depending on the product).

TIP As an alternative to installing a local instance on their development machines, Docker users can consider one of the many SQL Server containers available on DockerHub. Here's the link to the official SQL Server Docker image, released and maintained by Microsoft: https://hub.docker.com/_/ microsoft-mssql-server.

Regardless of the choice we make, there's no need to worry; we'll always be able to migrate our on-premise SQL Server database to a cloud-hosted Azure SQL database service whenever we want to, with minimal effort.

SQL Server Express and LocalDB

The SQL Server Express installation instructions are detailed in the appendix. In case we don't want to install a local SQL server instance on our development machine, we could take an alternative route by using SQL Server Express LocalDB—a lightweight SQL instance provided by Visual Studio that offers the same T-SQL language, programming surface, and client-side providers as the regular SQL Server Express without the need to install or configure (almost) anything. Such a solution can be great during development, because it immediately gives us a database with no additional work. But it comes with a huge set of limitations that make it unsuitable for production use, which is one of the goals we want to achieve with this book. For that reason, I suggest avoiding this "convenient" shortcut and sticking with a regular SQL Server edition instead.

When SQL Server installation is complete, we can connect to the newly installed instance by using one of the following free management tools:

- SQL Server Management Studio (SSMS)
- Azure Data Studio (ADS)

Both software applications allow us to connect to a SQL Server database and manage its contents (tables, users, agents, and so on), as well as perform queries and scripts. SSMS is available only for Windows and has a lot of features that can be used from the GUI. ADS has a portable, multiplatform, lightweight design and provides a rather minimal interface that allows us to perform only SQL queries (at least, for now).

TIP Starting with version 18.7, SSMS includes ADS as an internal module, accessible from the Tools menu.

For this book, we're going to use SSMS, because it provides a more graceful learning curve for SQL novices. But ADS might be a great alternative for two groups of people:

seasoned SQL developers who prefer to avoid the GUI-based approach and perform everything through SQL queries and scripts, and Linux users, because both SQL Server and ADS can be installed in Linux.

4.2.3   Installing SSMS or ADS

SSMS can be installed through the SQL Server installation wizard's additional components (SQL Server Management Tools section) or downloaded as a standalone package at http://mng.bz/pdKw. To use ADS, download it at http://mng.bz/OpBa. Both tools are easy to install and set up via the installation wizard and require no specific settings.

> **NOTE**   In the following sections, we're going to use SSMS to connect to SQL Server and create the database structure via its unique UI-based approach. All the SQL queries required to create the `MyBGList` database tables can be found in the GitHub repository for this chapter.

4.2.4   Adding a new database

Right after completing the installation process, launch SSMS. The Connect to Server pop-up window should appear. Because we're connecting to a locally hosted SQL Server instance, we're going to use the following settings:

- *Server type*—Database engine
- *Server name*—`<MACHINENAME>\SQLEXPRESS` (or `.\SQLEXPRESS` ; a single dot can be used as an alias for the local machine name)
- *Authentication*—Windows authentication or SQL Server authentication (depending on whether you chose Windows Authentication or Mixed Mode during the installation phase)
- *Username and password*—Leave them blank for Windows authentication, or use the `sa` account's credentials for Mixed Mode/SQL Server authentication

Next, click the Connect button to establish a connection with the SQL Server instance. From here, we can finally create our database by right-clicking the `Databases` folder in the left tree view and then selecting the New Database option (figure 4.4).

The New Database modal window opens, allowing us to give our new database a name and configure its core settings. For the sake of simplicity, we'll give it the `MyBGList` name and keep the default settings, as shown in figure 4.5.

Click the OK button to create the database, which will be added to the `Databases` folders as a new child node, with several subfolders: `Diagrams`, `Tables`, `Views`, and so on.

INTRODUCING LOGINS AND USERS

Now that we have the `MyBGList` database, we need to create a set of credentials (username and password) that can be put in a connection string to make our web API access it. To do that, we need to perform two tasks:

- Add a login to authenticate into our SQL Server local instance.
- Add a user to authorize the login into our `MyBGList` database.

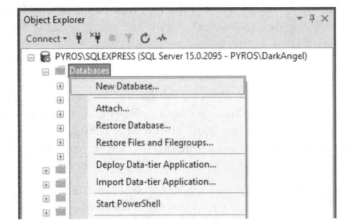

Figure 4.4   Adding a new SQL database in SSMS

Figure 4.5   Creating the MyBGList database in SSMS

The individual logins-and-users approach ensures a good security posture, because it gives us precise, granular control of who can access each database and to what extent. It's important to understand that logins must be added to the SQL Server instance and therefore affect the whole instance, whereas users pertain only to a specific database—in our case, MyBGList. For that reason, the same login could be theoretically linked to different users. That said, in our specific scenario, we'll create a login and a user with the same name and then link them.

ADDING THE SQL SERVER LOGIN

Because the Login entry must be added at the instance level, we need to use SQL
Server's main `Security` folder—not the folder of the same name inside the `MyBGList`
database. When we locate this folder, we right-click it and choose New Login from the
contextual menu to access the Login—New modal window, shown in figure 4.6.

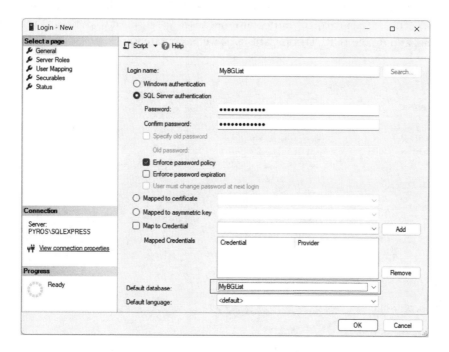

Figure 4.6   Adding the MyBGList login in SSMS

As we can see, the page is split into multiple pages. Figure 4.6 shows the General page,
where we need to define the login name, the authentication type, the password, and
so on. Here's a list of the settings that we'll take for granted throughout the rest of
the book:

- *Login Name*—`MyBGList`
- *Authentication*—SQL Server Authentication
- *Password*—MyS3cretP4$$ (or any other password you want to use)
- *Enforce Password Policy*—Enabled (unless you want to choose a weak password)
- *Enforce Password Expiration*—Disabled (unless you want the password to expire)
- *Default Database*—`MyBGList`

All the other settings can be left at their defaults.

> **WARNING**   If we chose Windows authentication during the SQL Server instal-
> lation phase (see the appendix), we need to enable the authentication mixed
> mode at the SQL Server instance level; otherwise, we won't be able to log in.

ADDING THE MYBGLIST DATABASE USER

Next, we switch to the User Mapping page. We can use this page as a shortcut to create an individual user for each existing database and have that user linked automatically to the login entry we're about to add. That's great, because it's precisely what we need to do now. Select the MyBGList database in the right panel, create the MyBGList user, and select the db_owner role in the Database Role Membership panel, as shown in figure 4.7. The db_owner role is important, because it's required to perform create, read, update, and delete (CRUD) operations as well as create tables.

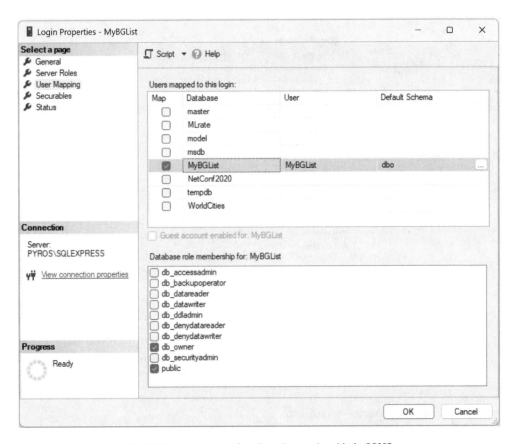

Figure 4.7   Adding the MyBGList user and setting the role membership in SSMS

All the other settings can be left at their default values. Click the OK button to add a new MyBGList login to the SQL Server instance and a new (linked) MyBGList User to the MyBGList database at the same time.

> **WARNING**   As always, feel free to change the Login and User settings, if you like. Be sure to remember your changes later, when we'll put them in a connection string to access our MyBGList database.

This section concludes the initial setup of our SQL database. Now we need to create the BoardGames, Domains, and Mechanics tables that will host our data, as well as the BoardGames_Domains and BoardGames_Mechanics junction tables to handle their many-to-many relationships.

4.3   *EF Core*

Now that we have a real data source accessible through a DBMS, it's time to introduce the software component that we'll be using to interact with it: EF Core, a set of technologies designed to help ASP.NET Core developers interact with a supported DBMS source in a standardized, structured way. This behavior is achieved through a set of ORM techniques that allow us to work with data at a higher abstraction level, using the C# programming language instead of having to write actual SQL queries.

> **NOTE** The EF Core version we're going to use in this book is the latest iteration of a project released more than a decade ago. The first version, called Entity Framework and included with .NET Framework 4.5 SP1, was released on August 11, 2008, and was followed by no fewer than 13 subsequent versions in 13 years. Not until version 4.1, which introduced Code First support, did the project establish itself in the ASP.NET developer communities, overcoming strong initial criticism due to many bugs, performance problems, and antipattern architectural choices. Since the introduction of EF Core 1.0, released under Apache License 2.0 and featuring a completely rewritten codebase as well as cross-platform compatibility, the component gained a lot of popularity and is now widely adopted for ASP.NET projects of all sizes.

4.3.1   *Reasons to use an ORM*

Before getting straight to the code, it could be wise to spend a couple of minutes answering the following question: do we really need an ORM? (We've chosen the SQL database approach, so why can't we use standard SQL code?) The whole idea of using a programming language such as C# to interact with an RDBMS instead of its built-in API (SQL queries) may seem odd. But assuming that we choose a good ORM, we have a lot to gain by taking this approach. Among other things, we can

- Reduce the development time and size of the code base
- Standardize our data retrieval strategies and thus reduce the number of mistakes
- Take advantage of several advanced RDBMS features out of the box (transactions, pooling, migrations, seeds, streams, security measures, and so on) without having to learn how to use them with bare SQL commands
- Minimize the number of string-manipulation methods, functions, and techniques required to write dynamic SQL commands programmatically

Consider the following SQL query:

```
UPDATE users SET notes = "this user has been disabled" WHERE id = 4;
```

If we want to assign the value set to the notes column dynamically by using C#, we could be tempted to write something like this:

```
var notes = "this user has been disabled";

// ... other code

$"UPDATE users SET notes = "{notes}" WHERE id = 4;";
```

This technique, however, will greatly increase the chance of a SQL injection unless we make sure that the notes variable content is escaped properly and/or completely under our control. To address this risk, we'd be forced to patch the dynamic query by using SQL parameters. When we use such a technique, the query gets executed through a system-stored procedure that separates the actual SQL commands from the array of parameters, keeping their values "isolated" from the execution context and eliminating the risk of injection. Here's how we could write the preceding SQL query to adopt this approach:

```
SqlDataAdapter myCommand = new SqlDataAdapter(
"UPDATE users SET notes = @notes", conn);
SQLParameter parm =
    myCommand.SelectCommand.Parameters.Add("@notes",
        SqlDbType.VarChar, 11);
Parm.Value = notes;
```

Alternatively, we could implement other viable (or "not-so-viable") countermeasures, such as creating a dedicated stored procedure for that task or escaping the notes variable manually. Inevitably, we'd end up putting such countermeasures in some helper class or method, in a desperate effort to centralize them—which would likely pose additional security risks in the future, because those workarounds might become outdated or less secure as time passes and new vulnerabilities are discovered. Here's how we can write the same query with EF Core (assuming that we've configured it properly):

```
var user = DbContext.Users.Where(u => u.Id == 4);
user.Notes = "this user has been disabled";
DbContext.SaveChanges();
```

We wrote some C# code here. The ORM will take care of everything, including the anti-injection countermeasures, and automatically generate the SQL required to interact with the database without our having to do (or know) anything about it.

> **NOTE** Don't get me wrong: SQL is a powerful language, and any developer who's experienced enough to use it to its full extent will probably be able to use it quickly and effectively to write any kind of query without an ORM. This level of theoretical and practical SQL knowledge isn't common among web developers, however. Most of them will have a much better learning curve if they're given the chance to interact with data in the same language they're using to write the backend code (C# in the preceding examples)—especially

if they can count on a software component that handles most of the complex work automatically and transparently.

It's important to understand that delegating the most complex SQL tasks to an ORM component doesn't mean that software developers won't need some SQL knowledge or that they don't need to learn anything about it anymore. The purpose of an ORM is not to throw SQL out of the picture, but to free developers from the need to reinvent the wheel with SQL, giving them more time to focus on what really matters: the source code.

It's also worth noting that most ORMs, including EF Core, even give the developers the chance to write queries to handle specific tasks, as well as analyze the ORM-generated queries. We'll make extensive use of these features throughout this book. Besides convenience and security benefits, notable advantages of ORM include the following:

- *Seamless DBMS switch*—Abstracting the database and its SQL syntax makes it easy to switch among the various supported DBMS products. Because we're not writing the queries manually, everything should work out of the box without our having to do anything other than reconfigure the ORM and change the connection string.
- *Query optimization*—The queries that the ORM creates automatically are generally more optimized than those written by the average software developer, often resulting in a performance gain. But the outcome depends on the ORM implementation, the database structure, and the query type.
- *Improved readability*—ORM-based statements are typically much more readable than parametrized SQL queries, as well as more succinct and easier to maintain.
- *Source control*—The ORM-related source code (and all its history) will be tracked and versioned automatically by the source control system, together with the rest of the code. This isn't always the case when we use stored procedures, which typically aren't tracked and are often changed on the fly by a database administrator directly on the database server(s).

As with any abstraction mechanism, some inevitable tradeoffs accompany the benefits of using an ORM, including the following:

- *Performance problems*—Using an ORM adds overhead to the whole system, which almost always results in a performance hit. Often, the query optimization benefit that we talked about earlier compensates for this drawback, but the actual effect depends on the given scenario.
- *Knowledge gap*—Adopting an ORM to address advanced (or less-advanced) SQL problems that we don't want to solve by ourselves could eventually take away most of our interest in learning and studying SQL, thus making us weaker developers in that portion of the stack.
- *Opaque data access layer*—Because the ORM "hides" the SQL queries, software developers won't have the chance to inspect low-level data retrieval techniques

merely by looking at the codebase. The only way to analyze the actual queries would be to launch the project in Debug mode and inspect the ORM-accessible properties (assuming that they're available) or have them logged somewhere.

- *Additional work*—Adopting an ORM and learning how to use it properly aren't easy tasks and often take a great deal of effort for all developers involved—perhaps even more than getting used to the raw SQL syntax.
- *Limited database support*—Most ORMs, including EF Core, come with limited database support, which inevitably reduces our options when we make the decision to use it.

Despite these drawbacks, adopting an ORM in data-oriented applications is widely considered to be good practice and will greatly help us optimize the development of our RESTful web API in terms of time, source-code size, security, and reliability.

4.3.2   *Setting up EF Core*

Without further ado, let's see how we can add EF Core to our existing code. Here's a list of tasks that we need to complete to achieve this result:

1 Install EF Core and the `dotnet-ef` command-line interface (CLI) tools, using the .NET Core CLI.
2 Explore the EF Core data modeling approaches, code-first and database-first, and their corresponding migrations and scaffolding tools.
3 Create a data model, following the EF Core conventions and rules for each approach.
4 Review the data model, and adjust it to our needs.

INSTALLING THE EF CORE PACKAGES AND TOOLS

As always, the required NuGet packages can be installed within Visual Studio, using the NuGet Package Manager or the Package Manager Console, or from the command line, using the .NET Core CLI. For simplicity, this time we'll use the .NET Core CLI, which requires us to open a command prompt, navigate to our project's root folder, and type the following commands:

```
> dotnet add package Microsoft.EntityFrameworkCore.SqlServer --version 6.0.11
> dotnet add package Microsoft.EntityFrameworkCore.Design --version 6.0.11
```

Right after that, let's also install the `dotnet-ef` CLI tools, a set of command-line features that we can use to perform design-time development tasks. Because we plan to use the EF Core's data modeling features, we're going to need these tools soon enough. Without leaving the command line, type the following command:

```
> dotnet tool install --global dotnet-ef --version 6.0.11
```

The `--global` switch ensures that the tools will be installed globally, allowing us to use them for all projects. To limit their use to this project only, remove that switch before executing the command. Next, run the following command to ensure that the `dotnet-ef` CLI tools have been installed properly:

```
> dotnet ef
```

If we did everything correctly, we should see ASCII output containing the EF logo and the installed version of the CLI tools. Now we can move to our next task.

EF CORE DATA MODELING TECHNIQUES

The EF Core data model can be created by means of two approaches:

- *Code-first*—Create the C# entity classes manually, and use them to generate the database schema, keeping it in sync with the source code by means of the EF CLI's migrations tool.
- *Database-first*—Generate the C# entity classes by reverse engineering them from an existing database schema, and keep them in sync with the database structure by using the EF CLI's scaffolding tool.

As we can see, the two techniques are based on different premises. When we use code-first, the EF Core data model is the "source of truth," meaning that all the change management tasks are always made there and then "replicated" to the database by means of the migrations tool. That approach is great if we don't have an existing database up and running, because it allows us to create the database schema from scratch and use C# to manage it without the need for specific SQL knowledge or database modeling tools. Conversely, database-first takes for granted that the source of truth is played by the database schema, so whenever we want to change our database's structure, we have to use raw SQL queries or database modeling tools such as SSMS and then replicate those changes to our C# entity classes using the scaffolding tool. This approach is often preferable when we have an existing database, maybe inherited from an existing application that our ASP.NET Core project is meant to replace.

Taking our concrete scenario into account, we currently have an empty database without any schema. So adopting the code-first approach might be the most logical choice.

4.3.3   *Creating the DbContext*

Let's start by creating a dedicated folder where we'll put everything related to our EF Core data model. In Visual Studio's Solution Explorer, right-click the `MyBGList` node, and create a new `/Models/` folder in the project's root.

The first class we need to create there is our application's `DbContext`, which represents the operational context between ASP.NET Core and the database—in other words, a database session abstraction that allows us to perform CRUD operations programmatically by using our C# code.

The best thing we can do to get the most from our application's `DbContext` class is to create it by following the EF Core conventions. We can easily do that by inheriting the `DbContext` base class, as shown in the following listing.

```
using Microsoft.EntityFrameworkCore;

namespace MyBGList.Models
{
    public class ApplicationDbContext : DbContext
    {
        public ApplicationDbContext(
            DbContextOptions<ApplicationDbContext> options)
            : base(options)
        {
        }

        protected override void OnModelCreating(ModelBuilder modelBuilder)
        {
            base.OnModelCreating(modelBuilder);

            // TODO: custom code here
        }
    }
}
```

This code is the boilerplate we're going to use as a basis to create our data model. Both the constructor and the OnModelCreating method are required by the DbContext base class we're inheriting from.

We placed a TODO comment inside the OnModelCreating method because that's the place where we can configure our model by using the ModelBuilder API (also known as the Fluent API), one of the three configuration methods made available by EF Core. The other two supported methods are conventions and data annotations. Before starting to code, let's take a minute to see how the three configuration methods work:

- *Fluent API*—The most powerful data modeling configuration method because it takes precedence over the other two, overriding their rules when they collide.
- *Data annotations*—A set of attributes that can be used to add metadata to the various entity classes, allowing us to specify individual configuration settings for each. Data annotations override conventions and are overridden by Fluent API.
- *Conventions*—A set of naming standards hard-baked into EF Core that can be used to handle the mapping between the Model and the database schema automatically, without the need to use the Fluent API or data annotations.

Each configuration method can be used independently to obtain the same outcome. In this book, we'll use the Fluent API for modelwide settings, data annotations for entity-specific settings, and conventions whenever we can. This approach will allow us to learn gradually how to use each technique without creating useless conflicts that would result in code bloat.

OUR FIRST ENTITY

It's time to create our first entity. In EF Core, an *entity* is a C# class representing a business object—in other words, an abstraction of a database record type. For that reason, each entity class has a structure that closely matches a corresponding database table. That's expected, because we'll use those entities to perform all CRUD operations and even to create our database schema, because we're committed to the code-first approach.

Let's use this knowledge to create an entity that can represent our `BoardGame` database table. We already know the structure of this table because we have the CSV file and even a database schema diagram (figure 4.8) that we can use as references for the various fields/columns we need to include.

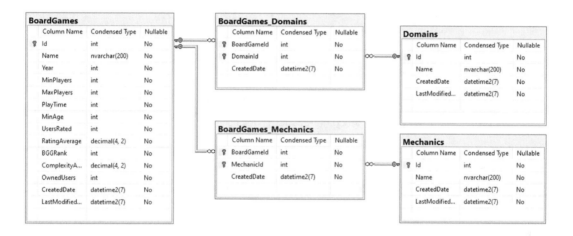

Figure 4.8   The MyBGList database schema diagram

The following listing shows the source code for our `BoardGame` entity class, which we can put in a new /Models/BoardGame.cs file.

Listing 4.2   `BoardGame.cs` file

```
using Microsoft.EntityFrameworkCore;
using System.ComponentModel.DataAnnotations;
using System.ComponentModel.DataAnnotations.Schema;

namespace MyBGList.Models
{
    [Table("BoardGames")]              Database
    public class BoardGame            table name
    {
        [Key]                         Database table's
        [Required]                    primary key
        public int Id { get; set; }
```

```
    [Required]
    [MaxLength(200)]
    public string Name { get; set; } = null!;

    [Required]
    public int Year { get; set; }

    [Required]
    public int MinPlayers { get; set; }

    [Required]
    public int MaxPlayers { get; set; }

    [Required]
    public int PlayTime { get; set; }

    [Required]
    public int MinAge { get; set; }

    [Required]
    public int UsersRated { get; set; }

    [Required]
    [Precision(4, 2)]
    public decimal RatingAverage { get; set; }

    [Required]
    public int BGGRank { get; set; }

    [Required]
    [Precision(4, 2)]
    public decimal ComplexityAverage { get; set; }

    [Required]
    public int OwnedUsers { get; set; }

    [Required]
    public DateTime CreatedDate { get; set; }

    [Required]
    public DateTime LastModifiedDate { get; set; }
    }
}
```

We did nothing special here. The class is mimicking the fields in the CSV file, because those fields are what we want to store in the database and retrieve with our web API. The only things missing are the Domains and Mechanics info, which will be stored in different database tables and therefore abstracted by means of their own EF Core entity types.

Before creating those classes, let's review the various attributes that we've added to the BoardGame entity type by using the data annotations configuration method:

- [Table("BoardGames")]—This attribute instructs EF Core to use the specified name for the database table related to this entity. Without it, the table name will be given by sticking to the EF Core conventions—that is, the class name will be used instead.

- [Key]—As its name implies, this attribute tells EF Core to set this field as the table's primary key.
- [Required]—Again, the attribute's name explains everything. These fields will be marked as required and won't accept a null value.
- [MaxLength(200)]—This attribute can be applied to the string and byte[] properties to specify the maximum character (or byte) length for its value. The assigned size will also set the size of the corresponding database column.
- [Precision(4,2)]—This attribute configures the precision of the data for that given field. It's used for mostly decimal types to define the number of allowed digits. The number before the comma defines the precision (the total number of digits in the value); the number after the comma represents the scale (the number of digits after the decimal point). By taking all that into account, we can see how our value of 4,2 indicates that we expect numbers with two digits before and two digits after the decimal point.

NOTE For additional info about data annotation attributes and a comprehensive list of them, read the official docs at http://mng.bz/Y6Da.

Now that we have a proper BoardGame entity class, we can delete the root-level BoardGame.cs file that we created in chapter 2; we don't need it anymore. Then we need to add a reference to the MyBGList.Models namespace at the top of the BoardGamesController.cs file so that the controller will be able to find (and use) the new model instead of the deleted dummy class:

```
using MyBGList.Models;
```

ADDING OTHER ENTITIES

Let's create the Domain entity. The code for this class is much simpler. The Domain record type requires only a few fields: a unique Id and Name, plus the CreationDate and LastModifiedDate. Create a new /Models/Domain.cs file, and fill it with the code in the following listing.

Listing 4.3 Domain.cs file

```
using System.ComponentModel.DataAnnotations;
using System.ComponentModel.DataAnnotations.Schema;

namespace MyBGList.Models
{
    [Table("Domains")]
    public class Domain
    {
        [Key]
        [Required]
        public int Id { get; set; }
```

```
        [Required]
        [MaxLength(200)]
        public string Name { get; set; } = null!;

        [Required]
        public DateTime CreatedDate { get; set; }

        [Required]
        public DateTime LastModifiedDate { get; set; }
    }
}
```

Nothing is new here. This entity is essentially a subset of the previous one. The same can be said of the Mechanic entity, which has the same fields as the previous one. The following listing shows the code that we can put in a new /Models/Mechanic.cs file.

Listing 4.4 Mechanic.cs file

```
using System.ComponentModel.DataAnnotations;
using System.ComponentModel.DataAnnotations.Schema;

namespace MyBGList.Models
{
    [Table("Mechanics")]
    public class Mechanic
    {
        [Key]
        [Required]
        public int Id { get; set; }

        [Required]
        [MaxLength(200)]
        public string Name { get; set; } = null!;

        [Required]
        public DateTime CreatedDate { get; set; }

        [Required]
        public DateTime LastModifiedDate { get; set; }
    }
}
```

Now we have the three main entities that will populate our data source. We need to add the required junction entities to JOIN them.

JUNCTION ENTITIES

As I said earlier, we're dealing with two many-to-many relationships here, because each Domain (and Mechanic) can be referenced to zero, one, or multiple BoardGames, and vice versa. Because we've opted for an RDBMS, we need to create two additional entities that EF Core will use to abstract (and create) the required junction tables.

We'll call them `BoardGames_Domains` and `BoardGames_Mechanics`, respectively, as we did with the database schema diagram (figure 4.8).

Let's start with the `BoardGames_Domains` entity. Create a new `/Models/BoardGames_Domains.cs` file, and fill its content with the source code in the following listing.

Listing 4.5   `BoardGames_Domains.cs` file

```
using System.ComponentModel.DataAnnotations;

namespace MyBGList.Models
{
    public class BoardGames_Domains
    {
        [Key]
        [Required]
        public int BoardGameId { get; set; }

        [Key]
        [Required]
        public int DomainId { get; set; }

        [Required]
        public DateTime CreatedDate { get; set; }
    }
}
```

This time, we didn't use the `[Table("<name>")]` attribute. The conventions naming standards are good enough for this table.

The same approach is required for the `BoardGames_Mechanics` entity, which features the same fields. The following listing contains the source code for the new `/Models/BoardGames_Mechanics.cs` file that we need to create.

Listing 4.6   `BoardGames_Mechanics.cs` file

```
using System.ComponentModel.DataAnnotations;

namespace MyBGList.Models
{
    public class BoardGames_Mechanics
    {
        [Key]
        [Required]
        public int BoardGameId { get; set; }

        [Key]
        [Required]
        public int MechanicId { get; set; }

        [Required]
        public DateTime CreatedDate { get; set; }
    }
}
```

As we can see by looking at this code, these two entity classes have two properties with the [key] attribute, meaning that we want their respective database tables to have a composite primary key. This approach is a common one used to deal with many-to-many junction tables, as each mapped relationship is almost always meant to be unique.

Composite primary keys are supported in EF Core, but they require an additional setting that only Fluent API support. Let's add that setting to our code before proceeding. Open the ApplicationDbContext.cs file, and add the following code to the existing OnModelCreating method, replacing the TODO comment:

```
protected override void OnModelCreating(ModelBuilder modelBuilder)
{
    base.OnModelCreating(modelBuilder);

        modelBuilder.Entity<BoardGames_Domains>()
            .HasKey(i => new { i.BoardGameId, i.DomainId });

        modelBuilder.Entity<BoardGames_Mechanics>()
            .HasKey(i => new { i.BoardGameId, i.MechanicId });
}
```

We can use the OnModelCreating method override to further configure and/or customize the model after all the default conventions defined in the entity types have been applied. Notice how we used the HasKey method to configure the composite primary key of the [BoardGames_Domains] and [BoardGames_Mechanics] tables.

Now that we've created these junction entities, a couple of questions arise. How can we tell EF Core to use the values that we'll store, using them to JOIN the BoardGames records with Domains and Mechanics? More important, is there a way to create a direct reference to these relationships from the BoardGames entity? The following sections answer these questions, starting with the second one.

NAVIGATION PROPERTIES

In EF Core, the term *navigation property* describes an entity property that directly references a single related entity or a collection of entities. To better understand this concept, consider the following two navigation properties, which we could add to the BoardGames_Domains entity class:

```
public BoardGame? BoardGame { get; set; }
public Domain? Domain { get; set; }
```

Each of these (nullable) properties is intended to be a direct reference to one of the entities handled by the junction. This technique can be useful, allowing us to handle the JOIN between tables transparently by using standard properties. But if we want EF Core to fill these properties properly, we need to make our DbContext aware of the corresponding relationships. In other words, we need to configure it by defining some rules. Because these rules affect multiple entities, we'll use the Fluent API to set them up. First, however, we need to add all the required navigation properties to our entities.

Let's start by adding the preceding properties to the `BoardGames_Domains` entity class. Then add the following two properties to the `BoardGames_Mechanics` entity class:

```
public BoardGame? BoardGame { get; set; }
public Mechanic? Mechanic { get; set; }
```

Now we need to reciprocate these references in the main entity classes. Open the /Models/BoardGame.cs file, and add the following properties after the last line of code:

```
public ICollection<BoardGames_Domains>? BoardGames_Domains { get; set; }
public ICollection<BoardGames_Mechanics>? BoardGames_Mechanics { get; set; }
```

Do the same in the /Models/Domain.cs file

```
public ICollection<BoardGames_Domains>? BoardGames_Domains { get; set; }
```

and in the /Models/Mechanic.cs file:

```
public ICollection<BoardGames_Mechanics>? BoardGames_Mechanics { get; set; }
```

Now that all entities have their navigation properties applied, we can use the Fluent API to configure them. Before proceeding with the code, let's briefly recap what we need to do:

- Define a one-to-many relationship between the `BoardGame` entity and `BoardGames_Domains` entity (using the `BoardGameId` foreign key), and define another one-to-many relationship between the `Domain` entity and `BoardGames_Domains` entity (using the `DomainId` foreign key).
- Define a one-to-many relationship between the `BoardGame` entity and `BoardGames_Mechanics` entity (using the `BoardGameId` foreign key), and define another one-to-many relationship between the `Mechanic` entity and `BoardGames_Mechanics` entity (using the `MechanicId` foreign key).
- Set up a cascade behavior for all these relationships so that all the junction records will be deleted when one of the related main records is deleted.

Relational database concepts and references
This plan, as well as this part of the chapter, takes for granted that you have the required RDBMS knowledge to handle many-to-many relationships and that you understand concepts such as foreign keys, constraints, and cascading rules. In case of problems, the following links can help you understand these topics better:

- http://mng.bz/GReJ
- http://mng.bz/zmZA

Let's put the plan into practice. Open the /Models/ApplicationDbContext.cs file, and put the following lines (marked in bold) in the `OnModelCreating` method, below the `HasKey` methods that we added earlier to configure the composite primary keys:

```
protected override void OnModelCreating(ModelBuilder modelBuilder)
{
    base.OnModelCreating(modelBuilder);

        modelBuilder.Entity<BoardGames_Domains>()
            .HasKey(i => new { i.BoardGameId, i.DomainId });

    modelBuilder.Entity<BoardGames_Domains>()
        .HasOne(x => x.BoardGame)
        .WithMany(y => y.BoardGames_Domains)
        .HasForeignKey(f => f.BoardGameId)
        .IsRequired()
        .OnDelete(DeleteBehavior.Cascade);

    modelBuilder.Entity<BoardGames_Domains>()
        .HasOne(o => o.Domain)
        .WithMany(m => m.BoardGames_Domains)
        .HasForeignKey(f => f.DomainId)
        .IsRequired()
        .OnDelete(DeleteBehavior.Cascade);

        modelBuilder.Entity<BoardGames_Mechanics>()
            .HasKey(i => new { i.BoardGameId, i.MechanicId });

    modelBuilder.Entity<BoardGames_Mechanics>()
        .HasOne(x => x.BoardGame)
        .WithMany(y => y.BoardGames_Mechanics)
        .HasForeignKey(f => f.BoardGameId)
        .IsRequired()
        .OnDelete(DeleteBehavior.Cascade);

    modelBuilder.Entity<BoardGames_Mechanics>()
        .HasOne(o => o.Mechanic)
        .WithMany(m => m.BoardGames_Mechanics)
        .HasForeignKey(f => f.MechanicId)
        .IsRequired()
        .OnDelete(DeleteBehavior.Cascade);
}
```

This code should be quite easy to understand. We wrote down our plan using the Fluent API, thus ensuring that EF Core will be able to fill all the navigation properties defined in our entities properly whenever we want to enforce such behavior. Now that we've set up the relationships between our entities, we need to make them accessible through our ApplicationDbContext class.

DEFINING THE DBSETS

In EF Core, entity types can be made available through the DbContext by using a container class known as DbSet. In a nutshell, each DbSet represents a homogenous set of entities and allows us to perform CRUD operations for that entity set. In other words, if the entity class represents a single record within a database table, we can say that the DbSet represents the database table itself.

DbSets are typically exposed by the DbContext through public properties, one for each entity. Here's an example that represents a DbSet for the BoardGame entity:

```
public DbSet<BoardGame> BoardGames => Set<BoardGame>();
```

Now that we know the back story, we're ready to switch back to the /Models/ ApplicationDbContext.cs file and add a DbSet for each of our entities at the end of the class in the following way (new lines marked in bold):

```
using Microsoft.EntityFrameworkCore;

namespace MyBGList.Models
{
    public class ApplicationDbContext : DbContext
    {

        // ... existing code

        public DbSet<BoardGame> BoardGames => Set<BoardGame>();
        public DbSet<Domain> Domains => Set<Domain>();
        public DbSet<Mechanic> Mechanics => Set<Mechanic>();
        public DbSet<BoardGames_Domains> BoardGames_Domains
            => Set<BoardGames_Domains>();
        public DbSet<BoardGames_Mechanics> BoardGames_Mechanics =>
    Set<BoardGames_Mechanics>();
    }
}
```

With that code, we can consider our EF Core data model to be ready. All we have to do now is to add the ApplicationDbContext class to our app's services container so that we can start using it.

4.3.4 Setting up the DbContext

In this section, we'll set up and configure an instance of our brand-new Application-DbContext class in our MyBGList web API project. As we should know at this point, this step must be performed within the Program.cs file. Before we jump to the code, however, it may be wise to spend a couple of minutes reviewing the role of a DbContext instance within an ASP.NET Core web application, which also determines its lifecycle. To do that, we need to understand the concept of a unit of work.

UNIT OF WORK

The best definition of *unit of work* is given by Martin Fowler, the software engineer who introduced the dependency injection design pattern in his Catalog of Patterns of Enterprise Application architecture (http://mng.bz/0yQv):

> *[A unit of work] maintains a list of objects affected by a business transaction and coordinates the writing out of changes and the resolution of concurrency problems.*

In a nutshell, a *unit of work* is a set of CRUD operations performed against a database during a single business transaction. From a RDBMS point of view, we can think of it as a transaction, with the sole difference being that it's handled at the application level instead of the database level.

In most ASP.NET Core web applications, a DbContext instance is meant to be used for a single unit of work that gets executed within a single HTTP request/response lifecycle. Although this approach is not required, it's widely acknowledged as good practice to ensure the atomicity, consistency, isolation, and durability (ACID) properties of each transaction. Here's a typical usage scenario:

1 The web API receives an HTTP GET request for a list of board games, which is handled by a controller (BoardGamesController) and a dedicated action method (Get).
2 The action method obtains a DbContext instance through dependency injection and uses it to perform a READ operation (resulting in a SELECT query) to retrieve the requested records.
3 The DbContext retrieves the (raw) data from the BoardGames database table and uses it to create a set of entities, which it returns to the calling action method.
4 The action method receives the resulting entities and returns them to the caller through a JSON-serialized data transfer object (DTO).
5 The DbContext instance gets disposed.

This example depicts a typical unit of work that performs a single read-only operation. Let's see what happens when we need to read and write data, such as when dealing with an HTTP PUT or POST request. For simplicity, we'll assume that such requests come from an authorized source such as a web-based management interface, using a secure token (or IP address) that was checked beforehand.

6 The web API receives an HTTP PUT request meant to globally replace the term "war" with the term "conflict" in all the board game's Mechanics. The request is handled by a dedicated Rename action method in the Mechanics-Controller, which accepts two parameters: oldTerm ("war") and newTerm ("conflict").
7 Again, the action method obtains a DbContext instance through dependency injection and uses it to perform a READ operation (resulting in a SELECT query) to retrieve the records to modify, using the oldTerm parameter passed by the request. The resulting records are used to create a set of Mechanic entities, which the DbContext returns to the action method, tracking them for changes.
8 The action method receives the resulting Mechanic entities and changes their names in a foreach cycle, using the newTerm parameter. These changes are tracked by the DbContext instance, because we're still operating within the same unit of work.

9 After the end of the `foreach` cycle, the action methods call the `DbContext`'s
   `SaveChanges` method to save the batch rename job.

10 EF Core detects the changes and persists them to the database.

11 The action method returns a successful response to the caller (in JSON format), typically with some details on what happened: number of modified records,
   task duration, and so on.

12 The `DbContext` instance is disposed.

Now that we know how the `DbContext` instance is meant to work, we're ready to set it
up within our `Program.cs` file.

CONFIGURING THE DBCONTEXT

With the following lines of code, which we can put in the `Program.cs` file, we'll register our `ApplicationDbContext` class as a scoped service in the ASP.NET Core service
provider and configure it to use a SQL Server database with a given connection string:

```
builder.Services.AddDbContext<ApplicationDbContext>(options =>
    options.UseSqlServer(
        builder.Configuration.GetConnectionString("DefaultConnection"))
    );
```

By following this pattern, the connection string is meant to be added in our `appsettings`
`.json` file—or in the `appsettings.Development.json` file, because we'll likely be
using a different connection string in production. Because a SQL Server connection
string contains the login user credentials (username and password) in clear text, however, doing that during development would likely expose our source code to vulnerability problems. If we plan to push our code to a GitHub repository, for example,
everyone who has access to it will be able to see and use those credentials. What can
we do to prevent that situation?

SECURELY STORING THE CONNECTION STRING

Securing the connection string, as well as any secrets we may have to use while working on our web API, is a critical requirement in software development. In our specific
scenario, to deal with our connection-string problem efficiently, we can consider the
following approaches:

- Put the connection string in the `appsettings.Development.json` file, and configure it to be excluded/ignored by our source control provider so that it won't
  be uploaded with the rest of the code.
- Put the connection string in an environment variable and put a reference to its
  name within the `appsettings` file, or use this reference directly from the
  source code, skipping the `appsettings` approach.
- Use Visual Studio's Secret Manager feature to store the connection string (and
  its credentials) securely in a separate, protected place.

All these methods are viable enough. But excluding a configuration file from source
control management may have other negative effects. What if we lose this file and

are unable to recover it? Currently, the file contains only a few lines, but it might grow in the future, possibly containing other configuration settings that could be difficult to retrieve.

As for the environment-variable pattern, I don't recommend using it. This approach will be harder to maintain as the number of keys to secure increases, which is likely to happen in almost all apps. Because we're using Visual Studio, the Secret Manager feature will help us solve all credential-related problems throughout the rest of the book—at least, during development.

INTRODUCING SECRET MANAGER

One of the best aspects of the Secret Manager feature is that it can be used from within the Visual Studio GUI. All we need to do is to right-click to the project's root folder in Solution Explorer and then choose the Manage User Secrets option from the contextual menu (figure 4.9).

Figure 4.9   Accessing the Visual Studio Secret Manager feature

As soon as we select that option, Visual Studio adds a `UserSecretsId` element within a `PropertyGroup` of our web API project's configuration file (the `MyBGList.csproj` file). Here's what the element looks like:

```
<UserSecretsId>
  cfbd4e7a-6cc3-470c-8bd3-467c993c69e6
</UserSecretsId>
```

By default, the inner text of that `UserSecretsId` element is a globally unique identifier (GUID). But this text is arbitrary and can be changed as long as it's unique to the project (unless we want more projects to share the same secrets). Right after adding the `UserSecretsId` value to our project, Visual Studio will automatically use it to generate an empty `secrets.json` file in the following folder:

```
C:\Users\<UserName>\AppData\Roaming\Microsoft
➥ \UserSecrets\<UserSecretsId>\secrets.json
```

When that's done, Visual Studio automatically opens that file for us from within the GUI in edit mode, where we can store our secrets securely. All the key/value pairs that we put in the `secrets.json` file override the corresponding key/value pairs in any `appsettings*.json` file (or are appended to them if they don't exist there), which means that if we put our connection string within the `secrets.json` file, it will be treated (and fetched by the source code) as though it's in the `appsettings.json` file,

regardless of the environment. Let's take advantage of this feature and put our connection string in the secrets.json file in the following way:

```
{
  "ConnectionStrings": {
    "DefaultConnection": "Server=localhost\\SQLEXPRESS;Database=MyBGList;
        User Id=MyBGList;Password=MyS3cretP4$$;
        Integrated Security=False;MultipleActiveResultSets=True;
        TrustServerCertificate=True"
  }
}
```

> **NOTE**   This connection string contains some common compatibility settings
> that ensure a good level of SQL Server and ASP.NET Core interoperability
> and should work in most scenarios. Be sure to change the sample password
> (MyS3cretP4$$) to the one that was used to create the Login user.

As we can see, we've created the same key/value pair conventional structure used by the
appsettings.json file, which is good practice, because we'll likely need to put these
values in a remotely-hosted appsettings.Production.json file when we deploy our
app in a production environment (chapter 12). Also, the structure we've used matches
the ASP.NET Core conventions of the GetConnectionString method that we used
in the Program.cs file to retrieve the connection-string value, so we're good to go.

> **NOTE**   For reasons of space, we won't delve further into Visual Studio's Secret
> Manager feature. For additional info about it and other usage scenario sam-
> ples, check out http://mng.bz/KlGO.

Now that our ApplicationDbContext class has been configured properly, we can use
it to create our database structure.

4.3.5   Creating the database structure

The code-first approach that we've chosen to adopt relies on generating the database
schema from the source code, using the EF CLI's migrations tool. As always, it could
be wise to briefly review the concept of migrations.

INTRODUCING MIGRATIONS

The EF Core migrations tool was introduced with the goal of keeping the database
schema in sync with the EF Core model by preserving data. Every time we need to create or update the schema, we can use the tool to compare the existing database structure with our current data model and generate a C# file containing the required set of
SQL commands to update it. This autogenerated file is called a *migration,* and per the
EF Core CLI default settings, it's created in a /Migrations/ folder.

   The current state of the model is stored in another autogenerated file called
<DbContext>ModelSnapshot.cs. That file is created in that same /Migrations/ folder
with the initial migration and gets updated with each subsequent migration. The

snapshot file allows EF Core to calculate the changes required to synchronize the database structure with the data model.

> **NOTE**   As we can easily guess, the migration tool knows what to do, and which database to check and/or update, by fetching our `ApplicationDbContext` and the connection string that we defined.

ADDING THE INITIAL MIGRATION

In our current scenario, because our `MyBGList` database is still empty, we need to create the initial migration, which will be used to create the database schema from scratch. To do that, open a command prompt window, navigate to the `MyBGList` project's root folder, and type the following command:

```
> dotnet ef migrations add Initial
```

If we did everything correctly, we should see the following output:

```
Build started...
Build succeeded.
info: Microsoft.EntityFrameworkCore.Infrastructure[10403]
    Entity Framework Core 6.0.11 initialized 'ApplicationDbContext'
    using provider 'Microsoft.EntityFrameworkCore.SqlServer:6.0.11'
    with options: None
Done. To undo this action, use 'ef migrations remove'
```

That "`Done`" message at the end means that the initial migration was created successfully. To confirm that, we can check for the presence of a new /Migrations/ folder with the two autogenerated files in it, as shown in figure 4.10. Now that our initial migration is ready, we need to apply it to our database.

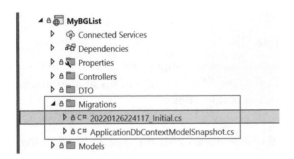

Figure 4.10   The new /Migrations/ folder with the autogenerated initial migration and snapshot files

UPDATING THE DATABASE

It's important to understand that when we add a migration, we only create the autogenerated files that will update our database structure according to our current data model. The actual SQL queries won't be executed until we apply that migration by using the `database update` EF Core CLI command. To apply our `Initial` migration to our `MyBGList` database, run the following command:

```
> dotnet ef database update Initial
```

TIP In this specific case, the `Initial` parameter could be omitted, because the `database update` command, when executed without a specific migration name, always updates the database up to the most recent migration. Specifying a name can be useful in some cases, such as reverting to a previous migration, which is a great way to roll back unwanted changes applied to the database schema.

After executing the command, we should see output containing the actual SQL queries run against the `MyBGList` database by the EF migrations tool, followed by another `"Done"` confirmation message to inform us that everything went well. As soon as we see that outcome, we can launch SQL Server Management Studio and connect to our `MyBGList` database to check what happened. If we did everything correctly, we should see the five database tables that correspond to our entities and all their expected columns, as well as the relationships, indexes, and foreign keys that match our data model (figure 4.11).

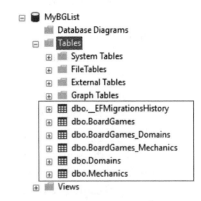

Figure 4.11 The database tables generated by the EF Core Migration tool

Now that our database structure is ready, we need to learn how to use our `ApplicationDbContext` class within our web API to interact with it. In chapter 5, we'll acquire this knowledge by accomplishing several data-related tasks, including the following:

- Importing the board game's CSV file, which we downloaded from Kaggle, into the `MyBGList` database
- Refactoring our `BoardGamesController`'s `Get` action method to serve the actual data through the `BoardGame` entities instead of the sample data we're currently using

4.4 Exercises

As always, the following exercises emulate some task assignments given by our product owner and addressed to the `MyBGList` development team—in other words, to us.

TIP The solutions to the exercises are available on GitHub in the `/Chapter_04/Exercises/` folder. To test them, replace the relevant files in your `MyBGList` project with those in that folder, and run the app.

4.4.1 Additional fields

Add the following properties to the `BoardGames` entity:

- `AlternateNames` (string, max length 200, not required)
- `Designer` (string, max length 200, not required)
- `Flags` (int, required)

Furthermore, add the following properties to the `Domains` and `Mechanics` entities:

- `Notes` (string, max length 200, not required)
- `Flags` (int, required)

4.4.2 *One-to-many relationship*

Add a new `Publisher` entity that will be used to list all the available board-game publisher (one for each `BoardGame`). The new entity is meant to have the `Publishers` table name and the following properties:

- `Id` (primary key, int, not null)
- `Name` (string, max length 200, required)
- `CreatedDate` (datetime, required)
- `LastModifiedDate` (datetime, required)

Next, create a one-to-many relationship between this entity and the `BoardGame` entity, adding the `PublisherId` property (int, required) to the `BoardGame` entity. Remember to add the navigation properties to the two entities, as well as to define the foreign keys, cascading rules, and `DbSet<Publisher>` in the `ApplicationDbContext` class, using the Fluent API.

4.4.3 *Many-to-many relationship*

Add a new `Category` entity to list all the available categories (one or more) for each `BoardGame`. The new entity is meant to have the `Categories` table name and the following properties:

- `Id` (primary key, int, not null)
- `Name` (string, max length 200, required)
- `CreatedDate` (datetime, required)
- `LastModifiedDate` (datetime, required)

Next, create a many-to-many relationship between this entity and the `BoardGame` entity, adding a `BoardGames_Categories` junction entity with the minimum number of required properties. Remember to add the navigation properties to the three entities, as well as to define the foreign keys, cascading rules, and `DbSets` for the `Category` and the `BoardGames_Categories` entities in the `ApplicationDbContext` class, using the Fluent API.

4.4.4 *Creating a new migration*

Using the EF Core Migration tool, create a new `Chapter4_Exercises` migration containing all the changes performed during the previous tasks. This task will also check the updated data model for consistency, ensuring that the preceding exercises have been done properly.

4.4.5 Applying the new migration

Apply the new `Chapter4_Exercises` migration, using the EF Core Migration tool. Then inspect the `MyBGList` database structure to ensure that all the new tables and columns were created.

4.4.6 Reverting to a previous migration

Roll back the database schema to its previous state by applying the `Initial` migration, using the EF Core Migration tool. Then inspect the `MyBGList` database structure to ensure that all the new tables and columns were removed.

Summary

- It's time to replace the fake sample data we've used so far with a proper data source managed by a DBMS.
  - First, however, it's strongly advisable to review the various SQL and NoSQL alternatives and pick a suitable one for our scenario.
- After careful analysis, installing a local instance of the Microsoft SQL Server Express edition seems to be a viable choice for development purposes.
  - It's also recommended to install SQL Server Management Studio (SSMS), a data modeling tool that allows us to perform various management tasks (creating databases, tables, and so on) by using the GUI.
- We're going to access our SQL database from our web API by using EF Core, a set of technologies designed to help developers interact with a DBMS source through a set of ORM techniques.
  - Using an ORM instead of writing raw SQL queries might have some drawbacks, but it offers strong benefits in terms of security, flexibility, optimizations, readability, and maintainability.
- After installing EF Core, we must create our `ApplicationDbContext` class, which represents the operational context between ASP.NET Core and the database.
  - We also need a set of entities, C# classes that represent the tables of our database and allow us to perform CRUD operations directly from the code.
- To allow the `ApplicationDbContext` to interact with the database, we need to instantiate it with a connection string, which we can store securely in our development environment using Visual Studio's *Secret Manager* feature.
- As soon as we set up the connection string, we can use the EF Core *migrations* tool to create our database structure from our current EF Core data model.

CRUD operations

This chapter covers

- Performing SELECT, INSERT, UPDATE, and DELETE queries with EF Core
- Handling requests using the HTTP GET, POST, PUT, and DELETE methods
- Implementing paging, sorting, and filtering using EF Core
- Using data-transfer objects (DTOs) to exchange JavaScript Object Notation (JSON) data with the client

In chapter 4, we dedicated ourselves to the installation, setup, and configuration of all the prerequisites for interacting with a database management system (DBMS), and we learned the means, techniques, and reasons to do that. Now that we have a database context and an object-relational mapper (ORM) up and running, we're ready to perform the typical data-related tasks: create, read, update, and delete (CRUD) operations, which are handled by INSERT, SELECT, UPDATE, and DELETE SQL queries, respectively. Performing these operations with Entity Framework Core (EF Core) allows our MyBGList web API application to interact with the DBMS we set up in chapter 4.

In this chapter, we'll take advantage of our data model to perform several read and write operations required by our concrete scenario, using the EF Core's `Application-DbContext` class. These tasks will help us develop the skills required to interact with our database throughout the rest of the book.

This chapter takes for granted that you already know the basic data manipulation language (DML) operations supported by most DBMSes and how they work. No specific SQL knowledge is required, however, because all these tasks will be handled by the Language Integrated Query (LINQ) component and the `IQueryable<T>` extension methods that it provides.

5.1 Introducing LINQ

Microsoft introduced LINQ in 2007 with the release of .NET Framework 3.5. The purpose of LINQ is to extend the programming language (C#, in our scenario) by allowing the use of *query expressions*—expressive statements that loosely resemble SQL syntax—to conveniently fetch, process, and manipulate data from any data source in a uniform, standardized, and consistent way. Any C# collection-type class can be queries in LINQ, as long as it implements the generic `IEnumerable<T>` interface.

> **TIP** This brief introduction recaps the core principles and features of LINQ. For additional info, I suggest reading the official documentation at http://mng.bz/91Yr.

The main advantage of LINQ is rather obvious: it allows developers to use a single unified query language to deal with different types of raw data sources (XML, DBMS, CSV, and more)—as long as an ORM is capable of "mapping" them to `Enumerable<T>` types. Being able to manipulate our data with C# objects instead of SQL queries is one of the main reasons why we're using EF Core, after all. We'll deal with those objects mostly by using LINQ standard methods, as well as an additional set of LINQ-based extension methods provided by EF Core.

5.1.1 Query syntax vs. method syntax

The best way to learn LINQ is to use it, which we're going to do often from now on. First, however, here's a quick overview of LINQ syntaxes. I use the plural form here because we can choose between two approaches: a declarative query syntax, which loosely resembles SQL queries, and a fluent method syntax, which looks more like standard C# methods. The best way to learn how these syntaxes work is to see them in action. Consider the following example:

```
var data = new [] {
    new BoardGame() {
        Id = 1,
        Name = "Axis & Allies",
        Publisher = "Milton Bradley",
        Year = 1981
    },
```

```
    new BoardGame() {
        Id = 2,
        Name = "Citadels",
        Publisher = "Hans im Glück",
        Year = 2000
    },
    new BoardGame() {
        Id = 3,
        Name = "Terraforming Mars",
        Publisher = "FryxGames",
        Year = 2016
    }
};
```

This array isn't new to us; it's the same one we've used to populate the `RestDTO` `<BoardGame[]>` return object of the `BoardGameController`'s `Get()` method since chapter 2. Suppose that you want to fetch all the board games published in 2000 from this array, using LINQ. Here's how we could do that by using query syntax:

```
var boardgames = from bg in data where bg.Year == 2000 select bg;
```

The syntax in bold looks rather like a typical SQL query. The statement will return an `IEnumerable<BoardGame>` containing all the board games that match the `where` condition (or an empty collection). Now let's perform the same task by using method syntax:

```
var boardgames = data.Where(bg => bg.Year == 2000);
```

Although the two statements will accomplish the same thing, the syntactical difference is quite evident. Query syntax, as its name suggests, looks like a SQL query, whereas method syntax is much like standard C# code, with lambda expressions used as method parameters.

> **NOTE** The `Where()` method used in this example is one of the many standard LINQ operators that can be used to form the LINQ pattern. Those operators provide several querylike capabilities: filtering, projection, aggregation, sorting, and more. For additional info about them, check out http://mng .bz/jmpe.

If you already know what lambda expressions are and how to use them, feel free to skip the next section. Otherwise, keep reading.

5.1.2   *Lambda expressions*

A *lambda expression* is a C# expressive operator that can be used to create an anonymous function in the following way:

```
(input) => { body }
```

The left part of the expression—the `input`—can be used to specify one or more input parameters. The right part—the `body`—contains one or more statements that return the function's expected result. The `input` and the `body` are connected by the `=>` lambda declaration operator. Here's a typical lambda expression:

```
(a, b) => { Console.WriteLine($"{a} says hello to {b}"); }
```

Whenever we have a single input and/or statement, we can omit the corresponding parentheses:

```
a => Console.WriteLine($"{a} says hello");
```

In case there are no input parameters, we can use empty parentheses in the following way:

```
() => Console.WriteLine($"Somebody says hello");
```

Although lambda expressions aren't specific to LINQ, they're used often with LINQ because of their versatility. Starting with C# 10 and ASP.NET 6, they got several syntactical improvements—attributes, explicit return types, natural delegate type inferring, and so on—that greatly improved their use with the Minimal API's `Map` methods. We took advantage of these enhancements in chapter 3, when we applied the Cross-Origin Resource Sharing (CORS) and cache attributes in the `Program.cs` file's `Map-Get()` from chapter 2:

```
app.MapGet("/error",
    [EnableCors("AnyOrigin")]
    [ResponseCache(NoStore = true)] () =>
    Results.Problem());
```

Lambda expressions play a pivotal role in ASP.NET Core, and we're going to use them extensively throughout this book.

> **TIP** For further info on lambda expressions, check out the official documentation at http://mng.bz/WA2W.

5.1.3 The IQueryable<T> interface

Now that we've introduced LINQ and the method syntax we're going to use, let's see how the LINQ queries built with EF Core are converted to a database-specific query language (such as SQL). The whole process relies on the `IQueryable<T>` interface provided by the `System.Linq` namespace, which can be used to create an in-memory-representation of the query that we want to execute against our database. Here's an example of how we can provide a `IQueryable<BoardGame>` instance from an instance of our `Application-DbContext`, which is supposedly referenced by the `_context` local variable:

```
var query = _context.BoardGames;
```

All we did was create a reference to the existing `BoardGames` property that we set up in chapter 4. This property is of `DbSet<BoardGame>` type: however, the `DbSet<T>` type implements the IQueryable<T> interface, thus exposing all the interface's public methods (and extension methods) due to *polymorphism.*

> **DEFINITION**   In object-oriented programming, the term *polymorphism* describes accessing objects of different types through the same interface. I don't delve into this topic, taking for granted that you already know it. For further info regarding polymorphism in C#, take a look at http://mng.bz/81OD.

The query variable holds an in-memory representation of a query that will retrieve all records present in the [BoardGames] database table. In our scenario (SQL Server), it will be converted to the following SQL query:

```
SELECT * FROM BoardGames;
```

In most cases, we don't want to access the whole sequence, but a portion of it. This scenario is one in which LINQ comes into play, thanks to the IQueryable<T> extension methods that it provides. We could add the Where() operator

```
var query = _context.BoardGames.Where(b => b.Year == 2020);
```

which will be converted to the following SQL query:

```
SELECT * FROM BoardGames WHERE Year = 2020;
```

Because LINQ operators can be chained, we can use many of them together in the following way:

```
var query = _context.BoardGames
    .Where(b => b.Year == 2020)
    .OrderBy(b => b.Name);
```

Alternatively, we can achieve the same result by adding them through separate lines:

```
var query = _context.BoardGames.Where(b => b.Year == 2020);
query = query.OrderBy(b => b.Name);
```

Both approaches result in the following SQL query:

```
SELECT * FROM BoardGames WHERE Year = 2020 ORDER BY Name;
```

The query representation built with the IQueryable<T> interface and LINQ operators is called an *expression tree.* It's important to understand that expression trees are converted to queries and sent to the database only when we execute the IQueryable<T>, which happens only when the results are consumed by the source code—in other words, when we use an operator that returns something that can be created or evaluated only by querying the database. To better understand this concept, consider this example:

```
var query = _context.BoardGames.Where(b => b.Year == 2020);
var bgArray = query.ToArray();
```

The first line of code creates an `IQueryable<T>` instance and builds an expression tree without the need to query the database. The second line of code, however, asks for an array of all the board games fetched with the preceding query, which can't be returned without executing such a query to the database and putting the resulting records in a new instance of the `BoardGame[]` type.

Our discussion of LINQ and `IQueryable<T>` ends here. We'll learn how to make good use of these powerful syntaxes while we work on our app's source code. First, we'll focus on using our `ApplicationDbContext` class inside our existing `MyBGList` app.

5.2 Injecting the DbContext

As we learned in chapter 4, each `DbContext` instance is meant to be used for a single unit of work that gets executed within a single HTTP request/response lifecycle. The best way to accomplish this task is to have an `ApplicationDbContext` instance injected into each controller that needs it so that the corresponding action methods will be able to use it.

A great example is our existing `BoardGameController`'s `Get()` method, which is still using some dummy, manually generated board-game data instead of fetching it from the DBMS. Here's what we're going to do to replace this mock behavior with the real deal:

- Update the `BoardGameController`'s constructor to obtain an `ApplicationDbContext` instance using dependency injection.
- Create a private variable that will locally store a reference to the `ApplicationDbContext` instance and make it accessible by the controller's action methods through its lifecycle.
- Change the `Get()` method implementation, replacing the dummy data with an actual data retrieval query against our `MyBGList` database, performed by using the `IQueryable<T>` extension methods.

The following listing shows how we can pull off that plan (new and modified lines in bold).

Listing 5.1 `BoardGameController.cs` **file**

```
using Microsoft.AspNetCore.Mvc;
using Microsoft.EntityFrameworkCore;
using MyBGList.DTO;
using MyBGList.Models;

namespace MyBGList.Controllers
{
    [Route("[controller]")]
    [ApiController]
    public class BoardGamesController : ControllerBase
    {
        private readonly ApplicationDbContext _context;    ⟵ Adds the ApplicationDbContext instance
```

```
                    private readonly ILogger<BoardGamesController> _logger;

                    public BoardGamesController(
                        ApplicationDbContext context,
      Adds the           ILogger<BoardGamesController> logger
ApplicationDbContext     )
      instance         {
                            _context = context;
                            _logger = logger;
                    }

                    [HttpGet(Name = "GetBoardGames")]
                    [ResponseCache(Location = ResponseCacheLocation.Any, Duration = 60)]
                    public RestDTO<BoardGame[]> Get()
                    {
                        var query = _context.BoardGames;          ◁——  Creates the
                                                                        IQueryable<T>
                        return new RestDTO<BoardGame[]>()                expression tree
                        {
      Executes the          Data = query.ToArray(),
     IQueryable<T>          Links = new List<LinkDTO> {
                                new LinkDTO(
                                    Url.Action(null, "BoardGames",
                                        null, Request.Scheme)!,
                                    "self",
                                    "GET"),
                            }
                        };
                    }
                }
            }
```

As we can see, the new code is much thinner and more readable. That's expected, because we got rid of the manually generated board games and replaced them with a couple of lines of code: the first one to create the IQueryable<T> expression tree and the second to execute it, using the ToArray() method introduced earlier. This method tells EF Core to perform the following tasks:

- Perform a Select query against the database to fetch all the records of the [Boardgames] table.
- Enumerate the resulting records to create an array of BoardGame entities.
- Return the resulting array to the caller.

Before going forward, let's delve into our current implementation to see whether we can improve it further.

5.2.1   *The sync and async methods*

The ToArray() method that we used to retrieve the BoardGame array operates in a synchronous way: the calling thread is blocked while the SQL query is executed in the database. Let's replace this method with its asynchronous counterpart provided by EF

Core. This change will make our BoardGameController's source code compliant with the async/await pattern enforced by ASP.NET Core, which is generally considered to be a best practice in terms of performance benefits. First, we need to perform the following updates to the Get() method:

1 Replace the method's signature (and return value) to make it async.
2 Change the ToArray() method to its ToArrayAsync() counterpart.

Here's how the new code looks (updated code in bold):

```
public async Task<RestDTO<BoardGame[]>> Get()
{
    var query = _context.BoardGames;

    return new RestDTO<BoardGame[]>()
    {
        Data = await query.ToArrayAsync(),
        Links = new List<LinkDTO> {
            new LinkDTO(
                Url.Action(null, "BoardGames", null, Request.Scheme)!,
                "self",
                "GET"),
        }
    };
}
```

As we can see, to use the ToArrayAsync() method and the await operator, we had to change not only the Get() method's signature (adding the async modifier), but also its return value (with a Task<TResult> type). In other words, we had to convert the Get() method from synchronous to asynchronous. All these changes will be handled by ASP.NET Core transparently because the async/await pattern is natively supported by the framework. Now we're ready to test what we've done.

Task-based Asynchronous Pattern (TAP)

Following the .NET standard, EF Core provides an asynchronous counterpart for any synchronous method that performs I/O operations, with the former always ending with the Async suffix. In our scenario, because we want to optimize our web service performances, performing the DB-related tasks by using the .NET's Task-based Asynchronous Pattern (TAP) is generally a good idea. This approach allows the system to free the main thread for other tasks, such as handling other incoming calls, while waiting for the asynchronous result, thus improving the efficiency of the web application. For additional info on the async/await pattern, check out the following URLs:

- http://mng.bz/ElwR
- http://mng.bz/Nmwd

5.2.2   *Testing the ApplicationDbContext*

To test our new `Get()` method, we can visit the following URL, the same one we've used
many times to retrieve our manually generated list of board games: https://localhost:
40443/BoardGames. Sadly, this time we get a rather disappointing JSON response;
the `data` array is empty (figure 5.1).

Figure 5.1 `BoardGameController`'s `Get()` **method returning an empty "data" array**

That result is hardly a surprise. We've replaced our dummy data with a real data-
retrieval query against a database table, which happens to be empty. To have such an
array populated again, we need to seed our database, using the CSV data set that we
downloaded in chapter 4.

5.3   *Seeding the database*

It's time to implement the first part of the CRUD acronym: create the data within the
DBMS. As soon as we do, our `BoardGameController` is able to read the data correctly,
paving the way for the remaining `Update` and `Delete` tasks.

SQL Server Management Studio, the management tool we learned to use in chapter 4, provides some built-in data import features that work with a lot of structured
and semistructured formats, including CSV files. But this tool isn't ideal when we need
to fill multiple tables from a single file, which is precisely our goal. For that reason, to
fulfill this requirement, we'll implement a dedicated `Controller` class (which we'll
call `SeedController`) and an action method that will read the CSV file programmatically and create all the corresponding records within our database tables, using EF
Core. Here's what we'll have to do:

1 Move (or copy) the `bgg_dataset.csv` file that we downloaded from Kaggle in
   chapter 4 to a dedicated folder within our ASP.NET Core project.
2 Install a third-party NuGet package that will allow us to read our CSV file and
   map its content to an `IEnumerable<T>` collection of C# objects.
3 Create a `BggRecord` Plain Old CLR Object (POCO) class that the third-party
   package will use to map the CSV records to C# objects and make them available
   through an `IEnumerable<BggRecord>` collection.
4 Add a `SeedController` to host the action method that will read the CSV file
   content and feed the database.

5   Implement the CSV reading process, using the third-party package.

6   Iterate through the resulting `IEnumerable<BggRecord>` collection, and use the data to create the entities and add them to their corresponding `MyBGList` database tables with EF Core.

5.3.1 Setting up the CSV file

The first thing we must do is put the `bgg_dataset.csv` file containing the board-game-related data in a location that will be accessible by our ASP.NET Core app. We create a new /Data/ subfolder in the `MyBGList` project's root folder and move (or copy) the file there.

This folder and its content won't be accessible by outside users because we didn't add `StaticFilesMiddleware` to the application's pipeline in the `Program.cs` file. But we'll be able to access the folder programmatically by using ASP.NET Core from any `Controller` using the built-in I/O interfaces.

5.3.2 Installing the CsvHelper package

Now that we can access the CSV file, we need to find a way to read it in an efficient (and effortless) way. Theoretically speaking, we could implement our own CSV parser, which would also be a great way to improve our C# I/O programming skills. Taking that route, however, would be like reinventing the wheel, because a lot of community-trusted third-party packages can perform this task.

> **NOTE** The "build versus buy" debate is a never-ending dilemma in the IT decision-making process, and software development is no exception. As a general rule, if we don't have specific requirements for customization, performance, security, and/or backward compatibility, using a community-trusted component developed by a third party instead of implementing something on our own is often reasonable, as long as the costs can be covered and/or the license allows it. We'll often do the same in this book because it allows us to focus on our main topic.

For that reason, in this scenario we'll handle this task with CsvHelper, an open source .NET library for reading and writing CSV files developed by Josh Close. This library will be our ORM for our `bgg_dataset.csv` file because we're going to use it to map each record in that file to a C# POCO class.

> **NOTE** CsvHelper is dual-licensed under MS-PL and Apache 2, so it can be used for free even for commercial purposes. As for its community trust level, the 3.6K stars on GitHub and the 81M NuGet downloads speak for themselves. To see the source code, check out the project's GitHub repository at https://github.com/JoshClose/CsvHelper.

To install the package, type the following line in the Package Manager console:

```
Install-Package CsvHelper -Version 30.0.1
```

To use the dotnet CLI (from the project's root folder), type

```
> dotnet add package CsvHelper --version 30.0.1
```

Alternatively, we can use the NuGet GUI provided by Visual Studio by right-clicking the MyBGList project in the Solution Explorer window and choosing Manage NuGet Packages from the contextual menu. As soon as we've got the CsvHelper package installed, we can move to the next step: create the C# POCO class that the library will use to map the CSV records.

5.3.3   *Creating the BggRecord class*

Call the class BggRecord, and place it in a new subfolder inside the existing /Models/ folder—the one that contains our EF Core entities. Create a new /Models/Csv/ subfolder, right-click it in the Solution Explorer window, and choose Add > New Item > Class (or press Shift+Alt+C) to add a new class file to the project. Call the new file BggRecord.cs, and open it for editing.

The CsvHelper library will use this class to map the contents of each record (row) in the bgg_dataset.csv file. We can use various techniques to configure the mapping process, such as using dedicated map types or a [Name] data attribute provided by the library. For simplicity, we're going to use the data attributes approach: add a property for each CSV record field, and decorate it with the name of the corresponding header column name.

We already know the structure of the CSV file, because we used it to design our DB schema in chapter 4. Let's review these header columns by opening the file with a text reader (such as Notepad) and looking at the first line:

```
ID;Name;Year Published;Min Players;Max Players;
Play Time;Min Age;Users Rated;Rating Average;
BGG Rank;Complexity Average;Owned Users;
Mechanics;Domains
```

From these semicolon-separated values, we can infer the list of the properties we need to add to the BggRecord class. More precisely, we need to create a property for each value, possibly using exactly the same name to ensure that the mapping process will work. When using that name isn't possible, perhaps due to space characters (which can't be used for C# property names), we can use the [Name] attribute to enforce the mapping. The following listing shows how the resulting class will eventually look.

Listing 5.2   BggRecord.cs **file**

```
using CsvHelper.Configuration.Attributes;

namespace MyBGList.Models.Csv
{
    public class BggRecord
    {
```

```
        [Name("ID")]
        public int? ID { get; set; }

        public string? Name { get; set; }

        [Name("Year Published")]
        public int? YearPublished { get; set; }

        [Name("Min Players")]
        public int? MinPlayers { get; set; }

        [Name("Max Players")]
        public int? MaxPlayers { get; set; }

        [Name("Play Time")]
        public int? PlayTime { get; set; }

        [Name("Min Age")]
        public int? MinAge { get; set; }

        [Name("Users Rated")]
        public int? UsersRated { get; set; }

        [Name("Rating Average")]
        public decimal? RatingAverage { get; set; }

        [Name("BGG Rank")]
        public int? BGGRank { get; set; }

        [Name("Complexity Average")]
        public decimal? ComplexityAverage { get; set; }

        [Name("Owned Users")]
        public int? OwnedUsers { get; set; }

        public string? Mechanics { get; set; }

        public string? Domains { get; set; }
    }
}
```

The class is similar to the BoardGame entity that we created in chapter 4, which is hardly a surprise, because most of the CSV record data is stored in the [BoardGames] database table. But the BggRecord class is expected to contain some additional info that we want to store in different tables.

Also, we intentionally defined all the properties as nullable because we can't rely on the correctness of the CSV file that we're using as a data source. In other words, we want our ORM to map the CSV record to this object even if some fields are missing instead of throwing an exception or skipping the whole line.

WARNING Our bgg_dataset.csv file has some missing fields. Some of these fields, such as UsersRated and OwnedUsers, can be replaced by a zero default value; others, such as ID and Name, require us to skip the whole record. We'll see how to deal with both scenarios later.

Now that we have the C# class that will be used to map the CSV records, we can create the controller where the whole CSV-importing and database-seeding process will take place.

5.3.4   *Adding the SeedController*

To create the SeedController, perform the following steps:

1 Add a new SeedController.cs file in the /Controllers/ folder, using the Visual Studio Add > Controller feature and the API Controller - Empty template.
2 Change the [Route] attribute default value from [Route("api/[controller]")] to [Route("[controller]")] so that the new controller's routing pattern will be consistent with the one used by the BoardGamesController.
3 Modify the default constructor by injecting an ApplicationDbContext instance using dependency injection, and store its reference in a local private variable as we did with the BoardGameController.

The following listing shows how the resulting SeedController class should look.

Listing 5.3   `SeedController.cs` file

```
using Microsoft.AspNetCore.Http;
using Microsoft.AspNetCore.Mvc;
using MyBGList.Models;

namespace MyBGList.Controllers
{
    [Route("[controller]")]
    [ApiController]
    public class SeedController : ControllerBase
    {
        private readonly ApplicationDbContext _context;

        private readonly ILogger<SeedController> _logger;

        public SeedController(
            ApplicationDbContext context,
            ILogger<SeedController> logger)
        {
            _context = context;
            _logger = logger;
        }
    }
}
```

We also added the same ILogger interface instance that we have in the BoardGames-Controller. We're definitely going to use it later on.

In addition to the `ApplicationDBContext` and `ILogger`, we need to request a third instance in this controller through dependency injection: the `IWebHostEnvironment`, an interface that provides information about the web hosting environment the ASP.NET Core web application is running in. We're going to need this interface to determine the web application's root path, which will be required to load the CSV file. The following listing shows the improved `SeedController` class.

Listing 5.4 `SeedController.cs` file (version 2)

```
using CsvHelper;
using CsvHelper.Configuration;
using Microsoft.AspNetCore.Http;
using Microsoft.AspNetCore.Mvc;
using Microsoft.EntityFrameworkCore;
using MyBGList.Models;
using MyBGList.Models.Csv;
using System.Globalization;

namespace MyBGList.Controllers
{
    [Route("[controller]")]
    [ApiController]
    public class SeedController : ControllerBase
    {
        private readonly ApplicationDbContext _context;

        private readonly IWebHostEnvironment _env;          ◄──┐ Adds a local
                                                               │ variable
        private readonly ILogger<BoardGamesController> _logger;

        public SeedController(
            ApplicationDbContext context,
            IWebHostEnvironment env,          ◄── Injects the
            ILogger<BoardGamesController> logger)   IWebHostEnvironment
        {
            _context = context;
            _env = env;          ◄──┐ Assigns the
            _logger = logger;       │ injected instance
        }
    }
}
```

We've already added the `using` directives for all the namespaces that we'll need later. Now that the `IWebHostEnvironment` is available, we can use it to determine the CSV file's path, load it into a `StreamReader` object, and pass it to a CsvHelper's `CsvReader` class instance that will read the file content. In other words, we're ready to read our `bgg_dataset.csv` file.

5.3.5   *Reading the CSV file*

It's time to see how we can use the CsvHelper library to read our CSV file. The whole importing-and-seeding task will be handled by a dedicated action method, so we'll be able to launch it whenever we want to populate our database. Because we're talking about an idempotent task, configuring this method so that it will accept only HTTP PUT requests seems to be the most logical choice.

> **DEFINITION**   *Idempotency* is a property of HTTP methods that ensures that executing subsequent identical requests will have the same effect on the server as executing the first one. Per RFC 7231, the following HTTP methods are considered to be idempotent: GET, HEAD, OPTIONS, TRACE, PUT, and DELETE. All server applications should implement the idempotent semantic correctly, as clients might expect it. For that reason, because we're dealing with a data seeding task, which will affect our database only the first time it's called, we should make sure that the process will be triggered only by an idempotent HTTP method such as PUT.

Here's a brief list of what our Put() action method is expected to do:

- Instantiate a CsvConfiguration object to set up some CSV properties (culture settings, delimiter, and so on).
- Create a StreamReader pointing to the CSV file.
- Create an instance of the CsvReader class, which will perform the CSV parsing and map each record to a BggRecord object.
- Iterate the resulting IEnumerable<BggRecord> collection, create the EF Core entities retrieving the relevant data from each BggRecord entry, and persist them into the database (if they don't exist yet).

The actual implementation of the SeedController's Put method takes several lines of code. For readability, we'll review it by splitting it into smaller blocks, following the four comments placed inside: Setup, Execute, Save, and Recap. As always, the full source code is in the GitHub repository for this chapter. Before reviewing the code, let's briefly review the attributes we used to decorate the method:

```
[HttpPut(Name = "Seed")]
[ResponseCache(NoStore = true)]
```

As I've explained before, we used the [HttpPut] attribute to ensure that the action method will handle only put requests, because it's handling an idempotent call. We also disabled the cache, using the [ResponseCache] attribute that we used earlier. Now let's move to the first part of the code, which is the Setup block:

```
var config = new CsvConfiguration(CultureInfo.GetCultureInfo("pt-BR"))
{
    HasHeaderRecord = true,
    Delimiter = ";",
};
```

```
using var reader = new StreamReader(
    System.IO.Path.Combine(_env.ContentRootPath, "Data/bgg_dataset.csv"));
using var csv = new CsvReader(reader, config);
var existingBoardGames = await _context.BoardGames
    .ToDictionaryAsync(bg => bg.Id);
var existingDomains = await _context.Domains
    .ToDictionaryAsync(d => d.Name);
var existingMechanics = await _context.Mechanics
    .ToDictionaryAsync(m => m.Name);
var now = DateTime.Now;
```

Here is where we prepare the objects that the CsvReader (the CSV parser component provided by the CsvHelper library) requires to perform its job:

- A CsvConfiguration object containing all the relevant info to read the CSV file: the culture to use for the decimal separator, the field delimiter, and so on.
- A StreamReader object built against the bgg_dataset.csv file, with the filesystem path determined thanks to the IWebHostingModel instance that we injected into the controller's constructor (and stored in the _env local variable).
- An instance of the CsvReader object itself.
- Three dictionaries that will contain the BoardGame, Domain, and Mechanic records are already present in the database, which we're going to use to avoid creating duplicates in case of multiple runs (ensuring idempotence). These dictionaries will be empty the first time we run the method, because the database is empty.
- A DateTime object representing the current date and time, which will be used to assign a value to the CreatedDate and LastModifiedDate properties of the EF Core entities we're going to create.

The StreamReader and the CsvReader objects have been declared with a using declaration, convenient C# syntax that ensures the correct use of IDisposable (and IAsyncDisposable) objects by disposing of them at the end of the scope. In this case, the end of the scope is the end of the method. Because these two objects implement the IDisposable interface, and we want to be sure that both of them will be released from memory at the end of the process, declaring them with the using keyword is the right thing to do. Let's proceed with the subsequent Execute block:

```
var records = csv.GetRecords<BggRecord>();
var skippedRows = 0;
foreach (var record in records)
{
    if (!record.ID.HasValue
        || string.IsNullOrEmpty(record.Name)
        || existingBoardGames.ContainsKey(record.ID.Value))
    {
        skippedRows++;
        continue;
    }
```

```
var boardgame = new BoardGame()
{
    Id = record.ID.Value,
    Name = record.Name,
    BGGRank = record.BGGRank ?? 0,
    ComplexityAverage = record.ComplexityAverage ?? 0,
    MaxPlayers = record.MaxPlayers ?? 0,
    MinAge = record.MinAge ?? 0,
    MinPlayers = record.MinPlayers ?? 0,
    OwnedUsers = record.OwnedUsers ?? 0,
    PlayTime = record.PlayTime ?? 0,
    RatingAverage = record.RatingAverage ?? 0,
    UsersRated = record.UsersRated ?? 0,
    Year = record.YearPublished ?? 0,
    CreatedDate = now,
    LastModifiedDate = now,
};
_context.BoardGames.Add(boardgame);

if (!string.IsNullOrEmpty(record.Domains))
    foreach (var domainName in record.Domains
        .Split(',', StringSplitOptions.TrimEntries)
        .Distinct(StringComparer.InvariantCultureIgnoreCase))
    {
        var domain = existingDomains.GetValueOrDefault(domainName);
        if (domain == null)
        {
            domain = new Domain()
            {
                Name = domainName,
                CreatedDate = now,
                LastModifiedDate = now
            };
            _context.Domains.Add(domain);
            existingDomains.Add(domainName, domain);
        }
        _context.BoardGames_Domains.Add(new BoardGames_Domains()
        {
            BoardGame = boardgame,
            Domain = domain,
            CreatedDate = now
        });
    }

if (!string.IsNullOrEmpty(record.Mechanics))
    foreach (var mechanicName in record.Mechanics
        .Split(',', StringSplitOptions.TrimEntries)
        .Distinct(StringComparer.InvariantCultureIgnoreCase))
    {
        var mechanic = existingMechanics.GetValueOrDefault(mechanicName);
        if (mechanic == null)
        {
            mechanic = new Mechanic()
            {
                Name = mechanicName,
```

```
            CreatedDate = now,
            LastModifiedDate = now
        };
        _context.Mechanics.Add(mechanic);
        existingMechanics.Add(mechanicName, mechanic);
    }
    _context.BoardGames_Mechanics.Add(new BoardGames_Mechanics()
    {
        BoardGame = boardgame,
        Mechanic = mechanic,
        CreatedDate = now
    });
    }
}
```

As its name clearly implies, this block is where most of the magic happens. The overall logic is summarized in the following key points:

- We use the GetRecords() method of the CsvReader object to obtain the IEnumerable<BggRecord> class, which is stored in a local records variable.
- We iterate the IEnumerable with a foreach block to cycle through all the mapped record objects. If the objects lack a required field (ID and/or Name) or have been added already, we skip the whole record, using the continue statement (and count the skip by using the skippedRows counter); otherwise, we keep going.
- We use the BggRecord data to create an instance of the BoardGame entity and add it to our ApplicationDbContext's DbSet<BoardGame>.
- We split the BggRecords's Domains field with the comma character, because we know that the domains related to each board game are referenced by a comma-separated string containing their names.
- For each of these names, we check whether we have already created a corresponding Domain entity using the GetValueOrDefault()method in the existing-Domains dictionary, which uses the domain name as the key to optimizing the lookup performances. If we find an existing Domain entity, we use it; otherwise, we create a new one and add it to the DbSet<Domains> and to the existing-Domains dictionary so that it will be found next time. Next, we create a new BoardGame_Domains entity to add a many-to-many relationship between the newly added BoardGame and each new or existing Domain.
- We repeat the preceding step for the mechanics, using the Mechanic, the existingMechanics dictionary, the DbSet<Mechanics>, and the BoardGame_Mechanics entities.

It's important to understand that we're not persisting anything in the database yet. All the preceding work is performed in-memory, with EF Core tracking all the added and/or related entities. The relationships are held using temporary key values that EF Core assigns automatically when it adds the entities, using the Add() method. These temporary values will be eventually converted to actual values when EF Core persists the entities in the database. This discussion brings us to the `Save` block:

```
await _context.SaveChangesAsync();
```

As we can see, we're just calling an `async` method that will persist all changes performed in the current execution context (the `ApplicationDbContext` instance) to the underlying database. There's not much more to say about this block, at least for now, but we'll have to improve it further in a short while. Now let's move to the last part of the code, which is the `Recap` block:

```
return new JsonResult(new
{
    BoardGames = _context.BoardGames.Count(),
    Domains = _context.Domains.Count(),
    Mechanics = _context.Mechanics.Count(),
    SkippedRows = skippedRows
});
```

This block is also simple to read. We set up a `JsonResult` containing some relevant info about the outcome of our data-seeding task. We do that by using a C# anonymous type, which is a convenient way to encapsulate a set of read-only properties in a single object without defining a type explicitly. We used this technique in previous chapters, so there's nothing to add.

Our `SeedController.Put()` method is ready. We have to launch it to see whether it works as expected. (Major spoiler: it doesn't.)

5.3.6   *Executing the SeedController*

Until this moment, we've executed our controllers (and Minimal API) methods by using the browser's address bar. We've done that because all the methods we've created so far are meant to handle HTTP GET requests. That's not the case for our Seed-Controller's `Put()` method, which requires an HTTP PUT. To execute it, we need an HTTP client of some sort. Here are a couple of suitable alternatives that we could use:

- *Postman*—An API platform for building and using APIs, available as an online web application or as a Windows app
- *cURL*—A command-line tool for getting or sending data, using URL syntax

Both would do the job, but the `Postman` web app can't reach the localhost-based address where our `MyBGList` web application currently runs. For simplicity, we'll opt for a third option that we already have available: the SwaggerUI, which includes a built-in testing platform that we can use to interact with all our API resources. Furthermore, because the UI is generated automatically from our `swagger.json` file, we don't have to input the actual URIs manually. All our API endpoints are already there, ready to be launched.

To access the SwaggerUI, type the following URL in a browser's address bar: https:// localhost:40443/swagger/index.html. Locate the PUT /Seed endpoint, and expand the HTML panel, using the handle on the right, to expose the Try It Out button, shown in figure 5.2.

Figure 5.2 Trying the PUT /Seed endpoint

Click Try It Out to access the Execute panel, which consists only of an Execute button because the endpoint doesn't require parameters. Click Execute to start the seeding process (figure 5.3).

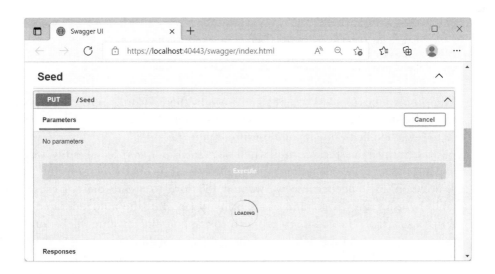

Figure 5.3 Executing the seeding process

The process will likely take a few minutes; we're reading approximately 20K CSV records, after all. Eventually, the Execute panel is updated with a black, console-like text box showing the outcome (figure 5.4).

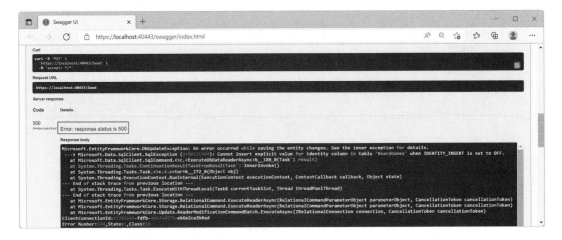

Figure 5.4   The PUT /Seed endpoint returning an error

As we can see, the seeding process failed (HTTP 500 response). The error message is shown in the response body, which is clearly visible in the text box. By reading the first lines, we should be able to identify the problem that caused the error:

```
Microsoft.EntityFrameworkCore.DbUpdateException:
An error occurred while saving the entity changes.
See the inner exception for details.
  ---> Microsoft.Data.SqlClient.SqlException (0x80131904):
Cannot insert explicit value for identity column
in table 'BoardGames' when IDENTITY_INSERT is set to OFF.
```

The problem lies in a `SqlException` thrown by the EF Core's SQL Client when trying to write to the `BoardGames` table. It seems that our SQL Server database doesn't allow us to set an explicit value in an identity column.

If we retrace the steps we took when we created our `BoardGame` entity, we can easily explain the error: we decorated the `BoardGame.Id` property by using the `[Key]` data annotation attribute because we wanted EF Core to create the corresponding DB table by using the `Id` column as its primary key. But the autogenerated migration script also assigns the `Identity` property to this column; its value will be automatically assigned (and autoincremented) by the database itself because the `IDENTITY_INSERT` flag is set to `OFF` by default. The error is clearly due to the fact that we're trying to assign an explicit value taken from the CSV record to the `Id` property manually instead of accepting the default value and having the database handle it. Now that we understand the root cause of our problem, we have two ways to fix it:

- Modify the Execute block of the SeedController.Put() method, removing the BoardGame.Id property assignment, thus leaving it to its default value.
- Modify the Save block of the SeedController.Put() method, altering the database's IDENTITY_INSERT flag to allow the manual insertion of identity values.

If we choose the first approach, we will lose the board game's existing IDs, which is not an option in our given scenario. The IDs are relevant info that we want to preserve by design. For that reason, we'll choose the other approach. Here's how we can refactor the Save block of the SeedController.Put() method to set the IDENTITY_INSERT flag value to ON right before saving our entities and then set it back to OFF:

```
// SAVE
using var transaction = _context.Database.BeginTransaction();
_context.Database.ExecuteSqlRaw("SET IDENTITY_INSERT BoardGames ON");
await _context.SaveChangesAsync();
_context.Database.ExecuteSqlRaw("SET IDENTITY_INSERT BoardGames OFF");
transaction.Commit();
```

As we can see by looking at this code, we've wrapped the three sets of commands—setting the flag to ON, inserting the entities, and setting the flag back to OFF—within a single transaction, ensuring that they'll be processed in an atomic manner. Because the IDENTITY_INSERT flag is specific to SQL Server, we had to perform the command by using the ExecuteSqlRaw() method, which executes a raw SQL command directly against the underlying database. In other words, we're bypassing the ORM, because EF Core doesn't provide a "managed" way to do that. That's not surprising, though, because we're working around a problem that is specific to the SQL Server engine.

Now that we've fixed our identity-related problem, we can launch the project, connect to the SwaggerUI, and launch the PUT /Seed endpoint again. This time, we should end up with an HTTP 200 response and the following response body:

```
{
  "boardGames": 20327,
  "domains": 8,
  "mechanics": 182,
  "skippedRows": 16
}
```

The seeding task was a success. Our database is filled with 8 domains, 182 mechanics, and more than 20K board games, with only 16 skipped CSV records with missing ID and/or Name. For simplicity, we'll ignore those "incorrect" records for now. We'll come up with a way to review (and possibly fix) them in the exercises at the end of this chapter.

5.4   Reading data

Now that our database has been filled with data, we can execute the `BoardGame-Controller`'s `BoardGames()` method—with the changes we applied at the beginning of this chapter—and see what has changed. If everything went according to our plan, we should see a lot of board games instead of the empty array we got last time.

Check it out by executing the following URL in a browser: https://localhost:40443/BoardGames. The outcome should be a huge JSON list of board games (figure 5.5).

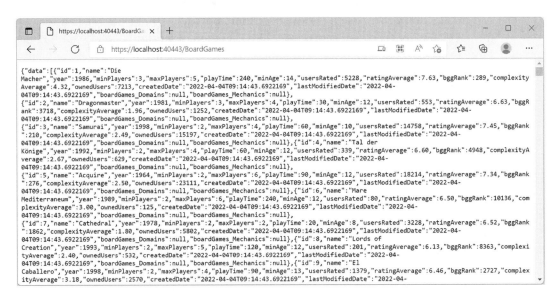

Figure 5.5   A long list of board games

This outcome clearly demonstrates that the second part of the CRUD operation—read—has been fulfilled. If we look at the scroll bar on the right, however, we see a potential problem with this output. A JSON object containing so many unordered records would likely be difficult for a typical client to use unless we provide a way to split the board-game data into discrete parts, sort it into a given (or configurable) order, and/or list only those board games that match certain conditions. In other words, we need to implement paging (or pagination), sorting, and filtering processes.

5.4.1   Paging

In a client-server programming context, the purpose of paging is to allow the client app to display a limited number of results on each page or view. We can use two techniques to achieve this result:

- *Client-side paging*—The client gets all the data from the server and uses the result to create a multipage UI that users can browse one page at a time.

- *Server-side paging*—The client creates a multipage UI that users can browse one page at a time. Each accessed page is populated by asking the server for only the relevant subset of the data.

If we apply this logic to our specific context, in which our web API plays the role of the server, we see that client-side paging requires an endpoint capable of returning all data in a single shot, with the client handling the actual job. In other words, we're already set!

Conversely, server-side paging requires some additional work. We need to improve our /BoardGames endpoint to return only the subset of board games that the user is supposed to see. This work is what we're going to do next, assuming that our web client requires this approach.

PageIndex, PageSize, RecordCount

To determine the subset of board games to return, our web API needs to know three values:

- PageIndex—The zero-based index of the page. When we adopt this naming convention, the first page has an index of 0, the second page has an index of 1, and so on. This value is almost always an input parameter, as it's meant to be passed by the client with the HTTP request.
- PageSize—The number of records contained on each page. This value is often an input parameter, because most clients allow the user to configure the number of items to display for each page. Sometimes, however, the server wants to force, override, limit, and/or restrict this number to control the size (and the performance hit) of the response.
- RecordCount—The total number of records, which can also be used to calculate the total number of available pages. This value is always calculated by the server, because the client has no way of knowing it in advance. But clients often need it, along with the actual data, to calculate the total number of pages (or records) to display to the user. A typical usage scenario for the RecordCount value is the page navigation UI component, which is commonly displayed as a list of clickable numbers and/or an array of PREV, NEXT, FIRST, and/or LAST buttons.

NOTE The PageIndex parameter is sometimes called PageNumber. When the latter name is used, the parameter typically adopts a one-based indexing convention: the first page is marked as 1, the second as 2, and so on. To keep things simple, because both C# and SQL Server work with zero-based indexes, we'll adopt zero-based indexing (and the PageIndex naming convention) throughout this book.

With all that in mind, we're now ready to refactor our GET /BoardGames method to take these values into account. We'll do the following things:

1 Add the pageIndex and pageSize input parameters, assuming that we want to give our clients the chance to determine both of them.

2   Change the EF Core implementation to return only the subset of records delimited by the pageIndex and pageSize values.

3   Calculate the RecordCount value and return it to the client along with the subset of requested data.

The following listing shows how we can pull off these tasks.

Listing 5.5   `BoardGameController.Get()` method (with paging)

```
[HttpGet(Name = "GetBoardGames")]
[ResponseCache(Location = ResponseCacheLocation.Any, Duration = 60)]
public async Task<RestDTO<BoardGame[]>> Get(
    int pageIndex = 0,
    int pageSize = 10)
{
    var query = _context.BoardGames
            .Skip(pageIndex * pageSize)
            .Take(pageSize);

    return new RestDTO<BoardGame[]>()
    {
        Data = await query.ToArrayAsync(),
        PageIndex = pageIndex,
        PageSize = pageSize,
        RecordCount = await _context.BoardGames.CountAsync(),
        Links = new List<LinkDTO> {
            new LinkDTO(
                Url.Action(
                    null,
                    "BoardGames",
                    new { pageIndex, pageSize },
                    Request.Scheme)!,
                "self",
                "GET"),
        }
    };
}
```

As we can see, the paging stuff is handled by the Skip() and Take() EF Core extension methods, which make good use of the new input parameters; as their names imply, they skip a number of records equal to the pageIndex multiplied by the pageSize and then take a number of records equal to the pageSize. Because the pageIndex is zero-based, this logic works even for the first page, which requires a skip of zero records.

> **NOTE**   We've set default values for the PageIndex and PageSize parameters (0 and 10, respectively) to ensure that our implementation will work even if the client's HTTP request doesn't set them explicitly. Whenever this happens, our API endpoint will serve only the first page of ten records.

Furthermore, we added the PageIndex, PageSize, and RecordCount properties to the RestDTO so that the client will receive them. While we were there, we updated the value of the Links property, adding a reference to the new pageIndex and pageSize variables, so that the property will keep matching the "self" endpoint URL. If we tried to build our project now, we would undoubtedly get a runtime error, because the Page-Index, PageSize, and RecordCount properties aren't present in the RestDTO class. Let's add them, as shown in the following listing, before proceeding.

Listing 5.6 `RestDTO.cs` file (with paging properties)

```
namespace MyBGList.DTO
{
    public class RestDTO<T>
    {
        public T Data { get; set; } = default!;

        public int? PageIndex { get; set; }

        public int? PageSize { get; set; }

        public int? RecordCount { get; set; }

        public List<LinkDTO> Links { get; set; } = new List<LinkDTO>();
    }
}
```

Now we can run our improved web API and perform a quick paging test.

TESTING THE PAGING PROCESS

Here are the URLs that we can use to retrieve the first three pages of board games, with each page holding five records:

- https://localhost:40443/BoardGames?pageIndex=0&pageSize=5
- https://localhost:40443/BoardGames?pageIndex=1&pageSize=5
- https://localhost:40443/BoardGames?pageIndex=2&pageSize=5

If we did everything correctly, we should receive a much smaller (and more readable) JSON object for each response, because the data array now contains a subset of five board games instead of the whole stack. We still have no way to sort the result of these "pages" in a given order, however. In the next section, we'll close this gap.

5.4.2 Sorting

Like paging, the sorting process can be implemented in two ways:

- *Using the DBMS*—The ORM appends a sorting statement (such as ORDER BY) to the query when asking the database for the data and receives the records already ordered.
- *Programmatically*—The ORM retrieves the unordered records and then sorts them in memory on the server side or even on the client side (assuming that we opted for client-side paging or no paging).

The DBMS approach is often preferable for performance reasons because it uses the indexes and caching strategies provided by the database engine. More important, it eliminates the need to fetch all the records from the database—a required task in sorting them programmatically. For that reason, we're going to follow this route.

> **NOTE** If we think about it for a moment, we see that the performance pitfalls of the programmatic sorting approach closely resemble those of client-side paging. In both cases, the actor performing the job needs to retrieve all the records, even when the goal is to return (or show) only some of them. This disadvantage is particularly evident when programmatic sorting is used in conjunction with paging; these unoptimized scenarios will likely take place in each page view.

The EF Core extension method we can use to delegate the sorting process to the database engine is called `OrderBy()` and can be used in the following way:

```
var results = await _context.BoardGames
                    .OrderBy(b => b.Name)
                    .ToArrayAsync();
```

The problem with this approach is that the `OrderBy()` extension method provided by EF Core requires a lambda expression as a parameter. No overloads accept a (dynamic) string value. If we want to allow the client to specify a sort column, we'll be forced to implement a cumbersome (and ugly) conditional statement, with a condition for each column. Here's a brief example (viewer discretion advised):

```
var query = _context.BoardGames.AsQueryable();
switch (orderBy)
{
    case "Name":
        query = query.OrderBy(b => b.Name);
        break;
    case "Year":
        query = query.OrderBy(b => b.Year);
        break;

    // TODO: add other cases (1 for each column we want to sort)

}
Data = await query.ToArrayAsync();
```

This approach isn't a good way to deal with our task. We need to find a way to apply that sorting statement dynamically, possibly using a string representation because that input value is likely to come from a client.

Luckily, we can achieve this result with another open source NuGet package designed with the precise intent to allow string-based query operations through LINQ providers. This package is Dynamic LINQ, developed by the ZZZ Projects community and released under the Apache-2.0 license. To install it, execute the following command in Visual Studio's Package Manager console:

```
Install-Package System.Linq.Dynamic.Core -Version 1.2.23
```

If you prefer to use the dotnet CLI (from the project's root folder), execute this command:

```
> dotnet add package System.Linq.Dynamic.Core --version 1.2.23
```

When the package has been installed, go back to the `BoardGameController.cs` file, and add the following `using` declaration to the top to make the Dynamic LINQ extension methods available for use:

```
using System.Linq.Dynamic.Core;
```

Now we can update the `Get()` method by adding a new `orderBy` input value that we can use to sort our records dynamically, using the DBMS engine. The following listing shows the improved method (new/updated code in bold).

Listing 5.7 `BoardGameController.Get()` **method (with paging and sorting)**

```
[HttpGet(Name = "GetBoardGames")]
[ResponseCache(Location = ResponseCacheLocation.Any, Duration = 60)]
public async Task<RestDTO<BoardGame[]>> Get(
    int pageIndex = 0,
    int pageSize = 10,
    string? sortColumn = "Name")
{
    var query = _context.BoardGames
            .OrderBy(sortColumn)
            .Skip(pageIndex * pageSize)
            .Take(pageSize);

    return new RestDTO<BoardGame[]>()
    {
        Data = await query.ToArrayAsync(),
        PageIndex = pageIndex,
        PageSize = pageSize,
        RecordCount = await _context.BoardGames.CountAsync(),
        Links = new List<LinkDTO> {
            new LinkDTO(
                Url.Action(
                    null,
                    "BoardGames",
                    new { pageIndex, pageSize },
                    Request.Scheme)!,
                "self",
                "GET"),
        }
    };
}
```

We've added a `sortColumn` string parameter for the client, which is consumed by the "string-based" overload of the `OrderBy()` extension method provided by Dynamic LINQ. The `OrderBy()` method instructs EF Core to add an `ORDER BY [sortColumn]` statement to the underlying database query and then apply skip-and-take paging to the ordered results.

> **WARNING**   In listing 5.7, we're passing the `sortColumn` GET parameter to the `OrderBy()` extension method without checking it properly. This approach is rather unsafe, as it's likely to lead to unexpected runtime errors and might even pose the risk of SQL injections (if the ORM isn't equipped to prevent them). I'll talk more about these kinds of problems and how to deal with them in chapter 6, which introduces data validation and exception handling.

ADDING A SORT ORDER

Before testing what we've done, let's improve our code further by adding a configurable sorting order. Sorting can be applied in two ways: ascending and descending. In general terms, *ascending* means smallest to largest (0–9, A–Z, and so on), whereas *descending* means largest to smallest (9–0, Z–A, and the like).

In most DBMSes, including SQL Server, the order can be set by the `ASC` and `DESC` keywords, with `ASC` being the default. In our current implementation, the `OrderBy()` method always sorts our records in ascending order, regardless of the column set with the `sortColumn` input parameter.

Suppose that we want to improve this behavior by allowing the client to choose the sort order instead of taking it for granted. Luckily, thanks to the Dynamic LINQ library, we can easily do that, because the `OrderBy()` overload we're using allows us to specify an optional, space-separated `ASC` or `DESC` keyword right after the column name. All we have to do is add a new `sortOrder` input parameter to our GET /Board-Games method:

```
public async Task<RestDTO<BoardGame[]>> Get(
    int pageIndex = 0,
    int pageSize = 10,
    string? sortColumn = "Name",
    string? sortOrder = "ASC")
```

We append it to the column name in the existing `OrderBy()` string parameter in the following way:

```
.OrderBy($"{sortColumn} {sortOrder}")
```

Now the client can set the sort column and the sort order. As always, we provided the new parameter with a suitable default value (`"ASC"`) that will be used whenever the client doesn't use that feature.

To test our sort, we can use the following URLs:

- https://localhost:40443/BoardGames?sortColumn=Name to retrieve the first ten records, sorted by Name (ascending)
- https://localhost:40443/BoardGames?sortColumn=Year to retrieve the first ten records, sorted by Year (ascending)
- https://localhost:40443/BoardGames?sortColumn=Year&sortOrder=DESC to retrieve the first ten records, sorted by Year (descending)

Next, we'll implement the last (but not least) read-related feature.

5.4.3 Filtering

Filtering doesn't need an introduction. We use it while surfing the web, because filtering is a pivotal feature of any search engine, as well as Wikipedia, Twitter, and any web (or nonweb) application that provides "browsable" data to users. Like sorting, filtering can be implemented by using the DBMS or programmatically, with the same caveats. For the same reasons, we'll take the DBMS-driven approach.

ADDING A FILTER LOGIC

Implementing a DBMS-driven filtering process in our existing GET /BoardGame endpoint is a rather easy task, especially considering that we have only a single string parameter to deal with: the board game's Name. Here's what we need to do:

1 Add a filterQuery input parameter, which the client(s) will use to specify the actual lookup query.
2 Use the filterQuery parameter in a new Where() operator that will instruct EF Core to retrieve only records with a matching Name from the database.

The following listing shows the implementation (new/updated code in bold).

Listing 5.8 `BoardGameController.Get()` method (with paging, sorting, and filtering)

```
[HttpGet(Name = "GetBoardGames")]
[ResponseCache(Location = ResponseCacheLocation.Any, Duration = 60)]
public async Task<RestDTO<BoardGame[]>> Get(
    int pageIndex = 0,
    int pageSize = 10,
    string? sortColumn = "Name",           Adds the
    string? sortOrder = "ASC",             filterQuery
    string? filterQuery = null)            parameter
{
    var query = _context.BoardGames.AsQueryable();
    if (!string.IsNullOrEmpty(filterQuery))
        query = query.Where(b => b.Name.Contains(filterQuery));
    var recordCount = await query.CountAsync();
    query = query
            .OrderBy($"{sortColumn} {sortOrder}")
            .Skip(pageIndex * pageSize)
            .Take(pageSize);
```

Handles the DbSet as an IQueryable object

Conditionally applies the filter

Determines the record count

```
    return new RestDTO<BoardGame[]>()
    {
        Data = await query.ToArrayAsync(),
        PageIndex = pageIndex,
        PageSize = pageSize,
        RecordCount = recordCount,
        Links = new List<LinkDTO> {
            new LinkDTO(
                Url.Action(
                    null,
                    "BoardGames",
                    new { pageIndex, pageSize },
                    Request.Scheme)!,
                "self",
                "GET"),
        }
    };
}
```

As we can see, this time we had to set a NULL default value for our new filterQuery parameter, because providing a "default" filter wouldn't make much sense. For that reason, we had to find a way to add the Where() operator conditionally so that it would be applied to the expression tree only if the filter query is null or empty. Two more things are worth noting:

- We had to use the AsQueryable() method to cast the DbSet<BoardGame> explicitly to an IQueryable<BoardGame> interface so that we could "chain" the extension methods to build the expression tree the way we did.
- We added a recordCount local variable and used it to pull the record count from the database sooner so that we could take the filter parameter into account before performing the paging tasks.

TESTING THE FILTERING PROCESS

We can use these URLs to test our brand-new filter behavior:

- https://localhost:40443/BoardGames?filterQuery=diplomacy to retrieve the top ten board games sorted by Name (ascending), with a Name containing "diplomacy" (spoiler: only five)
- https://localhost:40443/BoardGames?filterQuery=war to retrieve the first ten board games sorted by Name (ascending) with a Name containing "war"

5.5   *Updating and deleting data*

Now that we've learned how to create and read data, we're ready to tackle the last two parts of the CRUD acronym: update and delete. Those operations, like create, typically require elevated privileges to be used because they'll likely make permanent changes in the data source. I discuss this topic in chapter 9, which introduces authentication and authorization. For now, we'll stick to a sample implementation that allows us to learn the basics.

5.5.1   Updating a BoardGame

The first decision we should make is which HTTP method to use to perform the Update process. Should we use an idempotent HTTP method, as we did with `Seed-Controller.Put()`? The answer depends on how we plan to implement the Update process:

- If we can ensure that multiple identical Update operations will have the same outcome on the server, we can use an idempotent HTTP method such as PUT, which (according to RFCs 2616 and 7241) is meant to be used to create or replace a given, targeted resource by using a standardized intent.
- If we can't guarantee the prior result, we should use a nonidempotent HTTP method such as POST, which (according to the same RFCs) is meant to be used to create a new resource or otherwise interact with an existing resource by using a nonstandardized intent.

In our scenario, we can already answer this question. Because we intentionally created a `LastModifiedDate` column in our `BoardGames` table (and entity), we'll likely want to update it every time an update is performed on a record so we can keep track of it. Our Update operation will be nonidempotent because it will have a different, unique effect on our database each time it's executed. For that reason, we're going to use the HTTP POST method. Now that we've settled that matter, we can move to implementation.

CREATING THE BOARDGAMEDTO

The first thing to do is create a DTO that will allow authorized clients to send the board-game data to update.

> **Reasons to use a DTO**
>
> Theoretically speaking, instead of creating a DTO, we could use one of our existing classes: the EF Core's `BoardGame` entity that we've worked with since chapter 4 or the `BggRecord` entity that we created for the CsvHelper library. Using entities for DTOs, however, is widely considered to be bad practice: it breaks the single-responsibility principle, which states that every module, class, or function should have responsibility for a single part of that program's functionality.
>
> Entity classes are meant to be object wrappers for database tables and views. Directly using them to "configure" the JSON data output for our client-side app isn't a good idea, for several reasons. An entity might contain a lot of data that the user and/or the client-side app should never be able to see or transmit, such as password hashes, personal data, and so on. Masking or ignoring these properties would force the developer to overcomplicate the source code, eventually leading to a confusing codebase. In this book, we'll adopt the good practice of creating DTO objects whenever we need to transmit data from and to our clients within our API endpoints.

For simplicity, we'll implement a minimal `BoardGameDTO` class with three properties:

- `Id`, which will be used to locate the board-game record to update
- `Name` and `Year`, assuming that they're the only fields we want our clients to be able to update

Let's create a new `/DTO/BoardGameDTO.cs` file with the source code shown in the following listing.

Listing 5.9   `BoardGameDTO.cs` file

```
using System.ComponentModel;
using System.ComponentModel.DataAnnotations;

namespace MyBGList.DTO
{
    public class BoardGameDTO
    {
        [Required]
        public int Id { get; set; }

        public string? Name { get; set; }

        public int? Year { get; set; }
    }
}
```

Now that we have the DTO class, let's see how to make good use of it.

ADDING THE POST METHOD

The next step of the plan involves opening our `BoardGameController.cs` file and adding a new `Post()` action method that will do the following things:

1 Accept a JSON input with the same structure as the `BoardGameDTO` class.
2 Check for the existence of a board-game record with the given `Id`.
3 If the record is found, update its `Name` and/or `Year` accordingly, and also update the `LastModifiedDate` field to keep track of the `Update` operation.
4 Save the updated record in the DBMS.
5 Return a `RestDTO` object containing the relevant info to the client.

The following listing shows how we can implement all those features.

Listing 5.10   `BoardGameController`'s `Post` method

```
[HttpPost(Name = "UpdateBoardGame")]
[ResponseCache(NoStore = true)]
public async Task<RestDTO<BoardGame?>> Post(BoardGameDTO model)
{
    var boardgame = await _context.BoardGames
        .Where(b => b.Id == model.Id)
        .FirstOrDefaultAsync();
```

```
if (boardgame != null)
{
    if (!string.IsNullOrEmpty(model.Name))
        boardgame.Name = model.Name;
    if (model.Year.HasValue && model.Year.Value > 0)
        boardgame.Year = model.Year.Value;
    boardgame.LastModifiedDate = DateTime.Now;
    _context.BoardGames.Update(boardgame);
    await _context.SaveChangesAsync();
};

return new RestDTO<BoardGame?>()
{
    Data = boardgame,
    Links = new List<LinkDTO>
    {
        new LinkDTO(
                Url.Action(
                    null,
                    "BoardGames",
                    model,
                    Request.Scheme)!,
                "self",
                "POST"),
    }
};
}
```

Now we can test what we've done by using the SwaggerUI.

TESTING THE UPDATE PROCESS

Press F5 or click the Run button to execute the `MyBGList` project, which should auto-matically launch the browser with the SwaggerUI's main dashboard URL in the address bar: https://localhost:40443/swagger/index.html. Locate the `POST` /`BoardGames` end-point; expand its panel by using the right handle; and click Try It Out, as we did with the `PUT` /`Seed` endpoint earlier. This time, the SwaggerUI asks us to fill out the request body, because this method requires parameters (figure 5.6).

Fill out the JSON request with the following values to change the `Name` of the Risk board game (`Id` 181) to "Risk!" and the publishing `Year` from 1959 to 1980:

```
{
    "id": 181,
    "name": "Risk!",
    "year": 1980
}
```

Before executing the request, it could be wise to place a breakpoint at the start of the `Post()` method to check how the server will handle this request: once done, click the Execute button to perform the test. If everything goes as expected, we should end up with an HTTP 200 response and a `RestDTO<BoardGame>` object containing the

Figure 5.6   Trying the POST /BoardGames endpoint

BoardGame entity, with the newly updated Name, Year, and LastModifiedDate in its data property.

Now that we have proof that our method works, we can revert the changes by executing the POST /BoardGames endpoint a second time, with the following values in the JSON request body:

```
{
    "id": 181,
    "name": "Risk",
    "year": 1959
}
```

This code reverts the Risk board game to its original state except for the LastModifiedDate, which permanently keeps track of what we did.

5.5.2   *Deleting a BoardGame*

Unlike the Update process, which requires a nonidempotent HTTP method (in our scenario) because we had to deal with the LastModifiedDate, the Delete operation is almost always implemented with an idempotent approach. The reason is simple: assuming that the record to delete is targeted (typically by means of the Id primary key), executing the deletion multiple times against the same target (Id) should have the same effect on the server as executing it once. For that reason, we'll use the Http-Delete method, which (not surprisingly) is among the idempotent ones.

ADDING THE DELETE METHOD

Let's start with the usual plan. Here's what our new `Delete()` method should do:

1 Accept an integer-type input containing the `Id` of the board game we want to delete.

2 Check for the existence of a board-game record with the given `Id`.

3 If the record is found, delete it, and persist the changes in the DBMS.

4 Return a `RestDTO` object containing the relevant info to the client.

The following listing shows the implementation.

Listing 5.11 BoardGameController's Delete method

```
[HttpDelete(Name = "DeleteBoardGame")]
[ResponseCache(NoStore = true)]
public async Task<RestDTO<BoardGame?>> Delete(int id)
{
    var boardgame = await _context.BoardGames
        .Where(b => b.Id == id)
        .FirstOrDefaultAsync();
    if (boardgame != null)
    {
        _context.BoardGames.Remove(boardgame);
        await _context.SaveChangesAsync();
    };

    return new RestDTO<BoardGame?>()
    {
        Data = boardgame,
        Links = new List<LinkDTO>
        {
            new LinkDTO(
                    Url.Action(
                        null,
                        "BoardGames",
                        id,
                        Request.Scheme)!,
                    "self",
                    "DELETE"),
        }
    };
}
```

The source code looks loosely like the `Update` method, with less work to do; all we have to do is check for the `Id` key and act accordingly. Let's test whether the method works as expected by using the SwaggerUI.

TESTING THE DELETE PROCESS

Launch the MyBGList project, and have the browser point again to the SwaggerUI main dashboard's URL: https://localhost:40443/swagger/index.html. Locate the DELETE /BoardGames endpoint, expand its panel by using the handle, and click Try It Out.

This time, we're asked to specify a single Id parameter. Pay attention now: we're going to delete a board game from our database! But don't worry— we'll have it back shortly after performing the test.

> **TIP**   As always, it's strongly advisable to put a breakpoint at the start of the Delete method to keep track of what happens.

Let's use the Risk board game we updated (and reverted) earlier. Type 181 in the Id text box and click Execute to proceed. If everything goes the way it should, we'll receive an HTTP 200 response with the targeted board-game info in the RestDTO's data property—a sign that the board game has been found (and deleted).

To double-check, click Execute again. This time, the RestDTO's data property is null, confirming that the board game with Id 181 doesn't exist in the database. Now that the test is over, we may want to get the Risk board game back. We don't want to lose it, right? Luckily, we already have a convenient method that can bring it back.

RESEEDING THE DATABASE

If we think back to how we implemented the SeedController.Put() method, we should remember that it uses an existingBoardGames dictionary filled with existing records to identify and skip them by using the Id key, thus averting duplicate entries. Thanks to that dictionary, if we execute that method multiple times, all the records present in the CSV file will be skipped—except the Risk board game with Id 181, because it's not present anymore. In other words, all we need to do to add the Risk board game back to the database is execute the SeedController.Put() method.

Let's try that approach. Launch the MyBGList project again, access the SwaggerUI main dashboard, and execute the PUT /Seed endpoint. If everything works the way it should, we should have our Risk board game back in (almost) no time.

This chapter concludes our journey through CRUD operations. In the following chapters, we switch to error handling, data validation, and logging.

5.6   *Exercises*

The following exercises emulate some task assignments given by our product owner and addressed to the MyBGList development team (us).

> **TIP**   The solutions to the exercises are available on GitHub in the /Chapter_05/ Exercises/ folder. To test them, replace the relevant files in your MyBGList project with those in that folder, and run the app.

5.6.1   *Create*

Modify the SeedController's Put() method so that it accepts an optional Id parameter of an integer type. If such a parameter is present, the method will add only the board game that has that Id, skipping all the others; otherwise, it acts like it already does.

5.6.2 *Read*

Change the filtering behavior of the BoardGamesController's Get() method. Instead of returning the board games with a Name that contains the filterQuery, the method should return board games with a Name that starts with the filterQuery.

5.6.3 *Update*

Improve the capabilities of the BoardGamesController's Post method so that it can also update the following columns of the [BoardGames] table: MinPlayers, MaxPlayers, PlayTime, and MinAge. To implement this change properly, we also need to update the BoardGameDTO type.

5.6.4 *Delete*

Modify the BoardGamesController's Delete() method, replacing the current id integer parameter with a new idList string parameter, which clients will use to specify a comma-separated list of Id keys instead of a single Id. The improved method should perform the following tasks:

1 Ensure that every single id contained in the idList parameter is of an integer type.
2 Delete all the board games that match one of the given id keys.
3 Return a RestDTO<BoardGame[]?> JSON object containing all the deleted board games in the data array.

Summary

- CRUD operations strongly rely on the LINQ component provided by ASP.NET Core, which allows us to deal with different types of raw data sources by using a single, unified query language.
- To use LINQ effectively, we need to gain some knowledge of its syntax and method parameters and operators, as well as the interfaces where its extension methods apply:
  - IEnumerable<T>, which is implemented by most C# object collections.
  - IQueryable<T>, which is used to build expression trees that will eventually be translated into database queries and executed against the DBMS.
- To access our ApplicationDbContext within our controllers, we need to inject it by using dependency injection.
  - The injection can be done at the constructor level, where we can also assign the injected instance to a local property that will hold its reference for the controller's lifecycle, thus being accessible by all the action methods.
- When we have the ApplicationDbContext available, we can implement a create task that will seed our SQL Server database from a CSV data source of board games.
  - The seeding process can be implemented by using the CsvHelper NuGet package, which acts like an ORM for CSV files.

– The CsvHelper library will help us map the CSV records to DTO classes, which can be used to create the `BoardGame` entities and add them to the database.

- As soon as the create process is ready, we can execute it to feed our database with actual records.

  – Then we'll be able to implement the read, update, and delete operations as well. Each operation requires its own set of input parameters, HTTP method, and LINQ operators.

Data validation
and error handling

6

This chapter covers

- Overview of model binding and data validation
- Built-in and custom validation attributes
- ModelState validation approaches
- Error and exception handling techniques

For simplicity, up to this point we've assumed that the data coming from clients is always correct and adequate for our web API's endpoints. Unfortunately, this is not always the case: whether we like it or not, we often have to deal with erroneous HTTP requests, which can be caused by several factors (including malicious attacks) but always occur because our application is facing unexpected or unhandled behavior.

In this chapter, we'll discuss a series of techniques for handling unexpected scenarios during the client–server interaction. These techniques rely on two main concepts:

- *Data validation*—A set of methods, checks, routines, and rules to ensure that the data coming into our system is meaningful, accurate, and secure and therefore is allowed to be processed

- *Error handling*—The process of anticipating, detecting, classifying, and managing application errors that might happen within the program execution flow

In the upcoming sections, we'll see how we can put them into practice within our code.

6.1 Data validation

We know from chapter 1 that the primary purpose of a web API is to enable different parties to interact by exchanging information. In later chapters, we saw how to implement several HTTP endpoints that can be used to create, read, update, and delete data. Most (if not all) of these endpoints require an input of some sort from the calling client. As an example, consider the parameters expected by the GET /BoardGames endpoint, which we greatly improved in chapter 5:

- pageIndex–An optional integer value to set the starting page of the board games to return
- pageSize—An optional integer value to set the size of each page
- sortColumn—An optional string value to set the column to sort the returned board games
- sortOrder—An optional string value to set the sort order
- filterQuery—An optional string value that, if present, will be used to return only board games with a Name that contains it

All these parameters are optional. We've chosen to allow their absence—in other words, to accept incoming requests without them—because we could easily provide suitable default values in case they're not explicitly provided by the caller. For that reason, all the following HTTP requests will be handled in the same way and therefore will provide the same outcome (until the default values change):

- https://localhost:40443/BoardGames
- https://localhost:40443/BoardGames?pageIndex=0&pageSize=10
- https://localhost:40443/BoardGames?pageIndex=0&pageSize=10&sortColumn=Name&sortOrder=ASC

At the same time, we require some of these parameters' values to be compatible with a given .NET type instead of being raw strings. That's the case with pageIndex and pageSize, whose values are expected to be of type integer. If we try to pass even one of them with an incompatible value, such as the HTTP request https://localhost:40443/BoardGames?pageIndex=test, our application will respond with an HTTP 400 - Bad Request error without even starting to execute the BoardGamesController's Get action method:

```
{
  "type":"https://tools.ietf.org/html/rfc7231#section-6.5.1",
  "title":"One or more validation errors occurred.",
  "status":400,
  "traceId":"00-a074ebace7131af6561251496331fc65-ef1c633577161417-00",
  "errors":{
```

```
    "pageIndex":["The value 'string' is not valid."]
  }
}
```

We can easily see that by allowing and/or rejecting such requests, we're already performing some sort of data validation activity on those parameters by actively checking two important acceptance criteria:

- Providing an undefined value for each parameter is OK because we have server-defined fallbacks (the action method's default values).
- Providing a noninteger value for pageIndex and pageSize is not OK because we expect them to be of an integer type.

We're obviously talking about an implicit activity, because the null-checking and fall-back-to-default tasks are conducted by the framework under the hood, without our having to write anything. Specifically, we're taking advantage of the ASP.NET Core's model binding system, which is the mechanism that automatically takes care of all that.

6.1.1   Model binding

All the input data coming from HTTP requests—request headers, route data, query strings, form fields, and so on—is transmitted by means of raw strings and received as such. The ASP.NET Core framework retrieves these values and converts them from strings to .NET types automatically, saving the developer from the tedious, error-prone manual activity. Specifically, the model binding system retrieves the input data from the HTTP request query string and/or body and converts them to strongly typed method parameters. This process is performed automatically upon each HTTP request, but it can be configured with a set of attribute-based conventions according to the developer's requirements.

Let's see what model binding does under the hood. Consider the HTTP GET request https://localhost:40443/BoardGames?pageIndex=2&pageSize=50, which is routed to our BoardGamesController's Get action method:

```
public async Task<RestDTO<BoardGame[]>> Get(
  int pageIndex = 0,
  int pageSize = 10,
  string? sortColumn = "Name",
  string? sortOrder = "ASC",
  string? filterQuery = null)
```

The model binding system performs the following tasks:

- Identifies the presence of the pageIndex and pageSize GET parameters
- Retrieves their raw string values ("2" and "50"), converts them to integer types (2 and 50), and assigns the converted values to the corresponding action method's properties

- Identifies the absence of the sortColumn, sortOrder, and filterQuery GET parameters, and assigns a null value to the corresponding action method's properties so that the respective default values will be used instead

In a nutshell, the main purpose of the model binding system is to convert a given (raw string) source to one or more expected (.NET typed) targets. In our example, the raw GET parameters issued by the URL are the model binding's sources, and the action method's typed parameters are the targets. The targets can be simple types (integer, bool, and the like) or complex types (such as data-transfer objects [DTOs]), as we'll see later.

6.1.2   *Data validation attributes*

In addition to performing standard type conversion, model binding can be configured to perform several data validation tasks by using a set of built-in data annotation attributes included in the System.ComponentModel.DataAnnotation namespace. Here's a list of the most notable of those attributes:

- [CreditCard]—Ensures that the given input is a credit card number
- [EmailAddress]—Ensures that the given string input has an email address format
- [MaxLength(n)]—Ensures that the given string or array input has a length smaller than or equal to the specified value
- [MinLength(n)]—Ensures that the given string or array input has a length equal to or greater than the specified value
- [Range(nMin, nMax)]—Ensures that the given input falls between the minimum and maximum specified values
- [RegularExpression(regex)]—Ensures that the given input matches a given regular expression
- [Required]—Ensures that the given input has a non-null value
- [StringLength]—Ensures that the given string input doesn't exceed the specified length limit
- [Url]—Ensures that the given string input has a URL format

The best way to learn how to use these validation attributes is to implement them within our MyBGList web API. Suppose that we want (or are asked) to limit the page size of our GET /BoardGames endpoint to a maximum value of 100. Here's how we can do that by using the [Range] attribute:

```
public async Task<RestDTO<BoardGame[]>> Get(
    int pageIndex = 0,
    [Range(1, 100)] int pageSize = 10,       ◁────┐ Range validator
    string? sortColumn = "Name",                   │ (1 to 100)
    string? sortOrder = "ASC",
    string? filterQuery = null)
```

NOTE This change request is credible. Accepting any page size without limits means allowing potentially expensive data-retrieval requests, which could result in HTTP response delays, slowdowns, and performance drops, thus exposing our web application to denial-of-service (DoS) attacks.

This change would cause the URL https://localhost:40443/BoardGames?pageSize=200 to return an `HTTP 400 - Bad Request` status error instead of the first 200 board games. As we can easily understand, data annotation attributes can be useful whenever we want to put some boundaries around the input data without implementing the corresponding checks manually. If we don't want to use the `[Range]` attribute, we could obtain the same outcome with the following code:

```
if (pageSize < 0 || pageSize > 100) {
  // .. do something
}
```

That `"something"` could be implemented in various ways, such as raising an exception, returning an HTTP error status, or performing any other suitable error handling action. Manual approaches can be hard to maintain, however, and they're often prone to human error. For that reason, the best practice in working with ASP.NET Core is to adopt the centralized interface provided by the framework as long as we can use it to achieve what we need to do.

DEFINITION This approach is known as *aspect-oriented programming* (*AOP*), a paradigm that aims to increase the modularity of the source code by adding behavior to existing code without modifying the code itself. The data annotation attributes provided by ASP.NET are a perfect example because they allow the developer to add functionalities without cluttering the code.

6.1.3 *A nontrivial validation example*

The `[Range(1, 100)]` validator that we used to limit page size was easy to pull off. Let's try a more difficult change request. Suppose that we want (or are asked) to validate the `sortOrder` parameter, which currently accepts any string, to accept only a value that can be considered valid for its specific purpose, which is either `"ASC"` or `"DESC"`. Again, this change request is more than reasonable. Accepting an arbitrary string value for a parameter such as `sortOrder`, which is used programmatically to compose a LINQ expression with Dynamic LINQ, could expose our web application to dangerous vulnerabilities, such as SQL injections or LINQ injections. For that reason, providing our app a validator for these "dynamic" strings is a security requirement that we should take care of.

TIP For additional info regarding this topic, check out the StackOverflow thread at http://mng.bz/Q8w4.

Again, we could easily implement this change request by taking a programmatic approach, making the following "manual check" within the action method itself:

```
if (sortOrder != "ASC" && sortOrder != "DESC") {
  // .. do something
}
```

But we have at least two other ways to achieve the same outcome with the built-in validator interface provided by ASP.NET Core: using the [RegularExpression] attribute or implementing a custom validation attribute. In the upcoming sections, we'll use both techniques.

USING THE REGULAREXPRESSION ATTRIBUTE

The RegularExpressionAttribute class is one of the most useful and most customizable data annotation attributes because it uses the power and flexibility of regular expressions. The [RegularExpression] attribute relies on the .NET regular expression engine, represented by the System.Text.RegularExpressions namespace and its Regex class. This engine accepts regular expression patterns written using Perl 5-compatible syntax and uses them against the input string to determine matches, retrieve occurrences, or replace the matching text, depending on the method being used. Specifically, the attribute calls the IsMatch() method internally to determine whether the pattern finds a match in the input string, which is precisely what we need in our scenario.

Regular expressions

Regular expressions (also known as *RegEx* and *RegExp*) are standardized patterns used to match character combinations in strings. The technique originated in 1951 but became popular only during the late 1980s, thanks to the worldwide adoption of the Perl language (which has featured a regex library since 1986). Also, in the 1990s, the Perl Compatible Regular Expression (PCRE) library was adopted by many modern tools (such as PHP and Apache HTTP Server), becoming a de facto standard.

Throughout this book, we will rarely use regular expressions and only to a basic extent. To find out more about the topic, check the following website, which provides some insightful tutorials, examples, and a quick-start guide: https://www.regular-expressions.info.

Here's a suitable RegEx pattern that we can use to check for the presence of either the ASC or DESC string:

```
ASC|DESC
```

This pattern can be used within a [RegularExpression] attribute in our BoardGames-Controller's Get action method in the following way:

```
public async Task<RestDTO<BoardGame[]>> Get(
  int pageIndex = 0,
  [Range(1, 100)] int pageSize = 10,
  string? sortColumn = "Name",
```

```
[RegularExpression("ASC|DESC")] string? sortOrder = "ASC",
string? filterQuery = null)
```

Afterward, all incoming requests containing a `sortOrder` parameter value different from `"ASC"` and `"DESC"` will be considered to be invalid, resulting in an `HTTP 400 - Bad Request` response.

USING A CUSTOM VALIDATION ATTRIBUTE

If we don't want to fulfill our change request by using the `[RegularExpression]` attribute, we can achieve the same outcome with a custom validation attribute. All the existing validation attributes extend the `ValidationAttribute` base class, which provides a convenient (and overridable) `IsValid()` method that performs the actual validation tasks and returns a `ValidationResult` object containing the outcome. To implement our own validation attribute, we need to perform the following steps:

1 Add a new class file, which will contain our custom validator's source code.
2 Extend the `ValidationAttribute` base class.
3 Override the `IsValid` method with our own implementation.
4 Configure and return a `ValidationResult` object containing the outcome.

ADDING THE SORTORDERVALIDATOR CLASS FILE

In Visual Studio's Solution Explorer, create a new `/Attributes/` folder in the `MyBGList` project's root. Then right-click the folder, and add a new `SortOrderValidator-Attribute.cs` class file to generate an empty boilerplate within a new `MyBGList.Attributes` namespace. Now we're ready to implement our custom validator.

IMPLEMENTING THE SORTORDERVALIDATOR

The following listing provides a minimal implementation that checks the input string against the `"ASC"` and `"DESC"` values, returning a successful result only if an exact match of one of them occurs.

> **Listing 6.1**   `SortOrderValidatorAttribute`

```
using System.ComponentModel.DataAnnotations;

namespace MyBGList.Attributes
{
    public class SortOrderValidatorAttribute : ValidationAttribute
    {
        public string[] AllowedValues { get; set; } =
            new[] { "ASC", "DESC" };
        public SortOrderValidatorAttribute()
            : base("Value must be one of the following: {0}.") { }

        protected override ValidationResult? IsValid(
            object? value,
            ValidationContext validationContext)
        {
            var strValue = value as string;
            if (!string.IsNullOrEmpty(strValue)
```

```
            && AllowedValues.Contains(strValue))
            return ValidationResult.Success;

        return new ValidationResult(
            FormatErrorMessage(string.Join(",", AllowedValues))
        );
        }
    }
}
```

The code is easy to read. The input value is checked against an array of allowed string values (the AllowedValues string array) to determine whether it's valid. Notice that if the validation fails, the resulting ValidationResult object is instantiated with a convenient error message that will give the caller some useful contextual info about the failed check. Default text for this message is defined in the constructor, but we can change it by using the public ErrorMessage property provided by the Validation-Attribute base class in the following way:

```
[SortOrderValidator(ErrorMessage = "Custom error message")]
```

Also, we set the AllowedValues string array property as public, which gives us the chance to customize these values in the following way:

```
[SortOrderValidator(AllowedValues = new[] { "ASC", "DESC", "OtherString" })]
```

> **TIP** Customizing the allowed sorting values could be useful in some edge-case scenarios, such as replacing SQL Server with a database management system (DBMS) that supports a different sorting syntax. That's why we defined a set accessor for that property.

Now we can go back to our BoardGamesController's Get method and replace the [RegularExpression] attribute that we added earlier with our new [SortOrder-Validator] custom attribute:

```
using MyBGList.Attributes;

// …

public async Task<RestDTO<BoardGame[]>> Get(
  int pageIndex = 0,
  [Range(1, 100)] int pageSize = 10,
  string? sortColumn = "Name",
  [SortOrderValidator] string? sortOrder = "ASC",
  string? filterQuery = null)
```

IMPLEMENTING THE SORTCOLUMNVALIDATOR

Before going further, let's implement another custom validator to fix an additional security issue in the going BoardGamesControlle's Get action method: the sortColumn parameter. Again, we must deal with an arbitrary, user-provided string parameter used to build a LINQ expression tree dynamically, which could expose our web application to some LINQ injection attacks. The least we can do to prevent these kinds of threats is to validate that string accordingly.

This time, however, the "allowed" values are determined by the properties of the [BoardGame] database table, which is represented in our codebase by the BoardGame entity. We can take either of two approaches:

- Use fixed strings to hardcode all the BoardGame entity's property names and proceed as we did with the "ASC" and "DESC" values.
- Find a way to check the entity's property names dynamically against the given input string.

The first approach is easy to pull off by using a [RegularExpression] attribute or a custom attribute similar to the SortOrderValidator we created. This solution could be quite hard to maintain in the long run, however, especially if we plan to add more properties to the BoardGame entity. Furthermore, it won't be flexible enough to use with entities such as Domains, Mechanics, and so on unless we pass the whole set of "valid" fixed strings as a parameter each time.

The dynamic approach could be the better choice, especially considering that we can make it accept an EntityType property, which we can use to pass the entity type to check. Then it would be easy to use LINQ to iterate through all the EntityType's properties to check whether one of them matches the input string. The following listing shows how we can implement this approach in a new SortColumnValidator-Attribute.cs file.

Listing 6.2 SortColumnValidatorAttribute

```
using System.ComponentModel.DataAnnotations;

namespace MyBGList.Attributes
{
    public class SortColumnValidatorAttribute : ValidationAttribute
    {
        public Type EntityType { get; set; }

        public SortColumnValidatorAttribute(Type entityType)
            : base("Value must match an existing column.")
        {
            EntityType = entityType;
        }

        protected override ValidationResult? IsValid(
            object? value,
            ValidationContext validationContext)
        {
            if (EntityType != null)
            {
                var strValue = value as string;
                if (!string.IsNullOrEmpty(strValue)
                    && EntityType.GetProperties()
                        .Any(p => p.Name == strValue))
```

```
                    return ValidationResult.Success;
                }

                return new ValidationResult(ErrorMessage);
            }
        }
    }
```

As we can see, the core part of the `IsValid()` method's source code relies on the `Get-Properties()` method, which returns an array of `PropertyInfo` objects corresponding to the type's properties.

> **WARNING** The `IsValid()` method, as we have implemented it, will consider any property valid for sorting purposes, as long as it exists: although such an approach might work in our specific scenario, it's hardly the most secure choice when dealing with entities with private properties, public properties that contain personal or sensitive data, and the like. To better understand this potential problem, consider having a `User` entity with a `Password` property containing the password hash. We wouldn't want to allow clients to sort a list of users by using that property, right? These kinds of problems can be solved by tweaking the preceding implementation to exclude some properties explicitly or (better) by enforcing the good practice of always using DTOs instead of entity classes when interacting with clients unless we're 100 percent sure that the entity's data won't pose any threat.

The technique of programmatically reading/inspecting the code's metadata that we used here is known as *reflection*. It is supported in most programming frameworks through a set of dedicated libraries or modules. In .NET, this approach is available through the classes and methods provided by the `System.Reflection` namespace.

> **TIP** For additional info about the reflection technique, check out the following guide: http://mng.bz/X57E.

Now that we have our new custom validation attribute, we can use it in our Board-GamesController's `Get` method in the following way:

```
public async Task<RestDTO<BoardGame[]>> Get(
    int pageIndex = 0,
    [Range(1, 100)] int pageSize = 10,
    [SortColumnValidator(typeof(BoardGameDTO))] string? sortColumn = "Name",
    [SortOrderValidator] string? sortOrder = "ASC",
    string? filterQuery = null)
```

Notice that we used the `BoardGameDTO` instead of the `BoardGame` entity for the Sort-ColumnValidator's `EntityType` parameter, thus following the single-responsibility principle introduced in chapter 5. Using DTOs instead of entity types whenever we exchange data with clients is a good practice that will greatly increase the security posture of our web application. For that reason, I suggest always following this practice, even if it requires additional work.

6.1.4   *Data validation and OpenAPI*

Thanks to the introspection activity of the Swashbuckle middleware, the criteria followed by the model binding system are documented automatically in the autogenerated swagger.json file, which represents the OpenAPI specification file for our web API's endpoints (chapter 3). We can check out such behavior by executing the URL https://localhost:40443/swagger/v1/swagger.json and then looking at the JSON content of the file. Here's an excerpt containing the first two parameters of the GET /BoardGames endpoint:

```
{
  "name": "PageIndex",       ⇽───┐  Parameter name
  "in": "query",
  "schema": {
    "type": "integer",       ⇽───┘  Parameter type
    "format": "int32",       ⇽───   Parameter format
    "default": 0             ⇽──┐
  }                             │  Parameter
},                              │  default value
{
  "name": "PageSize",        ⇽───┐  Parameter name
  "in": "query",
  "schema": {
    "maximum": 100,
    "minimum": 1,
    "type": "integer",       ⇽───┘  Parameter type
    "format": "int32",       ⇽───   Parameter format
    "default": 10            ⇽──┐
  }                             │  Parameter
}                               │  default value
```

As we can see, everything worth noting about our parameters is documented there. Ideally, the clients that consume our web API will use this information to create a compatible user interface that can be used to interact with our data in the best possible way. A great example is the SwaggerUI, which uses the swagger.json file to create the input forms that we can use to test our API endpoints. Execute the URL https://localhost:40443/swagger/index.html, expand the GET /BoardGames endpoint panel by using the right handle, and check the list of parameters on the Parameters tab (figure 6.1).

The type, format, and default value info for each parameter are well documented. If we click the Try It Out button, we can access the edit mode of that same input form, where we can fill the text boxes with actual values. If we try to insert some clearly invalid data, such as strings instead of integers, and click the Execute button, the UI won't perform the call; instead, it shows the errors we need to correct (figure 6.2).

No request to the GET /BoardGame endpoint has been made (yet). The input errors were detected by the client-side validation techniques built by the SwaggerUI in the parameter info retrieved from the swagger.json file. All this happens automatically, without our having to code (almost) anything; we're using the framework's built-in features to their full extent.

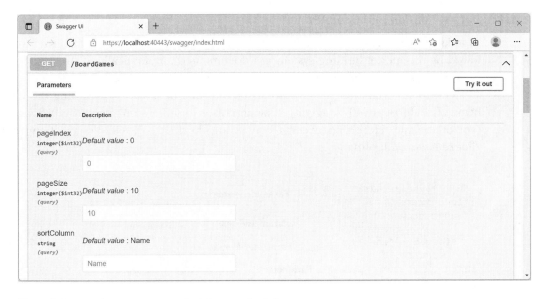

Figure 6.1 `GET /BoardGames` **endpoint parameter info**

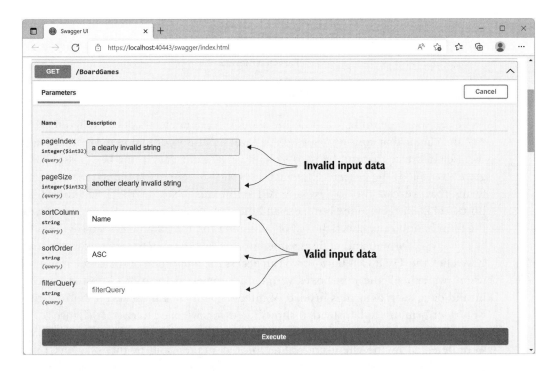

Figure 6.2 `GET /BoardGames` **input form with invalid data**

> ### Should we rely on client-side validation?
>
> It's important to understand that the client-side validation features of SwaggerUI are useful only for improving user experience and preventing a useless round trip to the server. Those features serve no security purpose, because they can be easily bypassed by any user who has some minimal HTML and/or JavaScript knowledge.
>
> The same can be said of all client-side validation controls, rules, and checks. They're useful for enhancing our application's presentation layer and blocking invalid requests without triggering their server-side counterparts, thus improving the overall performance of the client app, but they can't ensure or protect the integrity of our data. So we can't—and shouldn't—rely on client-side validation. In this book, because we're dealing with a web API, which represents the server-side companion of any client–server model we could imagine, we must always validate all the input data, regardless of what the client does.

BUILT-IN VALIDATION ATTRIBUTES

Most of the built-in validation attributes are natively supported by Swashbuckle, which automatically detects and documents them in the `swagger.json` file. If we look at our `swagger.json` file now, we'll see that the `[Range]` attribute is documented in the following way:

```
{
  "name": "pageSize",
  "in": "query",
  "schema": {
    "maximum": 100,          ⟵┐ Range attribute
    "minimum": 1,            ⟵┐ min value
    "type": "integer",         Range attribute
    "format": "int32",         max value
    "default": 10
  }
}
```

Here's how the `[RegularExpression]` attribute is documented:

```
{
  "name": "sortOrder",
  "in": "query",
  "schema": {
    "pattern": "ASC|DESC",   ⟵┐ RegularExpression
    "type": "string",          attribute's RegEx
    "default": "ASC"           pattern
  }
}
```

Clients can also use this valuable information to implement additional client-side validation rules and functions.

CUSTOM VALIDATION ATTRIBUTES

Unfortunately, custom validators aren't natively supported by Swashbuckle, which is hardly a surprise, because there's no chance that Swashbuckle would know how they work. But the library exposes a convenient filter pipeline that hooks into the swagger .json file generation process. This feature allows us to create our own filters, add them to the pipeline, and use them to customize the file's content.

> **NOTE** The Swashbuckle's filter pipeline is covered extensively in chapter 11. In this section, I provide only a small preview of this feature by introducing the IParameterFilter interface, because we need it to fulfill our current needs. For additional info about the interface, check out chapter 11 and/or the following URL: http://mng.bz/ydNe.

In a nutshell, here's what we need to do if we want to add our custom validation attribute's info to the swagger.json file:

1 Create a new filter class implementing the IParameterFilter interface for each of our custom validation attributes. Swashbuckle will call and execute this filter before creating the JSON block for all the parameters used by our controller's action methods (and Minimal API methods).

2 Implement the IParameterFilter interface's Apply method so that it detects all parameters decorated with our custom validation attribute and adds relevant info to the swagger.json file for each of them.

Let's put this plan into practice, starting with the [SortOrderValidator] attribute.

ADDING THE SORTORDERFILTER

In Visual Studio's Solution Explorer panel, create a new /Swagger/ folder, right-click it, and add a new SortOrderFilter.cs class file. The new class must implement the IParameterFilter interface and its Apply method to add a suitable JSON key to the swagger.json file, like the built-in validation attributes. The following listing shows how we can do that.

Listing 6.3   SortOrderFilter

```
using Microsoft.OpenApi.Any;
using Microsoft.OpenApi.Models;
using Swashbuckle.AspNetCore.SwaggerGen;
using MyBGList.Attributes;

namespace MyBGList.Swagger
{
    public class SortOrderFilter : IParameterFilter
    {
        public void Apply(
            OpenApiParameter parameter,
            ParameterFilterContext context)
        {
            var attributes = context.ParameterInfo?
```

```
                    .GetCustomAttributes(true)
                    .OfType<SortOrderValidatorAttribute>();          Checks whether
                                                                      the parameter has
              if (attributes != null)                                the attribute
              {
                  foreach (var attribute in attributes)
                  {
                      parameter.Schema.Extensions.Add(
                          "pattern",
                          new OpenApiString(string.Join("|",
                              attribute.AllowedValues.Select(v => $"^{v}$")))
                          );
                  }
              }
          }
      }
}
```

If the attribute is present, acts accordingly

Notice that we're using the "pattern" JSON key and a RegEx pattern as a value—the same behavior used by the [RegularExpression] built-in validation attribute. We did that to facilitate the implementation of the client-side validation check, assuming that the client will already be able to provide RegEx support when it receives the info (which happens to be "compatible" with our validation requirements). We could use a different key and/or value type, leaving the implementation details to the clients. Next, let's create another filter for our second custom validation attribute.

ADDING THE SORTCOLUMNFILTER

Add a new SortColumnFilter.cs class file within the /Swagger/ folder. This class will be similar to the SortOrderFilter class, with some minor differences: this time, we'll have to retrieve the names of the EntityType properties instead of the AllowedValues string array, which require some additional work. The following listing provides the source code.

Listing 6.4 `SortColumnFilter`

```
using Microsoft.OpenApi.Any;
using Microsoft.OpenApi.Models;
using Swashbuckle.AspNetCore.SwaggerGen;
using MyBGList.Attributes;

namespace MyBGList.Swagger
{
    public class SortColumnFilter : IParameterFilter
    {
        public void Apply(
            OpenApiParameter parameter,
            ParameterFilterContext context)
        {
            var attributes = context.ParameterInfo?
                .GetCustomAttributes(true)
                .OfType<SortColumnValidatorAttribute>();          Checks whether
                                                                   the parameter
                                                                   has the attribute
```

```
              if (attributes != null)
              {
                  foreach (var attribute in attributes)      ◁┐  If the attribute
                  {                                            │  is present, acts
                      var pattern = attribute.EntityType       │  accordingly
                          .GetProperties()
                          .Select(p => p.Name);
                      parameter.Schema.Extensions.Add(
                          "pattern",
                          new OpenApiString(string.Join("|",
                              pattern.Select(v => $"^{v}$")))
                          );
                  }
              }
          }
      }
}
```

Again, we used the "pattern" key and a RegEx pattern for the value, because even this validator is compatible with a RegEx-based client-validation check. Now we need to hook these filters to the Swashbuckle's middleware in the `Program.cs` file so that they'll be taken into account when the Swagger file is generated.

BINDING THE IPARAMETERFILTERS

Open the `Program.cs` file, and add the namespace corresponding to our newly implemented filters at the top:

```
using MyBGList.Swagger;
```

Scroll down to the line where we add the Swashbuckle's Swagger Generator middleware to the pipeline, and change it in the following way:

```
builder.Services.AddSwaggerGen(options => {         │  Adds the SortColumnFilter
    options.ParameterFilter<SortColumnFilter>();  ◁─┘  to the filter pipeline
    options.ParameterFilter<SortOrderFilter>();   ◁─┐
});                                                  │  Adds the SortOrderFilter
                                                     │  to the filter pipeline
```

Now we can test what we did by running our project in Debug mode and looking at the autogenerated `swagger.json` file, using the same URL as before (https://localhost :40443/swagger/v1/swagger.json). If we did everything correctly, we should see the `sortOrder` and `sortColumn` parameters with the "pattern" key present and filled in according to the validator's rules:

```
{
  "name": "sortColumn",
  "in": "query",
  "schema": {
    "type": "string",
    "default": "Name",                    │  SortColumnValidator's
    "pattern": "^Id$|^Name$|^Year$"   ◁──┘  RegEx pattern
```

```
      }
    },
    {
      "name": "sortOrder",
      "in": "query",
      "schema": {
        "type": "string",
        "default": "ASC",
        "pattern": "^ASC$|^DESC$"
      }
    }
```

SortOrderValidator's
RegEx pattern

It's important to understand that implementing custom validators can be a challenge—and an expensive task in terms of time and source-code lines. In most scenarios, we won't need to do that, because the built-in validation attributes accommodate all our needs. But being able to create and document them can make a difference whenever we deal with complex or potentially troublesome client-defined inputs.

6.1.5 Binding complex types

Up to this point, we've always worked with our action methods by using simple type parameters: integer, string, bool, and the like. This approach is a great way to learn how model binding and validation attributes work and is often the preferred approach whenever we deal with a small set of parameters. Several scenarios, however, can greatly benefit from using complex-type parameters such as DTOs, especially considering that the ASP.NET Core model binding system can handle them as well.

When the model binding's target is a complex type, each type property is treated as a separate parameter to bind and validate. Each property of the complex type acts like a simple type parameter, with great benefits in terms of code extensibility and flexibility. Instead of having a potentially long list of method parameters, we can box all the parameters into a single DTO class. The best way to understand the advantages is to put them into practice by replacing our current simple type parameters with a single, comprehensive complex type.

CREATING A REQUESTDTO CLASS

In Visual Studio's Solution Explorer panel, right-click the /DTO/ folder, and add a new RequestDTO.cs class file. This class will contain all the client-defined input parameters that we're receiving in the BoardGamesController's Get action method; all we have to do is to create a property for each of them, as shown in the following listing.

Listing 6.5 RequestDTO.cs file

```
using MyBGList.Attributes;
using System.ComponentModel;
using System.ComponentModel.DataAnnotations;

namespace MyBGList.DTO
{
    public class RequestDTO
```

```
        {
            [DefaultValue(0)]
            public int PageIndex { get; set; } = 0;                    Built-in
                                                                        validation
            [DefaultValue(10)]                                          attributes
            [Range(1, 100)]
            public int PageSize { get; set; } = 10;

            [DefaultValue("Name")]
            [SortColumnValidator(typeof(BoardGameDTO))]
            public string? SortColumn { get; set; } = "Name";    Custom
                                                                  validation
            [DefaultValue("ASC")]                                 attributes
            [SortOrderValidator]
            public string? SortOrder { get; set; } = "ASC";

            [DefaultValue(null)]
            public string? FilterQuery { get; set; } = null;
        }
    }
```

Default value attributes

Built-in validation attributes

Custom validation attributes

Notice that we've decorated each property with a [DefaultValue] attribute. This attribute enables the Swagger generator middleware to create the "default" key in the swagger.json file, because it won't be able to see the initial value that we set by using the convenient C# inline syntax. Luckily, this attribute is supported and provides a good workaround. Now that we have the RequestDTO class, we can use it to replace the simple type parameters of the BoardGamesController's Get method in the following way:

```
[HttpGet(Name = "GetBoardGames")]
[ResponseCache(Location = ResponseCacheLocation.Any, Duration = 60)]
public async Task<RestDTO<BoardGame[]>> Get(
    [FromQuery] RequestDTO input)                              The new complex-
{                                                              type parameter
    var query = _context.BoardGames.AsQueryable();
    if (!string.IsNullOrEmpty(input.FilterQuery))
        query = query.Where(b => b.Name.Contains(input.FilterQuery));
    query = query
            .OrderBy($"{input.SortColumn} {input.SortOrder}")
            .Skip(input.PageIndex * input.PageSize)
            .Take(input.PageSize);

    return new RestDTO<BoardGame[]>()
    {
        Data = await query.ToArrayAsync(),
        PageIndex = input.PageIndex,
        PageSize = input.PageSize,
        RecordCount = await _context.BoardGames.CountAsync(),
        Links = new List<LinkDTO> {
            new LinkDTO(
                Url.Action(
                    null,
                    "BoardGames",
                    new { input.PageIndex, input.PageSize },
```

```
                    Request.Scheme)!,
                "self",
                "GET"),
        }
    };
}
```

In this code, we use the `[FromQuery]` attribute to tell the routing middleware that we want to get the input values from the query string, thus preserving the former behavior. But we could have used any of the other available attributes:

- `[FromQuery]`—To get values from the query string
- `[FromRoute]`—To get values from route data
- `[FromForm]`—To get values from posted form fields
- `[FromBody]`—To get values from the request body
- `[FromHeader]`—To get values from HTTP headers
- `[FromServices]`—To get values from an instance of a registered service
- `[FromUri]`—To get values from an external URI

Being able to switch among parameter binding techniques by using an attribute-based approach is another convenient feature of the framework. We'll use some of these attributes later.

We had to use the `[FromQuery]` attribute explicitly because the default method for complex-type parameters is to get the values from the request body. We also had to replace all the parameters' references within the source code with the properties of the new class. Now the "new" implementation looks more sleek and DRY (Don't Repeat Yourself principle) than the preceding one. Moreover, we have a flexible, generic DTO class that we can use to implement similar GET-based action methods in the `BoardGamesController`, as well as in other controllers that we want to add in the future: `DomainsController`, `MechanicsControllers`, and so on. Right?

Well, no. If we take a better look at our current `RequestDTO` class, we see that it's not generic at all. The problem lies in the `[SortColumnValidator]` attribute, which requires a `type` parameter. As we can see by looking at the source code, this parameter is hardcoded to the `BoardGameDTO` type:

```
[SortColumnValidator(typeof(BoardGameDTO))]
```

How can we work around the problem? On first thought, we might be tempted to pass that parameter dynamically, maybe using a generic <T> type. This approach would require changing the `RequestDTO`'s class declaration to

```
public class RequestDTO<T>
```

which would allow us to use it in our action methods in the following way:

```
[FromQuery] RequestDTO<BoardGameDTO> input
```

Then we'd change the validator this way:

```
[SortColumnValidator(typeof(T))]
```

Unfortunately, that approach wouldn't work. In C#, attributes that decorate a class are evaluated at compile time, but a generic <T> class won't receive its final type info until runtime. The reason is simple: because some attributes could affect the compilation process, the compiler must be able to define them in their entirety at compile time. As a result, attributes can't use generic type parameters.

Generic attribute type limitations in C#

According to Eric Lippert (a former Microsoft engineer and member of the C# language design team), this limitation was added to reduce complexity in both the language and compiler code for a use case that doesn't add much value. His explanation (paraphrased) can be found in this StackOverflow answer given by Jon Skeet: http://mng.bz/Mlw8.

For additional info regarding this topic, check out the Microsoft guide to C# generics at http://mng.bz/JIOK.

This behavior could change in the future, because the .NET community often asks the C# language design team to reevaluate it.

If attributes can't use generic types, how can we work around the problem? The answer isn't difficult to guess: if the mountain won't go to Mohammed, Mohammed must go to the mountain. In other words, we need to replace the attribute approach with another validation technique that's supported by the ASP.NET framework. Luckily, such a technique happens to exist, and it goes by the name IValidatableObject.

IMPLEMENTING THE IVALIDATABLEOBJECT

The IValidatableObject interface provides an alternative way to validate a class. It works like a class-level attribute, meaning that we can use it to validate any DTO type regardless of its properties and in addition to all property-level validation attributes it contains. The IValidatableObject interface has two major advantages over the validation attributes:

- It isn't required to be defined at compile time, so it can use generic types (which allows us to overcome our problem).
- It's designed to validate the class in its entirety, so we can use it to check multiple properties at the same time and perform cross-validation and any other tasks that require a holistic approach.

Let's use the IValidatableObject interface to implement the sort-column validation check in our current RequestDTO class. Here's what we need to do:

1. Change the RequestDTO's class declaration so that it can accept a generic <T> type.
2. Add the IValidatableObject interface to the RequestDTO type.

3 Implement the `Validate` method of the `IValidatableObject` interface so that it will fetch the generic `<T>` type's properties and use their names to validate the `SortColumn` property.

The following listing shows how we can implement these steps.

Listing 6.6 `RequestDTO.cs` file (version 2)

```
using MyBGList.Attributes;
using System.ComponentModel;
using System.ComponentModel.DataAnnotations;

namespace MyBGList.DTO
{
    public class RequestDTO<T> : IValidatableObject          ◁┘  Generic Type and
    {                                                             IValidatableObject
        [DefaultValue(0)]                                         interface
        public int PageIndex { get; set; } = 0;

        [DefaultValue(10)]
        [Range(1, 100)]
        public int PageSize { get; set; } = 10;

        [DefaultValue("Name")]
        public string? SortColumn { get; set; } = "Name";

        [SortOrderValidator]
        [DefaultValue("ASC")]
        public string? SortOrder { get; set; } = "ASC";

        [DefaultValue(null)]
        public string? FilterQuery { get; set; } = null;         Validate method
                                                                  implementation
        public IEnumerable<ValidationResult> Validate(     ◁┘
            ValidationContext validationContext)
        {
            var validator = new SortColumnValidatorAttribute(typeof(T));
            var result = validator
                .GetValidationResult(SortColumn, validationContext);
            return (result != null)
                ? new [] { result }
                : new ValidationResult[0];
        }
    }
}
```

In this code, we see that the `Validate` method implementation presents a plot twist: we're using the `SortColumnValidator` under the hood! The main difference is that this time, we're using it as a "standard" class instance rather than a data annotation attribute, which allows us to pass the generic type as a parameter.

It almost feels like cheating, right? But that's not the case; we're recycling what we've already done. We can do that thanks to the fact that the `GetValidationResult` method exposed by the ValidationAttribute base class is defined as public, which allows us to create an instance of the validator and call it to validate the SortColumn property.

Now that we have a generic DTO class to use in our code, open the BoardGames-Controllers.cs file, scroll down to the Get method, and update its signature in the following way:

```
public async Task<RestDTO<BoardGame[]>> Get(
    [FromQuery] RequestDTO<BoardGameDTO> input)
```

The rest of the method's code doesn't require any change. We've specified the BoardGameDTO as a generic-type parameter so that the RequestDTO's Validate method will check its properties against the SortColumn input data, ensuring that the column set by the client to sort the data is valid for that specific request.

ADDING DOMAINSCONTROLLER AND MECHANICSCONTROLLER

Now is a good time to create a DomainsController and a MechanicsController, replicating all the features that we've implemented in the BoardGamesController so far. Doing this will allow us to make a proper test of our generic RequestDTO class and our IValidatableObject flexible implementation. We also need to add a couple of new DTOs, DomainDTO class and MechanicDTO, which will be along the lines of the BoardGameDTO class.

For reasons of space, I'm not listing the source code for these four files here. That code is available in the /Chapter_06/ folder of this book's GitHub repository, in the /Controllers/ and /DTO/ subfolders. I strongly suggest that you try to implement them without looking at the GitHub files, because this is a great chance to practice everything you've learned so far.

TESTING THE NEW CONTROLLERS

When the new controllers are ready, we can check them thoroughly by using the following URL endpoints (for the GET method),

- https://localhost:40443/Domains/
- https://localhost:40443/Mechanics/

as well as the SwaggerUI (for the POST and DELETE methods).

> NOTE Whenever we delete a domain or a mechanic, the cascading rules that we set for these entities in chapter 4 also remove all its references to the corresponding many-to-many lookup table. All board games will lose their relationship with that specific domain or mechanic (if they had it). To recover, we need to delete all the board games and then reload them by using the Seed-Controller's Put method.

UPDATING THE IPARAMETERFILTERS

Before we go further, we need to do one last thing. Now that we've replaced our simple type parameters with a DTO, the SortOrderFilter and SortColumnFilter won't be able to locate our custom validators anymore. The reason is simple: their current implementation is looking for them by using the `GetCustomAttributes` method of the `context.ParameterInfo` object, which returns an array of the attributes applied to the parameter handled by the filter. Now this `ParameterInfo` contains a reference of the DTO itself, meaning that the preceding method will return the attributes applied to the whole DTO class—not to its properties.

To fix the problem, we need to extend the attribute lookup behavior so that it also checks the attributes assigned to the given parameter's properties (if any). Here's how we can update the `SortOrderFilter`'s source code to do that:

```
var attributes = context.ParameterInfo
    .GetCustomAttributes(true)                              Retrieves the parameter's
    .Union(                              ◁────────          properties custom attributes
        context.ParameterInfo.ParameterType.GetProperties()
        .Where(p => p.Name == parameter.Name)
        .SelectMany(p => p.GetCustomAttributes(true))
    )
    .OfType<SortOrderValidatorAttribute>();
```

Notice that we used a `Union` LINQ extension method to produce a single array containing the custom attributes assigned to the `ParameterInfo` object itself, as well as those assigned to a property of that `ParameterInfo` object with the name of the parameter that the filter is currently processing (if any). Thanks to this new implementation, our filters will be able to find the custom attributes assigned to any complex-type parameter's property as well as to simple type parameters, ensuring full backward compatibility.

The `SortOrderFilter` has been fixed, but what about the `SortColumnFilter`? Unfortunately, the fix isn't so simple. The `[SortColumnValidator]` attribute isn't applied to any property, so there's no way that the `SortColumnFilter` can find it. We might think that we could work around the problem by adding the attribute to the `IValidatableObject`'s `Validate` method and then tweaking the filter's lookup behavior to include methods other than properties. But we already know that this workaround would fail; the attribute would still require a generic type parameter that can't be set at compile time. For reasons of space, we won't fix this problem now; we'll postpone this task until chapter 11, when we'll learn other API documentation techniques involving Swagger and Swashbuckle.

> **TIP** Before proceeding, be sure to apply the preceding patch to the `Sort-ColumnFilter` as well. The source code to add is identical, because both filters use the same lookup strategy. This patch may seem to be useless, because the `SortColumnFilter` isn't working (and won't work for a while), but keeping our classes up to date is good practice, even if we're not actively using or counting on them.

Our data validation journey is over, at least for now. In the next section, we'll learn how to handle validation errors and program exceptions.

6.2   *Error handling*

Now that we've implemented several server-side data validation checks, we've created a lot of additional failing scenarios for our web API, in addition to those normally provided in case of blatantly invalid HTTP requests. Each piece of missing, malformed, incorrect, or otherwise invalid input data, according to and limited by our validation rules that determine a model-binding failure, will be rejected by our web API with an HTTP 400 - Bad Request error response. We experienced this behavior at the start of this chapter when we tried to pass a string value to the pageIndex parameter instead of a numeric 1. The HTTP 400 status wasn't the only response from the server, however. We also got an interesting response body, which deserves another look:

```
{
    "type":"https://tools.ietf.org/html/rfc7231#section-6.5.1",
    "title":"One or more validation errors occurred.",
    "status":400,
    "traceId":"00-a074ebace7131af6561251496331fc65-ef1c633577161417-00",
    "errors":{
        "pageIndex":["The value 'string' is not valid."]
    }
}
```

As we can see, our web API doesn't only tell the client that something went wrong; it also provides contextual information about the error, including the parameter with the rejected value, using the HTTP API response format standard defined at https://tools.ietf.org/html/rfc7807, which appeared briefly in chapter 2. All this work is performed automatically by the framework under the hood; we don't have to do anything. This work is a built-in functionality of the [ApiController] attribute that decorates our controllers.

6.2.1   *The ModelState object*

To understand what the [ApiController] attribute is doing for us, we need to take a step back and review the whole model binding and validation system lifecycle. Figure 6.3 illustrates the flow of the various steps performed by the framework within a typical HTTP request.

Our point of interest starts right after the HTTP request arrives, and the routing middleware invokes the model binding system, which performs two relevant tasks in sequence:

- Binds the input values to the action method's simple type and/or complex-type parameters. If the binding process fails, an HTTP error 400 response is returned immediately; otherwise, the request goes to the next phase.
- Validates the model by using the built-in validation attributes, the custom validation attributes, and/or the IValidatableObject. The results of all the validation checks are recorded in the ModelState object, which eventually becomes valid (no validation errors occurred) or invalid (one or more validation errors

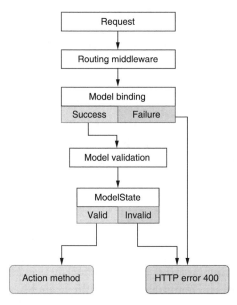

Figure 6.3   Model binding and validation lifecycle with the [ApiController] attribute

occurred). If the `ModelState` object ends up being valid, the request is handled by the action method; otherwise, an HTTP error `400` response is returned.

The important lesson is that both the binding errors and the validation errors are handled by the framework (using an HTTP `400` error response) without even calling the action method. In other words, the [ApiController] attribute provides a fully automated error-handling management system. This approach can be great if we don't have specific requirements, but what if we want to customize something? In the following sections, we'll see how to do that.

6.2.2   Custom error messages

The first thing we may want to do is define some custom error messages instead of the default ones. Let's start with the model binding errors.

CUSTOMIZING THE MODEL BINDING ERRORS

To change the default model binding error messages, we need to modify the settings of the `ModelBindingMessageProvider`, which can be accessed from the `Controllers-Middleware`'s configuration options. Open the `Program.cs` file, locate the `builder .Services.AddControllers` method, and replace the current parameterless implementation in the following way (new lines in bold):

```
builder.Services.AddControllers(options => {
    options.ModelBindingMessageProvider.SetValueIsInvalidAccessor(
        (x) => $"The value '{x}' is invalid.");
    options.ModelBindingMessageProvider.SetValueMustBeANumberAccessor(
        (x) => $"The field {x} must be a number.");
```

```
options.ModelBindingMessageProvider.SetAttemptedValueIsInvalidAccessor(
    (x, y) => $"The value '{x}' is not valid for {y}.");
options.ModelBindingMessageProvider.SetMissingKeyOrValueAccessor(
    () => $"A value is required.");
});
```

For simplicity, this sample changes only three of the many available messages.

CUSTOMIZING THE MODEL VALIDATION ERRORS

Changing the model validation error messages is easy because the Validation-
Attribute base class comes with a convenient ErrorMessage property that can be
used for that purpose. We used it when we implemented our own custom validators.
The same technique can be used for all built-in validators:

```
[Required(ErrorMessage = "This value is required.")]
[Range(1, 100, ErrorMessage = "The value must be between 1 and 100.")]
```

By doing that, however, we're customizing the error messages, not the ModelState validation process itself, which is still performed automatically by the framework.

6.2.3   *Manual model validation*

Suppose that we want (or are asked) to replace our current HTTP 400 - Bad Request with
a different status code in case of some specific validation failures, such as an HTTP 501 -
Not Implemented status code for an incorrect pageSize integer value (lower than 1 or
bigger than 100). This change request can't be handled unless we find a way to check
the ModelState manually (and act accordingly) within the action method. But we know
that we can't do that, because the ModelState validation and error handling process is
handled by the framework automatically thanks to the [ApiController] functionalities.
In case of an invalid ModelState, the action method won't even come into play; the
default (and unwanted) HTTP 400 error will be returned instead.

The first solution that might come to mind would be to get rid of the [Api-
Controller] attribute, which would remove the automatic behavior and allow us to
check the ModelState manually, even when it's invalid. Would that approach work? It
would. Figure 6.4 shows how the model binding and validation lifecycle diagram work
without the [ApiController] attribute.

As we can see, now the action method will be executed regardless of the Model-
State status, allowing us to inspect it, see what went wrong, and act accordingly, which
is precisely what we want. But we shouldn't commit to such a harsh workaround,
because the [ApiController] attribute gives our controller several other functionalities that we may want to preserve. Instead, we should disable the automatic Model-
State validation feature, which we can do by tweaking the default configuration
settings of the [ApiController] attribute itself.

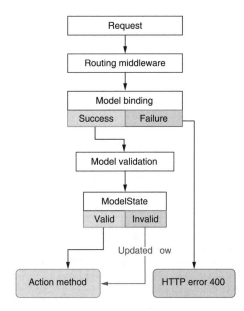

Figure 6.4   Model binding and validation lifecycle without the `[ApiController]` attribute

CONFIGURING THE APICONTROLLER'S BEHAVIOR

Open the `Program.cs` file, and locate the line where we instantiate the app local variable:

```
var app = builder.Build();
```

Place the following lines of code right above it:

```
builder.Services.Configure<ApiBehaviorOptions>(options =>
    options.SuppressModelStateInvalidFilter = true);

var app = builder.Build();
```

This setting suppresses the filter that automatically returns a `BadRequestObject-Result` when the `ModelState` is invalid. Now we can achieve what we want for all our controllers without removing the `[ApiController]` attribute, and we're ready to implement our change request by conditionally returning an `HTTP 501` status code.

IMPLEMENTING A CUSTOM HTTP STATUS CODE

For simplicity, suppose that the change request affects only the `DomainsController`. Open the `/Controllers/DomainsController.cs` file, and scroll down to the `Get` action method. Here's what we need to do:

1   Check the `ModelState` status (valid or invalid).
2   If the `ModelState` is valid, preserve the existing behavior.
3   If the `ModelState` isn't valid, check whether the error is related to the `pageSize` parameter. If that's the case, return an `HTTP 501` status code; otherwise, stick to the `HTTP 400`.

And here's how we can pull it off:

```
[HttpGet(Name = "GetDomains")]
[ResponseCache(Location = ResponseCacheLocation.Any, Duration = 60)]
public async Task<ActionResult<RestDTO<Domain[]>>> Get(          ◁──┐  New return value
    [FromQuery] RequestDTO<DomainDTO> input)                          │  (ActionResult<T>)
{
    if (!ModelState.IsValid)
    {
        var details = new ValidationProblemDetails(ModelState);
        details.Extensions["traceId"] =
            System.Diagnostics.Activity.Current?.Id
                ?? HttpContext.TraceIdentifier;
        if (ModelState.Keys.Any(k => k == "PageSize"))
        {
            details.Type =
                "https://tools.ietf.org/html/rfc7231#section-6.6.2";
            details.Status = StatusCodes.Status501NotImplemented;
            return new ObjectResult(details) {
                StatusCode = StatusCodes.Status501NotImplemented
            };
        }
        else
        {
            details.Type =
                "https://tools.ietf.org/html/rfc7231#section-6.5.1";
            details.Status = StatusCodes.Status400BadRequest;
            return new BadRequestObjectResult(details);
        }
    }
    // ... code omitted ...          ◁──┤  Code omitted for
}                                        reasons of space
                                         (unchanged)
```

Steps to perform if ModelState is invalid (marginal annotation pointing to the `if (!ModelState.IsValid)` block)

We can easily check the ModelState status by using the IsValid property, which returns true or false. If we determine that the ModelState isn't valid, we check for the presence of the "PageSize" key in the error collection and create a UnprocessableEntity or a BadRequest result to return to the client. The implementation requires several lines of code because we want to build a rich request body documenting the error details, including the reference to the RFC documenting the error status code, the traceId, and so on.

This approach forced us to change the action method's return type from Task<RestDTO<Domain[]>> to Task<ActionResult<RestDTO<Domain[]>>>, because now we need to handle two different types of responses: an ObjectResult if the ModelState validation fails and a JSON object in case it succeeds. The ActionResult is a good choice because thanks to its generic-type support, it can handle both types.

Now we can test the new behavior of the DomainsController's Get action method. This URL should return an HTTP 501 status code: https://localhost:40443/Domains?pageSize=101. This one should respond with an HTTP 400 status code: https://localhost:40443/Domains?sortOrder=InvalidValue.

Because we also need to check the HTTP status code, not the response body alone, be sure to open the browser's Network tab (accessible through Developer Tools in all Chrome-based browsers) before executing the URL—a quick, effective way to see the status code of each HTTP response in real time.

AN UNEXPECTED REGRESSION BUG

All is well so far—except for a nontrivial regression error that we unintentionally caused in all our controllers! To check out what I'm talking about, try to execute the two "invalid" URLs in the preceding section against the `BoardGamesController`'s `Get` method:

- https://localhost:40443/BoardGames?pageSize=101
- https://localhost:40443/BoardGames?sortOrder=invalidValue

The first URL returns 101 board games, and the second throws an unhandled exception due to a syntax error in dynamic LINQ. What happened to our validators?

The answer should be obvious: they still work, but because we disabled the `[Api-Controller]`'s automatic `ModelState` validation feature (and HTTP `400` response), all of our action methods are executed even if some of their input parameters are invalid, with no manual validation to fill the gap except the `DomainsController`'s `Get` action method! Our `BoardGamesController` and `MechanicsController`, as well as all `Domains-Controller` action methods other than `Get`, are no longer protected from insecure input. Don't panic, though; we can fix the problem.

Again, we may be tempted to remove the `[ApiController]` attribute from the `DomainsController` and work around our regression bug with no further hassle. Unfortunately, this approach won't do the trick; it will prevent the bug from affecting the other controllers but won't solve the problem for the `DomainsController`'s other action methods. Also, we'd lose the other useful features of `[ApiController]`, which was why we didn't get rid of it to begin with.

Think about what we did: disabled a feature of the `[ApiController]` for the entire web application because we didn't want it to trigger for a single controller's action method. That was the mistake. The idea was good; we need to refine the scope.

IMPLEMENTING AN IACTIONMODELCONVENTION FILTER

We can obtain what we want by using the convenient ASP.NET Core filter pipeline, which allows us to customize the behavior of the HTTP request/response lifecycle. We'll create a filter attribute that checks for the presence of the `ModelStateInvalidFilter` within a given action method and removes it. This setting will have the same effect as the configuration setting that we placed in the `Program.cs` file, but it will happen only for the action method that we'll choose to decorate with that filter attribute. In other words, we'll be able to disable the `ModelState` autovalidation feature conditionally (opt-out, default-in) instead of having to shut it down for everyone (default-out).

Let's put that theory into practice. Create a new `ManualValidationFilter-Attribute.cs` class file in the `/Attributes/` folder, and fill it with the source code in the following listing.

Listing 6.7   `ManualValidationFilterAttribute`

```
using Microsoft.AspNetCore.Mvc.ApplicationModels;
using Microsoft.AspNetCore.Mvc.Infrastructure;

namespace MyBGList.Attributes
{
    public class ManualValidationFilterAttribute
        : Attribute, IActionModelConvention
    {
        public void Apply(ActionModel action)
        {
            for (var i = 0; i < action.Filters.Count; i++)
            {
                if (action.Filters[i] is ModelStateInvalidFilter
                    || action.Filters[i].GetType().Name ==
                        "ModelStateInvalidFilterFactory")
                {
                    action.Filters.RemoveAt(i);
                    break;
                }
            }
        }
    }
}
```

Sadly, the `ModelStateInvalidFilterFactory` type is marked as `internal`, which prevents us from checking for the filter presence by using a strongly typed approach. We must compare the `Name` property with the literal name of the class. This approach is hardly ideal and might cease to work if the name changes in future releases of the framework, but for now, it will do the trick. Now that we have the filter, we need to apply it to our `DomainsController`'s `Get` action method like any other attribute:

```
[HttpGet(Name = "GetDomains")]
[ResponseCache(Location = ResponseCacheLocation.Any, Duration = 60)]
[ManualValidationFilter]
public async Task<ActionResult<RestDTO<Domain[]>>> Get(
    [FromQuery] RequestDTO<DomainDTO> input)
```

The new ManualValidationFilter attribute

Now we can delete (or comment out) the application-wide settings that caused the regression bug in the `Program.cs` file:

```
// Code replaced by the [ManualValidationFilter] attribute
// builder.Services.Configure<ApiBehaviorOptions>(options =>
//     options.SuppressModelStateInvalidFilter = true);
```

We've reenabled the automatic `ModelState` validation feature for all our controllers and methods, leaving in manual state only the single action method for which we've implemented a suitable fallback. We've found a way to fulfill our change request while fixing our unexpected bug—and without giving up anything. Furthermore, everything we did here helped us to gain experience and raised our awareness of the ASP.NET Core request/response pipeline, as well as the underlying model binding and validation mechanism. Our manual ModelState validation overview is over, at least for now.

6.2.4 *Exception handling*

The ModelState object isn't the only source of application errors that we might want to handle. Most application errors we'll experience with our web API will be due not to client-defined input data, but to unexpected behavior of our source code: null-reference exceptions, DBMS connection failures, data-retrieval errors, stack overflows, and so on. All these problems will likely raise exceptions, which (as we've known since chapter 2) will be caught and handled by the DeveloperExceptionPageMiddleware (if the corresponding application setting is true) and the ExceptionHandlingMiddleware (if the setting is false).

In chapter 2, when we implemented the UseDeveloperExceptionPage application setting, we set it to false in the generic appsettings.json file and to true in the appsettings.Development.json file. We used this approach to ensure that the DeveloperExceptionPageMiddleware would be used only when the app is executed in a development environment. This behavior is clearly visible in the code section of the Program.cs file where we add the ExceptionHandlingMiddleware to the pipeline:

```
if (app.Configuration.GetValue<bool>("UseDeveloperExceptionPage"))
    app.UseDeveloperExceptionPage();
else
    app.UseExceptionHandler("/error");
```

Let's disable this development override temporarily so that we can focus on how our web API is handling exceptions when dealing with actual clients (in other words, in production). Open the appSettings.Development.json file, and change the value of the UseDeveloperExceptionPage setting from true to false:

```
"UseDeveloperExceptionPage": false
```

Now our application will adopt the production error handling behavior even in development, allowing us to check what we're doing while updating it. In chapter 2, we set the ExceptionHandlingMiddleware's error handling path to the "/error" endpoint, which we implemented by using the following Minimal API MapGet method in the Program.cs file:

```
app.MapGet("/error",
    [EnableCors("AnyOrigin")]
    [ResponseCache(NoStore = true)] () =>
    Results.Problem());
```

Our current implementation consists of a single line of code that returns a Problem-Details object, which results in an RFC 7807-compliant JSON response. We tested this behavior in chapter 2 by implementing and executing the /error/test endpoint, which throws an exception. Let's execute it again to take another look at it:

```
{
  "type":"https://tools.ietf.org/html/rfc7231#section-6.6.1",
  "title":"An error occurred while processing your request.",
  "status":500
}
```

This simple yet effective response clearly shows that we've set up a decent exception-handling strategy for our production environment. Every time something goes wrong, or when we want to raise an exception within our code manually, we can be sure that the calling client will receive an HTTP 500 error status code together with a standard (and RFC 7807-compliant) response body.

At the same time, we can see that the overall outcome isn't informative. We're telling the client only that something went wrong by returning an HTTP 500 status code and a minimal response body that explains the error in human-readable form.

We're facing the same scenario that we experienced with the [ApiController]'s ModelState validation, an automatic behavior that might be convenient for most scenarios but could be limiting if we need to customize it further. We may want to return different status codes, depending on the exception being thrown. Or we may want to log the error somewhere and/or send an email notification to someone (depending on the exception type and/or context).

Fortunately, the ExceptionHandlingMiddleware can be configured to do all those things, and many more, with relatively few lines of code. In the following sections, we'll take a better look at the ExceptionHandlingMiddleware (we only scratched its surface in chapter 2, after all) and see how we can use it to its full extent.

WORKING WITH THE EXCEPTIONHANDLINGMIDDLEWARE

The first thing we can do to customize the current behavior is to provide the Problem-Details object with some additional details regarding the exception, such as its Message property value. To do that, we need to retrieve two objects:

- The current HttpContext, which can be added as a parameter in all Minimal API methods
- An IExceptionHandlerPathFeature interface instance, which allows us to access the originating exception in a convenient handler

Here's how we can do that (relevant code in bold):

```
app.MapGet("/error",
    [EnableCors("AnyOrigin")]
    [ResponseCache(NoStore = true)] (HttpContext context) =>
    {
        var exceptionHandler =
            context.Features.Get<IExceptionHandlerPathFeature>();
```

Adds the HttpContext

Retrieves the Exception handler

```
// TODO: logging, sending notifications, and more     ◁─┐ Performs other
                                                          error-related
var details = new ProblemDetails();                       management
details.Detail = exceptionHandler?.Error.Message;         tasks
details.Extensions["traceId"] =
    System.Diagnostics.Activity.Current?.Id
      ?? context.TraceIdentifier;
details.Type =
    "https://tools.ietf.org/html/rfc7231#section-6.6.1";
details.Status = StatusCodes.Status500InternalServerError;
return Results.Problem(details);
});
```

Sets the Exception message — points to the line `details.Detail = exceptionHandler?.Error.Message;`

After we perform this upgrade, we can launch our app and execute the `/error/test` endpoint to get a much more detailed response body:

```
{
  "type":"https://tools.ietf.org/html/rfc7231#section-6.6.1",
  "title":"An error occurred while processing your request.",
  "status":500,
  "detail":"test",
  "traceId":"00-7cfd2605a885fbaed6a2abf0bc59944e-28bf94ef8a8c80a7-00"
}
```

New JSON data — points to the `"detail":"test",` and `"traceId"` lines

Notice that we're manually instantiating a `ProblemDetails` object instance, configuring it for our needs, and then passing it to the `Results.Problem` method overload, which accepts it as a parameter. We could do much more than simply configure the `ProblemDetails` object's properties, however. We could also do the following:

- Return different HTTP status codes depending on the exception's type, as we did with the `ModelState` manual validation in the `DomainsController`'s `Get` method
- Log the exception somewhere, such as in our DBMS
- Send email notifications to administrators, auditors, and/or other parties

Some of these possibilities are covered in the upcoming chapters.

> **WARNING** It's important to understand that the exception-handling middleware will reexecute the request using the original HTTP method. The handler endpoint—in our scenario, the `MapGet` method handling the `/error/` path—shouldn't be restricted to a limited set of HTTP methods, because it would work only for them. If we want to handle exceptions differently based on the original HTTP method, we can apply different HTTP verb attributes to multiple actions with the same name. We could use `[HttpGet]` to handle `GET` exceptions only and `[HttpPost]` to handle `POST` exceptions only, for example.

EXCEPTION HANDLING ACTION

Instead of delegating the exception handling process to a custom endpoint, we can use the `UseExceptionHandler` method's overload, which accepts an `Action<IApplication-Builder>` object instance as a parameter. This approach allows us to obtain the same level of customization without specifying a dedicated endpoint. Here's how we can use the implementation that we currently have within our Minimal API's `MapGet` method using that overload:

```
app.UseExceptionHandler(action => {
    action.Run(async context =>
    {
        var exceptionHandler =
            context.Features.Get<IExceptionHandlerPathFeature>();

        var details = new ProblemDetails();
        details.Detail = exceptionHandler?.Error.Message;
        details.Extensions["traceId"] =
            System.Diagnostics.Activity.Current?.Id
                ?? context.TraceIdentifier;
        details.Type =
            "https://tools.ietf.org/html/rfc7231#section-6.6.1";
        details.Status = StatusCodes.Status500InternalServerError;
        await context.Response.WriteAsync(
            System.Text.Json.JsonSerializer.Serialize(details));    ◁──┐
    });                                                       JSON-serializing the
});                                                          ProblemDetails object
```

As we can see, the source code is almost identical to the `MapGet` method's implementation. The only real difference is that here, we need to write the response body directly into the HTTP response buffer; we must take care of serializing the `ProblemDetails` object instance to an actual JSON-formatted string. Now that we've had some practice with the various error handling approaches offered by the framework, we're ready to apply this knowledge to the topic of chapter 7: application logging.

6.3   *Exercises*

It's time to challenge ourselves with the usual list of hypothetical task assignments given by our product owner. The solutions to the exercises are available on GitHub in the `/Chapter_06/Exercises/` folder. To test them, replace the relevant files in your `MyBGList` project with those in that folder, and run the app.

6.3.1   *Built-in validators*

Add a built-in validator to the `Name` property of the `DomainDTO` object so that it will be considered valid only if it's not null, not empty, and contains only uppercase and lowercase letters (without digits, spaces, or any other characters). Examples of valid values are `"Strategy"`, `"Family"`, and `"Abstract"`. Examples of invalid values are `"Strategy Games"`, `"Children's"`, `"101Guides"`, `""`, and `null`.

In case of an invalid value, the validator should emit the error message `"Value must contain only letters (no spaces, digits, or other chars)"`. The Domains-Controller's `Post` method, which accepts a `DomainDTO` complex type as a parameter, can be used to test the HTTP response containing the validation outcome.

6.3.2   *Custom validators*

Create a [LettersOnly] validator attribute, and implement it to fulfill the same specifications given in section 6.3.1, including the error message. The actual value check
should be performed using either regular expressions or string manipulation techniques, depending on whether the custom UseRegex parameter is set to true or false
(default). When the custom validator attribute is ready, apply it to the Name property
of the MechanicDTO object, and test it with both the UseRegex parameter values available by using the MechanicsController's Post method.

6.3.3   *IValidatableObject*

Implement the IValidatableObject interface to the DomainDTO object, and use its
Valid method to consider the model valid only if the Id value is equal to 3 or if the
Name value is equal to "Wargames". If the model is invalid, the validator should emit
the error message "Id and/or Name values must match an allowed Domain." The
DomainsController's Post method, which accepts a DomainDTO complex type as a
parameter, can be used to test the HTTP response containing the validation outcome.

6.3.4   *ModelState validation*

Apply the [ManualValidatonFilter] attribute to the DomainsController's Post
method to disable the automatic ModelState validation performed by the [Api-
Controller]. Then implement a manual ModelState validation to return the following HTTP status codes conditionally whenever ModelState isn't valid:

- HTTP 403 - Forbidden—If the ModelState is invalid because the Id value isn't
  equal to 3 and the Name value isn't equal to "Wargames"
- HTTP 400 - Bad Request—If the ModelState is invalid for any other reason

If the ModelState is valid, the HTTP request must be processed as normal.

6.3.5   *Exception handling*

Modify the current /error endpoint behavior to return the following HTTP status
code conditionally, depending on the type of exception being thrown:

- HTTP 501 - Not Implemented—For the NotImplementedException type
- HTTP 504 - Gateway Timeout—For the TimeoutException type
- HTTP 500 - Internal Server Error—For any other exception type

To test the new error handling implementation, create two new MapGet methods,
using Minimal API and implement them so that they throw an exception of the corresponding type:

- /error/test/501 for the HTTP 501 - Not Implemented status code
- /error/test/504 for the HTTP 504 - Gateway Timeout status code

Summary

- Data validation and error handling allow us to handle most unexpected scenarios during the interaction between client and server, reducing the risk of data leaks, slowdowns, and other security and performance problems.

- The ASP.NET Core model binding system is responsible for handling all the input data coming from HTTP requests, including converting them to .NET types (binding) and checking them against our data validation rules (validating).

- We can assign data validation rules to input parameters and complex-type properties by using built-in or custom data annotation attributes. Furthermore, we can create cross-validation checks in complex types by using the `IValidatableObject` interface.

- The `ModelState` object contains the combined result of the data-validation checks performed against the input parameters. ASP.NET Core allows us to use it in two ways:
  - Processing it automatically (thanks to the `[ApiController]`'s autovalidation features).
  - Checking its values manually, which allows us to customize the whole validation process and the resulting HTTP response.

- Application-level errors and exceptions can be handled by using the `ExceptionHandlingMiddleware`. This middleware can be configured to customize the error handling experience according to our needs, such as
  - Returning different HTTP status codes and/or human-readable info depending on the exception's type.
  - Logging the exceptions somewhere (DBMS, text file, event registry, and so on).
  - Sending email notifications to the interested parties (such as system administrators).

Part 3

Advanced concepts

Congratulations on still being here! The knowledge you've acquired to this point gives you the right and privilege to access the most complex, but also the most rewarding, part of this book.

This part follows a modular approach. Each chapter provides a comprehensive overview of a specific topic that you may want to implement in our web API, depending on the scenario and your (or your product owner's) specific needs.

Chapter 7 introduces the concept of application logging, from its historical roots to the exponential growth of its importance gained within past few years. It also explains the differences between structured and unstructured logging and shows how to implement structured logging in ASP.NET Core by using the built-in ILogger interface or a third-party logging framework such as Serilog.

In chapter 8, we'll learn how to cache data on the server, on the client, and/or at an intermediate level by using a set of techniques available in ASP.NET Core, such as HTTP response caching, in-memory caching, and distributed caching (using SQL Server or Redis). These features, used correctly, can dramatically improve the performance of a web API, as well as greatly reduce the load on the server.

Chapter 9 features a comprehensive journey through authentication and authorization, from their abstract, high-level meanings to the concrete, practical programming tasks required to implement them. We'll learn how to implement a fully featured authentication process based on user accounts and JSON Web Tokens (JWT), as well as a role-based access control (RBAC) authorization strategy using the AuthorizeAttribute and IAuthorizationFilter provided by the framework.

Chapter 10 presents several notable API technologies that can be used as an alternative to REST and extensively explains how to implement two of them: GraphQL, a query language for APIs developed by Facebook, and gRPC, a language-agnostic remote procedure call architecture designed by Google.

By the end of this part, we'll have learned all that this book has to offer in terms of topics, programming skills, and techniques, except for the aspects related to deployment and release to production, which are covered in part 4.

7
Application logging

This chapter covers

- Application logging origin and purposes
- Logging techniques using the `ILogger` interface
- Differences between unstructured and structured logging
- Implementing an alternative logging framework with Serilog

The term *logging*, when used in an IT context, defines the process of keeping track of all the events occurring within the application (and their context information) in a structured, semistructured, and/or unstructured format, and outputting them to a dedicated view and/or storage channel. Such a channel is often called *secondary* to distinguish it from the primary output mechanism the software uses to communicate with the end user: the user interface (UI).

The primary purpose of logging is to keep track of the various interactions between the software and its users: state changes, access to internal resources, event handlers that trigger in response to user actions, exceptions thrown by internal modules, and so on. Because this activity monitoring task is performed while the application is running, each log entry is typically shown (or recorded) with a timestamp value representing the moment when the logged event occurred.

In this chapter, after a brief overview of the concept and importance of logging, we'll learn how to create a structured logging mechanism for our web API project by using the `ILogger` interface, as well as some third-party components that implement it.

7.1 Application logging overview

In computer science, *to log* refers to the sequential and chronological recording of the operations carried out by the system (as they are performed). These operations can be carried out by a plurality of actors: users, system administrators, automated scheduled tasks, and tasks originated by the system itself.

By extension, the term *log* also refers to the file (or set of files) in which these records are stored. When someone asks us to "check out the logs," we know that *logs* means the log files. Why do we use this verb, though? Where does it come from?

7.1.1 From boats to computers

When electronics didn't exist, the term *log* was used only to refer to a piece of wood. But its use as a synonym for *recording* didn't start with computers or information technology; it originated around the 18th century. In the nautical jargon of the time, *log* referred to a piece of wood attached to a rope that was left to float off the ship. The rope had a series of knots that the sailors would count to measure the speed of the ship at any moment; the speed was determined by the number of knots that were above the water. This rudimentary yet effective measuring instrument is the reason why the speed of boats is still expressed in knots today.

This technique was far from perfect, however. Sailors knew that the speed of the boat could have been influenced by several internal and external factors, such as sail or engine performance, atmospheric conditions, and wind strength and direction. For this reason, the log-based knot measurement task known as logging was repeated at regular intervals. Each logging activity was recorded in a special register along with other relevant information, such as time, wind, and weather—the context. This register, commonly called a *logbook*, was the first example of a proper log file. As we can see, this unique measurement technique provided not only the name, but also the foundation for the modern concept of logging.

The adoption of the logbook concept in computer jargon took place at the beginning of the 1960s and led to the introduction of related definitions, including *login* and *logout*. From that moment on, the importance of logging in the IT industry increased exponentially, leading to the birth of a new market sector (log management) that was worth more than $1.2 billion in 2022 and grows year after year. This expansion was clearly determined by the growing importance of the IT security, compliance, audit, monitor, business intelligence, and data analysis frameworks, which strongly rely on system and application logs.

7.1.2 Why do we need logs?

We may wonder what a logging system can do for our web API or why we should care about implementing it. The best way to address this concern is to enumerate the most important aspects of an application that can realistically benefit from a logging system:

- *Stability*—Log records allow us to detect and investigate bugs and/or unhandled exceptions promptly, facilitating the process of fixing them and minimizing the application's downtime.
- *Security*—The presence of a logging system helps us determine whether the system has been compromised and, if so, to what extent. The log records also allow us to identify the vulnerabilities found by the attacker and the malicious actions the attacker was able to perform by exploiting those vulnerabilities.
- *Business continuity*—The logging system can make system administrators aware of abnormal behaviors before they become critical and/or can inform them promptly about crashes via alarms, email messages, and other real-time notification-based alert processes.
- *Compliance requirements*—Most international IT security regulations, standards, and guidelines require precise logging policies. This approach has been further strengthened in recent years by the introduction of the General Data Protection Regulation (GDPR) on the territory of the European Union and other data protection regulations elsewhere.

It's important to understand that the act of "reading" the logs (and acting accordingly) doesn't have to be performed by human beings. A good logging practice always requires both manual checks and a monitoring system that can be configured to apply some preset remediations automatically in case of common incidents (restarting defective or nonfunctioning services, launching maintenance scripts, and so on). Most modern IT security software provides a highly automatable security operation center (SOC) framework and/or a security, orchestration, automation, and response (SOAR) integrated solution. All that considered, we can easily see that log management is not only a useful tool for keeping web (and nonweb) applications under control, but also an essential requirement to guarantee their overall reliability as well as a fundamental asset in IT security.

7.2 ASP.NET logging

Now that we've acknowledged the importance of logging, let's use the tools of the .NET framework to manage this important aspect of our application. These tools are the standardized, general-purpose logging APIs made available through the `ILogger` interface, which allows us to record the events and activities we want to log through a series of built-in and/or third-party logging providers.

Technically speaking, the `ILogger` API isn't part of .NET; it's located in an external `Microsoft.Extensions.Logging` NuGet package published and maintained by Microsoft. This package, however, is implicitly included in all ASP.NET Core applications, including the ASP.NET Core web API project template we've used to create our MyBG-List app. We can easily confirm that fact by looking at the BoardGamesController's source code.

Open the Controllers/BoardGamesController.cs file, and search for a reference to the ILogger interface. We should find it among the private properties of the controller's class:

```
private readonly ILogger<BoardGamesController> _logger;
```

As we can see, the interface accepts a generic type (TCategoryName). The name of the type will be used to determine the log category, a string value that will help us categorize the log entries coming from the various classes.

If we scroll down a bit farther, we see that the ILogger<BoardGamesController> object instance is obtained within the class constructor by the standard dependency injection (DI) pattern, which we should be used to by now:

```
public BoardGamesController(
    ApplicationDbContext context,
    ILogger<BoardGamesController> logger)
    {
        _context = context;
        _logger = logger;
}
```

Because all our controllers have been derived from this codebase, that same _logger private property (and injection pattern) should be present in our DomainsController and MechanicsController as well. We can already use the ILogger API. To demonstrate, let's take a couple of minutes to perform a simple test.

7.2.1   *A quick logging test*

Keeping the BoardGamesController.cs file open, scroll down to the Get action method's implementation, and add the following single line of code (in bold):

```
public async Task<RestDTO<BoardGame[]>> Get(
    [FromQuery] RequestDTO<BoardGameDTO> input)
    {
        _logger.LogInformation("Get method started.");    ◄── Our first
                                                              logging
        // ... rest of code omitted                          attempt
```

If we look at the suggestions given by Visual Studio's IntelliSense feature while writing this code, we notice that the API provides several logging methods: LogTrace, LogDebug, LogInformation (the one we used), LogWarning, LogError, and LogCritical, all of which correspond to the various log levels available. These methods are shortcuts for the generic Log method, which allows us to specify a LogLevel value explicitly. We can use this value to set the severity level of each log entry, choosing among several options defined by the LogLevel enumeration class.

Launch the project in Debug mode; open the Visual Studio Output window by choosing View > Output; and execute the `BoardGamesController`'s `Get` method via either SwaggerUI or https://localhost:40443/BoardGames. If everything goes as planned, immediately before receiving the HTTP response, we should see the following log entry in the Output window (along with several other lines):

```
MyBGList.Controllers.BoardGamesController: Information: Get method started.
```

That's the result of our first logging attempt. As we can see, the log entry contains the category (the controller's fully qualified class name), the chosen `LogLevel` (`Information`), and the log message that we specified when implementing it.

If we look at the other lines in the Output window, we can see a couple of other logs related to `EntityFrameworkCore`. We shouldn't be surprised, because we're using the same logging API that all other .NET and ASP.NET Core middleware and services use, along with any third-party package that has adopted it. That fact is great to know, because every configuration tweak we apply to the logging behavior of our application will affect not only our custom log entries, but also the logging capabilities provided by our components. Now that we've experienced how the `ILogger` API works in practice, let's take a couple of steps back to review its core concepts, starting with the `LogLevel` enumeration class.

7.2.2 Log levels

The `LogLevel` enum type is part of the `Microsoft.Extensions.Logging` namespace and defines the following available levels, in order of severity:

- *Trace* (0)—Information related to the application's internal activities and useful only for low-level debugging or system administration tasks. This log level is never used, because it can easily contain confidential data (such as configuration info, use of encryption keys, and other sensitive information that shouldn't be viewed or recorded by anyone).
- *Debug* (1)—Development-related information (variable values, stack trace, execution context, and so on) that's useful for interactive analysis and debugging purposes. This log level should always be disabled in production environments, as the records might contain information that shouldn't be disclosed.
- *Information* (2)—Informative messages that describe events or activities related to the system's normal behavior. This log level usually doesn't contain sensitive or nondisclosable information, but it's typically disabled in production to prevent excessive logging verboseness, which could result in big log files (or tables).
- *Warning* (3)—Information about abnormal or unexpected behaviors, as well as any other event or activity that doesn't alter the normal flow of the app.
- *Error* (4)—Informative messages about noncritical events or activities that have likely halted, interrupted, or otherwise hindered the standard execution flow of a specific task or activity.

- *Critical* (5)—Informative messages about critical events or activities that prevent the application from starting or that determine an irreversible and/or unrecoverable application crash.
- *None* (6)—No information is logged. Typically, this level is used to disable logging.

7.2.3   *Logging configuration*

We stumbled upon these LogLevel values in chapter 2, when we looked at our app-Settings files for the first time. Now it's time to explain their meaning. Open the appsettings.json file, and check out the root-level "Logging" key, shown in the following code snippet (nonrelevant parts omitted):

```
"Logging": {
  "LogLevel": {
    "Default": "Information",
    "Microsoft.AspNetCore": "Warning"
  }
}
```

These settings configure the logging behavior of the ILogger API for our application. More precisely, they specify the minimum level to log for each category, based on the numeric value of the LogLevel enumeration class, from Trace (0) to None (6).

As we can see, the Default category, which represents the default fallback setting, is set to Information, so it will log Information and higher levels (thus including Warning, Error, and Critical). Another setting, however, overrides these default rules for the Microsoft.AspNetCore category, which has been configured to log only Warning and higher levels. The purpose of this override is to exclude the Information level for the Microsoft.AspNetCore category, cutting out the logging of several unnecessary pieces of information regarding that namespace.

In more general terms, the category settings follow a simple set of rules based on *cascading* and *specificity* concepts (the most specific one is the one that will be used):

- Each category setting also applies to all its nested (child) categories. The logging settings for the Microsoft.AspNetCore category setting, for example, will also apply to all the categories starting with Microsoft.AspNetCore.* (such as Microsoft.AspNetCore.Http) unless they're overridden by specific rules.
- The settings applied to a specific category always override those configured for any top-level category pertaining to that same namespace, as well as the Default fallback category. If we add a settings key for the Microsoft.AspNet-Core.Http category with a value of Error, for example, we cut out the logging of all the Warning log events for that category, thus overriding the settings for the Microsoft.AspNetCore parent category.

It's important to remember that we can set up environment-specific logging configuration settings by using the appsettings.<EnvironmentName>.json files, as we did in chapter 2 when we created the UseDeveloperExceptionPage setting. This approach allows us to have verbose logging behavior for our `Development` environment while enforcing a more restrictive (and confidential) approach in our `Production` environment.

Suppose that we want (or are asked) to limit the logging verboseness for our `Production` environment while increasing the granularity of the `Development` logs. Here's what we need to do:

- *Production*—Log only `Warning` and higher levels for all categories except `MyBGList`, where we want to log the `Information` level as well.
- *Development*—Log `Information` and higher levels for all categories except `Microsoft.AspNetCore`, where we're interested only in `Warning` and higher levels, and `MyBGList`, where we want to log everything at `Debug` level and higher.

The first thing to do is to open the `appsettings.json` file, which is where we'll put the `Production` environment settings, and update it with the code in bold (nonrelevant part omitted):

```
"Logging": {
  "LogLevel": {
    "Default": "Warning",
    "MyBGList": "Information"
  }
}
```

Then we can proceed with the `appsettings.Development.json` file, which we need to update in the following way (nonrelevant part omitted):

```
"Logging": {
  "LogLevel": {
    "Default": "Information",
    "Microsoft.AspNetCore": "Warning",
    "MyBGList": "Debug"
  }
}
```

Now that we're familiar with the logging configuration settings, we may want to understand where all these log records go, because until now, we've seen them only in the Output window. To learn more, we need to know about logging providers.

7.2.4 Logging providers

A *logging provider* is a component that stores or displays logs. It receives the log records sent by the `ILogger` API based on the configuration settings—persists them somewhere.

The following sections provide an overview of the built-in logging providers—those provided by the framework. How many are there, what do they do, and how can we configure them? Then we'll review some third-party logging providers, which we can use to extend the capabilities of the `ILogger` API.

BUILT-IN LOGGING PROVIDERS

Here's a list of the default logging providers shipped by the .NET framework through the `Microsoft.Extensions.Logging` namespace:

- `Console`—Outputs the logs to the console. This provider allows us to view the log messages within the console window that ASP.NET Core opens to launch the `MyBGList.exe` process when we execute our app.
- `Debug`—Outputs the logs by using the `WriteLine` method provided by the `System.Diagnostics.Debug` class. When a debugger is connected, this provider allows us to view the log messages in the Visual Studio Output window, as well as store them in log files or registers (depending on the OS and the debugger settings).
- `EventSource`—Outputs the logs as runtime event traces so that they can be fetched by an event source platform such as Event Tracing for Windows or Linux Trace Toolkit next-gen.
- `EventLog`—Writes the logs in the Windows Event Log (available only for Windows operating systems).

Three more logging providers can send logs to various Microsoft Azure data stores:

- `AzureAppServicesFile`—Writes the logs to a text file within an Azure App Service filesystem (which needs to be set up and configured beforehand)
- `AzureAppServicesBlob`—Writes the logs to blob storage within an Azure Storage account (which needs to be set up and configured beforehand)
- `ApplicationInsights`—Writes the logs to an Azure Application Insights service (which needs to be set up and configured beforehand)

> **WARNING** The Azure providers aren't part of the runtime libraries and must be installed as additional NuGet packages. Because these packages are maintained and shipped by Microsoft, however, they're considered to be among the built-in providers.

Multiple logging providers can be attached to the `ILogger` API (enabled) at the same time, allowing us to store and/or display our logs in several places simultaneously. This is precisely what happens with the configuration shipped with all the ASP.NET Core web app templates, including the one we used to create our `MyBGList` web API project, which adds the following logging providers by default: `Console`, `Debug`, `EventSource`, and `EventLog` (Windows only).

The configuration line responsible for these default settings is the `WebApplication.CreateBuilder` method called at the start of the `Program.cs` file. If we want to change this behavior, we can use a convenient `ILoggingBuilder` interface instance made available by the `WebApplicationBuilder` object returned by that method.

Suppose that we want to remove the `EventSource` and `EventLog` providers while keeping the other ones. Open the `Program.cs` file, locate the preceding method, and add the following lines (in bold) that call:

```
var builder = WebApplication.CreateBuilder(args);
builder.Logging
    .ClearProviders()          ◄─────┐  Removes all registered
    .AddSimpleConsole()        ◄──────┤  logging providers
    .AddDebug();          ◄─┐
```

Adds the Debug logging provider

Adds the Console logging provider

Before we could get rid of those logging providers, we had to remove all the precon-figured ones (using the ClearProviders method). Then we added back only those that we want to keep.

CONFIGURING THE PROVIDERS

Most built-in logging providers can be configured programmatically via a dedicated overload of their add method that accepts an options object. Here's how we could configure the console provider to timestamp its log entries, using HH:mm:ss format and the UTC time zone:

```
builder.Logging
    .ClearProviders()
    .AddSimpleConsole(options =>     ◄──┐  Option-based
    {                                      configuration
        options.SingleLine = true;         added
        options.TimestampFormat = "HH:mm:ss ";
        options.UseUtcTimestamp = true;
    })
    .AddDebug();
```

We can check the new behavior immediately by launching our app in Debug mode, executing the BoardGamesController's Get method where we put our custom log message, and looking at the command prompt window hosting the MyBGList.exe pro-cess. If we did everything correctly, we should find our log message with its new look:

```
15:36:52 info:
MyBGList.Controllers.BoardGamesController[0] Get method started.
```

The HH:mm:ss timestamp is now clearly visible at the beginning of the line. But the option-based configuration method isn't the recommended way to configure the logging providers for the latest versions of .NET. Unless we have specific needs, it may be better to use a more versatile approach that uses the "Logging" section of the appsettings.json files—the same section that we used to configure the LogLevel.

Let's switch from the option-based configuration settings to this new method. The first thing to do is roll back the changes we made in the AddSimpleConsole method, reverting it to its parameterless overload in the following way:

```
builder.Logging
    .ClearProviders()
    .AddSimpleConsole()      ◄──┐  Option-based
    .AddDebug();                   configuration removed
```

Then we can open the `appsettings.json` file and add the following `Console` section block (nonrelevant part omitted):

```
"Logging": {
  "LogLevel": {
    "Default": "Warning",
    "MyBGList": "Information"          Console logging
  },                                   provider using the
  "Console": {              ◁─────────  appsettings.json file
    "FormatterOptions": {
      "SingleLine": true,
      "TimestampFormat": "HH:mm:ss ",
      "UseUtcTimestamp": true
    }
  }
}
```

We can use the same technique to override the `LogLevel` for specific logging providers. Here's how we could limit the verboseness of the `MyBGList` category by setting its `LogLevel` to `Warning` for the console logging provider only:

```
"Logging": {
  "LogLevel": {
    "Default": "Warning",
    "MyBGList": "Information"
  },                                   LogLevel settings
  "Console": {                         override for the
    "LogLevel": {          ◁─────────  Console provider
      "MyBGList": "Warning"
    },
    "FormatterOptions": {
      "TimestampFormat": "HH:mm:ss ",
      "UseUtcTimestamp": true
    }
  }
}
```

As we can see by looking at this code, we can override the settings specified in the generic `LogLevel` section by creating a new `LogLevel` subsection inside the logging provider configuration. We can confirm that the override works by executing our app from scratch (or hot-reloading it) and looking at the same command prompt window as before. We shouldn't see our custom log message, because it belongs to a `LogLevel` that we're not logging for that category anymore.

> **WARNING** The `appsettings`-based configuration approach can be convenient, as it allows us to customize the logging behavior of all our providers, and/or to set environment-specific rules, without having to update the `Program.cs` file. But this approach also requires some practice and study, because each provider has specific configuration settings. The `Debug` logging provider, for example, doesn't have the `TimestampFormat` and `UseUctTimestamp` settings, so those

values would be ignored if we tried to use them within a LogLevel:Debug section. This aspect will become evident when we configure third-party logging providers.

Let's remove the Logging:Console:LogLevel section from our appsettings.json file (in case we've added it) so that it won't hinder our upcoming tests.

7.2.5 *Event IDs and templates*

If we look again at the log message written in the MyBGList.exe console window by the console logging provider, we notice the presence of a numeric value within square brackets after the name of the class. That number, which happens to be [0] (zero) in our custom logging message, represents the event ID of the log. We can think of it as contextual info that we can use to classify a set of events that have something in common, regardless of their category. Suppose that we want (or are asked) to classify all logs related to our BoardGamesController's Get method with an event ID of 50110. The following sections show how we can implement that task.

SETTING CUSTOM EVENT IDs

To adopt such a convention, we need to replace our current implementation, switching to the LogInformation's method overload that accepts a given event ID as its first parameter (updated code in bold):

```
_logger.LogInformation(50110, "Get method started.");
```

If we launch our app in Debug mode and check the MyBGList.exe console window, we see the event ID in place of the previous value of 0:

```
15:43:15 info: MyBGList.Controllers.BoardGamesController[50110] Get method started.
```

Classifying our log messages can be useful, because it allows us to group them together (or filter them) whenever we need to perform some checks and/or audit activities. Having to set these numbers manually each time could be inconvenient, however, so let's create a CustomLogEvents class to define them in a centralized place.

In Visual Studio's Solution Explorer window, create a new /Constants/ root folder, and add a new CustomLogEvents.cs class file inside it. Then fill the new file with the content of the following listing.

Listing 7.1 CustomLogEvents class

```
namespace MyBGList.Constants
{
    public class CustomLogEvents
    {
        public const int BoardGamesController_Get = 50110;
        public const int BoardGamesController_Post = 50120;
        public const int BoardGamesController_Put = 50130;
        public const int BoardGamesController_Delete = 50140;
```

```
        public const int DomainsController_Get = 50210;
        public const int DomainsController_Post = 50220;
        public const int DomainsController_Put = 50230;
        public const int DomainsController_Delete = 50240;

        public const int MechanicsController_Get = 50310;
        public const int MechanicsController_Post = 50320;
        public const int MechanicsController_Put = 50330;
        public const int MechanicsController_Delete = 50340;
    }
}
```

Now we can go back to our `BoardGamesController` class and replace the numeric literal value with the constant that we created to reference it:

```
using MyBGList.Constants;          ◁──┐  New required
                                        │  namespace
// ... nonrelevant code omitted         │
                                              New constant
                                              instead of a
                                              literal value
_logger.LogInformation(CustomLogEvents.BoardGamesController_Get,   ◁──┘
    "Get method started.");
```

The new implementation is much more readable and less error-prone, because we don't have to type the numbers for each event ID within the code (and run the risk of typing them wrong).

> **NOTE**   Not all logging providers display the event ID, and not all of them put it in square brackets at the end of the line. The `Debug` provider doesn't show it, and other structured providers (such as the Azure ones) persist it in a specific column that we can choose to display or not.

USING MESSAGE TEMPLATES

The `ILogger` API supports a template syntax that we can use to build log messages, employing a string-formatting technique similar to the one provided by the `string` `.Format` C# method. Instead of using numbers to set the placeholders, however, we can use a name. Instead of doing this

```
string.Format("This is a {0} level log", logLevel);
```

we can do this:

```
_logger.LogInformation("This is a {logLevel} level log", logLevel);
```

The difference between the two approaches is that the latter is more human-readable; we immediately understand what the placeholder is for. If we need to use multiple placeholders in our template, we put their corresponding variables in the correct order, as in the following example:

```
_logger.LogInformation(
    "This is a {logLevel} level log of the {catName} category.",
    logLevel, categoryName);
```

We deliberately used the {catName} placeholder for the categoryName parameter to clarify that each placeholder will receive its value from the parameter that corresponds to its order, not to its name.

7.2.6 *Exception logging*

The ILogger API can also be used to log exceptions, thanks to some dedicated overloads provided by all the logging extension methods that accept an Exception? as a parameter. This feature can be convenient for our MyBGList application because we're handling exceptions through a centralized endpoint.

In chapter 6, being able to log our exceptions was one of the main reasons that led us to implement a centralized logging handling approach through the Exception-HandlerMiddleware. Now the time has come to turn this capability into something real.

Open the Program.cs file and scroll down to the Minimal API's MapGet method that handles the /error route. We need to provide an ILogger instance that we can use to log the exception's details. To obtain the ILogger instance, we could think about injecting an ILogger interface instance by using dependency injection in the following way:

```
app.MapGet("/error",
    [EnableCors("AnyOrigin")]
    [ResponseCache(NoStore = true)]
    (HttpContext context, ILogger logger)
```

Then we could use the logger variable within the MapGet method's implementation to perform our logging tasks. But because we're in the Program.cs file, we can use the default ILogger instance provided by the WebApplication object instead. This instance is accessible through the Logger property of the app local variable—the same variable that we use to add our middleware to the request pipeline. Here's how we can take advantage of this property to implement our exception logging change request:

```
// Minimal API
app.MapGet("/error",
    [EnableCors("AnyOrigin")]
    [ResponseCache(NoStore = true)] (HttpContext context) =>
    {
        var exceptionHandler =
            context.Features.Get<IExceptionHandlerPathFeature>();

        var details = new ProblemDetails();
        details.Detail = exceptionHandler?.Error.Message;
        details.Extensions["traceId"] =
            System.Diagnostics.Activity.Current?.Id
              ?? context.TraceIdentifier;
        details.Type =
            "https://tools.ietf.org/html/rfc7231#section-6.6.1";
        details.Status = StatusCodes.Status500InternalServerError;
```

```
app.Logger.LogError(                                    Exception
    exceptionHandler?.Error,                            logging
    "An unhandled exception occurred.");

return Results.Problem(details);
});
```

While we're here, we could create a new event ID for this specific task so that we'll be able to filter all the error log entries related to exceptions. Switch to the /Constants/CustomLogEvents.cs file, and add the following constant at the beginning of the class, right above the existing ones:

```
public const int Error_Get = 50001;
```

Now we can switch to the Program.cs file and change the LogError method implementation with the override accepting an eventId parameter:

```
using MyBGList.Constants;

// ... nonrelevant code omitted

app.Logger.LogError(                        Custom
    CustomLogEvents.Error_Get,              Event ID
    exceptionHandler?.Error,
    "An unhandled exception occurred.");
```

Now that we've gained confidence with the ILogger API, we're ready to talk about third-party logging providers, which allow us to persist these logs in structured data stores, such as our database management system (DBMS). First, however, we'll spend some valuable time examining the difference between structured and unstructured logging.

7.3   *Unstructured vs. structured logging*

All the built-in logging providers that we've briefly reviewed (except for the Azure ApplicationInsights provider, which we'll talk about later) have a common characteristic: they store (or show) the log information by using raw strings. In other words, the log records have the appearance of textual data that gets stored (or shown) in an unstructured way. The following list summarizes the differences between unstructured, semistructured, and structured data:

- *Unstructured data*—Raw data that isn't organized with a predefined data model, be it a database schema, a spreadsheet file with columns, a structured XML/JSON file, or anything else that allows splitting the relevant parts of the recorded data among fields—in other words, a plain text record.
- *Semistructured data*—Data that doesn't reside in a DBMS but comes with some organizational properties that make it easier to analyze, parse, and/or process the content (such as to seed an actual DBMS). A good example of semistructured data is the board game CSV file that we used in chapter 5 to seed our MyBGList database.

- *Structured data*—Data that has been organized into an addressable repository, such as a DBMS, and that is ready for effective analysis without our having to parse it. A typical example of structured data is a data set of records such as those that have populated our `MyBGList` tables since chapter 5.

We can say without doubt that the log records we've played with until now—thanks to the console's built-in provider—belong to the unstructured family. Is that a bad thing? Not necessarily, provided that we're fully aware of the benefits and drawbacks of this logging strategy.

7.3.1 Unstructured logging pros and cons

The unstructured logging approach undoubtedly has relevant advantages, including accessibility. We need a console or a text editor to view these records and fully understand their content. Furthermore, because the records are typically stored one after another, the log-reviewing phase is often rather quick and convenient, especially when we need to access the latest entries, maybe because we know that the event that triggered the log we're looking for occurred a short while ago.

Unfortunately, when things become more complicated, these benefits tend to disappear. If we need to retrieve a specific log entry without knowing when the relevant event occurred, or even whether it occurred, we might have a hard time finding it. Our only tools would be text-based search tools such as the Notepad Find feature and the Linux `grep` command. This task can become even more troublesome when these log files reach critical mass, which can happen quickly if we activate particularly verbose `LogLevels`. We all know how difficult it is to access and browse those gigantic files, not to mention perform search operations on them. Retrieving specific information from thousands of unstructured log entries can easily become a frustrating task; it's definitely not a quick and convenient way to get the job done.

> **NOTE** This problem is so well known in the IT ecosystem that it resulted in the birth of several log management tools that ingest unstructured log records and then aggregate, parse, and/or normalize them by using standard or user-defined patterns, rules, or schemas. These tools include Graylog, LogDNA, Splunk, and NewRelic.

In short, what's really lacking in the unstructured logging produced by most built-in logging providers is a feature that lets us filter those records in a practical way through one or more parameters, such as log level, event ID, transaction number, and a start/end date and time—in other words, to query them. We can overcome this limitation by adding a structured logging provider—a logging provider that allows us to write these records to a service that allows structured data storage, such as a DBMS.

7.3.2   *Structured logging advantages*

Following are the main benefits of a structured logging strategy:

- We don't need to rely on text-editor tools to read logs in manual mode.
- We don't need to write code to parse or process the logs in automatic mode.
- We can query the log records by using relevant fields, as well as aggregate them with external data. We could issue a JOIN query, for example, to extract only the logs triggered by user actions together with some relevant user data (such as user ID, name, and email address).
- We can extract and/or convert the logs in other formats, possibly including only the relevant information and/or omitting information that shouldn't be disclosed.
- Performance benefits, thanks to the indexing features of the DBMS, make the retrieval process more efficient even when we're dealing with a large number of records.

These benefits are a direct consequence of the fact that the log record is stored by using a predefined data structure. Some indirect benefits are also worth considering, determined by the fact that any structured logging provider is meant to rely on a data storage service that will ultimately store the data. These benefits vary depending on what type of data storage we choose. We could store our logs in various ways:

- Within our existing MyBGList database so that we can use EF Core to access it and keep all our application-relevant data in a single, centralized place
- In a separate database on the same DBMS instance (SQL Server) so that we can keep the log records logically separated from the board-game data while still being able to access them through EF Core to a certain extent
- In an external repository located elsewhere (such as a third-party service or DBMS) so that the log records are completely independent of the application's infrastructure and therefore more resilient against failures, leakage, tampering, and so on

As we can see, all these options are significant. We could even think about mixing those logging strategies, because the ILogger interface supports multiple logging providers, and most third-party providers support multiple output destinations.

> **TIP**   We could also keep the built-in logging providers that we configured earlier—Console and Debug—unless we want to remove or replace them. This approach would allow us to set up structured and unstructured logging at the same time.

That's enough theory. Let's see how we can add these valuable tools to our toolbox.

7.3.3 Application Insights logging provider

As I said earlier, the only built-in alternative that we could use to store event logs in a structured format is the Application Insights logging provider. In this section, we'll briefly see how we can set up this logging provider for our `MyBGList` web API. This task requires us to create an account in Microsoft Azure, the cloud provider that hosts the Application Insights service and makes it available. First, however, I'll briefly introduce Azure and Application Insights and discuss the benefits that cloud-based services such as Application Insights can bring to modern web applications such as our `MyBG-List` web API.

INTRODUCING MICROSOFT AZURE

Microsoft Azure (often referred to as MS Azure or simply Azure) is a public cloud computing platform owned and maintained by Microsoft. It was announced in 2008, formally released in 2010 as Windows Azure, and renamed in 2014. The platform relies on a huge network of Microsoft data centers worldwide. It offers more than 600 services provided through Software as a Service (SaaS), Platform as a Service (PaaS), and Infrastructure as a Service (IaaS) delivery models, using large-scale virtualization technologies. It follows the subscription-based approach used by its most notable competitors: Amazon Web Services (AWS) and Google Cloud Platform (GCP).

Azure services can be managed via a set of APIs that are directly accessible via the web and/or managed class libraries available for various programming languages. At the end of 2015, Microsoft also released the Azure Portal, a web-based management interface allowing users to manage most of the services in a visual graphical user interface (GUI). The release of the Azure Portal greatly helped Azure increase its market share, which (according to Canalys) reached 21 percent in the first quarter of 2022, with AWS at 33 percent and GCP at 8 percent.

> **TIP** The Canalys report is available at http://mng.bz/pdqK.

INTRODUCING APPLICATION INSIGHTS

Among the services made available by Azure is Azure Monitor, a comprehensive solution that can be used to collect and analyze logs, audit trails, and other performance-related output data from any supported cloud-based and on-premises environment or service, including web applications. The Azure Monitor feature dedicated to ingesting, monitoring, and analyzing the log and informative status messages generated by live web applications is called Application Insights.

> **NOTE** We could think of Application Insights as a Google Analytics of some sort. Instead of monitoring our web application's page views and sessions, however, it's meant to monitor and analyze its logs and status messages.

The presence of the Application Insights provider among the built-in logging providers is also the main reason why we've chosen to deal with Azure instead of AWS and GCP.

CREATING THE AZURE INSTANCE

Now that we know the basics of Azure and Application Insights, we can proceed with the service setup. To use the Application Insights service, we need to have a valid Azure account. Luckily, the service offers a basic pricing plan that has almost no charge until our log data becomes substantial.

TIP   To create a free account, go to https://azure.microsoft.com/en-us/free.

The first thing to do is log into the Azure Portal. Then use the search text box at the top of the main dashboard to find and access the Application Insights service. Click the Create button in the top-left corner of the screen to create a new Application Insights instance, as shown in figure 7.1.

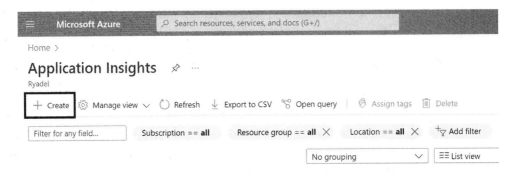

Figure 7.1   Creating a new instance

The creation process is simple and requires us only to set up a few parameters:

- *Subscription*—The Azure subscription to create this instance in. (If you don't have a subscription, you'll be asked to create a free one for a 30-day trial.)
- *Resource Group*—The Azure resource group to create this instance in.
- *Name*—The instance name.
- *Region*—The geographic region in which to create the instance.
- *Resource Mode*—Choose Classic if you want this Application Insights instance to have its own environment or Workspace-Based if you want to integrate it with an existing Log Analytics workspace. For simplicity, choose Classic (figure 7.2).

Click Review + Create to review these settings and then click Create to finalize the instance deployment process. As soon as the deployment is complete, click Go to Resource, which takes us to our new Application Insights instance's management dashboard, where we can retrieve the connection string (figure 7.3).

We're going to need that value when we configure the Application Insights logging provider so that it will be able to send log events to that instance. Let's store it in an appropriate place.

Home > Application Insights >

Application Insights   ⋯
Monitor web app performance and usage

PROJECT DETAILS

Select a subscription to manage deployed resources and costs. Use resource groups like folders to organize and manage all your resources.

Subscription * ⓘ	Microsoft MVP ⌄
⌐ Resource Group * ⓘ	(New) Manning ⌄
	Create new

INSTANCE DETAILS

Name * ⓘ	MyBGList ✓
Region * ⓘ	(Europe) West Europe ⌄
Resource Mode * ⓘ	(Classic) Workspace-based

Figure 7.2   Configuration settings

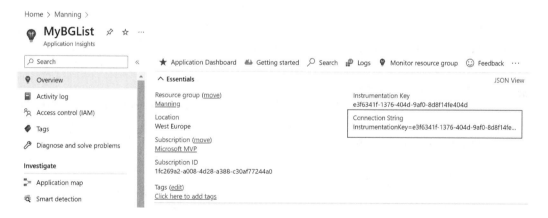

Figure 7.3   Retrieving the Application Insights connection string

STORING THE CONNECTION STRING

A great place to store the Application Insights connection string for development purposes is the `secrets.json` file, which we've been using since chapter 4. In the Visual Studio Solution Explorer window, right-click the project's root node and choose Manage User Secrets from the contextual menu. Here's the section block that we can add to the existing content, below the `ConnectionStrings` key (nonrelevant parts removed):

```
    "Azure": {
      "ApplicationInsights": {
        "ConnectionString": "<INSERT_CONNECTION_STRING_HERE>"    ⟵┐  Puts the
      }                                                               connection
    }                                                                 string here
```

Now we know where we'll retrieve the connection string when we configure the logging provider. First, however, we must install it.

INSTALL THE NUGET PACKAGES

Now that we have the MyBGList Application Insights instance in Azure and the connection string available, we can install the Application Insights logging provider NuGet
packages. As always, we can use Visual Studio's NuGet GUI, the Package Manager
Console window, or the .NET command-line interface (CLI). Here are the commands
to install them by using the .NET CLI:

```
> dotnet add package Microsoft.Extensions.Logging.ApplicationInsights --
      version 2.21.0

> dotnet add package Microsoft.ApplicationInsights.AspNetCore
        --version 2.21.0
```

> **NOTE** The version specified in the example is the latest stable version avail-
> able at this writing. I strongly suggest using that version as well to avoid having
> to deal with breaking changes, incompatibility problems, and the like.

The first package contains the provider itself, and the second is required to configure
it by using the appsettings.json file, as we did with the Console logging provider
earlier. When the packages are installed, we can configure the provider.

CONFIGURING THE LOGGING PROVIDER

The configuration part takes place in the Program.cs file of our app. Open that file,
locate the part where we defined the logging providers, and add the new one to the
loop in the following way:

```
builder.Logging
  .ClearProviders()
  .AddSimpleConsole()                          Adds the Application
  .AddDebug()                                  Insights logging
  .AddApplicationInsights(          ⟵┘         provider
    telemetry => telemetry.ConnectionString =
      builder
        .Configuration["Azure:ApplicationInsights:ConnectionString"],
      loggerOptions => { });
```

The new configuration line will activate the Application Insights logging provider for
our MyBGList web API. All we need to do now is to see whether it works.

TESTING THE APPLICATION INSIGHTS EVENT LOGS

Launch the project in Debug mode, and navigate to the /BoardGames endpoint to trigger some event logs. Then go back to the main dashboard of the Application Insights service in Azure, and choose Investigate > Transaction from the right menu. If we did everything correctly, we should see our application's event logs as TRACE event types, as shown in figure 7.4.

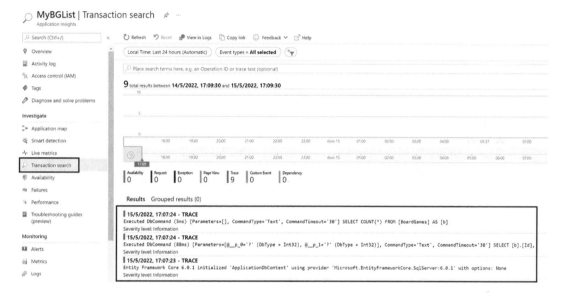

Figure 7.4   Application logs shown as TRACE event types

As we can see, the event logs are accessible in a structured format. We can even create some queries by using the GUI, such as filtering the entries with a severity level equal to or greater than a given value. That's a great improvement over unstructured logging!

This technique has a major limitation, however: the logging provider we added, as its name clearly implies, is limited to Azure's Application Insights service. We won't be able to store these structured logs anywhere else, such as within our existing SQL Server database or any other DBMS. To achieve this capability, we have to use a third-party logging provider that provides support for these kinds of output destinations.

7.4   Third-party logging providers

This section introduces Serilog, an open source logging library for .NET applications available on NuGet that allows us to store our application logs in several popular DBMSes (including SQL Server and MariaDB), as well as third-party services.

> **NOTE** We chose Serilog over other alternatives because it's one of the most popular third-party logging providers available, with more than 480 million

downloads and 1,000 stars on GitHub at this writing, as well as being open source (Apache 2.0 license).

After seeing how Serilog works, we'll see how to install it in our `MyBGList` web API project and make it work along with the built-in logging providers we already have.

7.4.1 Serilog overview

The first thing we must understand is that Serilog isn't only a logging provider that implements the `Microsoft.Extensions.Logging.ILogger` interface along with the other logging providers. It's a full-featured logging system that can be set up to work in two different ways:

- *As a logging API*—Replaces the .NET logging implementation (including the `ILogger` interface) with its own native interface
- *As a logging provider*—Implements the Microsoft extensions logging API (and extends it with several additional features) instead of replacing it

The main difference between these two architectural approaches is that the first one requires setting up a dependency on the `Serilog` interface in all our codebases, thus replacing the `ILogger` interface we've used up to now. Although this requirement isn't necessarily bad, I think that keeping the Microsoft logging API is generally a better choice because it's a better fit with the modular structure of a typical ASP.NET Core web app, ensuring a more flexible system. For that reason, we're going to follow the second approach. Regardless of how we choose to set it up, Serilog provides two main advantages over most other logging providers:

- *Enrichers*—A set of packages that can be used to add additional info automatically to log events (`ProcessId`, `ThreadId`, `MachineName`, `EnvironmentName`, and so on)
- *Sinks*—A selection of output destinations, such as DBMSes, cloud-based repositories, and third-party services

Because Serilog was built with a modular architecture, all enrichers and sinks are available via dedicated NuGet packages that we can install along with the library core package(s) whenever we need them.

7.4.2 Installing Serilog

For simplicity, we'll take for granted that in our scenario, we want to use Serilog to store our log events in our SQL Server database. We need to install the following packages:

- `Serilog.AspNetCore`—Includes the core Serilog package, integration into the ASP.NET Core configuration and hosting infrastructure, some basic enrichers and sinks, and the middleware required to log the HTTP requests
- `Serilog.Sinks.MSSqlServer`—The sink for storing event logs in SQL Server

To do that, we can use the NuGet GUI or the following commands in the Package Manager console:

```
> dotnet add package Serilog.AspNetCore --version 6.0.1
> dotnet add package Serilog.Sinks.MSSqlServer --version 6.0.0
```

TIP The versions are the latest stable versions available at the time of this writing. I strongly suggest using them as well to avoid having to deal with breaking changes, incompatibility problems, and the like.

7.4.3   Configuring Serilog

Configuration takes place in the Program.cs file of our app. We're going to use the UseSerilog extension method, provided by the Serilog.AspNetCore package, which will set Serilog as the main logging provider and set up the SQL Server sink with some basic settings. Open the Program.cs file, and add the following lines of code below the builder.Logging configuration settings we added earlier:

```
builder.Logging                    ◁─── Built-in
    .ClearProviders()                    logging provider
    .AddSimpleConsole()                  configuration
    .AddDebug()
    .AddApplicationInsights(
      telemetry => telemetry.ConnectionString =
        builder
          .Configuration["Azure:ApplicationInsights:ConnectionString"],
        loggerOptions => { });

builder.Host.UseSerilog((ctx, lc) => {        ◁─── Serilog
    lc.ReadFrom.Configuration(ctx.Configuration);      configuration
    lc.WriteTo.MSSqlServer(
      connectionString:
        ctx.Configuration.GetConnectionString("DefaultConnection"),
      sinkOptions: new MSSqlServerSinkOptions
      {
        TableName = "LogEvents",
        AutoCreateSqlTable = true
      });
    },
    writeToProviders: true);
```

This code requires us to add the following namespace references at the top of the file:

```
using Serilog;
using Serilog.Sinks.MSSqlServer;
```

Notice that we specified the same SQL Server connection string that we're using with EF Core. We did that because in this scenario, we want to use the same MyBGList database we're already using to store the board-game-related data.

NOTE Theoretically speaking, we could enforce a separation-of-concerns approach and create a dedicated logging database. Both approaches are perfectly viable, although they have pros and cons that could make them more or less viable in various circumstances. For simplicity, we'll assume that keeping everything in a single database is a valid choice for our scenario.

If we look at the code, we see that we named the table that will host the log records ("LogEvents"). Moreover, we configured the SQL Server sink to autocreate it in case it doesn't exist. This feature is a great built-in feature of that sink because it allows us to delegate the task without having to create the table manually, which would involve the risk of choosing the wrong data types. The autogenerated table will have the following structure:

```
[Id] [int] IDENTITY(1,1) NOT NULL
[Message] [nvarchar](max) NULL
[MessageTemplate] [nvarchar](max) NULL
[Level] [nvarchar](max) NULL
[TimeStamp] [datetime] NULL
[Exception] [nvarchar](max) NULL
[Properties] [nvarchar](max) NULL
```

Last but not least, we set the writeToProviders parameter to true. This option ensures that Serilog will pass the log events not only to its sinks, but also to the logging providers registered through the Microsoft.Extensions.Logging API, such as the built-in providers we configured earlier. This setting defaults to false because the Serilog default behavior is to shut down these providers and replace them with the equivalent Serilog sinks. We don't want to enforce this behavior, however, because we want to see how the built-in and third-party logging providers can be configured to work side by side. The configuration part is over, for the most part; now it's time to test what we've done so far.

7.4.4 Testing Serilog

Again, launch the MyBGList project in Debug mode, and execute the /BoardGame endpoint to trigger some log events. This time, instead of looking at the command-prompt output, we need to launch SQL Server Management Studio (SSMS) and connect to the MyBGList database. If everything worked properly, we should see a brand-new LogEvents table filled with structured event logs, as shown in figure 7.5.

If we take a closer look at the log events recorded in the table (in the bottom-right part of figure 7.5), we even see the log record related to the "custom" log event entry that we added to the BoardGameController. Our test was a success. We have a structured logging engine that records our log entries within our database.

7.4.5 Improving the logging behavior

In this section, we'll see how we can further improve our Serilog-based structured logging behavior with some of the many features provided by the library: adding columns, configuring the minimum logging level, customizing the log messages by using the Serilog template syntax, enriching our logs, and adding sinks.

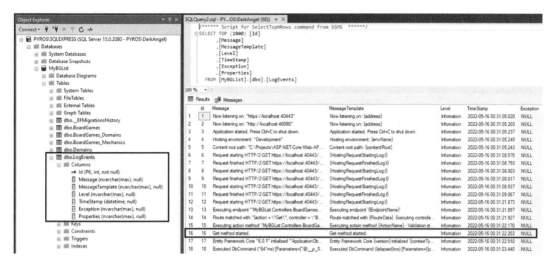

Figure 7.5 `LogEvents` **table filled with event logs**

ADDING COLUMNS

If we take a closer look at the log entries that fill the `LogEvents` table by using SSMS (figure 7.5), we notice that something is missing: columns to store the log record's source context (the namespace of the class that originated it) or the `EventId`. The reason is simple: instead of recording these values in dedicated columns, Serilog stores them in the `Properties` column. If we look at that column's value for our custom log entry, we see that both values are there, wrapped in an XML structure together with other properties (nonrelevant parts omitted):

```
<propertykey='EventId'>
  <structure type=''>
    <property key='Id'>
      50110
    </property>
  </structure>
</property>
<property key='SourceContext'>
  MyBGList.Controllers.BoardGamesController
</property>
```

Property value

Property name

Notice that `EventId` is a complex property because it can contain values of different types (`int`, `string`, and so on), whereas the `SourceContext` property hosts a simple `string` (the namespace of the class that originated the log record). Having these values stored within this XML semistructured format could be good enough for most scenarios. But Serilog also allows us to store these properties in their own individual columns. These features are enabled through an optional `columnOptions` parameter that can be specified in the configuration settings, so we can add a collection of `AdditionalColumns` and map them to these properties.

Suppose that we want to store the `SourceContext` property in a dedicated column. Here's how we can use the `columnOptions` parameter to do that:

```
builder.Host.UseSerilog((ctx, lc) => {
    lc.ReadFrom.Configuration(ctx.Configuration);
    lc.WriteTo.MSSqlServer(
        connectionString:
            ctx.Configuration.GetConnectionString("DefaultConnection"),
        sinkOptions: new MSSqlServerSinkOptions
        {
            TableName = "LogEvents",
            AutoCreateSqlTable = true
        },
        columnOptions: new ColumnOptions()          ⟵  Configures the
        {                                                columnOptions
            AdditionalColumns = new SqlColumn[]          optional parameter
            {
                new SqlColumn()
      Adds a column for   ⟶  {
      the SourceContext           ColumnName = "SourceContext",
      property                    PropertyName = "SourceContext",
                                  DataType = System.Data.SqlDbType.NVarChar
                }
            }
        }
    );
    },
    writeToProviders: true);
```

Now we need to delete the `LogEvents` table from the `MyBGList` database so that Serilog will be able to regenerate it with the new `SourceContext` column. Then we need to launch the `MyBGList` project in Debug mode, visit the `/BoardGame` endpoint to trigger the log records, and view the result in SSMS.

If everything worked as expected, we should see the new `SourceContext` column with the various namespaces, as shown in figure 7.6. (Don't worry if you can't read the text; the figure shows only where to find the new column.)

Figure 7.6   `LogEvents` table with the new SourceContext column

Now that we can look at these namespaces, we notice another problem. Why are we logging those log records with an `Information` level coming from the `Microsoft` `.AspNetCore` namespace? If we look at the `appsettings.Development.json` file, we see that we opted them out, using the `Logging:LogLevel` configuration key:

```
"Logging": {
  "LogLevel": {
    "Default": "Information",
    "Microsoft.AspNetCore": "Warning"
    "MyBGList": "Debug"
  }
},
```

The bold line clearly shows that we excluded all event logs with a `LogLevel` lower than `Warning`, which includes `Information` logs. If that's the case, why are we still logging them?

The answer is simple. Although Serilog can be configured via the `appsettings` `.json` file(s), like the built-in logging providers, it uses its own configuration section, which also replaces the `Logging` section used by the default logger implementation.

> **NOTE** The `Logging:LogLevel` section that we've had in our `appsettings.json` file(s) since chapter 2 is now useless, to the point that we could remove it (unless we want to disable Serilog and roll back to the default logger). That said, we'll keep that section for reference purposes.

The new configuration section is called "`Serilog`" and has a slightly different syntax. In the next section, we'll see how we can configure it.

Configuring the minimumLevel

To mimic the same `LogLevel` behavior that we configured in the `Logging` section, we need to add a new top-level "`Serilog`" section to the `appsettings.json` file below the existing "`Logging`" section. Here's how:

```
"Logging": {
  // omissis...
},
"Serilog": {
  "MinimumLevel": {
    "Default": "Warning",
    "Override": {
      "MyBGList": "Information"
    }
  }
}
```

Here is the corresponding section for the `appsettings.Development.json` file:

```
"Logging": {
  // omissis...
},
```

```
"Serilog": {
  "MinimumLevel": {
    "Default": "Information",
    "Override": {
      "Microsoft.AspNetCore": "Warning",
      "MyBGList": "Debug"
    }
  }
}
```

The `MinimumLevel` could also be configured programmatically in the `Program.cs` file (option-based approach) in the following way:

```
builder.Host.UseSerilog((ctx, lc) => {                                    Default
    lc.MinimumLevel.Is(Serilog.Events.LogEventLevel.Warning);   ◁────┐   MinimumLevel
    lc.MinimumLevel.Override(                                    ◁──  │   value
        "MyBGList", Serilog.Events.LogEventLevel.Information);        │

                                                        Overrides value for
    // ... omissis ...                                    specific sources
```

As we can see, we can configure a default behavior for all log event sources and then some namespace-based overrides, like the default logger settings.

> **WARNING** To determine the log level, Serilog doesn't use the `Microsoft` `.Extensions.Logging.LogLevel` enum. It uses the proprietary `Serilog.Events` `.LogEventLevel` enum, which features slightly different names: `Verbose`, `Debug`, `Information`, `Warning`, `Error`, and `Fatal`. The most relevant difference between the two enums is the absence of `Trace` and `None` in the Serilog counterpart, as well as the `Critical` level, which has been renamed `Fatal`.

The settings specified in the `MinimumLevel` section will be applied to all sinks. If we need to override them for a specific sink, we can use the `restrictedToMinimumLevel` setting in the `appsettings.json` files (configuration-based approach) in the following way:

```
"Serilog": {
  "WriteTo": [{
    "Name": "MSSqlServer",                              Sets up a minimum
    "Args": {                                           LogEventLevel for
      "restrictedToMinimumLevel": "Warning",   ◁──┘    this sink
    }
  }]
}
```

Or we can use the `Program.cs` file (option-based approach) in the following way:

```
lc.WriteTo.MSSqlServer(
    restrictedToMinimumLevel:                      ◁──┐   Sets up a minimum
        Serilog.Events.LogEventLevel.Information         LogEventLevel for
                                                         this sink
    // ... omissis ...
```

For our sample project, we'll keep the default behavior for all sinks. Therefore, we won't use the `restrictedToMinimumLevel` setting within our code.

MESSAGE TEMPLATE SYNTAX

Now that we've restored the logging level configuration, we can explore another great Serilog feature: the extended message template syntax. The default logger syntax provides an overload that allows us to use the standard .NET composite formatting feature, meaning that instead of writing this

```
_logger.LogInformation(CustomLogEvents.BoardGamesController_Get,
    "Get method started at " + DateTime.Now.ToString("HH:mm"));
```

we could write something like this

```
_logger.LogInformation(CustomLogEvents.BoardGamesController_Get,
    "Get method started at {0}", DateTime.Now.ToString("HH:mm"));
```

or this:

```
_logger.LogInformation(CustomLogEvents.BoardGamesController_Get,
    "Get method started at {0:HH:mm}", DateTime.Now);
```

The .NET composing formatting feature is powerful, but it has major drawbacks in terms of readability, especially when we have a lot of placeholders. For this reason, this feature is often neglected in favor of string interpolation (introduced in C# version 6), which provides a more readable, convenient syntax for formatting strings. Here's how we can implement the same logging entry as before by using string interpolation:

```
_logger.LogInformation(CustomLogEvents.BoardGamesController_Get,
    $"Get method started at {DateTime.Now:HH:mm}");
```

> **TIP**   For additional info about the .NET composing formatting feature, check out http://mng.bz/eJBq. For additional info regarding the C# string interpolation feature, see http://mng.bz/pdZw.

Serilog extends the .NET composing formatting feature with a message template syntax that not only fixes the readability problem, but also provides additional advantages. The fastest way to understand how the improved syntax works is to see how we could use it to write the previous log entry:

```
_logger.LogInformation(CustomLogEvents.BoardGamesController_Get,
    "Get method started at {StartTime:HH:mm}.", DateTime.Now);
```

As we can see, the message template syntax allows us to use string-based placeholders instead of numeric ones, which improves readability. But that's not all: all the placeholders will also be treated (and stored) as properties automatically, so we'll find them in the `Properties` column (within the XML structure). This convenient feature can be useful for performing query-based lookups within the log table, because all these values would be recorded in a semistructured (XML) fashion.

> **TIP** We could even store the values in dedicated columns by using the `column-Options` configuration parameter, as we did with `SourceContext` earlier, thus having them recorded in a structured way.

Thanks to this powerful placeholder-to-property feature, writing log messages with the Serilog's message template syntax is generally preferable to writing them with the C# string interpolation feature.

ADDING ENRICHERS

Now that we know the basics of Serilog's templating features, we can give our log records additional information regarding the application's context by using some of the enrichers provided by Serilog. Suppose that we want to add the following info to our logs:

- The name of the executing machine (equivalent to `%COMPUTERNAME%` for Windows systems or `$HOSTNAME` for macOS and Linux systems)
- The unique ID of the executing thread

To fulfill this request, we could write our log message(s) in the following way:

```
_logger.LogInformation(CustomLogEvents.BoardGamesController_Get,
    "Get method started [{MachineName}] [{ThreadId}].",          Adds
    Environment.MachineName,                                     placeholders
    Environment.CurrentManagedThreadId);
                                              Retrieves the
                          Retrieves the       MachineName
                          ThreadId
```

This approach retrieves these values and—thanks to the placeholder-to-property feature provided by the message template syntax—records them in the log record's `Properties` column. But we would be forced to repeat this code for every log entry. Furthermore, those values will also be present in the `Message` column, whether we want them there or not.

The purpose of Serilog's enrichers is to achieve the same outcome in a transparent way. To implement them, we need to install the following NuGet packages:

```
> dotnet add package Serilog.Enrichers.Environment --version 2.2.0
> dotnet add package Serilog.Enrichers.Thread --version 3.1.0
```

Then we can activate them, modifying the Serilog configuration in the `Program.cs` file in the following way (nonrelevant part omitted):

```
builder.Host.UseSerilog((ctx, lc) => {
    lc.ReadFrom.Configuration(ctx.Configuration);
    lc.Enrich.WithMachineName();                    Adds the Environment
    lc.Enrich.WithThreadId();                       enricher
```

Adds the
Thread
enricher

Now the `MachineName` and `ThreadId` properties will be created automatically in all our log records. Again, we can choose between keeping them in the `Properties` columns (semistructured) or store them in a structured format by adding a couple of columns, as we did for `SourceContext`.

ADDING OTHER SINKS

Before completing our Serilog journey, let's add another sink. Suppose that we want to write our log events to a custom text file. We can implement this requirement easily by using Serilog.Sinks.File, a sink that writes log events to one or more customizable text files. As always, the first thing to do is install the relevant NuGet package:

```
> dotnet add package Serilog.Sinks.File --version 5.0.0
```

Next, open the `Program.cs` file, and add the sink to the Serilog configuration in the following way:

```
builder.Host.UseSerilog((ctx, lc) => {
    lc.ReadFrom.Configuration(ctx.Configuration);
    lc.Enrich.WithMachineName();
    lc.Enrich.WithThreadId();
    lc.WriteTo.File("Logs/log.txt",              ⟵┐  Adds the sink,
                                                    │  specifying a file
                                                    │  path and name
        rollingInterval: RollingInterval.Day);   ⟵┐
                                                    │  Configures
                                                    │  the sink
    // ... non-relevant parts omitted ...
```

These settings will instruct the sink to create a `log.txt` file in the /Logs/ folder (creating it if it doesn't exist) with a rolling interval of one day. The *rolling interval* is the interval at which the sink will create a new file to store the logs. An interval of one day means that we'll have a single file for each day.

> **NOTE** The rolling interval also influences the filenames, because the sink— per its default behavior—will timestamp them accordingly. Our log filenames will be `log<yyyyMMdd>.txt`, such as `log20220518.txt`, `log20220519.txt`, and the like.

All we need to do to test the sink is launch our project in Debug mode, wait for it to load, and then check out the project's root folder. If everything went as expected, we should find a new /Logs/ folder containing a `log<yyyyMMdd>.txt` file with the logs formatted in the following way:

```
2022-05-18 04:07:57.736 +02:00 [INF]
    Now listening on: https://localhost:40443
2022-05-18 04:07:57.922 +02:00 [INF]
    Now listening on: http://localhost:40080
2022-05-18 04:07:57.934 +02:00 [INF]
    Application started. Press Ctrl+C to shut down.
2022-05-18 04:07:57.939 +02:00 [INF]
    Hosting environment: Development
```

The log entries are written by means of the default output template provided by the sink. If we want to customize the default template, we can use the `outputTemplate` configuration property. Suppose that we want to include the `MachineName` and `ThreadId` properties with which we enriched our logs a short while ago. Here's how we can achieve that:

```
lc.WriteTo.File("Logs/log.txt",
    outputTemplate:                                    ◁──┐   Defines a
        "{Timestamp:HH:mm:ss} [{Level:u3}] " +              custom output
        "[{MachineName} #{ThreadId}] " +                    template
        "{Message:lj}{NewLine}{Exception}",             ──┘
    rollingInterval: RollingInterval.Day);
```

The custom template results in the following outcome:

```
04:35:11 [INF] [PYROS #1] Now listening on: https://localhost:40443
04:35:11 [INF] [PYROS #1] Now listening on: http://localhost:40080
04:35:11 [INF] [PYROS #1] Application started. Press Ctrl+C to shut down.
04:35:11 [INF] [PYROS #1] Hosting environment: Development
```

As we can see, now the `MachineName` and `ThreadId` property values are present in each log entry.

> **TIP** For reasons of space, I won't dig further into Serilog. To find additional info about it, as well as its enrichers, sinks, and message template syntax, check out the library official wiki at https://github.com/serilog/serilog/wiki.

7.5   *Exercises*

It's time to challenge ourselves with the usual list of hypothetical task assignments given by our product owner.

> **NOTE** The solutions to the exercises are available on GitHub in the `/Chapter_ 07/Exercises/` folder. To test them, replace the relevant files in your `MyBG- List` project with those in that folder, and run the app.

7.5.1   *JSON console logging*

Replace the built-in simple console logging provider with the built-in JSON console logging provider.

7.5.2   *Logging provider configuration*

Set the JSON console logging provider's `TimeStampFormat` to log only hours and minutes (without seconds), using the UTC time zone and the options-based approach.

7.5.3   *Exception logging's new property*

In the exception handler Minimal API method, add a new `errorMessage` custom property to the error log message, using Serilog's message template syntax. The new property must contain the exception's `Message` value.

7.5.4 New Serilog enricher

Enrich the current log configuration by adding the `ThreadName` property. Then modify Serilog's file sink so that the `ThreadName` value will be written right after the `ThreadId` value, separated by a space.

7.5.5 New Serilog sink

Add another file sink below the existing one, with the following requirements:

- *Filename*—`/Logs/errors.txt`
- *Output template*—Same as the existing file sink
- *Log level to record*—`Error` and `Fatal` only
- *Rolling interval*—Daily

Summary

- *Logging* is the process of keeping track of all the events occurring within the application in a structured, semistructured, and/or unstructured format and sending them to one or more display and/or storage channels.
  - The term originated in the nautical field and has been used in IT since the 1960s.
- Application logging allows us to detect and fix bugs, unhandled exceptions, errors, and vulnerabilities, thus improving the stability and security of our apps.
  - Moreover, it greatly helps us identify abnormal behaviors before they become critical, which can be crucial for business continuity.
  - Furthermore, it's a requirement for most international IT security regulations, standards, and guidelines.
- The .NET Framework provides standardized, general-purpose logging APIs through the `Microsoft.Extensions.Logging` package and the `ILogger` interface, which allows us to record the events and activities we want to log through a series of built-in and/or third-party logging providers.
- Most of the .NET built-in providers store log events by using raw strings (unstructured format). Although this logging technique has some benefits, it's far from ideal, especially for dealing with a large amount of log records.
  - When that's the case, switching to a structured format is often wise, as it allows us to query those records for relevant info instead of having to parse and/or process them.
- Adopting a structured logging strategy in .NET is possible thanks to the Azure Application Insights logging provider, available through an external NuGet package maintained by Microsoft.
  - Application Insights works only within the Azure ecosystem, however, which can be a hindrance in terms of accessibility and customization.

- A great alternative way to implement structured logging in .NET is Serilog, an open source logging library for .NET applications available on NuGet.
  - Serilog can be used to store application logs in several popular DBMSes, as well as third-party services and other destinations.
  - The storage destination(s) can be defined by using a modular architecture built around *sinks*—sets of output handlers that can be installed and configured independently.
- Other notable Serilog features include
  - Additional columns, which can be used to add other structured properties to the log event table.
  - Enrichers, which extend the log data with other context info.
  - A powerful message template syntax, which allows us to customize the log messages and properties in a convenient, readable way.

Caching techniques

8

This chapter covers

- Caching overview
- HTTP response caching (client-side, intermediate, and server-side)
- In-memory caching
- Distributed caching (using SQL Server or Redis)

In information technology, the term *cache* describes a hardware component or a software mechanism that can be used to store data so that future requests that require such data can be served faster and—most important—without being retrieved from scratch. Good caching practices often result in performance benefits, lower latency, less CPU overhead, reduced bandwidth use, and decreased costs.

Based on this definition, we can understand that adopting and implementing a caching strategy can create many invaluable optimization advantages. These advantages are especially important for web applications and services (including web APIs), which often have to deal with recurring requests targeting the same resources, such as the same HTML page(s) or JSON result(s) accessed by multiple users. But introducing a caching mechanism also adds some complexity to our code and might easily cause unwanted side effects when we don't implement it properly.

Chapter 3 introduced the concept of caching, talking about server-side, client-side, and intermediate caching. This chapter expands those concepts and puts them in action with some implementation strategies. We'll start with a brief overview of the main benefits and downsides that caching can introduce. Then we'll learn how to use several caching mechanisms, natively provided by .NET and ASP.NET Core, that can implement caching on various levels:

- *Client-side and intermediate HTTP response caching*—Through HTTP response headers
- *Server-side HTTP response caching*—Using the `ResponseCachingMiddleware`
- *In-memory caching*—Using the `IMemoryCache` interface
- *Distributed caching*—Using the `IDistributedCache` interface

8.1   *Caching overview*

The first question we should ask ourselves before starting to code is what we should cache to begin with. This question isn't easy to answer, because choosing what to cache strongly depends on how our web application is meant to work—to put it even more clearly, what kind of client interactions (requests) it's meant to handle. Consider some common scenarios:

- A static website, which mostly relies on HTML, CSS, JS, and images, should typically focus on HTTP caching, possibly at the browser level and/or via a content-delivery network (CDN) because the server doesn't do much more than serve static resources. In other words, it requires client-side and/or intermediate HTTP response caching.
- A dynamic website, such as a WordPress blog, should focus on client-side and/or intermediate HTTP response caching, as it serves several static resources, and most of its HTML content (past blog articles) isn't subject to frequent changes. Because the web pages are built using PHP and data retrieved from a database management system (DBMS), however, it could benefit from server-side HTTP response, as well as in-memory and/or distributed caching for some expensive and/or highly recurrent DBMS queries.
- A RESTful web API, such as our `MyBGList` project, should use HTTP response caching to optimize the most frequently accessed `GET` endpoints and/or those that come with the default parameters. But because we can reasonably expect that most clients will configure their requests to retrieve only specific data (or only the data they're allowed to fetch, as we'll see in chapter 9), a good in-memory and/or distributed server-side caching strategy to relieve the burden on our DBMS could be even more relevant.

DEFINITION   A *content-delivery network* (*CDN*) is a geographically distributed network of proxy servers that can be used as a service to provide high availability and increase the performance of the content.

In a nutshell, when developing our caching strategy, we should always consider what we can reasonably expect from the clients and how these requests affect our web application's architecture. As a general rule, we should always aim to cache at the highest level we can get away with: HTTP response caching for static assets and frequently called endpoints that return the same response, in-memory or distributed caching to reduce DBMS calls. That said, a well-crafted web application often adopts a combination of all the preceding techniques to deal with the needs of each of its various sections in the best possible way.

8.2 HTTP response caching

As we've known since chapter 1, cacheability is one of the six guiding constraints of representational state transfer (REST):

> *Cache constraints require that the data within a response to a request be implicitly or explicitly labeled as cacheable or non-cacheable. If a response is cacheable, then a client cache is given the right to reuse that response data for later, equivalent requests.* (Roy Fielding's REST dissertation, 5.1.4; http://mng.bz/qdPK)

This small quote summarizes what we need to do to implement a proper HTTP response caching strategy. We already did that in chapter 3, when we introduced the [ResponseCache] attribute (part of the `Microsoft.AspNetCore.Mvc` namespace) and implemented it in several controller and Minimal API methods. Here's what we used in our controller's Get methods to label their responses as *cacheable*:

```
[ResponseCache(Location = ResponseCacheLocation.Any, Duration = 60)]
```

And we have labeled several other responses as *noncacheable*:

```
[ResponseCache(NoStore = true)]
```

The [ResponseCache] attribute is a convenient way to set the cache-control HTTP response header's directives, required by the HTTP 1.1 caching specifications (RFC 7234). These directives are honored by clients and intermediate proxies, fulfilling the REST constraint's requirements. Now, because we have used this header in all our controller's methods, we can proudly say that our MyBGList web API is already compliant with the cacheability constraint. Yay! Next, let's see how we can improve our current implementation.

8.2.1 Setting the cache-control header manually

The first question we should ask is whether we could set the cache-control header manually instead of relying on the [ResponseCache] attribute. We can do this easily by using the Response.Headers collection provided by the HttpContext, which happens to be writable. To demonstrate, add a new Minimal API method to the Program.cs file that uses it (listing 8.1).

```
app.MapGet("/cache/test/1",
    [EnableCors("AnyOrigin")]
    (HttpContext context) =>
    {
        context.Response.Headers["cache-control"] =        Sets the cache-
            "no-cache, no-store";                          control header
        return Results.Ok();
    });
```

This method handles the /cache/test/1 endpoint, adding a cache-control header's directive identical to the one added by the [ResponseCache(NoStore = true)] that we've used elsewhere. Setting such directives programmatically would be rather verbose, inconvenient, and hard to maintain, however. The [ResponseCache] attribute may be a better alternative unless we have specific caching needs that aren't supported by the high-level abstraction it provides.

8.2.2   *Adding a default caching directive*

Our REST cacheability constraint compliance relies on applying the [ResponseCache] attribute to all our controller and Minimal API methods. If we forget to use it somewhere, the corresponding response will have no cache-control header. We can easily test it by creating a second Minimal API caching test method without specifying any caching strategy:

```
app.MapGet("/cache/test/2",
    [EnableCors("AnyOrigin")]
    (HttpContext context) =>
    {
        return Results.Ok();
    });
```

Add this method to the Program.cs file, right below code listing 8.1. Then perform the following tasks:

1 Launch the project in Debug mode.
2 Open the browser's Development Tools panel by pressing F12.
3 Select the Network tab.
4 Navigate to the /cache/test/2 endpoint.
5 Check out the HTTP response headers on the Network tab.

We won't find any cache-control header for that response. Although this behavior isn't considered to be a direct violation of the constraint requirements, it's widely considered to be a data-security vulnerability because it leaves clients (and intermediate proxies) free to choose whether to cache the received content, which could contain sensitive information (passwords, credit cards, personal data, and so on). To avoid this problem, it may be wise to define a default caching directive that kicks in every time we don't use the [ResponseCache] attribute but is overwritten wherever that attribute is present—in other words, a fallback mechanism.

IMPLEMENTING A NO-CACHE DEFAULT BEHAVIOR

Suppose that we want to implement a no-cache default directive for our MyBGList web API that should kick in whenever the [ResponseCache] attribute isn't explicitly set. We can add to our app's HTTP pipeline custom middleware that will set the cache-control header by using the programmatic approach we used a while ago. Open the Program.cs file, scroll down to the line where we added the AuthorizationMiddleware, and add the code in the following listing below that line.

Listing 8.2 `Program.cs` file: Custom caching middleware

```
App.UseAuthorization();

app.Use((context, next) =>
{
    context.Response.Headers["cache-control"] =
        "no-cache, no-store";
    return next.Invoke();
});
```

Adds a default cache-control directive

This task is the first time we've implemented custom middleware—an easy task thanks to the Use extension method. We specify what to do with the HttpContext (and/or other injected services) and then pass the HTTP request to the next component in the pipeline.

> **NOTE** We've implemented nonblocking middleware, because we're passing the HTTP request to the subsequent component instead of terminating the pipeline (and providing an HTTP response), as blocking middleware would do. We saw this difference in chapter 1, which introduced blocking and non-blocking middleware.

TESTING THE NO-CACHE FALLBACK BEHAVIOR

To test our new caching fallback custom middleware, launch the project in Debug mode, and repeat the test that we performed a moment ago. This time, we should find the cache-control header with the no-cache, no-store fallback directive that we set up.

Now let's check whether the fallback strategy is overwritten by the [RequestCache] attribute (when present). Repeat the test, this time using the /BoardGames GET endpoint instead. If everything works as expected, we should find the cache-control header directive specified by the [RequestCache] attribute that we used for the BoardGamesController's Get action method,

```
cache-control: public,max-age=60
```

which confirms that our no-cache fallback behavior works as expected.

USING STRONGLY TYPED HEADERS

Now that we know that our custom middleware works, let's refine it. A potential weakness that we can spot by looking at the code is that we're taking a literal approach to setting the response header—an approach that's subject to human error. To improve this aspect, we can use the `GetTypedHeaders` method provided by the `HttpContext`
`.Response` object, which allows access to the response headers via a strongly typed approach. The following listing shows how we can update our current implementation by replacing those strings with strongly typed values.

> Listing 8.3   `Program.cs` file: Custom caching middleware (updated)

```
app.Use((context, next) =>                                       Uses the
{                                                                GetTypedHeaders
    context.Response.GetTypedHeaders().CacheControl =    ◁──┘    method
            new Microsoft.Net.Http.Headers.CacheControlHeaderValue()
            {
                NoCache = true,        Configures the cache settings
                NoStore = true         using strongly typed values
            };
    return next.Invoke();
});
```

The new code not only looks better, but also prevents us from having to type the headers manually, eliminating the risk of mistyping them.

8.2.3   *Defining cache profiles*

Thanks to the no-cache fallback behavior that we've set, we don't have to add a `[ResponseCache]` attribute to all our controller and Minimal API methods that we don't want our clients (and intermediate proxies) to cache. But we still have to duplicate these attributes whenever we want to configure different caching behavior. A good example is the `Get` methods of our `BoardGamesController`, `DomainsController`, and `Mechanics-Controller`, which repeat the `[ResponseCache]` attribute multiple times:

```
[ResponseCache(Location = ResponseCacheLocation.Any, Duration = 60)]
```

This approach is far from ideal, especially considering that the number of our controllers will likely increase over time. We likely want to centralize these directives to keep our codebase more DRY (Don't Repeat Yourself) and easier to maintain. We can achieve this goal by using cache profiles. This convenient `ControllerMiddleware` configuration option allows us to set up some predefined caching directives and then apply them by using a convenient name-based reference instead of repeating them. Let's test this neat feature by adding two cache profiles with the following names and behaviors:

- *NoCache*—Use whenever we want to prevent any client or intermediate proxy from caching the response.
- *Any-60*—Use when we want to tell everyone (clients and intermediate proxies) to cache the response for 60 seconds.

Open the `Program.cs` file, locate the line where we added the `ControllerMiddleware` by means of the `AddControllers` extension method, and add the options in the following listing at the end of the existing configuration settings.

Listing 8.4 `Program.cs` file: Cache profiles

```
builder.Services.AddControllers(options => {

    // ... non-relevant code omitted ...

    options.CacheProfiles.Add("NoCache",              ⊲──┐  Adds the
        new CacheProfile() { NoStore = true });             "NoCache" profile
    options.CacheProfiles.Add("Any-60",              ⊲──┐  Adds the
        new CacheProfile()                                   "Any-60" profile
        {
            Location = ResponseCacheLocation.Any,
            Duration = 60
        });
});
```

Now that we have two centralized cache profiles, we can apply them throughout our controllers. Open the `BoardGamesController.cs` file, and scroll down to the `Get` action method. Then change the current implementation of the `[ResponseCache]` attribute, replacing the caching values with a reference to the `"Any-60"` caching profile in the following way:

```
[HttpGet(Name = "GetBoardGames")]
[ResponseCache(CacheProfileName = "Any-60")]     ⊲──  Adds a reference to
public async Task<RestDTO<BoardGame[]>> Get(          the cache profile
```

To test what we've done, perform the following steps:

1 Launch the project in Debug mode.
2 Open the browser's Network tab.
3 Navigate to the /GetBoardGames endpoint.
4 Check out the `cache-control` header value.

If we did everything correctly, we should see the same directive that we had before:

```
cache-control: public,max-age=60
```

The only difference is that now the values are taken from the `"Any-60"` cache profile, meaning that we successfully centralized them. Now we can apply this technique to all our controllers, replacing the values of all the existing `[ResponseCache]` attributes with the name of the corresponding cache profile:

```
                                                          Use this to
                                                          prevent caching.
[ResponseCache(CacheProfileName = "NoCache")]     ⊲──┘
[ResponseCache(CacheProfileName = "Any-60")]      ⊲──  Use this to enforce 60-second
                                                          caching for anyone.
```

TIP   Technically speaking, instead of using the "NoCache" cache profile, we could remove the attribute and let our no-cache fallback behavior take care of the action methods we don't want to cache. But we won't do that. The fall-back is meant to act as a safety net against human errors, not to handle our standard caching settings.

8.2.4   *Server-side response caching*

When used alone, the [ResponseCache] attribute will take care of setting the appro-priate caching HTTP headers depending on the parameters being set for it. In other words, it handles HTTP response caching only for clients and intermediate proxies. But ASP.NET Core has a built-in component that can store the HTTP responses in a dedicated internal cache repository and serve them from that cache instead of reexe-cuting the controller's (or Minimal API's) methods. The name of this component is *response-caching middleware*. In the following sections, we'll see how we can add it to our application's pipeline and use it to implement server-side HTTP request caching.

UNDERSTANDING THE RESPONSE-CACHING MIDDLEWARE

The response-caching middleware allows our ASP.NET Core app to cache its own responses according to the same caching directives specified in the response headers by the [ResponseCache] attribute or by any other means. So we can say that it per-forms its caching job like an intermediate reverse proxy or a CDN service except that it runs on the server side instead of being an intermediate layer.

> **NOTE**   The middleware runs on the same server that hosts the ASP.NET Core application itself—not a trivial problem, because one of the main benefits of intermediate caching services (such as reverse proxies and CDNs) is that they're located elsewhere to avoid burdening the web server with additional overhead. This fact is important to consider when we choose whether to use this middleware, as we're going to see in a short while.

The fact that the response-caching middleware uses the HTTP response headers also means that when it's enabled, it seamlessly stacks on what we've already done. We don't have to specify additional caching settings or profiles unless we want to.

> **TIP**   The response-caching middleware will cache only HTTP responses using GET or HEAD methods and resulting in a 200 - OK status code. It ignores any other responses, including error pages.

ADDING SERVICES AND MIDDLEWARE

Setting up the response-caching middleware in our MyBGList web API requires us to add two lines to the app's Program.cs file. The first line adds the required services to the service collection. We can do this after all the existing services, right before the app's building phase, as shown in the following code snippet:

```
builder.Services.AddResponseCaching();          ◁┐  Adds the response-caching
                                                 │  middleware services
var app = builder.Build();
```

Scroll down to the line where we added the Cross-Origin Resource Sharing (CORS) middleware. Then add the response-caching middleware, using the convenient extension method in the following way:

```
app.UseCors();

app.UseResponseCaching();          Adds the response-
                                   caching middleware
```

NOTE To work, the CORS middleware must be called after the response-caching middleware.

CONFIGURING THE MIDDLEWARE

Thanks to these changes, our MyBGList web API is equipped with a server-side HTTP response caching mechanism. Also, we're reserving part of local memory to store the results of our cached responses, which could negatively affect the performance of our app. To prevent memory-shortage problems, we can fine-tune the middleware's caching strategies by changing its default settings, using the following public properties provided by the ResponseCachingOptions class:

- MaximumBodySize—Specifies the maximum cacheable size for the response body, in bytes. The default value is 64 * 1024 * 1024 bytes (64 MB).
- SizeLimit—Represents the size limit for the response-cache middleware, in bytes. The default value is 100 * 1024 * 1024 bytes (100 MB).
- UseCaseSensitivePaths—If set to true, caches the responses by using case-sensitive paths. The default value is false.

Here's how we can use these properties to halve the default caching size limits:

```
builder.Services.AddResponseCaching(options =>
{
                                              Sets max response
    options.MaximumBodySize = 32 * 1024 * 1024;    body size to 32 MB
    options.SizeLimit = 50 * 1024 * 1024;
});                                           Sets max middleware
                                              size to 50 MB
```

TIP For further information on the response-caching middleware, see http:// mng.bz/GRDV.

8.2.5 *Response caching vs. client reload*

All the HTTP response caching techniques that we've reviewed so far implement standard HTTP caching semantics. Although this approach is great from a RESTful perspective, it has an important consequence that can easily be seen as a downside. These techniques don't only follow the response cache headers; they also honor the request cache headers, including the cache-control headers set by web browsers when their user issues a reload and/or force-reload action:

```
Cache header set by a browser's reload

    cache-control: max-age=0        Cache header set by a
    cache-control: no-cache         browser's force reload
```

As a result, all clients are perfectly able to bypass this kind of cache. This situation is great from clients' perspective because they can force our app to serve them fresh content whenever they want to. But it also means that the cache won't benefit us in terms of performance (and overhead reduction) if we receive several of these requests in a short period, including those generated by malicious attempts such as distributed denial-of-service (DDoS) attacks.

Unfortunately, ASP.NET doesn't provide a way to overcome this problem. The intended response-caching behavior can't be overridden or set up to ignore the HTTP request header. If we want to overcome the client's will and take control of what should and shouldn't be cached, we must rely on alternative approaches, such as using a reverse proxy, a third-party caching package (such as `AspNetCore.Cache-Output`), or any other component or service that can be set up to ignore the HTTP request headers at will.

Otherwise, we might think of integrating our response-caching strategies with other caching techniques that aren't based on HTTP headers. The following sections introduce some of those techniques and show how we can implement them alongside what we've done so far.

8.3   *In-memory caching*

As its name implies, *in-memory caching* is a .NET caching feature that allows us to store arbitrary data in local memory. The mechanism is based on the `IMemoryCache` interface, which can be injected as a service (following the standard dependency injection pattern that we should be used to by now) and exposes some convenient `Get` and `Set` methods to interact with the cache by retrieving and storing data.

> **NOTE** Technically speaking, even the server-side HTTP response caching strategy based on the response-caching middleware we implemented earlier uses the `IMemoryCache` interface to store its caching data.

The `IMemoryCache` interface is part of the `Microsoft.Extensions.Caching.Memory` namespace, maintained by Microsoft and shipped with a dedicated NuGet package included in most ASP.NET Core templates.

> **WARNING** The `IMemoryCache` interface and its `Microsoft.Extensions.Caching.Memory` namespace shouldn't be confused with `System.Runtime.Caching`, a different NuGet package that provides an alternative in-memory cache implementation made available through a different class with a similar name (`MemoryCache`). Although both implementations provide similar functionalities, the `IMemoryCache` interface works natively with the ASP.NET Core dependency injection design pattern; thus, it's the recommended approach for ASP.NET Core applications.

In the following sections, we'll see how we can implement in-memory caching in our `MyBGList` web API and explore some typical use scenarios.

8.3.1   Setting up the in-memory cache

Again, the first thing to do is set up and configure the `MemoryCache` services in the service collections. Open the `Program.cs` file, and add the following line after all the existing services, right before the app's building phase:

```
builder.Services.AddMemoryCache();          ◁── Adds the
                                                MemoryCache service
var app = builder.Build();
```

The extension method supports an additional overload to accept a `MemoryCacheOptions` object that can be used to configure some caching settings, such as the following:

- `ExpirationScanFrequency`—A `TimeSpan` value that defines the length of time between successive scans for expired items
- `SizeLimit`—The maximum size of the cache, in bytes
- `CompactionPercentage`—The amount to compact the cache by when the `SizeLimit` value is exceeded

For simplicity, we'll stick with the default values.

8.3.2   Injecting the IMemoryCache interface

Now that we've enabled the `MemoryCache` service, we can inject an `IMemoryCache` interface instance into our controllers. We'll do that in the `BoardGamesController`. Open the `BoardGamesController.cs` file, and add a reference to the interface's namespace at the top of the file:

```
using Microsoft.Extensions.Caching.Memory;
```

Right after that reference, add a new private, read-only `_memoryCache` property below the constructor, in the following way:

```
private readonly IMemoryCache _memoryCache;
```

This property will host the `IMemoryCache` instance; we need to inject it into in the constructor, as we did with the `ApplicationDbContext` in chapter 5. The following listing shows how.

Listing 8.5   `BoardGamesController: IMemoryCache`

```
public BoardGamesController(
    ApplicationDbContext context,
    ILogger<BoardGamesController> logger,
    IMemoryCache memoryCache)              ◁── Injects the
{                                             IMemoryCache
    _context = context;
    _logger = logger;
    _memoryCache = memoryCache;           ◁── Stores the instance
}                                             in the local variable
```

That's all we need to do to give our app in-memory cache capability. In the next section, we'll learn how to use it.

8.3.3   *Using the in-memory cache*

The IMemoryCache instance is a singleton object that can be used to store arbitrary data as key-value pairs. The great thing about it is that it can store all objects, even nonserializable ones. It can store a collection of model entities retrieved from the database by using Entity Framework Core (EF Core), for example. The following sections define a practical scenario based on this behavior.

IMPLEMENTING AN IN-MEMORY CACHING STRATEGY

Suppose that we want to cache the board-game array returned by EF Core within our current BoardGamesController's Get method for 30 seconds. Because that method can be called by using multiple parameters that will affect the returned data, we also need to find a way to create a different cache key for each request with different parameters to avoid the risk of returning wrong data. Here's what we need to do:

1 Create a cacheKey string variable based on the GET parameters.
2 Check out the _memoryCache instance to see whether a cache entry for that key is present.
3 If a cache entry is present, we use it instead of querying the database; otherwise, retrieve the data by using EF Core, and set the cache entry with an absolute expiration of 30 seconds.

The following listing shows how we can pull off this plan.

Listing 8.6   BoardGamesController's Get method

```
[HttpGet(Name = "GetBoardGames")]
[ResponseCache(CacheProfileName = "Any-60")]
public async Task<RestDTO<BoardGame[]>> Get(
    [FromQuery] RequestDTO<BoardGameDTO> input)
{
    _logger.LogInformation(CustomLogEvents.BoardGamesController_Get,
        "Get method started.");

    var query = _context.BoardGames.AsQueryable();
    if (!string.IsNullOrEmpty(input.FilterQuery))
        query = query.Where(b => b.Name.Contains(input.FilterQuery));

    var recordCount = await query.CountAsync();

    BoardGame[]? result = null;
    var cacheKey = $"{input.GetType()}-{JsonSerializer.Serialize(input)}";
    if (!_memoryCache.TryGetValue<BoardGame[]>(cacheKey, out result))
```

Retrieves the IQueryable → (points to `var query = _context.BoardGames.AsQueryable();`)

Applies the filterQuery (if present) → (points to filter lines)

Retrieves the record count from the database → (points to `var recordCount = await query.CountAsync();`)

Declares the local variable to store board-game data (points to `BoardGame[]? result = null;`)

Checks the in-memory cache for the presence of the cache key (points to TryGetValue line)

Creates a unique cache key by using the RequestDTO (points to cacheKey line)

```
{
  query = query
    .OrderBy($"{input.SortColumn} {input.SortOrder}")
    .Skip(input.PageIndex * input.PageSize)
  .Take(input.PageSize);
  result = await query.ToArrayAsync();
  _memoryCache.Set(cacheKey, result, new TimeSpan(0, 0, 30));
}

return new RestDTO<BoardGame[]>()
{
  Data = result,
  PageIndex = input.PageIndex,
  PageSize = input.PageSize,
  RecordCount = recordCount,
  Links = new List<LinkDTO> {
    new LinkDTO(
      Url.Action(
        null,
        "BoardGames",
        new { input.PageIndex, input.PageSize },
        Request.Scheme)!,
      "self",
      "GET"),
  }
};
}
```

If no cached data exists, retrieves it from DB (and caches it)

Sets the cached (or newly retrieved) data in the RestDTO

Notice that the new implementation, despite adding some complexity to the code, is still strongly based on the previous one. We added only the part to create the cache key and the "cache-or-query" logic to use EF Core conditionally (only if a suitable cache entry isn't present) instead of always using it.

As for the cacheKey definition, we created a unique string by concatenating the RequestDTO<BoardGame> type name and its JavaScript Object Notation (JSON) serialized representation. The type name is retrieved with the built-in GetType method, and the serialization is obtained by the Serialize method of the JsonSerializer static class, which is part of the System.Text.Json namespace. (Remember to add its reference at the top of the file.) That method creates a JSON string from the input data-transfer object (DTO). By concatenating these two strings, we've provided ourselves a simple yet effective way to create a unique key for each request.

The rest of the code is straightforward and should be easy to understand. The "cache-or-query" logic relies on the convenient IMemoryCache's TryGetValue<T> method, which returns true if the cache entry exists (while conditionally setting the output parameter with the retrieved value) and false if it doesn't.

TIP In this example, the <T> generic type could be omitted when using the TryGetValue method, because it will be inferred automatically from the result local variable. We chose to specify it explicitly to clarify the cache-retrieval process.

The best thing we can do to test our new caching strategy is place a couple of break-points within the source code: one on the line where we call the TryGetValue method, and another one on the line that (if no cached data is found) will execute the data-retrieval process from the database by using EF Core (figure 8.1).

```
49    BoardGame[]? result = null;
50    var cacheKey = $"{input.GetType()}-{JsonSerializer.Serialize(input)}";
51    if (!_memoryCache.TryGetValue<BoardGame[]>(cacheKey, out result))
52    {
53        query = query
54                .OrderBy($"{input.SortColumn} {input.SortOrder}")
55                .Skip(input.PageIndex * input.PageSize)
56                .Take(input.PageSize);
57        result = await query.ToArrayAsync();
58        _memoryCache.Set(cacheKey, result, new TimeSpan(0, 0, 30));
59    }
```

Figure 8.1   Setting up the breakpoints to test the in-memory cache

Ideally, we can expect the first breakpoint to be hit every time the server receives the request (that is, when the HTTP response cache doesn't kick in), and the second one should be hit only when the app has nothing in cache for the incoming request, which should happen only once every 30 seconds for each request with the same set of parameters. Conversely, if the cache entry is present, that part of the code shouldn't be executed.

When the breakpoints have been placed, we can launch our project in Debug mode and call the /BoardGames GET endpoint without parameters, so that the default parameters will be used. Now, because this request has never been called before, the IMemoryCache instance should have no cache entries for it. As a result, both break-points should be hit in sequence. (Press F5 or click the Continue button when the first breakpoint activates to stop on the second one, as shown in figure 8.2.)

```
49    BoardGame[]? result = null;
50    var cacheKey = $"{input.GetType()}-{JsonSerializer.Serialize(input)}";
51    if (!_memoryCache.TryGetValue<BoardGame[]>(cacheKey, out result))
52    {
53        query = query
54                .OrderBy($"{input.SortColumn} {input.SortOrder}")
55                .Skip(input.PageIndex * input.PageSize)
56                .Take(input.PageSize);
57        result = await query.ToArrayAsync();   ≤ 197ms elapsed
58        _memoryCache.Set(cacheKey, result, new TimeSpan(0, 0, 30));
59    }
```

Figure 8.2   Both breakpoints are being hit because there's nothing in cache for this request.

The fact that the first breakpoint has been hit is hardly a surprise; we know that it's expected to be hit on every request. The important thing to notice is that the second breakpoint is being hit as well. The controller will query the DBMS by using EF Core to retrieve the entries for the first time, as we expect it to do.

So far, so good. Press F5 or click Continue a second time to hop off the second breakpoint and resume the app's execution; then wait for the controller to return its response and for the browser to show the JSON outcome. When the JSON result with the board-games data fills the browser's window, press Ctrl+F5 (while focusing the browser) to clear the cache, thus issuing a forced page reload. Again, the first break-point should be hit, because the forced reload should invalidate both the client-side and server-side HTTP response caches and reach the controller's Get method. But if we press F5 or click Continue within 30 seconds of the previous request, this time the second breakpoint isn't likely to be hit, and we'll receive a second response, identical to the previous one, without having to query the DBMS.

If we repeat this test after 30 seconds or more, the in-memory cache should expire, meaning that both breakpoints will be hit again. This simple yet effective test is more than enough to confirm that our in-memory caching implementation works as expected. Now that we've tested the in-memory cache mechanism, we're ready to move to distributed caching.

8.4 Distributed caching

In-memory caching has several advantages over HTTP caching in terms of management and customization, because we have full control of what to cache and what not to cache. But this technique also has some unavoidable downsides, most of which depend on the fact that the cache storage resides in the server's local memory.

Although this situation isn't a problem when our web app is running on a single server, it becomes a major problem for apps running on a server farm (that is, on multiple servers). In this scenario, each cached entry will be available only within the single server that set it up; any other server won't be able to retrieve it and will have to create its own. As a result, each server will have its own local in-memory cache with different expiration times. This behavior, besides being a waste of memory, can lead to cache inconsistencies, because the same user might navigate across different servers that could respond with different cached data (having stored it at different times).

The best thing we can do to avoid these drawbacks is to replace the local in-memory cache mechanism with a shared caching repository that can be accessed by multiple servers—in other words, a distributed cache. Switching from a local cache to a distributed cache provides the following advantages:

- *Consisted cached data*—Because all servers retrieve them from the same source
- *Independent lifetime*—Because it doesn't depend on any web server (won't reset whenever we need to restart it)
- *Performance benefits*—Because it's typically implemented by a third-party service and won't consume a web server's local memory

NOTE Although the first advantage affects only apps that are running on multiple servers, the other two advantages are likely to benefit even one-server app scenarios.

In the following sections, we'll set up a distributed cache mechanism in our MyBGList project, starting with the in-memory caching implementation we already have.

8.4.1 *Distributed cache providers overview*

The first thing to do when we want to set up a distributed caching strategy is choose the cache provider—the external service that will host the cached data. When we're dealing with ASP.NET Core web apps, the challenge usually boils down to the following two major alternatives:

- *A DBMS (such as SQL Server)*—The most obvious choice, especially considering that most web apps (including our MyBGList web API) already use it for data storage purposes, so most of the required stuff is already set up
- *A distributed key-value store (such as Redis or NCache)*—Another popular choice, because those storage services are typically fast (Redis can perform up to 110K SETs and 81K GETs per second), easy to set up and maintain, and can scale out at will

With that in mind, we'll implement a distributed caching strategy by using a popular provider for both SQL Server and Redis. Each can be easily installed by adding a reference to its own NuGet package, which implements the IDistributedCache interface (part of the built-in Microsoft.Extensions.Caching.Distributed namespace). This interface, like ILogger, IMemoryCache, and many others that we've used in previous chapters, provides a common set of methods that we can use to set up, configure, and manage the cache provider.

8.4.2 *SQL Server*

To use the SQL Server distributed cache provider, we need to install the NuGet package Microsoft.Extensions.Caching.SqlServer. As always, we can use Visual Studio's NuGet graphical user interface (GUI), Visual Studio's Package Manager console, or the command-line interface (CLI). I'll take for granted that you know how to do that. Then open the Program.cs file, and set up the distributed caching provider, using the standard, service-based approach that you should be used to by now.

CONFIGURING THE SQL SERVER CACHE SERVICE

In the Program.cs file, scroll down to the point where we added the in-memory cache by using the AddMemoryCache extension method, and add the lines in listing 8.7 immediately below it.

Listing 8.7 `Program.cs` **file: Distributed SQL Server cache service**

```
builder.Services.AddDistributedSqlServerCache(options =>       ◁────  Adds the SQL
{                                                                     Server distributed
    options.ConnectionString =                                       cache provider
        builder.Configuration.GetConnectionString("DefaultConnection");
    options.SchemaName = "dbo";
    options.TableName = "AppCache";
});
                                                              Configures the
                                                              provider's settings
```

Notice that the configuration process is loosely similar to what we did with Serilog in chapter 7. We're "recycling" the same connection string that we set up for EF Core in chapter 4 to use the same MyBGList database. But the distributed caching tasks will be performed against a new, dedicated database table called "AppCache".

> **NOTE** For reasons of space, I won't bother explaining the other configuration options. They're self-explanatory, and we don't need to change them for demonstration purposes. For additional info on the SqlServerCacheOptions class and its properties, see http://mng.bz/zmzr.

CREATING THE APPCACHE DB TABLE

This table doesn't exist in our database yet. To create it, we must install and then execute a specific sql-cache command, using the dotnet CLI in the project's root folder. Here's how we can install the sql-cache command:

```
dotnet tool install --global dotnet-sql-cache –version 6.0.11
```

> **WARNING** The version number here must match the .NET version (patch included) installed on the system. Otherwise the sql-cache create command that we're about to use will likely return an error.

Then execute the command in the following way:

```
dotnet sql-cache create "{connectionString}" dbo AppCache
```

Be sure to replace the {connectionString} placeholder with the value of the DefaultConnection key (including the username/password credentials) defined in the secrets.json file. Also be sure to replace any double backslash (such as in local-host\\MyBGList) with a single backslash (localhost\MyBGList); otherwise, the CLI command will fail. When executed correctly, the sql-cache command should create a new [AppCache] DB table in our MyBGList database with the following columns:

- Id: PK, nvarchar(449), not null
- Value: varbinary(max), not null
- ExpiresAtTime: datetimeoffset(7), not null
- SlidingExpirationInSeconds: bigint, null
- AbsoluteExpiration: datetimeoffset(7), null

Alternatively, we could create the table manually by using SQL Server Management Studio (SSMS).

ADDING THE DISTRIBUTEDCACHEEXTENSIONS

Unfortunately, the `IDistributeCache` interface doesn't come with the handy generic-type methods—`Get<T>`, `Set<T>`, and `TryGetValue<T>`—that we appreciated in the `IMemoryCache` interface; it provides only `Get` and `Set` methods to handle string and byte array values. Because we want to store strongly typed entity objects retrieved by the DBMS, using those methods as they are would force us to convert them to byte arrays, thus resulting in more code lines.

For that reason, we'll create our first extension method helper class, in which we'll implement the same methods provided by the `IMemoryCache` interface and extend the `IDistributedCache` interface with them. Here are the methods we're going to create:

- `TryGetValue<T>`, accepting a `cacheKey` string value and an `out` parameter of T type
- `Set<T>`, accepting a `cacheKey` string value, a value of `T` type, and a `TimeSpan` value representing the absolute expiration relative to the current time

In the project's root folder, create a new /Extensions/ directory and a new `Distributed-CacheExtensions.cs` file within it. Then fill the new file with the content of the following listing.

Listing 8.8   `DistributedCacheExtensions.cs` file

```csharp
using Microsoft.Extensions.Caching.Distributed;
using System.Text;
using System.Text.Json;

namespace MyBGList.Extensions
{
    public static class DistributedCacheExtensions
    {
        public static bool TryGetValue<T>(          ◁──┐ TryGetValue<T>
            this IDistributedCache cache,               │ implementation
            string key,
            out T? value)
        {
            value = default;
            var val = cache.Get(key);
            if (val == null) return false;
            value = JsonSerializer.Deserialize<T>(val);
            return true;
        }
                                              ┌── Set<T>
                                              │   implementation
        public static void Set<T>(          ◁─┘
            this IDistributedCache cache,
            string key,
            T value,
            TimeSpan absoluteExpirationRelativeToNow)
```

```
    {
        var bytes = Encoding.UTF8.GetBytes(JsonSerializer.Serialize(value));
        cache.Set(key, bytes, new DistributedCacheEntryOptions()
        {
            AbsoluteExpirationRelativeToNow = absoluteExpirationRelativeToNow
        });
    }
  }
}
```

Notice that both extension methods perform a conversion between the byte[] type (required by the IDistributedCache interface's default methods) and a JSON serialization of the cache value, which is passed as a T generic type. Thanks to these methods, we provided the IDistributedCache interface the same methods that we used when implementing the IMemoryCache interface, so we can use a similar approach to implement it.

INJECTING THE IDISTRIBUTEDCACHE INTERFACE

Now that we have the service enabled, the [AppCache] table ready, and our convenient extension methods, we can inject an IDistributedCache interface instance into one of our controllers, as we did with the IMemoryCache interface earlier. This time we'll use the MechanicsController. Open the MechanicsController.cs file, and add a reference to the required namespaces at the top of the file:

```
using Microsoft.Extensions.Caching.Distributed;
using MyBGList.Extensions;
using System.Text.Json;
```

Then add a new private, read-only _distributedCache property right below the constructor, in the following way:

```
private readonly IDistributedCache _distributedCache;
```

Now we need to inject an IDistributedCache instance into the constructor by using the dependency injection pattern, as we've already done several times. The following listing shows how.

Listing 8.9 MechanicsController: IDistributedCache

```
public MechanicsController(
    ApplicationDbContext context,
    ILogger<BoardGamesController> logger,
    IDistributedCache distributed)          ◁——— Injects the IDistributedCache
{
    _context = context;
    _logger = logger;
    _distributedCache = distributedCache;   ◁——— Stores the instance in the local variable
}
```

All that's left now is the implementation part in the `MechanicsController`'s `Get` method. The source code is provided in the following listing.

Listing 8.10   `MechanicsController's Get method`

```
[HttpGet(Name = "GetMechanics")]
[ResponseCache(CacheProfileName = "Any-60")]
public async Task<RestDTO<Mechanic[]>> Get(
    [FromQuery] RequestDTO<MechanicDTO> input)
{
  var query = _context.Mechanics.AsQueryable();
  if (!string.IsNullOrEmpty(input.FilterQuery))
    query = query.Where(b => b.Name.Contains(input.FilterQuery));

  var recordCount = await query.CountAsync();

  Mechanic[]? result = null;
  var cacheKey =
    $"{input.GetType()}-{JsonSerializer.Serialize(input)}";
  if (!_distributedCache.TryGetValue<Mechanic[]>(cacheKey, out result))
  {
    query = query
      .OrderBy($"{input.SortColumn} {input.SortOrder}")
      .Skip(input.PageIndex * input.PageSize)
            .Take(input.PageSize);
      result = await query.ToArrayAsync();
      _distributedCache.Set(cacheKey, result, new TimeSpan(0, 0, 30));
  }

  return new RestDTO<Mechanic[]>()
  {
      Data = result,
      PageIndex = input.PageIndex,
      PageSize = input.PageSize,
      RecordCount = recordCount,
      Links = new List<LinkDTO> {
        new LinkDTO(
          Url.Action(
            null,
            "Mechanics",
            new { input.PageIndex, input.PageSize },
            Request.Scheme)!,
          "self",
          "GET"),
      }
  };
}
```

Declares the result variable → `Mechanic[]? result = null;`

Creates the cache key from the GET parameters

Checks the cache for the existence of the key

If cache isn't present, retrieves the data and sets it

As we can see, the actual `IDistributedCache` implementation is almost identical to what we did in the `BoardGamesController`'s `Get` method for the `IMemoryCache` interface. Such optimization could be done thanks to the extension methods provided by the DistributedCacheExtensions class, which handle the byte[] conversion tasks internally, allowing us to focus on the caching set and retrieval logic in the action method's source code. Now we need to test what we've done.

TESTING THE DISTRIBUTED CACHE

To test our distributed cache implementation, we can perform the same tasks that we did when we tested the IMemoryCache. Obviously, we won't be able to test it by using multiple web servers, but that's not an problem: as long as we can prove that the data is stored and retrieved properly on our third-party service (SQL Server) by our single-server app, we can take for granted that the same behavior will work in a multiserver scenario.

Let's proceed with the test. Open the MechanicsController.cs file, and place a couple breakpoints within the source code: one on the line where we call the TryGet-Value method and another one on the first line between the curly brackets, as we did with the BoardGamesController.cs file (refer to figure 8.1). When the breakpoints have been placed, launch the project in Debug mode, and call the /Mechanics GET endpoint without parameters so that the default parameters will be used.

Because that request is the first in the past 30 seconds, the IDistributedCache instance should find no valid cache entries, so both breakpoints should be hit (refer to figure 8.2). Wait for the JSON outcome to show up in the browser; then press Ctrl+F5 (while focusing the browser) to issue a forced page reload within the next 30 seconds. If everything works as expected, this time only the first breakpoint will be hit because the actual data will be loaded from the distributed cache.

Wait 30 seconds or more to make the distributed cache expire; then refresh the page again. This time, both breakpoints should be hit again, proving that the retrieval-and-expiration logic works and concluding our distributed cache test.

8.4.3 *Redis*

Implementing a Redis-based distributed cache requires us to perform three major tasks:

1 Set up a Redis server we can use to test the distributed cache mechanism.
2 Install the NuGet package required to handle the Redis distributed cache provider.
3 Change the distributed cache settings in the Program.cs file, replacing the SQL Server provider with the Redis provider.

In the following sections, we'll take care of all those tasks.

> **NOTE** The implementation in the MechanicsController.cs file won't require any change because we're changing the underlying provider, not the IDistributedCache uniform interface that will handle the caching behavior.

SETTING UP A REDIS SERVER

The quickest thing we can do to provide ourselves a Redis server is to create a free account in Redis Enterprise Cloud, the fully managed cloud service offered by Redis on its official website. To obtain it, perform the following steps:

1 Visit the https://redis.com website.
2 Click the Try Free button to access the subscription form.
3 Create an account by using Google or GitHub or by filling out the subscription form.
4 Select a cloud vendor and region to create the Redis instance (figure 8.3).
5 Click the Let's Start Free button to activate the free plan.

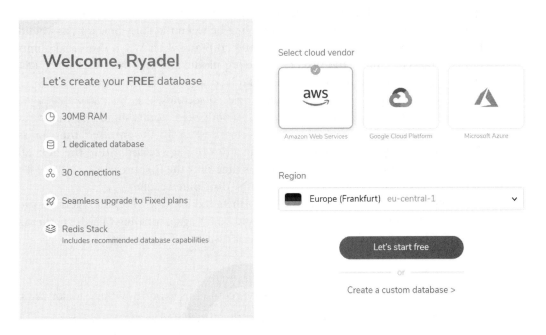

Figure 8.3   Selecting the cloud vendor and region in Redis Cloud

The website creates our Redis database instance and shows its entry in the service's main dashboard. Click the new instance to access its configuration settings, where we can take note of the public endpoint (figure 8.4) we'll use to access it.

Next, we need to scroll farther down that page's Configuration tab until we reach the Security panel, where we can retrieve the default user password (figure 8.5). The Public Endpoint and Default User Password values are all we need to assemble the Redis connection string.

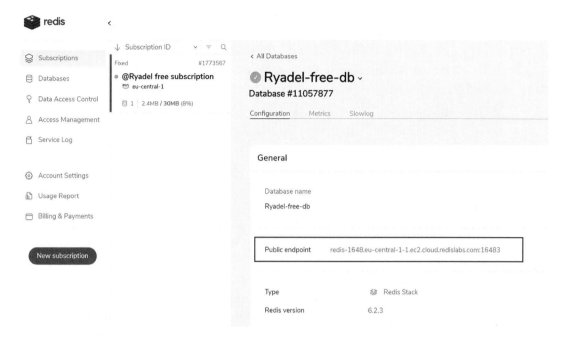

Figure 8.4 Retrieving the Redis database's public endpoint

Figure 8.5 Retrieving the Redis database's default user password

ADDING THE REDIS CONNECTION STRING

Because the Redis connection settings are reserved data, we're going to store them securely, using Visual Studio's User Secrets feature, which we used in previous chapters. On the Solution Explorer panel, right-click the project's root node, and choose the Manage User Secrets option from the contextual menu to access the secrets.json file for our `MyBGList` project. Add the following section to the JSON content below the "Azure" section that we added in chapter 7:

```
"Redis": {
  "ConnectionString": "<public endpoint>,password=<default password>"
}
```

Replace the `<public endpoint>` and `<default password>` placeholders with the values retrieved from the Redis Cloud dashboard panel. Now that we have the Redis storage service, as well as the connection string required to connect to it, we're ready to install the NuGet package and configure the distributed cache service by using the Redis provider.

INSTALLING THE NUGET PACKAGE

The NuGet package we need to use the Redis distributed cache provider is `Microsoft.Extensions.Caching.StackExchangeRedis`. When we're done installing it, we can switch to the `Program.cs` file to set up and configure the service.

CONFIGURING THE REDIS CACHE SERVICE

Open the `Program.cs` file, and locate the point where we set up and configured the SQL Server distributed cache provider. Comment out the SQL Server settings, and replace them with the following Redis-related code:

```
builder.Services.AddStackExchangeRedisCache(options =>      ◁—— Adds the Redis
{                                                                distributed cache
    options.Configuration =                                      provider
        builder.Configuration["Redis:ConnectionString"];   ◁——
});
                                        Configures the provider's
                                          connection settings
```

> **NOTE** Again, I won't delve into the other configuration options; the default settings are viable for this sample, demonstrative scenario. For additional info regarding the `RedisCacheOptions` class and its properties, check out http://mng.bz/0yBm.

If we did everything correctly, the new distributed cache provider should work with the same implementation that we set up in the `MechanicsController`; we don't have to change anything because the `IDistributedCache` interface is the same.

To test the new provider, we can perform the same two-breakpoints procedure that we used to test our previous SQL Server distributed cache implementation. For reasons of space, I won't mention it again. That said, it could be wise to repeat the test to ensure that everything works as expected.

> **TIP** For further information regarding the ASP.NET Core distributed cache, see http://mng.bz/Kld4.

Our application cache journey is over. Rest assured that we've only scratched the surface of a complex topic; to explore it further, check out the official Microsoft guides that I've referenced throughout the chapter.

8.5 Exercises

The time has come to challenge ourselves with a cache-related list of hypothetical task assignments given by our product owner. As always, dealing with these tasks will greatly help us memorize and remember the concepts covered and the techniques learned throughout this chapter.

> **TIP** The solutions to the exercises are available on GitHub in the /Chapter_08/ Exercises/ folder. To test them, replace the relevant files in your MyBGList project with those in that folder, and run the app.

8.5.1 HTTP response caching

Change the HTTP response cache behavior of the MechanicsController's Get method to make it comply with the following requirements:

- It must be cacheable only by clients (private).
- The cache must expire after 2 minutes.

8.5.2 Cache profiles

Add a new cache profile with the same settings specified in the preceding exercise, give it the name Client-120. Then apply the new cache profile to the BoardGames-Controller's Get method, replacing the existing cache profile.

8.5.3 Server-side response caching

Change the response-caching services settings in the following way:

- Set the largest cacheable size for the response body to 128 MB.
- Set the size limit for the response-cache middleware to 200 MB.
- Set the request paths as case-sensitive.

8.5.4 In-memory caching

Currently, the RecordCount property of the RestDTO object returned by the Board-GamesController's Get method is always retrieved from the DBMS. Change the current implementation to cache it as well, along with the result variable. To achieve this result without altering the existing caching strategy, consider the following approach:

1. Declare a new dataTuple variable of Tuple type.
2. Use it to group the recordCount and the result variables.
3. Cache the new dataTuple variable instead of the result variable, applying the set-and-retrieval logic to both variables grouped within it.

> **TIP** To find out more about the C# Tuple type and learn how to use it to group multiple data elements, check out the guide at http://mng.bz/918a.

8.5.5   *Distributed caching*

Change the name of the SQL Server distributed cache provider's caching table from [AppCache] to [SQLCache] at application level. Then create the new table in the DBMS, using the sql-cache CLI command. Don't delete the previous table so that you can revert the changes after completing the exercise.

Summary

- When developing a caching strategy, we should always consider what we can expect from clients and how their requests can affect our web application.
  - With that in mind, we should aim to cache at the highest level we can get away with. In ASP.NET Core, we can do this by using several caching mechanisms provided by the framework, including
    - HTTP response cache (client-side and server-side)
    - In-memory cache
    - Distributed cache
- HTTP response caching is useful mostly for static assets and frequently called endpoints that return the same response, whereas in-memory and distributed caching greatly reduce DBMS calls and the overhead caused by heavy-lifting business logic tasks.
  - Adopting a wise, balanced combination of all these techniques is typically the way to go when developing web applications.
- In ASP.NET Core, HTTP response caching is typically implemented by the [ResponseCache] attribute, which provides a high-level abstraction of the HTTP response caching headers.
  - The [ResponseCache] attribute settings can be defined inline and/or centralized within the app's main configuration file through the cache profiles feature.
  - If used alone, the [ResponseCache] attribute will take care of client-side response caching only. When coupled with the response-caching middleware, it also handles the server-side response-caching behavior of the web app.
- In-memory caching gives the developer more control of the caching data because it doesn't honor the HTTP request cache headers, so the clients can't refresh or invalidate it. It also has several other advantages:
  - It can be used to store objects of any type, including entities retrieved from the DBMS.
  - It's easy to set up, configure, and implement in any ASP.NET Core app thanks to the built-in IMemoryCache interface.
  - It's great for dealing with web apps hosted on a single server.
- In multiple-server scenarios, in-memory caching could lead to performance drawbacks and cache inconsistency problems. Distributed caching is an effective way to prevent that problem, because it relies on an external service that

makes the cache storage accessible simultaneously by all the web servers without affecting their local memory.

- – In ASP.NET Core, distributed caching can be set up and configured by using a DBMS (such as SQL Server) or key-value storage (such as Redis).
- – Each supported distributed cache provider comes with dedicated NuGet packages that implement the built-in `IDistributedCache` interface internally, allowing us to choose the provider we like most (and/or switching providers at will) without changing the app's implementation logic.

Authentication and authorization

This chapter covers

- Understanding authentication and authorization
- Getting an overview of ASP.NET Core Identity
- Implementing authentication via user accounts and JSON Web Tokens
- Enabling authorization with `AuthorizeAttribute` and `IAuthorizationFilter`
- Understanding the role-based access control (RBAC) authorization strategy

The ASP.NET Core web API that we've built throughout the previous chapters has taken solid shape. Before we publish it, however, we must address some major security permissions problems that we intentionally left open. If we take a closer look at our `BoardGamesController`, `DomainsController`, and `MechanicsController`, we can see that they all have some `Post` and `Delete` methods that anyone could use to alter our valuable data. We don't want that, do we?

For that reason, before even thinking about deploying our web API over the internet and making it publicly accessible, we need to find a way to restrict the use of those methods to a limited set of authorized users. In this chapter, we'll learn how to do that by using ASP.NET Core Identity, a built-in API that can be used to manage users, roles, claims, tokens, policies, authorization-related behaviors, and other features.

9.1 Basic concepts

Before I delve into the code, it's appropriate to provide a general overview of the concepts of *authentication* and *authorization*. Although the two terms are often used in the same context, they have distinct, precise meanings.

9.1.1 Authentication

In information security, *authentication* refers to the act of verifying the correct identity of a computer, software, or user. We could say that authentication is a mechanism to verify that an entity (or a person) is what it claims (or they claim) to be.

The authentication process is of utmost importance for any web app or service that needs to identify its users uniquely, for whatever reason—to restrict access to some (or all) user data, collect personal info, log and/or track users' actions while they use the service, be aware of whether they're logged in, disconnect them after a certain inactive period, and so on.

Also, authentication often plays an important role in enhancing the data protection, security, and monitoring capabilities of the web service (and the organization behind it). Uniquely verifying the identity of a connecting subject means that all the actions performed within the system can be traced back to their authors with reasonable certainty, facilitating compliance with the organization's accountability policies.

> **Accountability**
>
> Accountability is a key principle of ISO/IEC 27001, the well-known international standard that offers a systematic approach to designing, implementing, and operating an information security management system within an organization.
>
> The connection between authentication and accountability is also underlined by most European Union privacy authorities. According to the Italian Data Protection Authority, "... the sharing of credentials prevents the actions performed in a computer system from being attributed to a specific person in charge, with prejudice also to the owner, deprived of the possibility of checking the work of such relevant technical figures" (provision 4/4/2019).

Most web apps, web services, and IT devices require their users to fulfill an authentication process of some sort before granting them access. This process might involve unlocking our smartphone using a fingerprint, logging into a Facebook or LinkedIn account, publishing a photo on Instagram—all forms of authentication processes, even though some of them are performed under the hood because users gave consent to their devices to store their credentials and use them automatically.

Several authentication techniques are available nowadays, such as a username (or email) and password; one-time pins (OTPs) sent to email or mobile devices; one-time security codes generated by personal authentication apps; and biometric scans such as fingerprint, retina, and/or voice. I won't cover all those techniques in this chapter, but several online resources can provide more information about these topics.

> **TIP**   For further details on authentication in ASP.NET Core apps, check out http://mng.bz/jm6y.

9.1.2   *Authorization*

In general terms, *authorization* refers to the permission or power to perform, carry out, or exercise certain rights. In the IT field, *authorization* is defined as the process by which a system makes it possible to assign access privileges (also known as *permissions*) to individual computers, software, or users (or groups). These tasks typically are handled through the implementation of access policies, claims, or permission groups that allow or prohibit each relevant action or activity (reading, writing, deleting, and so on) within a given set of logical spaces (filesystem folders, drive network, database, sections of a website, web API endpoints, and so on). In practical terms, authorization is often provided or denied by defining a series of access control lists (ACLs) that specifies

- The access type(s) allowed for a specific resource (read, write, delete, and so on)
- Which computers, software, or users (or groups) are granted or denied access

Although authorization is orthogonal and independent from authentication, the two concepts are inherently entwined. If a system is unable to identify its users, it won't be able to match them properly against its ACLs and therefore grant or deny access to its resources. For that reason, most access control mechanisms are designed to require both authentication and authorization. More precisely, they do the following:

- Assign the lowest possible authorization permissions to nonauthenticated (anonymous) users. These permissions typically include accessing the public (unrestricted) content, as well as the login page, module, or form.
- Authenticate users who perform a login attempt successfully.
- Check their ACLs to assign the proper access privileges (permissions) to authenticated users.
- Authorize users to access the restricted content or not, depending on the permissions given to them or to the group(s) they belong to.

The authentication and authorization flows described in this scenario are depicted in figure 9.1. The figure mimics the behavior of a typical web application with a set of resources that can be accessed only by authorized users.

In the figure, the authentication process is meant to happen before authorization, because the latter requires the former to perform its job. But this scenario isn't

Authentication

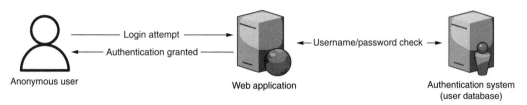

Authorization

Figure 9.1 Authentication and authorization flow

necessarily true. If an anonymous user tries to access a restricted resource, the authorization system will kick in before authentication, denying access to the nonauthenticated users and likely driving the web application to redirect the user to the login page. In some edge-case scenarios, there could even be resources meant to be accessible only by anonymous users (not authenticated ones). A typical example is the login page, because an authenticated user should never be allowed to perform additional login attempts until logging out.

> **NOTE** Connecting all these dots, we should see that authentication and authorization are distinct, separate, and independent things, even if they're ultimately meant to work together. Even if authorization could work without knowing the identity of the connecting party (as long as it has a feasible ACL for nonauthenticated users), it requires an authentication mechanism to fulfill the rest of its job.

Now that we have the general picture, we need to understand how to implement a viable authentication and authorization mechanism in our web API. As we learned earlier, in a typical web application the authentication process, often represented by a login phase, is expected to happen before the authorization part. When the user has successfully logged in, we get to know that user's permissions and authorize them to go (or not go) anywhere.

But we also (likely) know that the HTTP protocol is stateless. Each request is executed independently, without any knowledge of the requests that were executed before it. Everything that the client and server do within a request/response cycle, including all data sent and/or received, is meant to be lost at the end of the response unless the client and server are equipped with some mechanisms to store this data somewhere.

> **NOTE** These mechanisms aren't part of the HTTP protocol, but they typically take advantage of some of its features; in other words, they're built over it. Good examples are the caching techniques we saw in chapter 8, which can be implemented on the client side and/or the server side. These techniques use a specific set of HTTP headers, such as `Cache-Control`, to instruct the caching service what to do.

If we connect these two facts, we see that we have a problem: if each request doesn't know what happened before it, how can we know whether the user has been authenticated? How can we keep track of the outcome of the request/response cycle triggered by the login form—that is, the login result and (if successful) the user's identity? The next section briefly introduces some methods that overcome this problem.

IMPLEMENTATION METHODS

The most popular ways to set up HTTP authentication in modern web services and applications are sessions/cookies, bearer tokens, API keys, signatures, and certificates. Most of these techniques need no introduction for the average web developer, but it could be wise to spend some time describing how they work:

- *Sessions/cookies*—This method relies on a key/value storage service, typically located on the web server or on an external server or cluster. This service is used by the web application to store the user authentication info (the session), assigning it an autogenerated unique `sessionId`. Then the `sessionId` is sent to the browser via a cookie so that it will be resent on all subsequent requests and used on the server to retrieve the user's session and act accordingly (perform authorization-based checks) in a seamless, transparent way.
- *Bearer tokens*—This method relies on an encrypted token generated by the authentication server and containing the relevant authorization info. This token is sent to the client, which can use it to perform subsequent requests (until it expires) by setting it within the `Authorization` HTTP header without the need for further authentication attempts.
- *API keys*—The service that operates the web API gives its users a `ClientID` and `ClientSecret` pair (or gives them the chance to generate them) that can be used to access the API. Typically, that pair is sent via the `Authorization` HTTP header upon each request. Unlike the bearer token, however, which requires no authentication (more on that later), `ClientID` and `ClientSecret` are typically used to authenticate the requesting user every time, as well as to authorize that user.
- *Signatures and certificates*—These two authentication methods perform a hash of the request, using a previously shared private key and/or Transport Layer Security (TLS) certificate. This technique ensures that no intruder or middleman

can act as the requesting party, because they won't be able to "sign" the HTTP request. These approaches are great for security, but they can be quite hard to set up and implement for both parties, which restricts their use to services that require particularly high data-protection criteria.

Which of these methods should we use for our `MyBGList` web API? As always, we should consider the pros and cons of each alternative. Here's a quick breakdown:

- Session/cookies are clearly out of the picture, as they would negate our RESTful purposes, such as the *statelessness* constraint that we've known since chapter 3.
- Bearer tokens offer a decent security posture and are easy to implement, especially considering that ASP.NET Core Identity supports them out of the box (almost).
- API keys grant an even better security posture, but they require a lot of additional work, such as providing a dedicated management website or API set to enable users to manage them properly.
- Signatures and certificates are great from a security perspective, but they require even more additional work that could cause us some delays and/or raise overall costs.

Because we're dealing with board games, not with sensitive data, the bearer-token approach seems to be our best bet, at least from a cost/benefit perspective. The good thing about this choice is that it shares most of the work required to implement the API key approach. It's a perfect opportunity to learn the ASP.NET Core Identity basic techniques and put them in practice by building a viable authentication and authorization mechanism for most web APIs. The next section describes how bearer tokens work.

> **WARNING** The main purpose of this chapter and its source-code samples is to provide an overview of the various authentication and authorization mechanisms available for a web API and give general guidance on how to implement some of them with ASP.NET Core Identity. It's crucial to understand, however, that these methods are the primary targets of hacking attempts, denial-of-service (DoS) attacks, and several other malicious activities performed by third parties that could easily exploit pitfalls, implementation mistakes, nonupdated libraries, zero-day bugs, and the like. For that reason, if your web API and/or its underlying data source(s) contains personal, sensitive, or valuable data, consider strengthening your security posture by integrating or improving our code samples, using the security-related hyperlinks that I provide with them, as well as other authoritative tutorials on each subject.

BEARER TOKENS

Token-based authentication (also called *bearer authentication*) is one of the most-used approaches for web APIs. When implemented properly, it provides acceptable security standards without breaking the statelessness REST constraint.

Token-based authentication still requires users to authenticate themselves (perform the login) with a username and password. After the authentication process succeeds, however, instead of creating a persistent session, the server generates an encrypted

authorization token containing some relevant info about the outcome, such as a reference to the user identity (the userId), some info about the connecting client, the
token expiration date, and so on. This token, once retrieved by the client, can be set in
the Authorization HTTP header of any subsequent request to gain access to restricted
(authorized) resources until it expires. The process is summarized in figure 9.2.

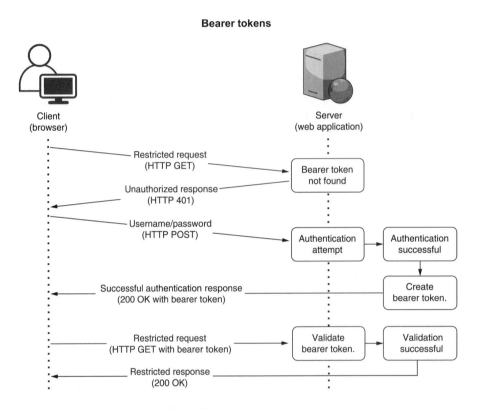

Figure 9.2   Bearer-token authorization flow

As we can see, no data is stored by the server. As for the client, implementation may
vary: the token can be stored locally (and reused until it expires) or discarded after
first use. The main advantage of bearer tokens is that they're a self-contained authorization mechanism because their existence automatically implies a successful authentication attempt. A single token can be used to authorize restricted requests addressed
to multiple web APIs and/or services, even if they're hosted elsewhere and/or have
no access to the user login data, as long as they share the same issuer signing key used
by the authentication service that generated them.

> **NOTE**   This versatility (and performance benefit) is also the cause of a main
> security flaw: after tokens are issued, they can't be invalidated (or updated)
> easily. If a third party manages to steal and use a token, they'll be able to

perform authorized requests until the token expires. Further, developers, system administrators, and users can't get rid of that token easily, even if they know that it's been compromised. Even disabling the originating user wouldn't do the trick, because that token is the result of an authentication process that took place when that user was still active. The best workaround for this security problem is to reduce the lifespan of these tokens as much as possible (ideally, to a few minutes) so that the attacker won't have much time to act.

Now that we've chosen a path for our concrete scenario and understood how it's supposed to work, it's time to familiarize ourselves with the framework that we'll use to implement it.

9.2   ASP.NET Core Identity

The ASP.NET Core Identity API provides a set of interfaces and high-level abstractions that can be used to manage and store user accounts in any ASP.NET Core app. Although it can be used with any database and/or object-relational mapping/mapper (ORM), the framework already provides several classes, helpers, and extension methods that allow us to use all its features with an Entity Framework Core (EF Core) data model, which makes it perfect for our current scenario.

> **NOTE**   The ASP.NET Core Identity source code is open source and available on GitHub at http://mng.bz/WAmx.

In the following sections, we'll learn how to use ASP.NET Core Identity to provide authentication capabilities to our existing `MyBGList` web API project. (Authorization will come next.) To achieve this goal, we'll perform the following steps:

1   Install the required NuGet packages.
2   Create a new `MyBGListUser` entity class to handle user data such as username and password.
3   Update our existing `ApplicationDbContext` to enable it to deal with the new user entity.
4   Add and apply a new migration to update our underlying database with the database tables required by ASP.NET Core Identity.
5   Set up and configure the required identity services and middleware in the `Program.cs` file.
6   Implement a new controller to handle the registration process (to create new users) and the login process (to assign temporary access tokens to existing users).

9.2.1   Installing the NuGet packages

To add ASP.NET Core Identity functionalities to our project, we need the following NuGet packages:

- `Microsoft.Extensions.Identity.Core`, containing the membership system and the main classes and services to handle the various login features we need

- `Microsoft.AspNetCore.Identity.EntityFrameworkCore`, the ASP.NET Core Identity provider for EF Core
- `Microsoft.AspNetCore.Authentication.JwtBearer`, containing middleware that enables ASP.NET Core applications to handle JSON Web Tokens (JWTs)

As always, we can choose to install the NuGet packages that we need within Visual Studio, using the NuGet Package Manager or the Package Manager console, or from the command line, using the .NET Core command-line interface (CLI). To use the CLI, open a command prompt, navigate to the project's root folder, and type the following commands:

```
> dotnet add package Microsoft.Extensions.Identity.Core --version 6.0.11
> dotnet add package Microsoft.AspNetCore.Identity.EntityFrameworkCore --
➥ version 6.0.11
> dotnet add package Microsoft.AspNetCore.Authentication.JwtBearer --
➥ version 6.0.11
```

Now we can start coding something, starting with the `ApplicationDbContext` class that we created in chapter 4.

9.2.2   *Creating the user entity*

Now that we've have installed the identity packages, we need to create a new entity class representing the users we want to authenticate and authorize. The name of this entity will be `ApiUser`.

> **NOTE** Ideally, we could call this entity `User`, but that generic name would create some nasty conflicts with other built-in properties (such as `Controller-Base.User`). To avoid that problem, I highly recommend opting for a more distinctive name.

Because we're using ASP.NET Core Identity, the best thing we can do to implement our new entity is extend the default implementation provided by the framework to deal with identity users, represented by the `IdentityUser` class (part of the `Microsoft.AspNetCore.Identity` namespace). Create a new /Model/ApiUser.cs class file, and fill it with the following code:

```
using Microsoft.AspNetCore.Identity;

namespace MyBGList.Models
{
    public class ApiUser : IdentityUser
    {
    }
}
```

That's all. We don't need to implement anything more for now, because the `Identity-User` class already contains all the properties we need: `UserName`, `Password`, and so on.

TIP For reasons of space, I won't provide an extensive description of the `IdentityUser` default class. To find out more about it (and its properties), see the definition at http://mng.bz/8182.

Now that we have a dedicated entity to handle our users, we can update our `ApplicationDbContext` class to make good use of it.

9.2.3   Updating the ApplicationDbContext

In chapter 4, when we created our `ApplicationDbContext` class, we extended the `DbContext` base class. To make it capable of handling our new `ApiUser` entity, we need to change it with another base class that includes the ASP.NET Core Identity function-alities we need. The name of this base class is (as you might guess) `IdentityDbContext`, and it's part of the `Microsoft.AspNetCore.Identity.EntityFrameworkCore` NuGet package that we installed earlier. Here's how we can do that (updated code in bold):

```
using Microsoft.AspNetCore.Identity.EntityFrameworkCore;      ⊲──┐ Required
                                                                 │ namespace
// ... existing code

public class ApplicationDbContext : IdentityDbContext<ApiUser>
```

The new **IdentityDbContext<TUser>** base class

Notice that the new base class requires an object of `TUser` type, which must be a class of `IdentityUser` type. Specifying our `ApiUser` entity there instructs EF Core, powered by the ASP.NET Core Identity extension package, to use its identity functionalities on it.

9.2.4   Adding and applying a new migration

Now that we've made our `ApplicationDbContext` aware of our new user entity, we're ready to add a new migration to update our underlying SQL Server database, creating the database tables required by ASP.NET Core Identity by using the code-first approach that we learned in chapter 4. Open a new command prompt, navigate to the `MyBGList` project's root folder, and type the following to create a new migration:

```
> dotnet ef migrations add Identity
```

Then type this command to apply the migration to our `MyBGList` database:

```
> dotnet ef database update Identity
```

If everything went well, the CLI commands should display text documenting the suc-cessful result of both tasks. We can double-check the outcome by opening SQL Server Management Studio (SSMS) to see whether the new ASP.NET Core Identity tables have been created. The expected result is shown in figure 9.3.

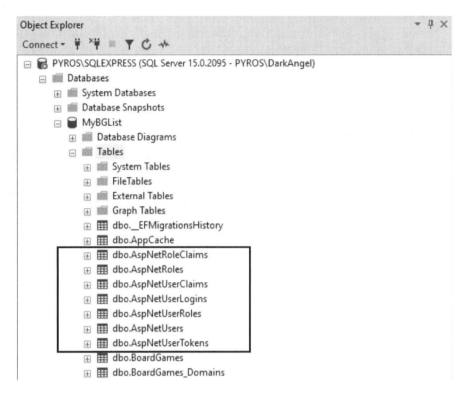

Figure 9.3   ASP.NET Core Identity tables

As per the ASP.NET Core Identity default behavior, all the identity database tables have an AspNet prefix—generally a good thing, because it allows us to distinguish them easily from the other tables.

Managing migrations (and dealing with migration-based errors)

The migrations feature is one of the distinctive strengths of EF Core, as it allows developers to incrementally update the DB schema to keep it in sync with the application's data model while preserving the existing data in the database, as well as roll back to a previous state at any time as we do with source control. But this feature can be hard to maintain in the long run, especially if we accidentally delete one of the incremental files generated by the dotnet-ef tool. When this happens, any attempt to update the existing database schema by using the CLI will likely return a SQL error, such as "table/column/key already exists". The only way to avoid seeing this error message is to preserve all the migration files. That's why we followed the good practice of generating them within a folder located inside the project, ensuring that they'll be put under source control along with the rest of the code.

Despite these countermeasures, in some edge-case scenarios, the migrations' incremental mechanism might break irreparably; we wouldn't be able to recover and/or roll back to safety. Whenever this happens, or if we lose a migration file without being able to recover it, the best thing we can do is reset all the migrations and create a new one that's in sync with our current database schema. This process, which involves some manual work, is called *squashing*, and is explained in detail in the Microsoft official guide at http://mng.bz/EIjl.

If we want to change the table names, we could do that by overriding the default values in the `ApplicationDbContext`'s `OnModelCreating` method as follows (but don't do this in your code):

```
modelBuilder.Entity<ApiUser>().ToTable("ApiUsers");
modelBuilder.Entity<IdentityRole<string>>().ToTable("ApiRoles");
modelBuilder.Entity<IdentityRoleClaim<string>>().ToTable("ApiRoleClaims");
modelBuilder.Entity<IdentityUserClaim<string>>().ToTable("ApiUserClaims");
modelBuilder.Entity<IdentityUserLogin<string>>().ToTable("ApiUserLogins");
modelBuilder.Entity<IdentityUserRole<string>>().ToTable("ApiRoles");
modelBuilder.Entity<IdentityUserToken<string>>().ToTable("ApiUserTokens");
```

This code would replace the `AspNet` prefix with `Api`. But we won't do that in our code samples; we'll keep the default prefix.

9.2.5 *Setting up the services and middleware*

Now we need to set up and configure some services and middleware within our `Program.cs` file. We need to add the following:

- *The identity service*—To perform the registration and login processes
- *The authorization service*—To define the rules for issuing and reading JWTs
- *The authentication middleware*—To add the JWT reading task to the HTTP pipeline

Let's start with the identity service.

ADDING THE IDENTITY SERVICE

Here's what we need to do:

1 Add the ASP.NET Core Identity service to the service container.
2 Configure the minimum security requirements for user passwords (aka password strength).
3 Add the ASP.NET authentication middleware.

Open the `Program.cs` file, find the section where we added the `DbContext` to the service container, and add the code in listing 9.1 right below it (new lines in bold).

Listing 9.1   Program.cs file: Identity service

```
using Microsoft.AspNetCore.Identity;          ⟵—┐  Required namespace

builder.Services.AddDbContext<ApplicationDbContext>(options =>
    options.UseSqlServer(
        builder.Configuration.GetConnectionString("DefaultConnection"))
    );

builder.Services.AddIdentity<ApiUser, IdentityRole>(options =>   ⟵—┐  Adds the
{                                                                      Identity
                                                                       service
    options.Password.RequireDigit = true;
    options.Password.RequireLowercase = true;          Configures
    options.Password.RequireUppercase = true;          password
    options.Password.RequireNonAlphanumeric = true;    strength
    options.Password.RequiredLength = 12;              requirements
})
    .AddEntityFrameworkStores<ApplicationDbContext>();
```

As we can see, we're telling ASP.NET Identity to accept only passwords that have

- At least one lowercase letter
- At least one uppercase letter
- At least one digit character
- At least one nonalphanumeric character
- A minimum 12 characters

These security standards will grant our users a decent level of authentication security for our non-data-sensitive scenario. The next step is setting up the authentication service.

ADDING THE AUTHENTICATION SERVICE

In our scenario, the authentication service has the following purposes:

- Defining JWTs as the default authentication method
- Enabling the JWT bearer authentication method
- Setting up the JWT validation, issuing, and lifetime settings

The following listing contains the relevant code, which we can place in the Program.cs file right below the identity service.

Listing 9.2   Program.cs file: Authentication service

```
using Microsoft.AspNetCore.Authentication.JwtBearer;   |  Required
using Microsoft.IdentityModel.Tokens;                  |  namespaces

builder.Services.AddAuthentication(options => {   ⟵—┐  Adds the
    options.DefaultAuthenticateScheme =                  Authentication
    options.DefaultChallengeScheme =                     service
    options.DefaultForbidScheme =
    options.DefaultScheme =
    options.DefaultSignInScheme =
```

```
        options.DefaultSignOutScheme =
            JwtBearerDefaults.AuthenticationScheme;
    }).AddJwtBearer(options => {
        options.TokenValidationParameters = new TokenValidationParameters
        {
            ValidateIssuer = true,
            ValidIssuer = builder.Configuration["JWT:Issuer"],
            ValidateAudience = true,
            ValidAudience = builder.Configuration["JWT:Audience"],
            ValidateIssuerSigningKey = true,
            IssuerSigningKey = new SymmetricSecurityKey(
              System.Text.Encoding.UTF8.GetBytes(
                  builder.Configuration["JWT:SigningKey"])          )
        };
    });
```

Sets the default authorization-related schemes

Adds the JWT Bearer authentication scheme

Configures JWT options and settings

The JWT Bearer option section is the most interesting part of the code, because it determines how the authentication service should validate the token. As we can see, we're asking to validate the Issuer, the Audience, and the key used by the issuer to sign the token (IssuerSigningKey). Performing these checks will greatly reduce the chance for a malicious third party to issue or forge a valid token.

Notice that instead of specifying these parameters directly in the code, we used a reference to our configuration file(s). We need to update those files now so that the source code will be able to retrieve those values.

UPDATING THE APPSETTINGS.JSON FILE

Open the appsettings.json file, and add the following top-level section, right below the existing SeriLog key:

```
"JWT": {
  "Issuer": "MyBGList",
  "Audience": "MyBGList",
  "SigningKey": "MyVeryOwnTestSigningKey123$"
}
```

As always, be sure to change the sample values with your own values if you plan to deploy your web API in a publicly accessible production environment.

> **TIP** Moving the SigningKey in the secret.json file would ensure an even better security posture. Be sure to do that unless you're working on a sample app like this one.

Now that our services have been set up properly, we're almost done with our Program.cs file. All that's missing now is the authentication middleware.

ADDING THE AUTHENTICATION MIDDLEWARE

In the Program.cs file, scroll down to the existing line

```
app.UseAuthorization();
```

and add the ASP.NET Core authentication middleware immediately before it:

```
app.UseAuthentication();          ◁──┐  New authentication
app.UseAuthorization();           ◁──┤  middleware
        Existing authorization       │
              middleware             │
```

We've known since chapter 2 that middleware order is important, because middleware sequentially affects the HTTP request pipeline. For that reason, be sure to call `Use-Authentication()` before `UseAuthorization()`, because our app needs to know which authentication scheme and handler are used to authorize the request. Now that we've set up and configured the ASP.NET Core Identity service and the authentication middleware, we're ready to implement the action methods that our users will use to create their accounts (register) and then authenticate themselves (log in).

9.2.6 *Implementing the AccountController*

In this section, we're going to create a new `AccountController` and populate it with two action methods: `Register` (to create new users) and `Login` (to authenticate them). Both methods require some required input parameters to perform their work. The `Register` method, for example, needs the data of the user who wants to create an account (username, password, email, and so on), whereas the `Login` method needs to know only the username and password. Because the `AccountController` will have to handle some specific ASP.NET Core identity-related tasks, we're going to need the following services, which we've never used before:

- `UserManager`—Provides the APIs for managing users
- `SignInManager`—Provides the APIs for logging users in

Both services are part of the `Microsoft.AspNetCore.Identity` namespace. We're going to need the first one for the `Register` method and the second to deal with the `Login`. Furthermore, because we also need to read the JWT settings that we specified in the `appsettings.json` configuration file(s), we're going to need the IConfiguration interface as well. As always, all these dependencies will be made available via dependency injection.

Let's start with empty boilerplate in the controller itself. Create a new Account-Controller.cs C# class file in the project's /Controllers/ folder, and fill it with the code in the following listing.

Listing 9.3 `AccountController` boilerplate

```
using Microsoft.AspNetCore.Mvc;
using Microsoft.EntityFrameworkCore;
using MyBGList.DTO;
using MyBGList.Models;
using System.Linq.Expressions;
using System.Linq.Dynamic.Core;
using System.ComponentModel.DataAnnotations;
```

```
using MyBGList.Attributes;
using System.Diagnostics;
using Microsoft.AspNetCore.Identity;          ASP.NET
using Microsoft.IdentityModel.Tokens;         Core Identity
using System.IdentityModel.Tokens.Jwt;        namespaces
using System.Security.Claims;

namespace MyBGList.Controllers
{                                              ┌─ Route
    [Route("[controller]/[action]")]     ◄─────┘  attribute
    [ApiController]
    public class AccountController : ControllerBase
    {
        private readonly ApplicationDbContext _context;

        private readonly ILogger<DomainsController> _logger;

        private readonly IConfiguration _configuration;

  ┌──▷ private readonly UserManager<ApiUser> _userManager;

        private readonly SignInManager<ApiUser> _signInManager;   ◄──┐
                                                                      │
        public AccountController(                                     │
            ApplicationDbContext context,                            │
            ILogger<DomainsController> logger,                       │
            IConfiguration configuration,                            │
  ├──▷      UserManager<ApiUser> userManager,                        │
            SignInManager<ApiUser> signInManager)   ◄────────────────┤
        {                                                            │
            _context = context;                                      │
            _logger = logger;                                        │
            _configuration = configuration;                         │
  └──▷      _userManager = userManager;                              │
            _signInManager = signInManager;   ◄──────────────────────┘
        }

        [HttpPost]
        [ResponseCache(CacheProfileName = "NoCache")]
        public async Task<ActionResult> Register()   ◄──┐ Register
        {                                                │ method
            throw new NotImplementedException();
        }

        [HttpPost]
        [ResponseCache(CacheProfileName = "NoCache")]
        public async Task<ActionResult> Login()   ◄──┐ Login
        {                                             │ method
            throw new NotImplementedException();
        }
    }
}
```

UserManager API points to `private readonly UserManager<ApiUser> _userManager;` and `_userManager = userManager;`

SignInManager API points to `private readonly SignInManager<ApiUser> _signInManager;`, `SignInManager<ApiUser> signInManager)`, and `_signInManager = signInManager;`

Notice that we've defined a [Route] attribute with an action-based routing rule ("[controller]/[action]") because we must deal with two HTTP POST methods that we need to distinguish. Thanks to that rule, our methods will have the following endpoints:

```
/Account/Register
/Account/Login
```

Other than that, we've set up a local instance for the _userManager, _signInManager, and _configuration objects (through dependency injection), and created the two not-implemented methods. In the following sections, we'll implement these two methods (and their DTO), starting with Register.

IMPLEMENTING THE REGISTER METHOD

If we look at the [AspNetUsers] table that ASP.NET Core Identity created for us in our SQL Server database, we see the parameters we need to create a new user (figure 9.4).

This table is meant to store the records for the ApiUser entity that we created earlier, which is an extension of the IdentityUser default class. If we check that entity, we see that it has a public property for each of the table columns—hardly a surprise, because we have used the EF Core code-first approach to create the table in the first place.

Now that we know the data we need to acquire from the users who want to create a new account, we can implement the DTO object that will "transport"

Figure 9.4   AspNetUsers database table

them, thereby putting the lessons in chapter 6 into practice. Create a new Register-DTO.cs C# class file in the project's /DTO/ folder, and fill it with the code shown in listing 9.4. For simplicity, we'll require our registering users to send us three types of info: a valid username, the password they want to use to perform the login, and their email address.

Listing 9.4   RegisterDTO class

```
using System.ComponentModel.DataAnnotations;

namespace MyBGList.DTO
{
    public class RegisterDTO
    {
        [Required]
        public string? UserName { get; set; }
```

```
        [Required]
        [EmailAddress]
        public string? Email { get; set; }

        [Required]
        public string? Password { get; set; }
    }
}
```

Now that we have our DTO, we can use it to implement our `AccountController`
`.Register` method, which is expected to handle the following tasks:

1 Accept a `RegisterDTO` input.
2 Check the `ModelState` to ensure that the input is valid.
3 If the `ModelState` is valid, create a new user (logging the result), and return
   Status Code 201 – Created; otherwise, return Status Code 400 – Bad Request
   documenting the errors.
4 If the user creation fails, or if any exception occurs during the whole process,
   return Status Code 500 – Internal Server Error, and return the relevant
   error message.

The following listing shows how we can implement these tasks.

Listing 9.5 `AccountController.Register` method

```
[HttpPost]
[ResponseCache(CacheProfileName = "NoCache")]
public async Task<ActionResult> Register(RegisterDTO input)
{
    try
    {                                          ⟵── Checks
                                                    ModelState and
        if (ModelState.IsValid)     ⟵────────────  acts accordingly
        {
            var newUser = new ApiUser();
            newUser.UserName = input.UserName;
Attempts    newUser.Email = input.Email;
to create   var result = await _userManager.CreateAsync(
the user        newUser, input.Password);
Checks the  if (result.Succeeded)
result and  {
acts            _logger.LogInformation(
accordingly         "User {userName} ({email}) has been created.",
                    newUser.UserName, newUser.Email);
                return StatusCode(201,
                    $"User '{newUser.UserName}' has been created.");
            }
            else
                throw new Exception(
                    string.Format("Error: {0}", string.Join(" ",
                        result.Errors.Select(e => e.Description))));
        }
```

```
        else
        {
            var details = new ValidationProblemDetails(ModelState);
            details.Type =
                "https://tools.ietf.org/html/rfc7231#section-6.5.1";
            details.Status = StatusCodes.Status400BadRequest;
            return new BadRequestObjectResult(details);
        }
    }
    catch (Exception e)          ⟵——|  Catches any exception
    {                                 |  and returns the error
            var exceptionDetails = new ProblemDetails();
            exceptionDetails.Detail = e.Message;
            exceptionDetails.Status =
                StatusCodes.Status500InternalServerError;
            exceptionDetails.Type =
                "https://tools.ietf.org/html/rfc7231#section-6.6.1";
            return StatusCode(
                StatusCodes.Status500InternalServerError,
                exceptionDetails);
    }
}
```

This code shouldn't be difficult to understand. The only new stuff is the use of the
UserManager service and its CreateAsync method, which returns an object of Identity-
Result type containing the result or the error(s) that occurred. Now that we have a
Register method, we can test it by trying to create a new user.

CREATING A TEST USER

Launch the project in Debug mode, and as always, wait for the SwaggerUI starting
page to load. Then we should see a new POST Account/Register endpoint that we can
expand, as shown in figure 9.5.

Figure 9.5   The `/Account/Register` **endpoint in SwaggerUI**

We can test the new method by clicking the Try It Out button in the top-right corner. As soon as we do, we'll be able to fill the sample JSON with actual `username`, `email`, and `password` values. Let's do a first test with the following values:

```
{
  "userName": "TestUser",
  "email": "TestEmail",
  "password": "TestPassword"
}
```

The request should return `HTTP Status Code 400`, with a response body explaining the error reason (invalid email format):

```
{
  "type": "https://tools.ietf.org/html/rfc7231#section-6.5.1",
  "title": "One or more validation errors occurred.",
  "status": 400,
  "errors": {
    "Email": [
      "The Email field is not a valid e-mail address."
    ]
  }
}
```

This response means that the `ModelState` validation is working properly. So far, so good. Now let's fix the email field and perform a new test with the following values:

```
{
  "userName": "TestUser",
  "email": "test-user@email.com",
  "password": "TestPassword"
}
```

Now the request should return `HTTP Status Code 500`, with a response body explaining the new error reason (invalid password format):

```
{
  "type": "https://tools.ietf.org/html/rfc7231#section-6.6.1",
  "status": 500,
  "detail": "Error: Passwords must have at least one non alphanumeric
  character. Passwords must have at least one digit ('0'-'9')."
}
```

The error warns us that the password isn't strong enough—another confirmation that our validation checks are working. Now we can fix that last problem and perform a third (and ideally last) test with the following values:

```
{
  "userName": "TestUser",
  "email": "test-user@email.com",
  "password": "MyVeryOwnTestPassword123$"
}
```

We should receive a confirmation message saying that the user has been created.

> **NOTE** Feel free to replace the username and/or password in the examples with your own values. But be sure to take note of them—especially the password, as the `UserManager.CreateAsync` method will store it as a nonreversible hash value in the `[AspNetUsers].[PasswordHash]` column.

Now we're done with the `Register` part. Let's move on to the `Login` method.

IMPLEMENTING THE LOGIN METHOD

Our mission is to create a suitable `LoginDTO` and use it to implement the `Login` action method. Let's start with the `LoginDTO` class, which (as we should know by now) requires only two properties: `UserName` and `Password` (see the following listing).

Listing 9.6   LoginDTO class

```
using System.ComponentModel.DataAnnotations;

namespace MyBGList.DTO
{
    public class LoginDTO
    {
        [Required]
        [MaxLength(255)]
        public string? UserName { get; set; }

        [Required]
        public string? Password { get; set; }
    }
}
```

Now we can implement the `AccountController.Login` method, which needs to take care of the following tasks:

1 Accept a `LoginDTO` input.
2 Check the `ModelState` to ensure that the input is valid; otherwise, return `Status Code 400 – Bad Request` documenting the error.
3 If the user exists and the password matches, generate a new token, and send it to the user along with `Status Code 200 – OK`.
4 If the user doesn't exist, the password doesn't match, and/or any exception occurs during the process, return `Status Code 401 – Unauthorized`, and return the relevant error message.

The following listing contains the source code for these tasks.

Listing 9.7   AccountController's login method

```
[HttpPost]
[ResponseCache(CacheProfileName = "NoCache")]
public async Task<ActionResult> Login(LoginDTO input)
```

```
{
    try                                          Checks
    {                                            ModelState and
        if (ModelState.IsValid)      ◁──┘        acts accordingly
        {
            var user = await _userManager.FindByNameAsync(input.UserName);
            if (user == null
                || !await _userManager.CheckPasswordAsync(
                    user, input.Password))
                throw new Exception("Invalid login attempt.");
            else
            {
                var signingCredentials = new SigningCredentials(
                    new SymmetricSecurityKey(
                        System.Text.Encoding.UTF8.GetBytes(
                            _configuration["JWT:SigningKey"])),
                    SecurityAlgorithms.HmacSha256);

                var claims = new List<Claim>();
                claims.Add(new Claim(
                    ClaimTypes.Name, user.UserName));

                var jwtObject = new JwtSecurityToken(
                    issuer: _configuration["JWT:Issuer"],
                    audience: _configuration["JWT:Audience"],
                    claims: claims,
                    expires: DateTime.Now.AddSeconds(300),
                    signingCredentials: signingCredentials);

                var jwtString = new JwtSecurityTokenHandler()
                    .WriteToken(jwtObject);

                return StatusCode(
                    StatusCodes.Status200OK, jwtString);
            }
        }
        else
        {
            var details = new ValidationProblemDetails(ModelState);
            details.Type =
                "https://tools.ietf.org/html/rfc7231#section-6.5.1";
            details.Status = StatusCodes.Status400BadRequest;
            return new BadRequestObjectResult(details);
        }
    }
    catch (Exception e)          ◁──┐   Catches any exception
    {                                   and returns the error
        var exceptionDetails = new ProblemDetails();
        exceptionDetails.Detail = e.Message;
        exceptionDetails.Status =
            StatusCodes.Status401Unauthorized;
        exceptionDetails.Type =
                "https://tools.ietf.org/html/rfc7231#section-6.6.1";
        return StatusCode(
```

Generates the signing credentials →

Sets up the user claims →

Instantiates a JWT object instance →

Generates the JWT encrypted string

Returns the JWT to the caller →

```
            StatusCodes.Status401Unauthorized,
            exceptionDetails);
    }
}
```

Again, this code should be easy to understand—except for the JWT generation section, which deserves some additional explanation. That section can be split into four parts, which I've separated with spaces, each of which sets a variable that plays a distinctive role in the JWT creation process:

- `signingCredentials`—This variable stores the JWT signature, encrypted with a HMAC SHA-256 cryptographic algorithm. Notice that the `SigningKey` is retrieved from the configuration settings, as with the authorization service in the `Program.cs` file earlier. This approach ensures that the writing and reading process will use the same value, meaning that the signing key will match.
- `claims`—This variable stores a list of claims for the user for whom we're generating the JWT. The authorization process will use these claims to check whether the user is allowed to access each requested resource (more on that later). Notice that for now, we're setting a single claim that corresponds to the user's `UserName` property. We'll add more claims soon.
- `jwtObject`—This variable stores an instance of the JWT itself (as a C# object) by putting together the signing credentials, the list of claims, the `issuer` and `audience` values retrieved by the configuration file(s), and a suitable expiration time (300 seconds).
- `jwtString`—This variable stores the encrypted string representation of the JWT. This value is the one we need to send back to the clients so that they can set it in the `Authorization` header in their subsequent requests.

NOTE We're using a couple of other `UserManager` methods: `FindByNameAsync` and `CheckPasswordAsync`. Because their names are self-explanatory, it shouldn't be difficult to understand what they do.

With this method, our `AccountController` is ready, and so is the authentication part of our implementation. Now we need to test it.

AUTHENTICATING THE TEST USER

To test the `AccountController`'s Login method, we can use the `TestUser` that we created with the `Register` method. Launch the project in Debug mode, access the SwaggerUI main dashboard, and select the new `POST Account/Login` endpoint (figure 9.6).

Click Try It Out in the top-right corner, and fill the sample JSON with the username and password values for the test user we created:

```
{
  "userName": "TestUser",
  "password": " MyVeryOwnTestPassword123$"
}
```

Account ⌄

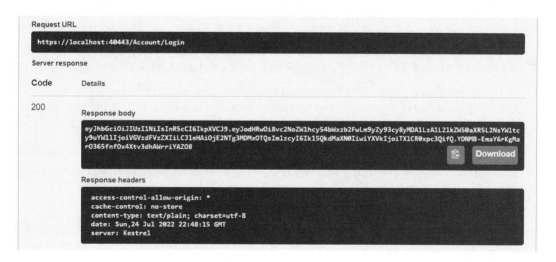

Figure 9.6 `/Account/Login` **endpoint in SwaggerUI**

If we did everything correctly, we should receive a `Status Code 200 - OK` response with the JWT in the response body (figure 9.7).

Request URL

`https://localhost:40443/Account/Login`

Server response

Code	Details
200	**Response body**

```
eyJhbGciOiJIUzI1NiIsInR5cCI6IkpXVCJ9.eyJodHRwOi8vc2NoZW1hcy54bWxzb2FwLm9yZy93cy8yMDA1LzA1L21kZW50aXR5L2NsYW1tc
y9uYW1lIjoiVGVzdFVzZXIiLCJleHAiOjE2NTg3MDMxOTQsImlzcyI6Ik15QkdaMaXN0IiwiYXVkIjoiTX1CR0xpc3QifQ.YDNMB-EmaY6rKgMa
rO365fnfOx4Xtv3dhAWrriYAZO8
```

Response headers

```
access-control-allow-origin: *
cache-control: no-store
content-type: text/plain; charset=utf-8
date: Sun,24 Jul 2022 22:48:15 GMT
server: Kestrel
```

Figure 9.7 `/Account/Login` **response with JWT**

Now our web API is equipped with a working authentication mechanism, consisting of a registration and login process handled through ASP.NET Core Identity. In the next section, we'll define some authorization rules based on it.

9.3   *Authorization settings*

In this section, we'll use the JWT generated by the `AccountController`'s `Login` method to restrict some of our API endpoints to authorized users. To obtain this outcome, we need to take care of two distinct aspects:

- *Client-side*—Add an `Authorization` HTTP header containing our JWT to properly emulate some "authorized" requests using our test client of choice (SwaggerUI).
- *Server-side*—Set up some authorization rules to make some of our existing controller's (and Minimal API's) action methods accessible only to callers that have a valid JWT with the required claims.

9.3.1   *Adding the authorization HTTP header*

Because our `AccountController`'s `Login` method returns a JWT in plain text, the most effective thing we can do is update our existing Swashbuckler SwaggerUI configuration to make it accept an arbitrary string that, if present, will be put in the `Authorization` HTTP header before the request is performed. As always, the required updates will be performed within the `Program.cs` file.

Handling the authorization header from the client side

The technique we're about to implement is intended to emulate what an actual REST client would do while performing requests. JWT aren't meant to be handled manually. Most client-side JavaScript frameworks, such as Angular and React, provide (or allow the use of) HTTP interceptors that can be used to attach arbitrary headers, such as the `Authorization` header with a previously fetched token, to all the requests before they're dispatched.

For additional info on HTTP interceptors, check out the following URLs:

- Angular (built-in interface): https://angular.io/api/common/http/HttpInterceptor
- Axios (for React and other frameworks): https://axios-http.com/docs/interceptors

---

We need to add a new security definition to tell Swagger the type of protection we want for our API and a new security requirement to enforce it globally. The following listing shows how.

Listing 9.8   `Program.cs` file: Swagger's bearer tokens setup

```
using Microsoft.OpenApi.Models;        ◁────┐  Required
                                             │  namespace
// ... existing code

builder.Services.AddSwaggerGen(options => {
    options.ParameterFilter<SortColumnFilter>();
    options.ParameterFilter<SortOrderFilter>();
```

```
options.AddSecurityDefinition("Bearer", new OpenApiSecurityScheme
    {
        In = ParameterLocation.Header,
        Description = "Please enter token",
        Name = "Authorization",
        Type = SecuritySchemeType.Http,
        BearerFormat = "JWT",
        Scheme = "bearer"
    });

options.AddSecurityRequirement(new OpenApiSecurityRequirement
    {
        {
            new OpenApiSecurityScheme
            {
                Reference = new OpenApiReference
                {
                    Type=ReferenceType.SecurityScheme,
                    Id="Bearer"
                }
            },
            Array.Empty<string>()
        }
    });
});
```

New Swagger security definition

New Swagger security requirement

Thanks to this update, a new Authorize button with a padlock icon will appear in the top-right corner of the SwaggerUI (figure 9.8). If we click it, a pop-up window will appear, giving us the chance to insert a bearer token to use in the `Authorization` HTTP header.

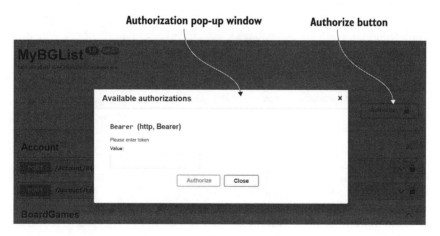

Figure 9.8   SwaggerUI Authorize button and pop-up window

That's precisely what we need to add JWTs to our requests. Now that the client-side part of the job is done, we can switch to the server side.

9.3.2   *Setting up the [authorize] attribute*

We must choose which API endpoints should be left available to everyone (as they already are) and which to restrict, limit, or block. The typical approach is to allow public/anonymous access to read-only endpoints that don't disclose reserved data and restrict everything else to authenticated (and authorized) users. Let's use common logic to design a given implementation scenario based on the product owner's explicit request. Suppose that we want to maintain unrestricted access to all action methods except the following:

- BoardGamesController—Post, Delete
- DomainsController—Post, Delete
- MechanicsController—Post, Delete
- SeedController—Put

We can easily see that all these methods are designed to apply permanent changes to our database, so putting them behind authorization rules makes a lot of sense. We definitely don't want some anonymous users to delete, update, or otherwise alter our board-game data!

To put our plan into practice we can decorate these methods with the [Authorize] attribute, part of the Microsoft.AspNetCore.Authorization namespace. This attribute can be applied to controllers, action methods, and minimal API methods to set specific authorization rules based on authentication schemes, policies, and/or roles. These rules can be configured with the attribute's parameters (as we'll see in a short while). When used without parameters, in its most basic form, the [Authorize] attribute will restrict access to authenticated users regardless of their permissions.

Because we haven't defined any policy or role for our users yet, we can start our implementation journey by using the parameterless behavior of the attribute. Open the following controllers: BoardGamesController, DomainsController, Mechanics-Controller, and SeedController. Then add the [Authorize] attribute to their Post, Delete, and Put methods, as follows:

```
using Microsoft.AspNetCore.Authorization;      Required
                                               namespace
// ... existing code

Authorize    [Authorize]
attribute     [HttpPost(Name = "UpdateBoardGame")]
              [ResponseCache(CacheProfileName = "NoCache")]
              public async Task<RestDTO<BoardGame?>> Post(BoardGameDTO model)
```

Now all our action methods that might alter our data will be accessible only to authenticated users.

CHOOSING THE DEFAULT ACCESS BEHAVIOR

It's important to understand that by applying the [Authorize] attribute to some specific action methods, we're implicitly setting a default-allow, opt-block logic for nonauthorized users. In other words, we're saying that all action methods are allowed for anonymous access except for those restricted with the [Authorize] attribute. We can reverse this logic to default-block, opt-allow by setting the [Authorize] attribute to the whole controller and then selectively using the [AllowAnonymous] attribute for the action methods that we do want to make accessible to everyone.

Both behaviors can be viable, depending on the specific use case. In general terms, the more restrictive approach (default-block, opt-allow) is considered to be safer, being less prone to human (developer) error. Typically, forgetting an [Authorize] attribute is worse than forgetting an [AllowAnonymous] attribute, because it could easily result in a data breach.

In our sample scenario, protecting the individual action methods might be acceptable, at least for those controllers with hybrid access behavior (anonymous and restricted action methods). The exception is the SeedController, which is intended to host only restricted action methods. In that case, setting the [Authorize] attribute at controller level would be more appropriate. Let's do that before moving on. Open the SeedController.cs file, and move the [Authorize] attribute from the action method to the controller:

```
[Authorize]
[Route("[controller]")]
[ApiController]
public class SeedController : ControllerBase
```

Thanks to this update, all action methods that we'll add to this controller will be restricted to authorized users automatically. We don't have to remember to do anything else.

ENABLING MINIMAL API AUTHORIZATION

Before moving to the testing phase, we should see how the [Authorize] attribute can be used in Minimal API with no additional effort. Let's add a Minimal API method to handle a new /auth/test/1 endpoint that will be accessible to authorized users only. The following listing contains the source code.

Listing 9.9 `Program.cs` file: `/auth/test/1` Minimal API endpoint

```
using Microsoft.AspNetCore.Authorization;

// ... existing code

app.MapGet("/auth/test/1",
    [Authorize]
    [EnableCors("AnyOrigin")]
    [ResponseCache(NoStore = true)] () =>
    {
        return Results.Ok("You are authorized!");
    });
```

Now we're finally ready to test what we've done so far.

9.3.3   *Testing the authorization flow*

Launch the project in Debug mode, and access the SwaggerUI dashboard. As always, this client is the one we're going to use to perform our tests.

The first thing we should do is check whether the authorization restrictions are working properly. The /auth/test/1 Minimal API endpoint that we added is a perfect candidate for that task because it can be called with a simple GET request that won't affect our data. We'll call that endpoint with SwaggerUI and ensure that it returns a Status Code 401 - Unauthorized response, as shown in figure 9.9.

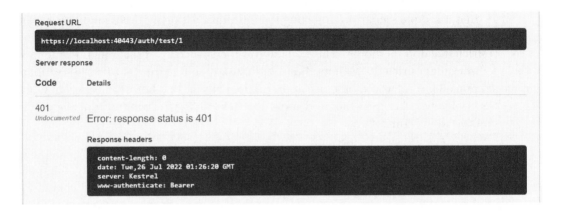

Figure 9.9   /auth/test/1 **endpoint returning** Status Code 401 - Unauthorized

So far, so good. A 401 - Unauthorized response is expected for any method with an [Authorize] attribute because we're not authenticated yet. Let's fill this gap and try again. Perform the following steps:

1 Call the Account/Login endpoint with our test user's username and password values, as we did when we tested it earlier, to receive a valid JWT.
2 Copy the JWT to the clipboard by selecting it and pressing Ctrl+C.
3 Click the Authorize button that we added to show the pop-up window.
4 Paste the JWT in the input text box within the pop-up window, and click Authorize to set it up for the next requests.

Now we can call the /auth/test/1 endpoint and see whether the bearer token allows us to perform this request. If everything goes well—and if we perform the test within 300 seconds, before the token expires—we should see a 200 - OK status code and a "You are authorized!" message in the response body, as shown in figure 9.10.

This outcome demonstrates that our JWT-based authentication and authorization flow is working; we've successfully restricted some methods to authorized users. Our authorization rules are still basic, however. We can distinguish between only anonymous

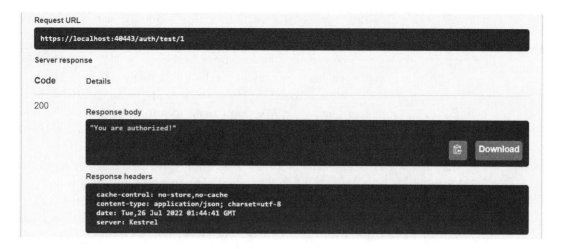

Figure 9.10 `/auth/test/1` **endpoint returning status code** `200 - OK`

and authenticated users, considering the latter to be authorized without further checks. Ideally, we should give our web API a more granular access control system that allows us to set up additional authorization behaviors, such as authorizing only some users to do something. In the next section, we'll do that by implementing a role-based claims mechanism.

9.4 Role-based access control

Suppose that we want to create different ACLs to support the following authenticated user types:

- *Basic users*—They should be allowed to access the read-only endpoints and nothing else, like the anonymous (not registered) users.
- *Moderators*—They should have access to the read-only and the update endpoints without being able to delete anything or to seed the database.
- *Administrators*—They should be able to do anything (read, update, delete, and seed).

The way things are now, all authenticated users are treated like administrators: they can do anything, because the `[Authorize]` attribute checks only that basic state. To change this behavior, we need to find a way to organize these users into different groups and assign specific authorizations to each group. In ASP.NET Core, we can achieve this result by using roles.

Role-based access control (*RBAC*) is a built-in authorization strategy that offers a convenient way to assign different permissions to different users. Each role behaves like a group, so we can add users to it and set up specific authorization rules for it. When the rules are defined, they'll be applied to all users who have that particular role.

Implementing the RBAC strategy is a great way to deal with our assignment because it allows us to categorize users. In a nutshell, here's what we need to do:

- *Register additional users.* We need at least two of them: a `TestModerator` and a `TestAdministrator`, each one representing the user type we want to support.
- *Create a predefined set of roles.* Based on our requirements, we need two of them: `Moderator` and `Administrator`. We don't need to add a role for basic users because they're expected to have the same permissions as anonymous users and the parameterless `[Authorize]` attribute already takes care of them.
- *Add users to roles.* Specifically, we need to assign the `TestModerator` user to the Moderator role and the TestAdministrator user to the administrator role.
- *Add role-based claims to JWT.* Because the JWT contains a collection of the authenticated user's claims, we need to put the user's roles in these claims so that the ASP.NET Core authorization middleware will be able to acknowledge them and act accordingly.
- *Set up role-based authorization rules.* We can perform this task by updating the `[Authorize]` attribute in the action methods that we want to restrict to moderators and administrators, so that they require the presence of the corresponding role-related claims in the JWT.

9.4.1   *Registering new users*

The first thing to do should be easy to pull off, because we did it when we tested the `Account/Register` endpoint by creating the `TestUser` account. We have to execute that same endpoint twice to add two more users. Here are the JSON values we can use to create the `TestModerator` account:

```
{
  "userName": "TestModerator",
  "email": "test-moderator@email.com",
  "password": "MyVeryOwnTestPassword123$"
}
```

And here are the values for the `TestAdministrator` account:

```
{
  "userName": "TestAdministrator",
  "email": "test-administrator@email.com",
  "password": "MyVeryOwnTestPassword123$"
}
```

NOTE   As always, feel free to change the usernames and/or passwords.

That's it for users. Let's proceed with roles.

9.4.2   *Creating the new roles*

The most convenient way to create roles is to use the `RoleManager` API, part of the `Microsoft.AspNetCore.Identity` namespace. We're going to use its `CreateAsync` method, which accepts an `IdentityRole` object as a parameter and uses it to create a new record in the persistence store—in our scenario, the [AspNetRoles] database table—assigning an unique `Id` to it. Here's how we can implement it:

```
await _roleManager.CreateAsync(new IdentityRole("RoleName"));
```

As we can see, the `IdentityRole` object's constructor accepts a value of type `string` representing the role name. After we create the role, we'll need to use this name within the code to refer to it. For that reason, defining these names as constants might be a good idea.

ADDING THE ROLENAMES CONSTANTS

To define these names as constants, create a new `RoleNames.cs` file in the `/Constants/` folder, and fill it with the code in the following listing.

Listing 9.10 `/Constants/RoleNames.cs` file

```
namespace MyBGList.Constants
{
    public static class RoleNames
    {
        public const string Moderator = "Moderator";
        public const string Administrator = "Administrator";
    }
}
```

These constants will allow us to refer to our roles by using a strongly typed approach instead of literal strings every time, preventing human error. Now we can write the code to create those roles. Because we're talking about a database-seeding task that will likely be executed only once, the best place to put it is in our `SeedController`. But using the existing `Put` method (which we implemented in chapter 5 to insert the board-game data into the database) would be bad practice, because it would break the single-responsibility principle. Instead, we should refactor the `SeedController` to create distinct endpoints (and action methods) for the two tasks we want it to handle. We'll rename the existing endpoint `/Seed/BoardGameData` and create a new `/Seed/AuthData` for the new seeding task.

REFACTORING THE SEEDCONTROLLER

To refactor the `SeedController`, open the `/Controllers/SeedController.cs` file, and modify the existing code as shown in the following listing (updated lines in bold).

Listing 9.11 `/Controllers/SeedController.cs` file: Class refactoring

```
using Microsoft.AspNetCore.Authorization;      | Required
using Microsoft.AspNetCore.Identity;           | namespaces

// ... existing code
```

```
namespace MyBGList.Controllers
{                                                    New attribute-
    [Authorize]                                      based routing
    [Route("[controller]/[action]")]                 behavior
    [ApiController]
    public class SeedController : ControllerBase
    {

        // ... existing code

        private readonly RoleManager<IdentityRole> _roleManager;

        private readonly UserManager<ApiUser> _userManager;

        public SeedController(
            ApplicationDbContext context,
            IWebHostEnvironment env,
            ILogger<SeedController> logger,
            RoleManager<IdentityRole> roleManager,
            UserManager<ApiUser> userManager)
        {                                                        RoleManager
            _context = context;                                 API
            _env = env;
            _logger = logger;
            _roleManager = roleManager;
            _userManager = userManager;
        }

        [HttpPut]                                        Existing Put action
        [ResponseCache(CacheProfileName = "NoCache")]    method renamed
        public async Task<IActionResult> BoardGameData() BoardGameData
        {
            // ... existing code
        }

        [HttpPost]
        [ResponseCache(NoStore = true)]
        public async Task<IActionResult> AuthData()      New AuthData
        {                                                action method
            throw new NotImplementedException();
        }
    }
}
```

UserManager API (annotation pointing to `private readonly UserManager<ApiUser> _userManager;` and `_userManager = userManager;`)

This code should be easy to understand. We changed the controller's routing rules to make the endpoints match the action names; then we injected the RoleManager and UserManager APIs that we'll need to create and assign roles. Finally, we renamed the existing Put action method BoardGameData and added a new AuthData action method to handle the role-creation task.

Notice that we didn't implement the new method, instead focusing on the Seed-Controller's refactoring part of the job. Now we can proceed with the implementation of the `AuthData` action method, replacing the "not implemented" code with the code in the following listing.

Listing 9.12 `/Controllers/SeedController.cs` file: `AuthData` method

```
[HttpPost]
[ResponseCache(NoStore = true)]
public async Task<IActionResult> AuthData()
{
    int rolesCreated = 0;
    int usersAddedToRoles = 0;

    if (!await _roleManager.RoleExistsAsync(RoleNames.Moderator))
    {
        await _roleManager.CreateAsync(
            new IdentityRole(RoleNames.Moderator));
        rolesCreated++;
    }
    if (!await _roleManager.RoleExistsAsync(RoleNames.Administrator))
    {
        await _roleManager.CreateAsync(
            new IdentityRole(RoleNames.Administrator));
        rolesCreated++;
    }

    var testModerator = await _userManager
        .FindByNameAsync("TestModerator");
    if (testModerator != null
        && !await _userManager.IsInRoleAsync(
            testModerator, RoleNames.Moderator))
    {
        await _userManager.AddToRoleAsync(testModerator,
            RoleNames.Moderator);
        usersAddedToRoles++;
    }

    var testAdministrator = await _userManager
        .FindByNameAsync("TestAdministrator");
    if (testAdministrator != null
        && !await _userManager.IsInRoleAsync(
            testAdministrator, RoleNames.Administrator))
    {
        await _userManager.AddToRoleAsync(
            testAdministrator, RoleNames.Moderator);
        await _userManager.AddToRoleAsync(
            testAdministrator, RoleNames.Administrator);
        usersAddedToRoles++;
    }

    return new JsonResult(new
    {
        RolesCreated = rolesCreated,
        UsersAddedToRoles = usersAddedToRoles
    });
}
```

Creates the roles

Adds users to roles

As we can see, we included some checks to ensure that

- Roles will be created only if they don't exist yet.
- Users will be added to roles only if they do exist and are not already in.

These controls will prevent the code from throwing errors if the action method is called more than once.

> **TIP**   The `TestAdministrator` user has been added to multiple roles: `Moderator` and `Administrator`. That's perfectly fine for our assignment, because we want administrators to have the same privileges as moderators.

9.4.3   *Assigning users to roles*

Because we've already created the `TestModerator` and `TestAdministrator` users, assigning them to new roles will be an easy task. We need to launch our project in Debug mode, access the SwaggerUI, and execute the `/Seed/AuthData` endpoint.

Because we previously set the `[Authorize]` attribute to the whole `SeedController`, however, if we try to call that endpoint without a valid JWT, we'll receive a `401 – Unauthorized` status code. To avoid that result, we have two choices:

- Authenticate ourselves with the `/Account/Login` endpoint (any user will do the trick), and then set the resulting JWT in the SwaggerUI's Authorize pop-up window.
- Comment out the `[Authorize]` attribute before executing the project and calling the `/Seed/AuthData` endpoint, and then uncomment it.

Regardless of the route we take, assuming that everything goes well, we should receive a `200 – OK` status code with the following JSON response body:

```
{
  "rolesCreated": 2,
  "usersAddedToRoles": 2
}
```

We've successfully created our roles and added our users to them. Now we need to ensure that we put these roles in the bearer token so that the authorization middleware can check their presence and act accordingly.

9.4.4   *Adding role-based claims to JWT*

To add the roles to the bearer token, we need to open the `/Controllers/Account-Controller.cs` file and then update the `Login` action method, adding a claim for each role that the successfully authenticated user belongs to. The following code snippet shows how (new lines in bold):

```
// ... existing code

var claims = new List<Claim>();
claims.Add(new Claim(
    ClaimTypes.Name, user.UserName));
```

```
claims.AddRange(
    (await _userManager.GetRolesAsync(user))
        .Select(r => new Claim(ClaimTypes.Role, r)));

// ... existing code
```

As we can see, the JWT of an authenticated user now contains zero, one, or even multiple role-based claims, depending on the number of roles the user belongs to. Those claims will be used to authorize that user's requests or not, depending on how we configure the authorization rules for each controller and/or action method.

9.4.5 *Setting up role-based auth rules*

Now that we've ensured that our authenticated user's JWT will contain a claim for each of their roles (if any), we can update our existing [Authorize] attributes to take roles into account. Let's start with the moderator role. Open the BoardGames-Controller, DomainsController, and MechanicsController files, and change the existing [Authorize] attribute applied to their update method in the following way:

```
[Authorize(Roles = RoleNames.Moderator)]
```

This code will change the attribute's behavior. Instead of authorizing all authenticated users regardless of their roles, now the attribute will authorize only users with the Moderator role. Because we're adding a reference to the RoleNames static class, we also need to add the following namespace reference at the top of each controller's file:

```
using MyBGList.Constants;
```

Let's repeat this process for the administrator role. Change the existing [Authorize] attribute applied to the controller's delete method in the following way:

```
[Authorize(Roles = RoleNames.Administrator)]
```

Then open the SeedController, and update its [Authorize] attribute (which we applied to the controller itself) with the preceding one, as restricting that controller to administrators is part of our assignment.

9.4.6 *Testing the RBAC flow*

To perform a harmless test, instead of using the existing endpoint, which would make some permanent changes in our data, we can create two new Minimal API test methods with the authorization rules we want to check. Open the Program.cs file, and add the following code right below the method handling the /auth/test/2 endpoint that we added earlier:

```
app.MapGet("/auth/test/2",
    [Authorize(Roles = RoleNames.Moderator)]
    [EnableCors("AnyOrigin")]
```

```
        [ResponseCache(NoStore = true)] () =>
        {
            return Results.Ok("You are authorized!");
        });

app.MapGet("/auth/test/3",
        [Authorize(Roles = RoleNames.Administrator)]
        [EnableCors("AnyOrigin")]
        [ResponseCache(NoStore = true)] () =>
        {
            return Results.Ok("You are authorized!");
        });
```

Now we can perform the following test cycle, which strongly resembles the one we designed for our first authorization flow. From the SwaggerUI main dashboard, perform the following steps:

1 Call the `Account/Login` endpoint with the `TestUser`'s username and password to receive a valid JWT.

   This user doesn't belong to any role.

2 Copy the JWT to the clipboard, click the SwaggerUI's Authorize button, copy its value to the input text box in the pop-up window, and click the Authorize button to close the pop-up window.

3 Call the `/auth/test/2` and `/auth/test/3` endpoints.

   If everything works as expected, we should get a `401 - Unauthorized` status code, because those endpoints are restricted to moderators and administrators, and `TestUser` isn't one of them, because it has none of the corresponding roles.

4 Repeat steps 1, 2, and 3 for the `TestModerator` account.

   This time, we should receive a `200 - OK` status code for the `/auth/test/2` endpoint and a `401 - Unauthorized` status code for the `/auth/test/3` endpoint. The former is restricted to moderators (which we are), and the latter is for administrators only (which we are not).

5 Repeat steps 1, 2, and 3 for the `TestAdministrator` account.

   This time, we should get a `200 - OK` status code for both endpoints, because that account belongs to the `Moderator` and `Administrator` roles.

9.4.7   *Using alternative authorization methods*

As we saw while working on it, the RBAC approach that we implemented relies on a claim of type role (`ClaimTypes.Role`) to perform its authorization checks. If the JWT token contains such a claim, and the claim's content matches the [`Authorize`] attribute's requirements, the user is authorized.

A lot of other claim types, however, can be assigned and checked to determine whether the user is authorized. We could authorize only users who have a mobile-phone number, for example, by using a `ClaimTypes.MobilePhone`, and we could perform such a check instead of, or in addition to, the users' given roles.

CLAIMS-BASED ACCESS CONTROL

This approach, called *claims-based access control (CBAC)*, includes the same features offered by RBAC and many more, because it can be used to check for any claim (or set of claims) at the same time.

> **NOTE** We could say that RBAC is nothing more and nothing less than a high-level abstraction of CBAC based on a single specific claim of `ClaimTypes.Role`.

Unlike RBAC, which is easy and fast to implement thanks to the `Role` property of the `[Authorize]` attribute, claims requirements are policy-based, so they must be explicitly declared by defining and registering a policy in the `Program.cs` file. Here's how we can add a `"ModeratorWithMobilePhone"` policy that will check for the presence of both the `Moderator` role and the mobile-phone number:

```
builder.Services.AddAuthorization(options =>
{
    options.AddPolicy("ModeratorWithMobilePhone", policy =>
        policy
            .RequireClaim(ClaimTypes.Role, RoleNames.Moderator)
            .RequireClaim(ClaimTypes.MobilePhone));
});
```

Checks for the Claim with a given value

Checks for the Claim presence only

> **NOTE** This technique is roughly the same one that we used to register the CORS policies in chapter 3.

Paste the preceding code snippet into the `Program.cs` file below the `builder.service AddAuthentication` lines to configure the authentication services. Then we can set the policy as a parameter of the `[Authorize]` attribute in the following way:

```
[Authorize(Policy = "ModeratorWithMobilePhone")]
```

This policy requires some modifications to the following parts of our existing code:

- The `RegisterDTO` class, to allow a registering user to add their `MobilePhone` number
- The `AccountController`'s `Register` action method, to save the `MobilePhone` value in the database (if present)
- The `AccountController`'s `Login` action method, to conditionally add a claim of `ClaimTypes.MobilePhone` to the JWT token containing the user's mobile phone number (if present)

I'm not going to use this approach in this book. I'm showing it briefly only because it can be useful for implementing some specific authorization requirements.

POLICY-BASED ACCESS CONTROL

Although CBAC is more versatile than RBAC, it allows us to check for the presence of only one of multiple claims and/or their specific value(s). What if the claim value isn't a single value, or if we need a more complex check? We may want to define a policy to authorize only users with an age equal to or greater than 18, and we won't be able to do that by checking for the presence of a claim of `ClaimTypes.DateOfBirth` or for a specific date-of-birth value.

Whenever we need to perform this kind of check, we can use the *policy-based access control (PBAC)* approach—the most complex and versatile authorization method provided by the `Microsoft.AspNetCore.Authorization` namespace. This technique is similar to CBAC, as it also requires a declarative approach—that is, declaring policies in the `Program.cs` file. But instead of checking for the mere presence (and, optionally, values) of one or multiple claims, it uses a more generic interface composed by one or more requirements (`IAuthorizationRequirement`) and requirement handlers (`IAuthorizationHandler`).

> **NOTE** This interface is also used under the hood by the CBAC's `Require-Claim` method. We could say that both RBAC and CBAC are simplified implementations of PBAC based on preconfigured policies.

I'm not going to use PBAC in this book, as it would require implementing some sample requirements and requirement handlers classes. But I'll briefly introduce the `RequireAssertion` method, which is a convenient way to configure and build policy-based authorization checks by using an anonymous function. Here's how we can use this method to define an "equal to or greater than 18" policy:

```
options.AddPolicy("MinAge18", policy =>
    policy
        .RequireAssertion(ctx =>
            ctx.User.HasClaim(c => c.Type == ClaimTypes.DateOfBirth)
            && DateTime.ParseExact(
                "yyyyMMdd",
                ctx.User.Claims.First(c =>
                        c.Type == ClaimTypes.DateOfBirth).Value,
                System.Globalization.CultureInfo.InvariantCulture)
            >= DateTime.Now.AddYears(-18)));
```

The added value is the `AuthorizationHandlerContext` object exposed by the `Require-Assertion` method, which contains a reference to the `ClaimsPrincipal` representing the current user. The `ClaimsPrincipal` class can be used not only to check for the presence and/or value of any claim, but also to use, transform, and/or convert those values to fulfill all our needs. Again, this policy could be used as a parameter of some hypothetical [Authorize] attributes to restrict some controllers, action methods, and/or Minimal API methods to users over 18 years of age in the following way:

```
[Authorize(Policy = "MinAge18")]
```

This policy would also require a lot of refactoring of our existing code, because we currently don't ask about (and collect) the registering user's date of birth. For that reason, I'll stop here, leaving the preceding code for reference purposes only.

> **Some useful authorization-related references**
>
> For additional info about the `[Authorize]` attribute and how to use it, see the guide at http://mng.bz/Nmj2.
>
> To learn more about RBAC, CBAC, and PBAC, check out the following guides:
>
> - http://mng.bz/DZj9
> - http://mng.bz/IJnM
> - http://mng.bz/Bl8g

This section concludes our test run, as well as our journey into ASP.NET Core authentication and authorization. It's important to understand that we've only scratched the surface of these vast and complex topics. The sample source code that we've put together throughout this chapter may be good enough for some basic web APIs without sensitive or valuable data, but it won't likely be appropriate for more complex scenarios unless we back it up with some additional security measures.

As for ASP.NET Core Identity, we've only scratched the surface of what the framework can do, from PBAC to non-JWT bearers, not to mention built-in integration with third-party authorization providers and protocols such as OAuth2, which I haven't dealt with for reasons of space. Nonetheless, the extensive overview that this chapter provides should still help us understand how ASP.NET Core authentication and authorization work and how to implement them in a typical web API scenario.

9.5   Exercises

The best way to imprint what we've learned in this chapter is to challenge ourselves with some identity-related upgrade tasks that our product owner may want to assign to us. As always, the solutions to the exercises can be found on GitHub in the /Chapter_09/Exercises/ folder. To test them, replace the relevant files in your MyBGList project with those in that folder, and run the app.

9.5.1   Adding a new role

Add a new "SuperAdmin" role to the static class that we're using to define the role names, using a strongly typed approach. Then modify the SeedController's AuthData method to ensure that the new role will be created if it doesn't already exist.

9.5.2   Creating a new user

Create a new "TestSuperAdmin" user, using the Account/Register endpoint, as we did with the TestUser, TestModerator, and TestAdministrator users. Feel free to choose your own password (but make sure you'll remember it for future use).

9.5.3   Assigning a user to roles

Modify the SeedController's AuthData method to assign the Moderator, Administrator, and SuperAdmin roles to the TestSuperAdmin user.

9.5.4 *Implementing a test endpoint*

Add a new /auth/test/4 endpoint, using Minimal API, and restrict its access to autho-rized users with the SuperAdmin role.

9.5.5 *Testing the RBAC flow*

Use the Account/Login endpoint to recover a JWT for the TestSuperAdmin account, and use it to try to access the /auth/test/4 endpoint and ensure that the new user and role work as expected.

Summary

- *Authentication* is a mechanism to verify that an entity (or a person) is what it (or they) claims to be. *Authorization* defines what an entity (or person) is capable of doing.
  - Both processes play a pivotal role in any web app or service that needs to restrict access to content, data, and/or endpoints.
- In most implementation methods, the authentication process typically happens before the authorization process, because the system needs to identify the call-ing client before assigning its permissions set.
  - But some authentication techniques, such as bearer tokens, enforce a self-contained authorization mechanism, thus allowing the server to authorize the client without having to authenticate it every time.
  - Bearer tokens' self-contained authorization approach has several advantages in terms of versatility but may raise some security problems if the server or the client can't protect the token from third-party access.
- The ASP.NET Core Identity framework provides a rich set of API and high-level abstractions that can be used to manage and store user accounts in any ASP.NET Core app, which makes it a great choice for implementing an authentication and authorization mechanism in any ASP.NET Core app.
  - Furthermore, it can be easily integrated with EF Core thanks to several built-in classes, helper, and extension methods.
- ASP.NET Core Identity provides several ways to perform authorization checks:
  - *RBAC*, which is easy to implement and often good enough for most needs.
  - *CBAC*, which is slightly more complex to implement yet more versatile, because it can be used to check for any claim.
  - *PBAC*, the underlying structure used by RBAC and CBAC, which can be accessed directly to set up more advanced authorization requirements.
- Authentication and authorization are complex topics, especially from an IT security perspective, because they're the primary targets of hacking attempts, DoS attacks, and other malicious activities.
  - For that reason, the techniques described in this chapter should be used with great care, always checking for updates, and used with the best practices pro-vided by the ASP.NET Core community and IT security standards.

Beyond REST

This chapter covers

- Overview of some notable REST drawbacks
- GraphQL introduction (pros and cons)
- GraphQL implementation with HotChocolate
- Overview of gRPC Remote Procedure Call (gRPC)
- gRPC implementation with `Grpc.AspNetCore`
- Other REST alternatives

As we've known since chapter 1, the REST architectural paradigm has been the most popular web API architecture for several years, thanks mostly to its scalability, flexibility, and portability, not to mention the huge adoption of the JavaScript Object Notation (JSON) data-exchange format by the IT world. But if we could take a closer look at all the REST web APIs in use nowadays, we'd likely see that only a fraction of them are RESTful. Most REST implementations adhere to only some of the guiding constraints defined by Roy Fielding which we reviewed in chapter 3 and have implemented throughout this book. Nonetheless, all of them have been developed with the REST standard in mind.

This indisputable success is more than justified. When it comes to designing and implementing a web service, REST is almost always a great choice, especially if we're looking for simplicity, versatility, and performance—the top reasons why it has replaced SOAP almost everywhere. But it's also important to understand that REST is not the only choice we have or even the best possible alternative in any given circumstance.

In this chapter, we'll take a comprehensive look at two alternatives: Facebook's GraphQL and Google Remote Procedure Call (gRPC). Both provide a different way of implementing web APIs and offer some advantages over the REST standard in specific scenarios. We'll see how we can implement them in ASP.NET Core with the help of some third-party NuGet packages, and we'll use them to interact with our board-game-related data as we do with our current REST-based approach.

10.1 REST drawbacks

Before considering the alternative approaches, let's acknowledge some well-known downsides and limitations of the REST standard. Rest assured that I'm not going to reveal some major blocking problems that could affect any web API, regardless of its use. The drawbacks I'm about to introduce may have little or no impact in most scenarios, depending on how our data is structured and how our clients are supposed to use it.

But in several circumstances, these limitations could result in nontrivial performance problems, as well as force us to design our endpoints and data-retrieval logic in a suboptimal way. The best way to understand what I mean is to take a close look at the data-fetching capabilities of the `MyBGList` web API that we've been working on—from the client point of view.

10.1.1 Overfetching

Whenever we want to retrieve the data of some board games, we need to issue a GET request to the `/BoardGames` endpoint (with some optional input parameters). By performing this call, we obtain a JSON-serialized `RestDTO` object containing the JSON representation of some `BoardGame` entities (paged, sorted, and/or filtered, depending on the input parameters) fetched from the underlying SQL database. We know this behavior all too well, because we've called the `/BoardGames` endpoint many times during our test rounds, and we also know that each of these entities contains several properties.

What if we need only some of them? We may want to populate a list of board games in which we display only each game's `Title` and possibly a hyperlink to each game's detail page, for which we also require the game's `Id`. But our current endpoint doesn't provide a mechanism that lets us choose the properties we need to fetch; we need to get them all. This scenario is an example of *overfetching*, which means that our clients are often forced to retrieve more data than they need.

> **NOTE** If we think about it, we can see how a certain amount of overfetching will inevitably be present in all our endpoints, because all of them are designed to return the whole entity and all its properties. Unless the client

requires all of them, every data-retrieval request received by our web API will ultimately result in some unnecessary data traffic.

This much unnecessary data traffic might have a negligible affect on most small services, but it can become a serious performance hit for large-scale, enterprise-level web APIs. To mitigate this problem, we could adopt some countermeasures, such as the following:

- *Exclude some entity properties from the JSON outcome by decorating them with the* [Json-Ignore] *data attribute, which works the way its name implies.* The attribute works like an on/off switch for all requests of all clients, however, so those "excluded" properties won't be available to anyone.

- *Create alternative endpoints with DTO classes containing only a fraction of the entity's properties, ideally matching the client's needs.* This approach, however, will inevitably complicate our web API codebase, eventually leading to code bloat, disorganization, and maintenance troubles, not to mention usability problems due to the presence of multiple endpoints returning similar yet not identical data.

- *Refactor our current endpoint(s) to allow the client to select the properties it wants to retrieve (and/or exclude those it doesn't need).* Implementing this workaround, however, will greatly increase the complexity of our action method's source code, as well as the public interface of our endpoints. Furthermore, we'll be forced to abandon our strongly typed entities and data-transfer objects (DTOs) in favor of anonymous objects or dynamic types unless we want to conditionally set their properties or leave them null. Both approaches can lead to interface errors, undesirable behaviors, and source code that's full of bad practices and hard to maintain.

There's no easy way to avoid overfetching as long as we're using a RESTful web API.

10.1.2 Underfetching

Let's go back to the list of board games we want to populate. That list is supposed to contain the Title of each board game, which is also a hyperlink to an endpoint showing the details for that single board game. Currently, we don't have an endpoint that returns a single board game, but we could easily implement one. Let's do that.

The action plan is simple: we need to receive the board game Id and return a RestDTO object containing the matching board game (if any). Open the /Controller/BoardGamesController.cs file, and paste the code in the following listing right below the existing BoardGames method.

Listing 10.1 BoardGamesController.cs file: GetBoardGame method

```
[HttpGet("{id}")]
[ResponseCache(CacheProfileName = "Any-60")]
public async Task<RestDTO<BoardGame?>> GetBoardGame(int id)
```

```
{
    _logger.LogInformation(CustomLogEvents.BoardGamesController_Get,
        "GetBoardGame method started.");

    BoardGame? result = null;
    var cacheKey = $"GetBoardGame-{id}";
    if (!_memoryCache.TryGetValue<BoardGame>(cacheKey, out result))
    {
        result = await _context.BoardGames.FirstOrDefaultAsync(bg => bg.Id
== id);
        _memoryCache.Set(cacheKey, result, new TimeSpan(0, 0, 30));
    }

    return new RestDTO<BoardGame?>()
    {
        Data = result,
        PageIndex = 0,
        PageSize = 1,
        RecordCount = result != null ? 1 : 0,
        Links = new List<LinkDTO> {
            new LinkDTO(
                Url.Action(
                    null,
                    "BoardGames",
                    new { id },
                    Request.Scheme)!,
                "self",
                "GET"),
        }
    };
}
```

This code doesn't contain anything new: we're accepting a board game's Id as input, using it to retrieve the board-game entry from the database, and returning it to the caller (if it does exist) within a RestDTO object. Let's test it. Launch our app in Debug mode, locate the new GET /BoardGames/{id} endpoint in the SwaggerUI, expand the panel, and click the Try It Out button to execute it. Set the id input value to 30 to receive the following response object:

```
{
    "id": 30,
    "name": "Dark Tower",
    "year": 1981,
    "minPlayers": 1,
    "maxPlayers": 4,
    "playTime": 90,
    "minAge": 10,
    "usersRated": 1261,
    "ratingAverage": 6.82,
    "bggRank": 2534,
    "complexityAverage": 1.81,
    "ownedUsers": 1655,
    "createdDate": "2022-04-04T09:14:43.6922169",
```

```
   "lastModifiedDate": "2022-04-04T09:14:43.6922169",
   "boardGames_Domains": null,
   "boardGames_Mechanics": null
}
```

Again, we're receiving all the properties of the resulting board-game entry, which is fine for our current needs, because now we need that data to create a detail view. Notice, however, that the last two properties—boardGames_Domains and boardGames_Mechanics—are set to null. Does that mean that the Dark Tower board game doesn't belong to any domain and doesn't implement any mechanic? No. Those properties are null simply because the data is stored in different database tables and linked through a many-to-many relationship (as we learned in chapters 4 and 5). That data isn't part of the BoardGame entity unless we explicitly include it in the query—a typical example of underfetching.

> **NOTE** Those properties are null even when we retrieve a list of board games by using the GET /BoardGames endpoint, because we're not explicitly including the related entities there as well. We didn't for a good reason: we'd end up overfetching and creating a considerable performance affect, considering that this endpoint might be used to return a considerable number of board games.

Again, we have several ways to work around this problem, such as the following:

■ *Add the missing data to the existing endpoint by explicitly using the* Include() *method provided by Entity Framework Core (EF Core).* This approach could be viable for endpoints that return a single entity, such as the new one we added, but it can't be done for those that return multiple results, for obvious performance reasons. We could minimize this drawback by linking the Include behavior to the presence of some new input parameters we might add, but this approach would eventually lead to the complexity and maintenance problems resulting from overfetching.

■ *Create alternative endpoints that return aggregate data to match the client's actual needs, such as* /GetBoardGamesWithRelatedData. Again, this approach is the same one we could use to deal with overfetching, but it has the same drawbacks: code bloat, maintenance, and usability problems.

■ *Create additional endpoints that return the missing data and that the client can call right after the existing one (or in a parallel thread) to retrieve everything it needs, such as* /GetDomainsByBoardGameId *and* /GetMechanicsByBoardGameId. This approach is typically more elegant, reusable, and tidy than the alternative-endpoints approach. But it forces clients to perform several HTTP requests (creating a additional overhead and a performance hit), as well as do a lot of additional work to combine/aggregate the data coming from the various endpoints.

As with overfetching, there's no easy way to get rid of underfetching problems when working with a RESTful web API. The only thing we can do is find an acceptable compromise among the number of endpoints, their intrinsic complexity (which often can be measured in terms of input parameters), and the specific requirements of the various clients.

This explains why the RESTful API and most general-purpose Software as a Service (SaaS) platforms that need to accommodate thousands of clients with many different needs (PayPal, MailChimp, TrustPilot, Google Analytics, and so on) often end up being surprisingly complex, with lots of endpoints and input parameters. That's also why the undisputable dominance of the REST API architecture has been challenged in the past few years by some modern alternatives. In the next sections, we're going to review some of those alternatives and see how we can implement them with ASP.NET Core.

10.2   *GraphQL*

Let's start our journey with GraphQL, a query language for APIs created by Facebook in 2012 for internal use and then open-sourced in 2015. After its public release, the language gained a lot of popularity throughout the web developer community and was quickly followed by several implementations for most popular programming languages, including JavaScript, Go, PHP, Java, Python, and Ruby.

GraphQL's success is due mostly to its great flexibility; it allows clients to receive data by using a single declarative query to a single endpoint. In other words, each client can ask for the data fields it needs and receive them (and only them) within a single request/response cycle, avoiding the risk of overfetching and underfetching without having to perform multiple HTTP requests at the same time.

10.2.1   *GraphQL advantages*

To better understand the differences between REST and GraphQL, take a look at figure 10.1. Notice that REST forces us to deal with multiple API endpoints, each of them retrieving data from our database management system (DBMS) by using our implementation strategy and sending a nonconfigurable JSON-serialized result set, eventually leading to a certain amount of overfetching and/or underfetching. As we learned earlier, we can mitigate these problems by adding endpoints. That solution, however, will inevitably require our clients to perform multiple round trips, as well as add complexity and increase development time. Conversely, GraphQL gives us the chance to deal with a single endpoint that will accept a single, standardized data-retrieval query, process and execute it against the DBMS by using its internal engine, and return a combined set of JSON data, avoiding overfetching, underfetching, and multiple round trips.

> **NOTE**   Both the query and the resulting data will have the same JSON structure, generated by the GraphQL runtime using the standards given by the GraphQL specs. We'll learn more about these specs (and how to use them) in a short while.

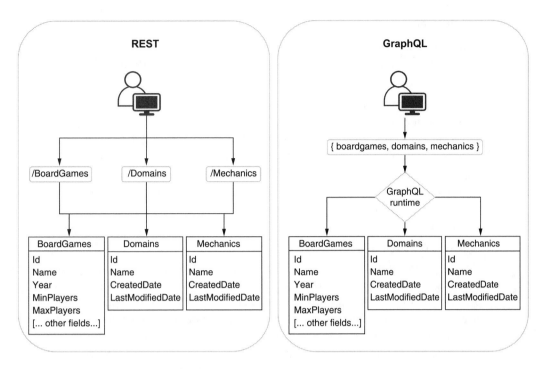

Figure 10.1   REST and GraphQL comparison

This approach is particularly beneficial for developers (and for the web API codebase in general), as it requires only a single endpoint. Furthermore, because the data is retrieved via a standardized query syntax, there's no need to implement filtering, sorting, and ordering features manually, based on custom input parameters. All the hard work is done by the underlying GraphQL runtime, assuming that the clients adopt the GraphQL specs.

> **NOTE**   The GraphQL specs are available at https://spec.graphql.org. For additional info regarding GraphQL, code samples, use cases, and FAQs, check out the official website at https://graphql.org.

Here's another notable advantage for developers: because clients can define the exact data they need from the server, the data model can be changed and improved over time with the risk of client-side incompatibilities, possibly even without releasing a new API version. Being able to add fields to the model without breaking the frontend code is a great added value for most microservices, especially if they feed data to multiple clients built with different frameworks (such as websites and mobile apps).

10.2.2 *GraphQL drawbacks*

Although GraphQL has many advantages over traditional REST APIs, it also has some key disadvantages. We can group these disadvantages into three categories: caching, performance, and complexity.

CACHING PROBLEMS

As we learned in chapter 8, RESTful APIs can use the built-in caching features provided by the HTTP protocol to implement client, intermediate, and/or server-side response caching. GraphQL comes with no native caching support, so we'd need to implement our own standard or rely on third-party libraries. Moreover, implementing an efficient cache mechanism won't be an easy task, because all requests are addressed to a single endpoint that's supposed to return highly customized (hence, often different) data sets.

PERFORMANCE PROBLEMS

Despite their well-known overfetching and underfetching problems, RESTful APIs are typically fast when it comes to issuing a single request to a given endpoint. As long as the data model is thin and/or the number of required round trips is low, the REST architecture can provide great performance and minimal server-side overhead.

Although GraphQL is also meant to be efficient, its underlying engine will likely require some additional overhead. Furthermore, because the data-retrieval queries are issued by the clients, there's an increased risk of performance loss due to time-consuming or nonoptimized requests. We can mitigate this problem to some extent by implementing (or adopting) a highly efficient GraphQL runtime. But processing custom, client-made queries and executing them against the DBMS is a complex job that can easily lead to unexpected scenarios (circular references, nested loops, nonindexed column lookups, and so on) that could slow or even crash the server.

COMPLEXITY PROBLEMS

RESTful APIs are easy to learn and implement, thanks mostly to the built-in support provided by most development frameworks, as well as the overall simplicity of the underlying HTTP-based approach and its widespread adoption. GraphQL often comes with no built-in support, has a steeper learning curve, and is still unknown to most developers. Furthermore, it still lacks some important features out of the box—caching, file uploads, and error handling, for example—that are likely to require additional work. Implementing these features (or finding viable workarounds) won't be as easy as with REST, because community support is still relatively limited. The increased complexity also affects clients. Writing a GraphQL query is much harder than calling a typical REST endpoint, especially if we want to avoid overfetching and underfetching, which is one of the main reasons to use it.

FINAL WORDS

With all its pros and cons, GraphQL provides a viable solution to the most relevant drawbacks of REST APIs. Although it's not suitable for all scenarios, it can be a valid alternative for dealing with big scalable projects that have rapidly changing data models, as long as the developers are up to the task. In the following sections, we accept the challenge by implementing a full-featured GraphQL API using ASP.NET Core to handle our `MyBGList` data model.

10.2.3 *Implementing GraphQL*

Because ASP.NET Core comes with no built-in GraphQL support, we have to identify and choose a suitable third-party library that does the heavy lifting unless we want to implement this feature by ourselves. We need a component that's able to perform the following steps:

1 Expose a GraphQL API endpoint that clients will use to send their queries.
2 Process the incoming requests (with GraphQL queries) against our `MyBGList` data model.
3 Retrieve the requested data from the underlying DBMS.
4 Provide a suitable HTTP response with the resulting data.

Ideally, steps 2 and 3 (the GraphQL runtime tasks) should be performed with EF Core, which would allow us to preserve our existing data model and everything we've done so far. It's evident that implementing all these requirements from scratch isn't a good idea; that approach would require a considerable amount of work (and source code), not to mention knowledge that we don't have (yet). That's why we'll opt for the third-party-libraries route.

CHOOSING THE GRAPHQL LIBRARY

As of today, we have two main third-party alternatives to choose between: GraphQL.NET (https://github.com/graphql-dotnet/graphql-dotnet) and HotChocolate (https://github .com/ChilliCream/hotchocolate). Both packages are open source (MIT-licensed), production-ready, and well-regarded in the ASP.NET developer community. Because we have to make a choice, we'll go with HotChocolate. It provides a couple of convenient features for our scenario, such as the following:

- A built-in GraphQL integrated development environment (IDE) called Banana-CakePop, which we can use to test the API endpoint without installing a dedicated client, as we've done with SwaggerUI
- Native EF Core support, which is precisely what we're looking for

Now that we've made our choice, we can move to installation.

INSTALLING HOTCHOCOLATE

As always, to install the HotChocolate NuGet packages, we can use the Visual Studio's NuGet graphical user interface (GUI), the Package Manager console window, or the .NET command-line interface (CLI). Here are the commands to install them by using the .NET CLI:

```
dotnet add package HotChocolate.AspNetCore --version 12.15.2
dotnet add package HotChocolate.AspNetCore.Authorization --version 12.15.2
dotnet add package HotChocolate.Data.EntityFramework --version 12.15.2
```

NOTE   This version is the latest stable version as of this writing. I strongly suggest using that version to avoid breaking changes, incompatibility problems, and the like.

As we might easily guess, the first package contains the GraphQL services and middleware. The second and third packages contain some useful extension sets that we can use to integrate ASP.NET Core Authorization and EF Core seamlessly into HotChocolate, which will allow us to reuse a lot of work (and source code).

When the package installation is done, try to build the project. If the Implicit Using feature is enabled (the default for most VS2022 C# templates), the RequestDTO object could raise some compiler errors due to an ambiguous reference to the [DefaultValue] attribute. To fix that error, replace the Using statement

```
using System.ComponentModel;
```

with

```
using DefaultValueAttribute = System.ComponentModel.DefaultValueAttribute;
```

which resolves the ambiguity and makes the errors disappear.

TIP   For further info on the Implicit Using feature, introduced with C# version 10, check out http://mng.bz/71mx.

SETTING UP THE GRAPHQL SCHEMA

Now that we've installed HotChocolate, the first thing need we need to do is set up the GraphQL schema, which defines how we want to expose data to our client and the create, read, update, and delete (CRUD) operations we want to allow. The GraphQL schema is typically composed of one or more root operation types that allow clients to perform read, write, and subscription tasks:

- Query—Exposes all the possible data-retrieval queries that we want to make available to our clients. This class serves as a centralized access layer of our data model, with one or more methods corresponding to the various ways to retrieve them.
- Mutation—Allows clients to perform Insert, Update, and/or Delete operations on our data model.
- Subscription—Enables a real-time messaging mechanism that clients can use to subscribe to various events and be notified of their occurrence.

The Query root type must always be present, whereas Mutation and Subscription are optional. Furthermore, Query and Mutation root types are stateless, whereas the Subscription type must be stateful because it needs to preserve the document, variables, and context over the lifetime of each active subscription.

TIP   For a detailed overview of Query, Mutation, and Subscription root operation types, see http://mng.bz/rdMZ.

To keep things simple, we'll implement only the `Query` and `Mutation` root operation types. These types will allow us to mimic the CRUD functionalities provided by the RESTful approach we've been working with.

ADDING THE QUERY TYPE

Let's start with the `Query`. In Visual Studio's Solution Explorer window, create a new /GraphQL/ top-level folder in our `MyBGList` project; then add a new `Query.cs` file to it. We need to create a public method for each entity in our data model that we want our clients to access by using GraphQL, mapping it to its corresponding `DbSet`. The following listing shows how.

Listing 10.2   /GraphQL/Query.cs file

```
using MyBGList.Models;

namespace MyBGList.GraphQL
{
    public class Query
    {
        [Serial]
        [UsePaging]
        [UseProjection]
        [UseFiltering]
        [UseSorting]
        public IQueryable<BoardGame> GetBoardGames(        ⟵── Entry point for
            [Service] ApplicationDbContext context)              BoardGames
            => context.BoardGames;

        [Serial]
        [UsePaging]
        [UseProjection]
        [UseFiltering]
        [UseSorting]
        public IQueryable<Domain> GetDomains(        ⟵── Entry point
            [Service] ApplicationDbContext context)         for Domains
            => context.Domains;

        [Serial]
        [UsePaging]
        [UseProjection]
        [UseFiltering]
        [UseSorting]
        public IQueryable<Mechanic> GetMechanics(        ⟵── Entry point
            [Service] ApplicationDbContext context)            for Mechanics
            => context.Mechanics;
    }
}
```

Two things in this code are worth noting:

- Each method is mapped to an EF Core `DbSet`, returning it as an `IQueryable` object that GraphQL runtime will use under the hood to retrieve the records from the DBMS.

- Each method has some data annotation attributes that we've never seen before. As we can easily guess, those attributes are part of HotChocolate and allow us to use some powerful built-in features without having to implement them explicitly.

The following list describes the purpose of each attribute:

- [Serial]—This attribute configures the GraphQL runtime to execute certain tasks in serial mode rather than in parallel mode, as required by our current ApplicationDbContext implementation. This approach will likely have some performance effects, but it's an acceptable choice for our sample scenario because it allows us to reuse our source code without refactoring it.
- [UsePaging]—This attribute adds pagination middleware that allows the GraphQL runtime to paginate results by using the Cursor Connections Specification, a standardized pagination approach adopted by GraphQL specs.
- [UseProjection]—This attribute adds dedicated middleware that will project the incoming GraphQL queries to database queries through IQueryable objects.
- [UseFiltering]—This attribute adds filtering middleware that allows the requesting clients to use filters, which will be translated into Language Integrated Query (LINQ) queries (using the IQueryable object) and then to DBMS queries (using EF Core) by the GraphQL runtime. The available filters will be inferred automatically by the runtime (and shown to the clients) by looking at the IQueryable entity types, as SwaggerUI does with the available REST endpoints.
- [UseSorting]—This attribute adds sorting middleware that allows the requesting clients to sort results by using a sorting argument, which will be translated into LINQ queries and then into DBMS queries under the hood.

Before continuing, it might be wise to understand why we're using the [Serial] attribute. When we use the AddDbContext<T> command to register our ApplicationDbContext as a scoped service, a single instance of the class is created and used for the entirety of any given HTTP request. This approach is a good one for typical REST APIs because each endpoint is expected to perform a single DBMS query and return a resulting result set. That's not the case with GraphQL; the runtime will likely have to perform multiple sets of queries and combine the resulting data into a single aggregate response. These queries, per the runtime's default behavior, are executed in parallel for performance reasons, making our DbContext crash with one of the following exceptions (depending on its current state):

- A second operation started on this context before a previous operation was completed
- Cannot access a disposed object

Both exceptions are due to the fact that our current DbContext implementation isn't thread-safe. The [Serial] attribute provides a workaround by forcing the runtime to resolve the queries one after another (serial mode). Alternatively, we could replace our current DbContext registration technique with an approach based on the

`AddDbContextFactory` extension method, registering a factory instead of a single scoped instance. That said, using the attribute, as we did, is a viable workaround for our sample project. The `AddDbContextFactory` approach would likely be the preferred route for production-level GraphQL APIs.

> ## HotChocolate data attributes
> For further information about HotChocolate data attributes, check out the following pages of the official docs:
>
> - http://mng.bz/Vp60
> - http://mng.bz/xdYY
> - http://mng.bz/Zo4a
> - http://mng.bz/AlR7
> - http://mng.bz/2awm

Now that we've added our `Query` root operation type, we're ready to deal with the `Mutation` type.

ADDING THE MUTATION TYPE

Add a new `Mutation.cs` file in the `/GraphQL/` folder; this folder is where we'll put the source code for the `Mutation` root operation type. We're going to create a public method for the `Update` and `Delete` tasks of our `BoardGames`, `Domains`, and `Mechanics` entities (six methods total). This time, the implementation part will be slightly more complex because we're going to use the DTO objects that we created in chapter 5 instead of the raw entity classes, which forces us to map the properties we want to update manually.

> **NOTE** The source code of the `/GraphQL/Mutation.cs` file is long. For that reason, I've split it into three parts—one for each affected entity. The full source code is available in the GitHub repository for this chapter.

The following listing provides the first part of the source code, containing the namespace and class declaration as well as the `Update` and `Delete` methods for the Board-Game entity.

Listing 10.3 `/GraphQL/Mutation.cs` file: `BoardGame` methods

```
using HotChocolate.AspNetCore.Authorization;
using Microsoft.EntityFrameworkCore;
using MyBGList.Constants;
using MyBGList.DTO;
using MyBGList.Models;

namespace MyBGList.GraphQL
{
    public class Mutation
```

```
        {
            [Serial]
            [Authorize(Roles = new[] { RoleNames.Moderator })]
            public async Task<BoardGame?> UpdateBoardGame(
                [Service] ApplicationDbContext context, BoardGameDTO model)
            {
                var boardgame = await context.BoardGames
                    .Where(b => b.Id == model.Id)
                    .FirstOrDefaultAsync();
                if (boardgame != null)
                {
                    if (!string.IsNullOrEmpty(model.Name))
                        boardgame.Name = model.Name;
                    if (model.Year.HasValue && model.Year.Value > 0)
                        boardgame.Year = model.Year.Value;
                    boardgame.LastModifiedDate = DateTime.Now;
                    context.BoardGames.Update(boardgame);
                    await context.SaveChangesAsync();
                }
                return boardgame;
            }

            [Serial]
            [Authorize(Roles = new[] { RoleNames.Administrator })]
            public async Task DeleteBoardGame(
                [Service] ApplicationDbContext context, int id)
            {
                var boardgame = await context.BoardGames
                    .Where(b => b.Id == id)
                    .FirstOrDefaultAsync();
                if (boardgame != null)
                {
                    context.BoardGames.Remove(boardgame);
                    await context.SaveChangesAsync();
                }
            }
        }
```

Updates a BoardGame → (points to `public async Task<BoardGame?> UpdateBoardGame(`)

Deletes a BoardGame → (points to `public async Task DeleteBoardGame(`)

The code in the following listing contains the Update and Delete methods for the Domain entity, which are almost identical to their BoardGame counterparts.

Listing 10.4   /GraphQL/Mutation.cs file: Domain methods

```
        [Serial]
        [Authorize(Roles = new[] { RoleNames.Moderator })]
        public async Task<Domain?> UpdateDomain(
            [Service] ApplicationDbContext context, DomainDTO model)
        {
            var domain = await context.Domains
                .Where(d => d.Id == model.Id)
                .FirstOrDefaultAsync();
            if (domain != null)
            {
                if (!string.IsNullOrEmpty(model.Name))
                    domain.Name = model.Name;
```

Updates a Domain → (points to `public async Task<Domain?> UpdateDomain(`)

```
                    domain.LastModifiedDate = DateTime.Now;
                    context.Domains.Update(domain);
                    await context.SaveChangesAsync();
                }
                return domain;
            }


            [Serial]
            [Authorize(Roles = new[] { RoleNames.Administrator })]
```
Deletes
a Domain ⊢▷
```
            public async Task DeleteDomain(
                [Service] ApplicationDbContext context, int id)
            {
                var domain = await context.Domains
                    .Where(d => d.Id == id)
                    .FirstOrDefaultAsync();
                if (domain != null)
                {
                    context.Domains.Remove(domain);
                    await context.SaveChangesAsync();
                }
            }
```

The following listing shows the methods for the `Mechanic` entity, which follows the same approach.

Listing 10.5   /GraphQL/Mutation.cs file: Mechanic methods

```
            [Serial]
            [Authorize(Roles = new[] { RoleNames.Moderator })]
```
Updates
a Mechanic ⊢▷
```
            public async Task<Mechanic?> UpdateMechanic(
                [Service] ApplicationDbContext context, MechanicDTO model)
            {
                var mechanic = await context.Mechanics
                    .Where(m => m.Id == model.Id)
                    .FirstOrDefaultAsync();
                if (mechanic != null)
                {
                    if (!string.IsNullOrEmpty(model.Name))
                        mechanic.Name = model.Name;
                    mechanic.LastModifiedDate = DateTime.Now;

                    context.Mechanics.Update(mechanic);
                    await context.SaveChangesAsync();
                }
                return mechanic;
            }


            [Serial]
            [Authorize(Roles = new[] { RoleNames.Administrator })]
```
Deletes
a Mechanic ⊢▷
```
            public async Task DeleteMechanic(
                [Service] ApplicationDbContext context, int id)
            {
                var mechanic = await context.Mechanics
                    .Where(m => m.Id == id)
```

```
            .FirstOrDefaultAsync();
        if (mechanic != null)
        {
            context.Mechanics.Remove(mechanic);
            await context.SaveChangesAsync();
        }
    }
  }
}
```

This implementation is similar to what we did in the `BoardGamesController`, `Domains-Controllers`, and `MechanicsController` when we implemented the `Update` and `Delete` methods in chapter 5. But it's important to understand one thing: the `[Authorize]` data attribute that we're using to restrict the access of the GraphQL's `Update` and `Delete` methods to moderators and administrators, respectively, is part of the `Hot-Chocolate.AspNetCore.Authorization` namespace. Therefore, it differs from the one we used in our controllers (which are part of the `Microsoft.AspNetCore.Authorization` namespace).

> **NOTE** The two attributes have the same name, but they accept a different `Roles` parameter type. The built-in Microsoft attribute wants a string, whereas the one provided by HotChocolate requires a string array. Otherwise, the attributes provide the same functionalities (that is, restricting a method to certain roles, claims, and/or policies, as we learned in chapter 9).

Again, we used the `[Serial]` attribute to ensure that the `Mutation` tasks will be executed in serial mode, for the reasons I explained earlier. With this class, our GraphQL schema is ready. Now we need to add the required services and middleware to our HTTP pipeline by updating the `Program.cs` file.

ADDING SERVICES AND MIDDLEWARE

Open the `Program.cs` file, and locate the part where we added the `ApplicationDbContext` as a service by using the `builder.Services.AddDbContext` method. We're going to add the GraphQL services right after those code lines, as follows.

Listing 10.6   `Program.cs` file: GraphQL services

```
using MyBGList.GraphQL;          ◁——  Adds the root
                                        types namespace
// [...]

builder.Services.AddGraphQLServer()      ◁——|  Registers the GraphQL
    .AddAuthorization()                        server as a service
    .AddQueryType<Query>()             ◁——
    .AddMutationType<Mutation>()   ◁——     Binds the Query
    .AddProjections()          ◁——             root type

  Adds                    Adds              Binds the
  authorization           projections       Mutation
  support                 functions         root type
```

```
    .AddFiltering()
    .AddSorting();
```

Adds filtering functions

Adds sorting capabilities

Let's switch to middleware. Scroll down a bit, and add the following line of code right below the `app.UseAuthorization()` method:

```
app.MapGraphQL();
```

The middleware accepts various configuration settings. But the default behaviors are good enough for our scenario, including the path of the GraphQL endpoint, which is `/graphql`.

This section concludes our HotChocolate setup and configuration task. It's time to see whether what we've done works and learn how to use GraphQL to interact with our data.

10.2.4 Working with GraphQL

Among the many good reasons why we picked HotChocolate is that it comes with BananaCakePop, a neat GraphQL client that we can use to interact with the GraphQL API we set up by using a convenient, web-based interface. To access the client's main dashboard, launch the project in Debug mode, and point your browser to GraphQL's default endpoint: https://localhost:40443/graphql. If everything goes well, we should see the page shown in figure 10.2.

Figure 10.2   BananaCakePop's main dashboard

Click the Create Document button; confirm the default connection settings in the pop-up window that appears; and click the Apply button to open a new tab, which we'll use to write our first GraphQL queries.

QUERY TEST

Let's start with a simple query that retrieves the top three board games, sorted by Id (in ascending order):

```
query {
  boardGames(order: { id: ASC }, first:3 ) {
    nodes {
      id
      name
      year
    }
  }
}
```

Copy and paste the query into the Operations tab (left part of the screen), and click the Run button to send it to the server. If everything works as it should, we should see the following outcome in the Response tab (right part of the screen):

```
{
  "data": {
    "boardGames": {
      "nodes": [
        {
          "id": 1,
          "name": "Die Macher",
          "year": 1986
        },
        {
          "id": 2,
          "name": "Dragonmaster",
          "year": 1981
        },
        {
          "id": 3,
          "name": "Samurai",
          "year": 1998
        }
      ]
    }
  }
}
```

It works! Notice that the response's nodes array contains only the Id, Name, and Year properties for each board-game entry, matching the properties that we included in the query. This result demonstrates that we're receiving only what we asked for, without any overfetching. Let's perform another test with a more complex query:

```
query {
  boardGames(order: { id: ASC }, first:3 ) {
    nodes {
      id
      name
      year
      boardGames_Domains {
        domain {
          name
        }
      }
      boardGames_Mechanics {
        mechanic {
          name
        }
      }
    }
  }
}
```

This time, we're asking for not only some board-game properties, but also for some info about their domains and mechanics. In other words, we're using the many-to-many relationships that we defined in chapter 4 to fetch data from three different entities (corresponding to three different database tables) within a single request.

Cut and paste the preceding query into BananaCakePop, and click Run to see the outcome. If everything goes as expected, we should see the domains and mechanics info for each board game, as shown in figure 10.3.

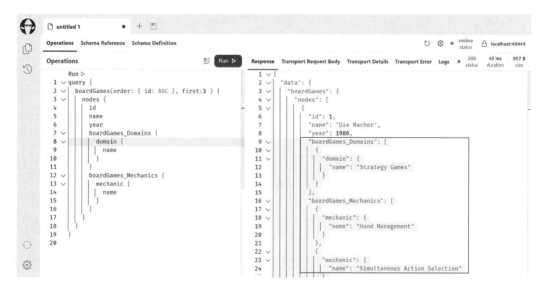

Figure 10.3   Requesting board games, domains, and mechanics together

Again, we can see that the response contains all the fields we asked for (and no more) for the three related entities. There's no need for additional requests or round trips because we don't have an underfetching problem to address.

MUTATION TEST

Let's complete this testing round with a mutation. This task is a bit trickier than the preceding one, because the `Mutation` class methods are protected by the `[Authorize]` data attribute. To call those methods without getting a `401 – Unauthorized` HTTP status code, we need to retrieve the bearer token that we set up in chapter 9 and use it within our request.

   To keep things simple, we won't implement the login functionalities in GraphQL. We'll perform the login from the SwaggerUI, as we did in chapter 9, and retrieve the JSON Web Token (JWT) from there. For reasons of space, I won't show how to do that here; feel free to check out chapter 9 for further guidance.

> **WARNING** Be sure to perform the login with the `TestModerator` or `Test-Administrator` user, as we need an account with the `Moderator` role to perform our mutation tests.

After retrieving the token, go back to the main BananaCakePop dashboard, and click the plus (+) button near the top-right corner of the screen to open a new tab (A in figure 10.4). This time, before closing the Connection Settings pop-up window by clicking Apply, select the Authorization tab, select the `Bearer` type, and paste the JWT in the Token text box within the form, as shown in figure 10.4.

Figure 10.4   BananaCakePop Authorization settings

Next, click Apply, and cut/paste the following mutation into the Operations tab. This mutation is expected to change the Name of a BoardGame entity with an Id equal to 1 from "Die Macher" to "Die Macher (v2)" and return the updated name:

```
mutation {
  updateBoardGame(model: {
    id:1
    name:"Die Macher (v2)"
  }) {
    name
  }
}
```

Click Run again to execute the code against the GraphQL server. If everything goes well, we should receive the following response:

```
{
  "data": {
    "updateBoardGame": {
      "name": "Die Macher (v2)"
    }
  }
}
```

This response shows that the mutation worked well, because the returned name corresponds to the updated one.

> **WARNING** Don't forget that you have only 5 minutes to use the JWT from the moment you retrieve it by using the /Login endpoint, because we set its expiration time to 300 seconds in chapter 9. If you need more time, feel free to increase that value.

To further confirm that our update has been performed, open a third tab (no authentication required this time), and run the following query to retrieve the Name of the board game with an Id equal to 1:

```
query {
  boardGames(where: { id: { eq: 1 } }) {
    nodes {
      name
    }
  }
}
```

This query will allow us to receive the updated name:

```
{
  "data": {
    "boardGames": {
      "nodes": [
```

```
    {
      "name": "Die Macher (v2)",
    }
  ]
 }
}
}
```

That's it for GraphQL. Now let's move on to gRPC.

10.3   *Google Remote Procedure Call*

gRPC is a language-agnostic, cross-platform, open source, high-performance Remote Procedure Call architecture designed by Google in 2015 to ensure high-speed communication among microservices. Its main architectural differences with REST are that gRPC uses the HTTP/2 protocol for transport instead of HTTP/1.1, and it uses protocol buffers (protobuf) as the data-exchange format instead of JSON.

10.3.1 *gRPC pros*

Most of the advantages of gRPC are related to performance:

- *Lightweight*—The framework can run on almost any hardware (as long as HTTP/2 is supported).
- *Low latency*—The handshake optimizations granted by the HTTP/2 protocol ensures latency considerably lower than that of HTTP/1.1-based approaches such as REST and GraphQL.
- *Low network use*—The protobuf binary serialization ensures reduced network use (considerably lower than REST and GraphQL).
- *Better communication model*—Unlike REST and GraphQL, both of which are limited to the HTTP/1.1 request-response communication model, gRPC takes advantage of the bidirectional, streaming, multiplexing communication features granted by HTTP/2.

Thanks to these benefits, gRPC APIs are reportedly seven to ten times faster than REST APIs, according to a well-known test published by Ruwan Fernando in 2019. The full article, including test methodology and results, is available at http://mng.bz/1M8n.

Otherwise, gRPC features most of the relevant benefits of REST and GraphQL. It's platform- and language-agnostic, has multiplatform support, has software development kits (SDKs) available for many programming languages and development frameworks, and has a well-established (and growing) developer community.

10.3.2 *gRPC cons*

Like REST and GraphQL, gRPC has some notable drawbacks, such as the following:

- *Complexity*—Implementing a gRPC-based API is a lot more difficult and much slower than implementing an equivalent REST API. The complex use of the

HTTP/2 protocol and the efforts required to implement the protobuf-based messaging system create a steep learning curve for most developers, even when they're using third-party libraries that do most of the hard work.

- *Compatibility*—Most clients are unable to support gRPC out of the box, including browsers, because they don't expose built-in APIs to control HTTP/2 requests with JavaScript. This problem has been mitigated by the introduction of gRPC-Web, an extension that makes gRPC compatible with HTTP/1.1, but this workaround still lacks a good level of support. (Most client-side frameworks don't support it.)

- *Readability*—Because protobuf compresses gRPC messages before the transmission phase, humans can't read the data exchanged by clients and servers without using dedicated tools. This fact is a huge downside compared with human-readable formats such as JSON and Extensible Markup Language (XML), as it makes it difficult to perform important development tasks such as writing requests manually, debugging, logging/analyzing the transferred data, and inspecting payloads.

- *Caching*—gRPC responses are hard to cache through intermediaries such as reverse proxies and/or content-delivery networks (CDNs). Furthermore, the gRPC specs don't provide standards, best practices, and/or guidelines for caching. This problem could be less serious in most gRPC-friendly scenarios, such as real-time data streaming microservices, but it's a nontrivial drawback for most web APIs, which is a major barrier to widespread adoption.

- *Overfetching and underfetching*—The gRPC architecture is based on requests accepting strongly typed input parameters and returning a predefined data structure, like REST. It doesn't provide native support for a declarative query language, and it doesn't have a runtime that projects the received input values to IQueryable objects or DBMS queries. As a result, it's subject to the same overfetching and underfetching problems as most RESTful APIs, even if the streaming and bidirectional communication capabilities granted by HTTP/2 minimize the number of required round trips.

All in all, we can say that gRPC is a great alternative to REST for specific use cases that require lightweight services, great performance levels, real-time communication, and low-bandwidth usage. But the lack of browser support strongly limits its use, especially if our web API aims to provide data to external websites, services, and apps that may unable to handle it properly.

Next, we'll see how to implement gRPC with ASP.NET Core. Unlike what we did with REST and GraphQL, this time we'll have to implement both the server and the client.

10.3.3 *Installing the NuGet packages*

ASP.NET Core provides gRPC support through the `Grpc.AspNetCore` NuGet package, developed and maintained by Google. The package contains the following libraries:

- `Grpc.AspNetCore.Server`—A gRPC server for .NET
- `Grpc.Tools`—The code-generation toolset
- `Google.Protobuf`—The protobuf serialization library

As always, the package can be installed by using the NuGet Package Manager GUI, the Package Manager console, or the dotnet CLI with the following command:

```
> dotnet add package Grpc.AspNetCore --version 2.50.0
```

10.3.4 *Implementing the gRPC Server*

Let's start with the server. Here's a list of the tasks that we'll need to do:

- *Add a protobuf file.* gRPC uses protocol buffer (protobuf) files to describe its interface definition language (IDL) and messaging structure. For that reason, we're going to need to set one up.
- *Update the project file.* After adding the protobuf file, we'll need to set it up within our project file so that the .NET compiler can use it autogenerate some base classes (stubs) for our gRPC server and client.
- *Implement the gRPC service.* We're going to extend the autogenerated gRPC server base class to create our own service, which will interact with our data by using EF Core.
- *Set up the project file.* As soon as the gRPC server is ready, we'll need to update our `Program.cs` file to add it to the HTTP pipeline, as well as register the main gRPC services in the service collection.

ADDING THE PROTOBUF FILE

The first thing to do is add a protobuf file, which will contain the message and service descriptions for our gRPC implementation. Start by creating a new /gRPC/ folder in our project's root folder, which will contain our protobuf file and our gRPC server class. Then right-click the folder, and add a new protocol buffer file, calling it `grpc.proto` (lowercase is recommended). You can use the "proto" query to search for it among the available templates, as shown in figure 10.5.

Next, we can use the new `grpc.proto` file to describe the interface that our gRPC server and client will use to exchange data. The syntax to use is called "proto3" (protobuf version 3) and is different from C# yet conceptually similar.

> **TIP** For reasons of space, I won't explain the "proto3" syntax in detail. For a reference guide, check out http://mng.bz/Pxjv.

Listing 10.7 shows how we can use the "proto3" syntax to define a single `GetBoard-Game` method accepting a `BoardGameRequest` input type and returning a `BoardGame-Response` output type.

Figure 10.5   Add a new protocol buffer file with Visual Studio.

Listing 10.7   `/gRPC/grpc.proto` file

```
syntax = "proto3";

option csharp_namespace = "MyBGList.gRPC";

package Grpc;                                                    Data-retrieval
                                                                     method
service Grpc {
  rpc GetBoardGame (BoardGameRequest) returns (BoardGameResponse);
}

message BoardGameRequest {              Input type
  int32 id = 1;                         definition
}

message BoardGameResponse {             Output type
  int32 id = 1;                         definition
  string name = 2;
  int32 year = 3;
}
```

Notice that the `BoardGameRequest` and `BoardGameResponse` types closely resemble the C# DTO classes that we've used since chapter 5 to process our requests. They're DTOs as well.

> **NOTE**   The numbers placed after the equal sign of each type's property aren't their default values (as would be the case C#), but their index. In the case of the `BoardGameResponse` type, the `id` property has an index of 1, name has 2, and year has 3. The protobuf serialization library will use these index values to serialize and compress the actual values.

SETTING UP THE PROJECT FILE

Now that we have our protobuf file, we need to set it up in our `MyBGList` project file so that the .NET compiler will locate and compile it. First, from Solution Explorer, right-click the project's root node, and choose Edit Project File from the contextual menu to open the `MyBGList.csproj` file. Next, add the following reference near the end of the file, before the `</Project>` closing tag:

```
<ItemGroup>
    <Protobuf Include="gRPC/grpc.proto" />
</ItemGroup>
```

This reference tells the .NET compiler to code-generate the client and server stubs.

> **TIP**   For additional info on the protobuf/gRPC code-generation features and their integration into the .NET building phase, see http://mng.bz/JlBa.

Now that we've laid out the basis, we can implement the service that our gRPC server will use to accept and process the incoming request.

IMPLEMENTING THE GRPCSERVICE

Create a new `/gRPC/GrpcService.cs` file, which will host our gRPC service implementation. This time, we'll be able to use C# syntax. (Yay!) We're going to create the single `GetBoardGame` data-retrieval method that we defined in the `grpc.proto` file, with its input and output types, to allow our clients to fetch some sample board-game data. The following listing shows how.

Listing 10.8   `/gRPC/GrpcService.cs` file

```csharp
using Grpc.Core;
using Microsoft.EntityFrameworkCore;
using MyBGList.Models;

namespace MyBGList.gRPC
{
    public class GrpcService : Grpc.GrpcBase          // Extends the codegen service base class
    {
        private readonly ApplicationDbContext _context;

        public GrpcService(ApplicationDbContext context)     // Injects the ApplicationDbContext
        {
            _context = context;
        }

        public override async Task<BoardGameResponse> GetBoardGame(     // Implements the GetBoardGame method
            BoardGameRequest request,
            ServerCallContext scc)
        {
            var bg = await _context.BoardGames               // Retrieves board-game data by using EF Core
                .Where(bg => bg.Id == request.Id)
                .FirstOrDefaultAsync();
            var response = new BoardGameResponse();
            if (bg != null)
            {
                response.Id = bg.Id;
                response.Name = bg.Name;
```

```
            response.Year = bg.Year;
        }
        return response;      ◁──┐  Returns the
    }                            │  BoardGameResponse
}                                │  type
}
```

This code should be easy to understand. Notice that it looks like one of our controllers, which isn't a surprise because it's meant to do roughly the same jobs under the hood: accepting a request, retrieving the data, and returning a response. Now that we have our service, we can map it to our `Program.cs` file and register the gRPC main services to make our server accept the incoming calls.

SETTING UP THE PROGRAM FILE

Let's start by registering the gRPC main services in the service collection. Open the `Program.cs` file, locate the part where we added the GraphQL services (`AddGraphQL-Server`), and add the following line right below it to enable gRPC:

```
builder.Services.AddGrpc();
```

Next, scroll down to the part where we added the GraphQL endpoint mapping (`Map-GraphQL`), and add the following line below it to map our new service in the ASP.NET routing pipeline:

```
app.MapGrpcService<GrpcService>();
```

Our gRPC server-side implementation is complete. Now we need a sample client to test it.

10.3.5 *Implementing the gRPC client*

Implementing a gRPC client with ASP.NET Core typically requires creating a new project with the same NuGet packages and a new protobuf file similar to the one we defined for our server (as client and server protobuf files need to share interfaces). This approach would decouple the client and server's source code, ensuring that each component will fulfill its role while relying on its own separate, independent codebase. But it would also require more time and coding effort.

To keep things simple, we'll create a new `GrpcController` that will act as a client. This approach will allow us to reuse the existing `/gRPC/grpc.proto` file without having to copy it or move it to a separate project. At the end of the day, we'll have a gRPC server and client in the same ASP.NET Core project, which is perfectly fine for testing purposes.

ADDING THE GRPCCONTROLLER

Create a new `/Controllers/GrpcController.cs` file to contain our gRPC client implementation. We need to define a single action method that will instantiate the gRPC client, perform the request to the gRPC service endpoint, and return the results. In other words, the action method will act as a wrapper for the actual gRPC client.

The added value of this approach is that we'll be able to deal with readable input and output values, as the serialization and compression tasks will happen within the action method. The following listing provides the source code.

Listing 10.9   /Controllers/GrpcController.cs file

```csharp
using Microsoft.AspNetCore.Mvc;
using Grpc.Net.Client;
using MyBGList.gRPC;

namespace MyBGList.Controllers
{
    [Route("[controller]/[action]")]
    [ApiController]
    public class GrpcController : ControllerBase
    {
        [HttpGet("{id}")]
        public async Task<BoardGameResponse> GetBoardGame(int id)
        {
            using var channel = GrpcChannel
                .ForAddress("https://localhost:40443");
            var client = new gRPC.Grpc.GrpcClient(channel);
            var response = await client.GetBoardGameAsync(
                            new BoardGameRequest { Id = id });
            return response;
        }
    }
}
```

Instantiates the gRPC client → `var client = new gRPC.Grpc.GrpcClient(channel);`

Sets up the gRPC channel → `using var channel = GrpcChannel.ForAddress("https://localhost:40443");`

Performs the client-to-server call → `var response = await client.GetBoardGameAsync(...`

Returns the received response → `return response;`

As we can see, the controller's implementation is thin. We don't have services to inject—not even our `ApplicationDbContext`. But we're supposed to retrieve our data from the gRPC server instead of using EF Core. Now that we have our client, we can test the gRPC data-retrieval flow.

TESTING IT

Launch the project in Debug mode, and access the SwaggerUI dashboard. Locate the /Grpc/GetBoardGame/{id} endpoint, handled by the GrpcController's GetBoard-Game action method that wraps our gRPC client. Expand the endpoint's panel, click the Try It Out button, enter 1 in the Id text box, and click Execute to perform the request (figure 10.6).

Right after executing this code, check the Server Response panel below to see the resulting JSON output. Notice that we're receiving the board game id, name, and year data in the endpoint's response body:

```json
{
    "id": 1,
    "name": "Die Macher (v2)",
    "year": 1996,
}
```

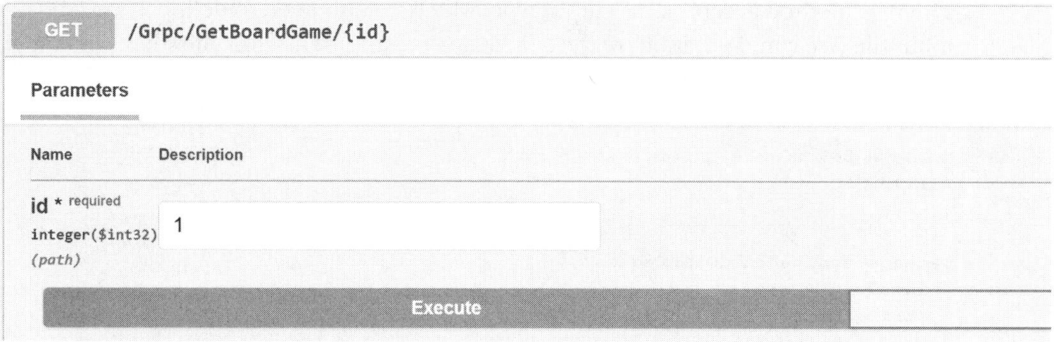

Figure 10.6 Executing the `/Grpc/GetBoardGame` endpoint that wraps the gRPC client

Those values were fetched by the underlying gRPC client through a connection established with the gRPC server, so our sample gRPC implementation is working properly.

10.3.6 Adding Authorization support

Before moving on to the next topic, let's see how our sample gRPC implementation handles the ASP.NET Core authorization framework. The gRPC services fully support the `[Authorize]` attribute we learned to use in chapter 9, so we already know what to do. In the following section, we'll use our acquired knowledge to perform the following tasks:

1 Define a new gRPC endpoint that will allow our clients to update board-game data by using gRPC.
2 Implement the new endpoint in our existing `GrpcService`, using the `[Authorize]` attribute to limit its use to users who have the `Moderator` role.
3 Update the `GrpcController` by adding a new action method that will act as a wrapper for the client that calls the new gRPC endpoint.

DEFINING THE NEW ENDPOINT

Open the /gRPC/grpc.proto file, and add the new `UpdateBoardGame` gRPC endpoint in the following way (new lines in bold):

```
// ... existing code

service Grpc {
  rpc GetBoardGame (BoardGameRequest) returns (BoardGameResponse);
  rpc UpdateBoardGame (UpdateBoardGameRequest) returns (BoardGameResponse);
}

// ... existing code
```

The new method accepts a new input type, which we also need to define within the pro-tobuf file. We can do that below the `BoardGameRequest` definition (new lines in bold):

```
// ... existing code

message BoardGameRequest {
  int32 id = 1;
}

message UpdateBoardGameRequest {
  int32 id = 1;
  string name = 2;
}

// ... existing code
```

Now that we've defined the interface, we can implement it in our `GrpcService`.

IMPLEMENTING THE NEW ENDPOINT

Open the /gRPC/GrpcService.cs file, and add the method in listing 10.10 right below the existing one. The code features the same data-retrieval and update logic that we've used several times.

> **Listing 10.10   /gRPC/GrpcService.cs file: UpdateBoardGame method**

```
using Microsoft.AspNetCore.Authorization;    │ Required
using MyBGList.Constants;                     │ namespaces

// ... existing code
                                                    ┐ Role-based
[Authorize(Roles = RoleNames.Moderator)]      ◄─────┘ access control
public override async Task<BoardGameResponse> UpdateBoardGame(
    UpdateBoardGameRequest request,
    ServerCallContext scc)
{
    var bg = await _context.BoardGames
        .Where(bg => bg.Id == request.Id)
        .FirstOrDefaultAsync();
    var response = new BoardGameResponse();
    if (bg != null)
    {
        bg.Name = request.Name;
        _context.BoardGames.Update(bg);
        await _context.SaveChangesAsync();
        response.Id = bg.Id;
        response.Name = bg.Name;
        response.Year = bg.Year;
    }
    return response;
}
```

To keep things simple, our sample method will update only the board game's `Name` data. But any additional field can be added to the interface without much effort.

Now that the server-side part is ready, we can move to the controller that wraps our gRPC client.

UPDATING THE GRPCCONTROLLER

The most convenient thing to do is add another wrapper that will instantiate a dedicated gRPC client for the new method. Open the /Controllers/GrpcController.cs file, and add another action method (as in the following listing) right below the existing one (relevant lines in bold).

Listing 10.11 /Controllers/GrpcController.cs file: UpdateBoardGame method

```
using Grpc.Core;            ◁——— Required
                                  namespace
// ... existing code

[HttpPost]
public async Task<BoardGameResponse> UpdateBoardGame(
    string token,           ◁——— Accepts the bearer
    int id,                       token as input value
    string name)
{                                              Creates a headers
                                               metadata object
    var headers = new Metadata();       ◁——
    headers.Add("Authorization", $"Bearer {token}");    ◁——— Adds the
                                                              Authorization
    using var channel = GrpcChannel                           header with
        .ForAddress("https://localhost:40443");               the token
    var client = new gRPC.Grpc.GrpcClient(channel);
    var response = await client.UpdateBoardGameAsync(
                        new UpdateBoardGameRequest {
                            Id = id,
                            Name = name
                        },
                        headers);       ◁——— Appends the
    return response;                          headers metadata
}                                            to the request
```

The new action method accepts the bearer token among input values, along with the id of the board game we want to update and the new name that we want to assign to it. The implementation is straightforward and should pose no problems.

TESTING THE NEW ENDPOINT

To test the new gRPC endpoint, we need to retrieve a bearer token, which we can do by using our existing REST /Account/Login endpoint.

> **WARNING** Be sure to perform the login with the TestModerator or Test-Administrator user, as we need an account with the Moderator role to perform our mutation tests.

As soon as we have the token, we can call the /UpdateBoardGame endpoint from the SwaggerUI, filling in all the relevant form fields (figure 10.7).

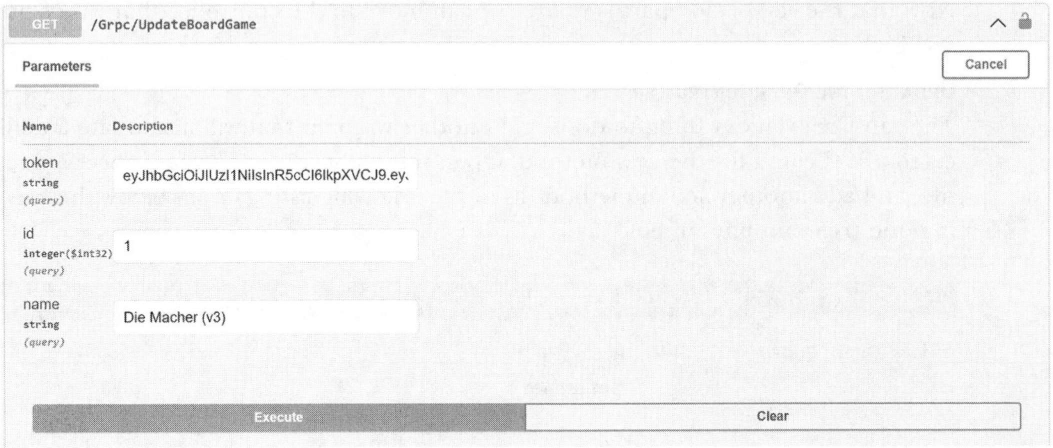

Figure 10.7   Calling `/UpdateBoardGame` **from the SwaggerUI**

If everything is working as expected, we should receive the following response body:

```
{
  "id": 1,
  "name": "Die Macher (v3)",
  "year": 1986
}
```

This response means that the name change has been applied. This task concludes our gRPC implementation sample.

> **TIP**   For more information on the ASP.NET Core gRPC integration, see https://docs.microsoft.com/en-us/aspnet/core/grpc.

10.4   *Other REST alternatives*

Facebook's GraphQL and gRPC aren't the only modern alternatives to REST. Several other promising data exchange technologies, architectures, and standards are gaining more attention from the developer community. The following sections briefly mention the most notable ones, as well as documenting current .NET Core support for each one.

10.4.1   *Newline Delimited JSON (NDJSON)*

NDJSON is a simple yet effective solution for storing, transferring, and streaming multiple JSON objects delimited by a newline separator (\n) or a return plus a newline separator pair (\r\n). The technique takes advantage of the fact that the JSON format doesn't allow newline characters within primitive values and doesn't require them elsewhere. (Most JSON formatters suppress them by default, because they have no purpose other than making the formatted data easier for humans to read.) ASP.NET support is granted by some third-party NuGet packages, such as `Ndjson.AsyncStreams` by Tomasz Pęczek. The package can be downloaded at https://github.com/tpeczek/ Ndjson.AsyncStreams.

10.4.2 Falcor

Falcor is a JSON-based data platform developed by Netflix and open-sourced in 2015 (under the Apache 2.0 license). Falcor operates as a layer between the client and the server, providing a single endpoint that clients can use to send JSON-formatted queries and receive exactly the data they need. The overall concept is similar to GraphQL, but instead of having a schema and static types, Falcor uses a single huge virtual JSON object that represents the data model and a specialized router that fetches the values requested by clients to one or more backend services.

Like GraphQL, Falcor prevents clients from problems such as overfetching, underfetching, and multiple round trips to gather the required data. ASP.NET support has been initially granted by the Falcor.NET NuGet Package (https://github .com/falcordotnet/falcor.net), developed by Craig Smitham for the .NET Framework 4.x around 2015. But the implementation is still in developer-preview status, was never ported to ASP.NET Core, and hasn't received updates for many years. For additional information on Falcor, check out the project's official page on GitHub at https:// netflix.github.io/falcor.

10.4.3 Thrift

Apache Thrift is an IDL and binary communication protocol developed by Facebook and released in 2020 as an open source project in the Apache Software Foundation. Like gRPC, it's based on a proprietary descriptor file that contains the interfaces for services and DTOs. The compiler uses the description file to generate the source code for the destination language (such as C#), obtaining the codegen stubs that can be extended to implement the server and client. Thrift can operate over HTTP/2, HTTP 1.1/1.0, and WebSocket, and it supports several data transmission protocols, including binary and JSON.

ASP.NET Core support is granted through the Apache Thrift IDL compiler (available for Windows and Linux) and the Thrift C# library, which can be compiled directly from the Thrift source code or obtained in a precompiled version through several third-party NuGet packages, such as `ApacheThrift`, `apache-thrift-netcore`, `thrift-csharp`, `Apache.Thrift`, and `Tnidea.Thrift`.

For additional information about Thrift, check out the project's official page at https://thrift.apache.org. For a comprehensive coverage of the Apache Thrift framework, see Randy Abernethy's *Programmer's Guide to Apache Thrift* at http://mng.bz/wPOa.

10.5 Exercises

The following exercises emulate some task assignments given by our product owner and addressed to the `MyBGList` development team—in other words, to us.

NOTE The solutions to the exercises are available on GitHub in the /Chapter_ 10/Exercises/ folder. To test them, replace the relevant files in your MyBG- List project with those in that folder, and run the app.

10.5.1 *Write a new GraphQL query*

Write a new GraphQL query that fetches the following data from the GraphQL end- point (and only that data), respecting all the following requirements:

- Retrieve only the board games with a Name starting with "War".
- Order the results by their names, in ascending order.
- Get only the top ten results.
- For each board game, retrieve the following fields: Id, Name, Year, MinPlayers, MaxPlayers, and PlayTime.
- For each board game, also retrieve the Id and Name of each related domain and mechanic.

TIP Feel free to check the GraphQL Query and Mutation syntax official ref- erence at https://graphql.org/learn/queries.

NOTE Be sure to test the query by using the BananaCakePop web client to ensure that it works.

10.5.2 *Fetch GraphQL data for a mutation*

Write a new GraphQL query that fetches the Id of the board game with a Name equal to "Axis & Allies" and "Year" equal to 2004. (One game should match both condi- tions.) After retrieving the Id, write a new GraphQL mutation to change its name to "Axis & Allies: Revised".

NOTE Again, feel free to check the GraphQL Query and Mutation syntax offi- cial reference (see section 10.5.1).

Be sure to execute the mutation with the BananaCakePop web client (retrieving and using a suitable bearer token) to ensure that the changes will be saved in the DBMS. Then roll back all the changes by setting the board game's Name back to its previous value.

10.5.3 *Implement new gRPC server features*

Improve the gRPC protobuf file to support the following methods: GetDomain, Update- Domain, GetMechanic, and UpdateMechanic. For each method, define the required input and output type, following the same pattern we used to implement the Board- GameRequest, UpdateBoardGameRequest, and BoardGameResponse types. Be sure to use the [Authorize] attribute to make the UpdateDomain and UpdateMechanic meth- ods accessible only to users with the Moderator role.

10.5.4 *Add new gRPC client wrappers*

Improve the GrpcController file by adding the following action methods: GetDomain, UpdateDomain, GetMechanic, and UpdateMechanic. Each action method must act like a wrapper for a gRPC client performing the call to the gRPC server, following the same pattern we used to implement the GetBoardGame and UpdateBoardGame action methods. Again, use the [Authorize] attribute to limit access to the update methods to the Moderator role.

10.5.5 *Test the new gRPC features*

Use the SwaggerUI to execute the new gRPC wrappers we created in section 10.5.4 to ensure that they work. At the same time, ensure that all the update methods are accessible only to users with the Moderator role.

Summary

- The REST architectural style has been the most popular web API architecture for years, thanks mostly to its scalability, flexibility, and portability, which led to worldwide success and enthusiastic adoption among the developer community. But it's not the only choice for implementing a web API or even the best alternative in every circumstance.
  - REST has a lot of benefits, yet it also has undeniable drawbacks such as overfetching and underfetching. These drawbacks can easily lead to nontrivial performance problems, forcing developers to define many additional endpoints and forcing clients to perform multiple round trips to fetch the data they need.
- GraphQL is a query language for APIs created by Facebook as a workaround for some known REST limitations.
  - Its success is due mostly to its great flexibility; it allows clients to receive highly personalized data sets by using a single declarative query to a single endpoint, avoiding the risk of underfetching and overfetching without the need for multiple round trips and/or many endpoints.
  - It's well supported by ASP.NET Core thanks to several open source NuGet packages, such as HotChocolate.
- gRPC is a high-performance RPC architecture designed to ensure high-speed communication among microservices.
  - Unlike REST and GraphQL, it uses the HTTP/2 protocol instead of HTTP/1.1, and protocol buffers instead of JSON.
  - Despite being considerably faster than REST and GraphQL, it has some drawbacks (such as complexity, poor readability, and lack of some relevant features) that limit its adoption to some specific use cases.
  - gRPC can be used in any ASP.NET Core app thanks to the Grpc.AspNetCore NuGet package.

- GraphQL and gRPC aren't the only alternatives to REST. Several other promising data exchange solutions are available:
  - Newline Delimited JSON (NDJSON), a simple yet effective solution for storing, transferring, and streaming multiple JSON objects delimited by newlines
  - Falcor, a JSON-based data platform developed by Netflix that offers features similar to GraphQL but has a different underlying architecture
  - Thrift, an interface definition language and binary communication protocol developed by Facebook that works like gRPC and has a similar architecture

Part 4

Toward production

We're approaching the end of the road. Our ASP.NET Core project is now a full-featured web API that—with some minor tweaks and perks—could fulfill the sample purposes we expect it to serve.

In this part, we'll learn the concepts and activities necessary to publish our web API project: setting up the documentation, adopting a suitable security approach, choosing the cloud provider, and (most important) dealing with the release and deployment aspects of ASP.NET Core.

Chapter 11 emphasizes the importance of good API documentation for potential users of a web API. It also reviews some important API documentation best practices and shows how to implement them with Swagger/OpenAPI and the Swashbuckle set of libraries for ASP.NET Core, with several source-code examples.

Then there'll be nothing left to do but get our web API project ready to be released into production, and that's what chapter 12 is all about. In that chapter, we learn how to adopt a consistent deployment plan built around a secure, risk-based approach. Then we proceed to implement that plan with the help of a step-by-step guide through the relevant phases: setting up a content-delivery network, creating a Windows Server virtual machine in Microsoft Azure, installing and configuring Internet Information Services, and deploying the web API to Windows Server with Visual Studio. At the end of all this work, we'll be able to serve our web API project through the internet and access it worldwide by using a public hostname address.

API documentation

In chapter 1, when we tried to define an application programming interface (API), we referred to it as a software platform that exposes tools and services that different computer programs can use to interact by exchanging data. Starting from this definition, we could say that the purpose of an API (including a web API) is to create a common place where independent and often-unrelated systems can meet, greet, and communicate by using a commonly accepted standard. These "actors" are mostly computer programs—such as websites, mobile apps, and microservices—that are implemented by other developers. For that reason, whoever takes on the task of designing, creating, and releasing a web API must acknowledge the existence and needs of a new type of user: the third-party developer, which brings us to this chapter's topic.

In modern software development, documenting an interface, middleware, a service, or any product that's intended to be a means to an end isn't considered to be an option anymore: it's a design requirement as long as we want to increase or speed its adoption. It's also the quickest possible way to make an interested third party able to fully understand the value of our work. This aspect has become so important in recent years that it favored the definition of a new design field: developer experience (DX), the user experience from a developer's point of view. By taking DX into account, I'll dedicate this chapter to identifying best practices for API documentation and show how we can put them in practice with the help of the many tools made available by ASP.NET Core.

11.1   *Web API potential audience*

The technical documentation of a product is useful only to the extent that it meets the needs and expectations of those who read it. For this reason, the first thing to do is identify our web API potential audience: the stakeholders who are expected to choose and/or use it. When referring to them, I usually break them into three main types, using names taken from construction slang.

11.1.1   *Prospectors*

Prospectors are passionate developers and IT enthusiasts who are willing to give our web API a try without a compelling need beyond personal interest, knowledge gaining, testing/reviewing purposes, and so on. This group is important if we want our web API to be a general-purpose product that we intend to release to the public (or part of it); their feedback will likely have an immediate effect on the developer community, possibly bringing in contractors and builders (see sections 11.1.2 and 11.1.3, respectively).

11.1.2   *Contractors*

Contractors are the IT analysts, solution architects, and backend designers who take responsibility for creating products, solving problems, or addressing potential challenges that our web API could help them deal with. Although typically, they don't get down to implementation, they often serve as decision-makers, since they have authority, handle the budget, and/or possess the required know-how to suggest, choose, or dictate which components to use (unless they let builders choose them).

11.1.3   *Builders*

Builders are software developers who choose (or are instructed) to use our web API to solve a specific problem. They represent the most technical part of our audience and can be difficult to satisfy, because dealing with our API is part of their working assignment, and they often have limited time to get the job done. Builders will have to learn to work with our web API practically; they're the third-party developers I mentioned earlier.

After reading those descriptions, it may seem obvious to think that our documentation should focus on builders, who are the end users of our web API. This premise is valid. Most of the API documentation best practices we'll deal with in this chapter will take this approach into account. But we shouldn't forget about the other two audience types, as the success of our project may also depend on them.

11.2 API documentation best practices

Developers are peculiar types of users. They're analytical, precise, and demanding, especially if we consider that they typically want to use our API to achieve major goals: implementing requirements, solving problems, and so on. Whenever they find themselves unable to achieve their goals due to poorly written documentation, there's a high chance they'll think that the API isn't good enough—and brutal as it may sound, they'll be right. At the end of the day, APIs are only as good as their documentation, which inevitably has a huge influence on adoption and maintainability.

What do we mean by good documentation, and how can we achieve it? No single answer is valid in all cases. But a few good practices can help us to find a viable way to achieve what we want, such as the following:

- *Adopting an automated description tool*—So that our documentation won't become stale or outdated if we forget to update it along with our web API's source code
- *Describing endpoints and input parameters*—So that our audience not only acknowledges their existence, but also learns their purposes and how to use them
- *Describing responses*—So that our audience knows what to expect when calling each endpoint and how to handle the outcome
- *Adding request and response samples*—To save our audience a huge amount of development time
- *Grouping endpoints into sections*—To better separate users' different scopes, purposes, and roles
- *Excluding reserved endpoints*—To prevent users from being aware of their existence and/or trying to call them
- *Emphasizing authorization requirements*—To let our audience distinguish between publicly accessible operations and those that are restricted to authorized users
- *Customizing the documentation context*—Such as choosing the appropriate names, icons, and metadata to help users find the required info

The following sections talk more about these concepts and show how to implement them in our `MyBGList` web API.

11.2.1 Adopt an automated description tool

If we want to satisfy a third-party developer, we must ensure that our API documentation will always be updated. Nothing is more frustrating than dealing with missing specifications, nonexistent operations or endpoints, wrong parameters, and the like. Outdated documentation will make our users think our API is broken, even if it's not.

NOTE A poorly (or wrongly) documented web API is technically broken, because a third party has no chance to see that it works as expected. That's the reason behind our initial statement that API documentation is a design requirement, not an option or an add-on. This concept is true even for internal APIs that are expected to be used only by internal developers, because the lack of proper documentation will eventually affect new employees, potential partners, maintenance tasks, handover processes, outsourcers, and so on.

The need to automate the documentation process is particularly strong for RESTful APIs, because the REST architectural standard doesn't provide a standardized mechanism, schema, or reference for that purpose. This is the main reason behind the success of Open API (formerly known as Swagger), an open source specification for automated API documentation released by SmartBear Software in 2011 with the purpose of solving that problem.

We've known about Swagger/OpenAPI since chapter 2, because Visual Studio's ASP.NET Core web API template, which we used to create our MyBGList project, includes the services and middleware of Swashbuckle, a set of services, middleware, and tools for implementing OpenAPI within ASP.NET Core. We've also experienced its autodiscovery and description capabilities, which granted us a code-generated OpenAPI 3.0 description file (swagger.json) and an interactive, web-based API client (SwaggerUI) that we've used to test our endpoints. Because we're already using Swashbuckle, we could say that we're set. In the following sections, however, we're going to extend its capabilities to meet our needs.

11.2.2 Describe endpoints and input parameters

If we look at our SwaggerUI main dashboard, we see that our current "documentation" consists merely of a list of endpoints and their input variables, without a single description of what each method does. Our audience will have to infer the endpoint's use, as well as the purpose of each request header and/or input parameter, from the names, which isn't the best possible way to showcase, valorize, or promote our work.

NOTE If our API adheres to the RESTful good practice of using HTTP verbs to identify the action type, it'll provide other useful hints about the use of each endpoint — at least to users who have the required know-how.

Conversely, we should adopt a standardized way to create a concise yet relevant description of each endpoint and its input variables. This practice will not only save builders time, but also give prospectors and contractors a better grip on how the API works and what it can do. Swashbuckle provides two ways to add custom descriptions to our endpoints and input parameters:

- Use an Extensible Markup Language (XML) documentation file autogenerated by the .NET compiler from the standard triple-slash, XML-formatted comments that we can add inside our C# classes.

- Use the `[SwaggerOperation]` data attribute, provided by the optional `Swashbuckle` `.AspNetCore.Annotations` NuGet package.

Each technique has benefits and downsides. In the next section, we'll see how to implement both techniques.

11.2.3 Add XML documentation support

The XML documentation approach can be useful, convenient, and fast to implement if we've already added comments in our source code by using the triple-slash syntax provided by C#. I'm talking about a neat C# feature that allows developers to create code-level documentation by writing special comment fields indicated by triple slashes. This feature is also used by some integrated development environments (IDEs), such as Visual Studio, that automatically generate XML elements to describe various code parts, such as `<summary>` (for methods), `<param>` (for input parameters), and `<returns>` (for return values).

> **NOTE** For additional info regarding C# XML documentation comments, check out http://mng.bz/qdy6. For a complete reference on the supported XML tags, see http://mng.bz/7187.

The best way to learn how to use this feature is to put it in practice. Open the `/Controllers/AccountController.cs` file, locate the `Register` action method, position the cursor above it (and all its attributes), and type the slash (/) character above it three times. As soon as you add the third slash, Visual Studio should generate the following XML comment boilerplate:

```
/// <summary>
///
/// </summary>
/// <param name="input"></param>
/// <returns></returns>
[HttpPost]
[ResponseCache(CacheProfileName = "NoCache")]
public async Task<ActionResult> Register(RegisterDTO input)
```

Notice that the autogenerated XML structure identifies the name of the `RegisterDTO` input parameter of the action method. Now that we have the boilerplate, let's fill it. Here's how we can document our `AccountController`'s `Register` endpoint:

```
/// <summary>
/// Registers a new user.
/// </summary>
/// <param name="input">A DTO containing the user data.</param>
/// <returns>A 201 - Created Status Code in case of success.</returns>
```

Right after that, scroll down to the `Login` action method, and do the same thing. Here's a suitable description we can use to document it:

```
/// <summary>
/// Performs a user login.
/// </summary>
/// <param name="input">A DTO containing the user's credentials.</param>
/// <returns>The Bearer Token (in JWT format).</returns>
```

Save and close `AccountController`. Next, tell the compiler to use the XML comments we've added, as well as any other comment of that type that's present in our code, to generate an XML documentation file.

GENERATING XML DOCUMENTATION FILES

To enable this feature, we need to update our `MyBGList` project's configuration file. Right-click the project's root node in the Solution Explorer window, and choose the Edit Project File option from the contextual menu to open the `MyBGList.csproj` file. Next, add the following code at the bottom of the file, below the `<ItemGroup>` block that we added in chapter 10 to include the protobuf file:

```
// ... existing code

<ItemGroup>
  <Protobuf Include="gRPC/grpc.proto" />
</ItemGroup>

<PropertyGroup>
  <GenerateDocumentationFile>true</GenerateDocumentationFile>
  <NoWarn>$(NoWarn);1591</NoWarn>
</PropertyGroup>

// ... existing code
```

Now the compiler will generate the XML documentation file whenever we build the project.

Overcoming the CS1591 warnings

The `<NoWarn>` element that we used in the preceding code will suppress the CS1591 warnings that the `GenerateDocumentationFile` switch will raise for any public types and members without a three-slash comment. We've chosen to shut them down globally in our sample project because we don't need that advice, but it could be useful to keep it up if we want to ensure that we comment/document everything.

For further info on the `GenerateDocumentationFile` switch, see http://mng.bz/mJdn.

The last thing we need to do is configure Swashbuckle to fetch the XML documentation file's contents.

CONFIGURING SWASHBUCKLE

To read our project's XML documentation file, Swashbuckle needs to know its full path and file name that corresponds to our project's name (with an `.xml` extension).

Instead of writing it manually, we can determine and build this path automatically by using `Reflection`, a C# technique that allows us to retrieve metadata on types at runtime. This programmatic approach is generally preferable, as it ensures better code maintainability than using literal strings, so we'll opt for it. Open the `Program.cs` file, locate the `AddSwaggerGen()` method, and add the following code within its configuration block (new lines in bold):

```
using System.Reflection;          ◁──── Required
                                          namespace
// ... existing code

                                                            Builds the XML
                                                            documentation
builder.Services.AddSwaggerGen(options =>                   filename
{
    var xmlFilename =                              ◁────
        $"{Assembly.GetExecutingAssembly().GetName().Name}.xml";
    options.IncludeXmlComments(System.IO.Path.Combine(  ◁──── Assembles the XML
        AppContext.BaseDirectory, xmlFilename));                documentation file
                                                                full path
    // ... existing code
```

Notice that in this code, we're using `Reflection` to build an XML filename that matches the project's name and then using it to construct the XML file's full path. Next, we'll test what we've done to see whether it works.

TESTING THE XML DOCUMENTATION

Run the project in Debug mode, and look at the SwaggerUI main dashboard, where we should see the same descriptive strings that we used in the three-slash comments (figure 11.1).

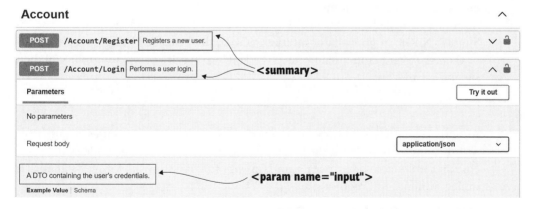

Figure 11.1 XML documentation fetched by Swashbuckle and used in SwaggerUI

Notice that the summary appears right after the endpoint definition. The description is shown inside the endpoint's expandable panel.

EVALUATING XML DOCUMENTATION PROS AND CONS

Being able to translate all our code-level comments to API documentation automatically allows us to kill two birds with one stone. If we're used to writing comments to describe our classes and methods (a developer's good practice), we can reuse a lot of work. Furthermore, this approach can be particularly useful for internal developers, because they'll be able to read our API documentation directly from the source code without even having to look at the `swagger.json` file and/or SwaggerUI.

But this notable benefit could easily become a downside. If we want to keep the internal source code documentation (for internal developers) separate from the public API documentation (for third-party developers/end users), for example, we could find this approach to be limited, not to mention that involves potential risk of an involuntary data leak. Code-level comments are typically considered to be confidential by most developers, who could likely use them to keep track of internal notes, warnings, known problems/bugs, vulnerabilities, and other strictly reserved data that shouldn't be released to the public. To overcome such a problem, we might think about using the `[SwaggerOperation]` data attribute alternative, which provides better separation of concerns between internal comments and API documentation, along with some neat additional features that we may want to use.

11.2.4 *Work with Swashbuckle annotations*

In addition to XML documentation, Swashbuckle provides an alternative, attribute-based feature for adding custom descriptions to our web API endpoints. This feature is handled by an optional module called `Swashbuckle.AspNetCore.Annotations`, available with a dedicated NuGet package. In the following sections, we'll learn how to install and use it.

INSTALLING THE NUGET PACKAGE

As always, to install the Swashbuckle annotations' NuGet packages, we can use Visual Studio's NuGet graphical user interface (GUI), the Package Manager console window, or the .NET command-line interface (CLI). Here are the commands to install them in the .NET CLI:

```
dotnet add package Swashbuckle.AspNetCore.Annotations --version 6.4.0
```

After installation, we'll be able to use some data annotation attributes to enhance our API documentation. We'll start with `[SwaggerOperation]`, which allows us to set up custom summaries, descriptions, and/or tags for our controller's action methods, as well as Minimal API methods.

USING THE [SWAGGEROPERATION] ATTRIBUTE

Because our `AccountController`'s action methods have already been documented via XML, this time we're going to use the `BoardGamesController`. Open the /Controllers/ `BoardGamesController.cs` file, and add the attributes to the four existing action methods as shown in listing 11.1 (new lines in bold).

Listing 11.1   `/Controllers/BoardGamesControllers.cs` file: Adding annotations

```
using Swashbuckle.AspNetCore.Annotations;          ⟵┐ Required
                                                    │ namespace
// ... existing code

[HttpGet(Name = "GetBoardGames")]
[ResponseCache(CacheProfileName = "Any-60")]          Adds the
┌─▷ [SwaggerOperation(                                 endpoint
│       Summary = "Get a list of board games.",  ⟵──┘ summary
│       Description = "Retrieves a list of board games " +   ⟵
│       "with custom paging, sorting, and filtering rules.")]
│   public async Task<RestDTO<BoardGame[]>> Get(
│
│       // ... existing code
│
│   [HttpGet("{id}")]
│   [ResponseCache(CacheProfileName = "Any-60")]         Adds the
┌─▷ [SwaggerOperation(                                    endpoint
│       Summary = "Get a single board game.",   ⟵──┘     summary
│       Description = "Retrieves a single board game with the given Id.")]  ⟵
│   public async Task<RestDTO<BoardGame?>> Get(int id)
│
[Swagger-  // ... existing code                                    Adds the
Operation]                                                          endpoint
attribute  [Authorize(Roles = RoleNames.Moderator)]                description
│   [HttpPost(Name = "UpdateBoardGame")]
│   [ResponseCache(CacheProfileName = "NoCache")]         Adds the
┌─▷ [SwaggerOperation(                                    endpoint
│       Summary = "Updates a board game.",   ⟵──┘         summary
│       Description = "Updates the board game's data.")]   ⟵
│   public async Task<RestDTO<BoardGame?>> Post(BoardGameDTO model)
│
│       // ... existing code
│
│   [Authorize(Roles = RoleNames.Administrator)]
│   [HttpDelete(Name = "DeleteBoardGame")]
│   [ResponseCache(CacheProfileName = "NoCache")]         Adds the
└─▷ [SwaggerOperation(                                    endpoint
        Summary = "Deletes a board game.",   ⟵──┘         summary
        Description = "Deletes a board game from the database.")]   ⟵
    public async Task<RestDTO<BoardGame?>> Delete(int id)

    // ... existing code
```

Now that we know how to use Swashbuckle annotations to describe our operations, let's do the same with their input parameters.

USING THE [SWAGGERPARAMETER] ATTRIBUTE

To set a description for input parameters, we can use the `[SwaggerParameter]` attribute, which is the counterpart to Swashbuckle annotations of the XML documentation's `<param>` tag. But whereas the XML tag must be defined at method level and then bound to its corresponding parameter by means of the name attribute, the

[SwaggerParameter] annotation must be defined above the parameter it's meant to describe.

To understand how it works, let's implement it. While keeping the BoardGames-Controller.cs file open, locate the Get() method, and add a [SwaggerParameter] to the existing input parameter in the following way (new lines in bold):

```
public async Task<RestDTO<BoardGame[]>> Get(
    [FromQuery]
    [SwaggerParameter("A DTO object that can be used " +
        "to customize the data-retrieval parameters.")]
    RequestDTO<BoardGameDTO> input)
```

Adds the [SwaggerParameter]

Now that the descriptive attributes have been set, we need to enable the Swashbuckle annotations feature globally by updating our Swagger configuration.

ENABLING ANNOTATIONS

To enable Swashbuckle annotations, open the Program.cs file, and add the following configuration setting to the existing AddSwaggerGen() method:

```
builder.Services.AddSwaggerGen(options =>
{
    options.EnableAnnotations();

    // ... existing code
```

Enables the Swashbuckle annotations feature

ADDING MINIMAL API SUPPORT

The [SwaggerOperation] attribute, as well as the whole Swashbuckle annotations feature, works even with Minimal API methods. Let's add some of those methods to the loop. Keeping the Program.cs file open, scroll down to the three Minimal API methods that we implemented in chapter 9 to test the ASP.NET Core authorization capabilities. Then add the [SwaggerOperation] attribute to them as shown in the following listing (new lines in bold).

Listing 11.2   Program.cs file: Adding annotations to Minimal API methods

```
using Swashbuckle.AspNetCore.Annotations;

// ... existing code

app.MapGet("/auth/test/1",
[Authorize]
[EnableCors("AnyOrigin")]
[SwaggerOperation(
    Summary = "Auth test #1 (authenticated users).",
    Description = "Returns 200 - OK if called by " +
    "an authenticated user regardless of its role(s).")]
[ResponseCache(NoStore = true)] () =>

// ... existing code
```

Required namespace

[SwaggerOperation] attribute

Adds the endpoint summary

Adds the endpoint description

```
app.MapGet("/auth/test/2",
[Authorize(Roles = RoleNames.Moderator)]
[EnableCors("AnyOrigin")]
[SwaggerOperation(
    Summary = "Auth test #2 (Moderator role).",
    Description = "Returns 200 - OK status code if called by " +
    "an authenticated user assigned to the Moderator role.")]
[ResponseCache(NoStore = true)] () =>

// ... existing code

app.MapGet("/auth/test/3",
[Authorize(Roles = RoleNames.Administrator)]
[EnableCors("AnyOrigin")]
[SwaggerOperation(
    Summary = "Auth test #3 (Administrator role).",
    Description = "Returns 200 - OK if called by " +
    "an authenticated user assigned to the Administrator role.")]
[ResponseCache(NoStore = true)] () =>

// ... existing code
```

Adds the endpoint summary

[Swagger-Operation] attribute

Adds the endpoint description

Adds the endpoint summary

Now we're ready to test what we've done.

TESTING ANNOTATIONS

To test our new annotations, run our project in Debug mode, and take a look at the SwaggerUI main dashboard, where we should be able to see them (figure 11.2).

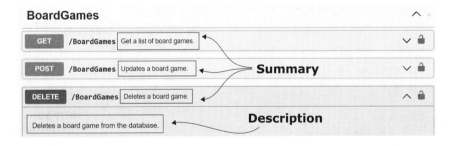

Figure 11.2   OpenAPI annotations added via the [SwaggerOperation] attribute

As we can see, the overall result is much like what we achieved by using the XML documentation approach. But there are some notable differences between what we can document with each technique. XML documentation, for example, allows us to describe examples (using the <example> element), which currently isn't supported by Swashbuckle annotations. At the same time, the Swashbuckle annotations feature can be extended with custom schema filters to support virtually any documentation option mentioned in the Swagger/OpenAPI specifications. In the following sections, we'll use both approaches in a complementary way to get the most out of them.

11.2.5 *Describe responses*

The same descriptive approach used for endpoints and input parameters should be also applied to our web API responses. This approach applies not only to the returned JavaScript Object Notation (JSON) data, but also to HTTP status codes (which should always be used according to their meaning) and relevant response headers (if any).

Again, to describe our responses, we can use the `<response>` XML documentation tag or the dedicated `[SwaggerResponse]` Swashbuckle annotation attribute. In the following sections, we'll take both of these approaches.

USING XML DOCUMENTATION

As we did earlier with the `<param>` tag, which can be used multiple times to describe each input parameter, we can create a `<response>` tag for any HTTP Status Code returned by the method. Each XML `<response>` tag requires a `code` attribute (to determine the HTTP Status Code of the response it describes) and a text-based value containing the actual description. To test it, again open the /Controllers/Account-Controller.cs file, and append the following `<response>` tags to the existing XML documentation comment block for the `Register` method (new lines in bold):

```
/// <summary>                                                    HTTP Status Code
/// Registers a new user.                                        201 description
/// </summary>
/// <param name="input">A DTO containing the user data.</param>
/// <returns>A 201 - Created Status Code in case of success.</returns>
/// <response code="201">User has been registered</response>       ◄
/// <response code="400">Invalid data</response>          ◄        HTTP Status
/// <response code="500">An error occurred</response>     ◄        Code 400
                                                                   description
                                       HTTP Status Code
                                       500 description
```

Next, scroll down to the `Login` method, and append the following `<response>` tags there as well:

```
/// <summary>                                                    HTTP Status Code
/// Performs a user login.                                       200 description
/// </summary>
/// <param name="input">A DTO containing the user's credentials.</param>
/// <returns>The Bearer Token (in JWT format).</returns>
/// <response code="200">User has been logged in</response>       ◄
/// <response code="400">Login failed (bad request)</response>    ◄
/// <response code="401">Login failed (unauthorized)</response>
     HTTP Status Code                              HTTP Status Code
     401 description                               400 description
```

To test what we've done, launch the project in Debug mode, access the SwaggerUI main dashboard, and expand the `Account/Register` and `Account/Login` endpoints. If we did everything properly, we should see our response description, as shown in figure 11.3.

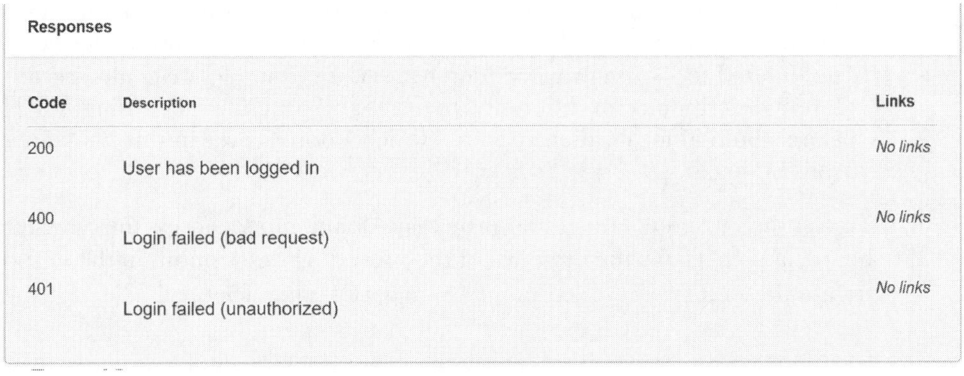

Responses		
Code	**Description**	**Links**
200	User has been logged in	*No links*
400	Login failed (bad request)	*No links*
401	Login failed (unauthorized)	*No links*

Figure 11.3 **Response descriptions for the** `/Account/Login` **endpoint**

Now that we know how to obtain this outcome by using XML documentation comments, let's see how to achieve the same thing with the [SwaggerResponse] data annotation attribute.

USING SWASHBUCKLE ANNOTATIONS

The [SwaggerResponse] attribute, like its <response> XML tag counterpart, can be added multiple times to the same method for the purpose of describing all the results, HTTP status codes, and response types that the affected method might send back to the client. Furthermore, it requires two main parameters:

- The HTTP status code for the response to describe
- The description we want to show

The best way to learn how to use it is to see it in action. Open the Program.cs file, scroll down to the /auth/test/1 Minimal API endpoint, and add a new [Swagger-Response] attribute to describe its unique response in the following way:

```
app.MapGet("/auth/test/1",
    [Authorize]
    [EnableCors("AnyOrigin")]
    [SwaggerOperation(
        Summary = "Auth test #1 (authenticated users).",
        Description = "Returns 200 - OK if called by " +
        "an authenticated user regardless of its role(s).")]
    [SwaggerResponse(StatusCodes.Status200OK,
        "Authorized")]
    [SwaggerResponse(StatusCodes.Status401Unauthorized,
        "Not authorized")]
```

HTTP Status Code 201 description

HTTP Status Code 401 description

Notice that we used the StatusCodes enum provided by the Microsoft.AspNetCore .Http namespace, which allows us to specify the HTTP status codes by using a strongly typed approach.

NOTE   One advantage of using the attribute-based method is that it grants us all the benefits provided by C# and ASP.NET Core features, including—yet not limited to—strongly typed members. As an example, we could specify different descriptions for different languages and/or cultures by using ASP.NET Core's built-in localization support (which I don't cover in this book for reasons of space).

To test the attribute, launch the project in Debug mode, access the SwaggerUI dashboard, and check for the presence of the preceding descriptions in the Responses section of the /auth/test/1 endpoint's SwaggerUI panel (figure 11.4).

Responses

Code	Description	Links
200	Authorized	No links
401	Not authorized	No links

Figure 11.4   Response descriptions for the /auth/test/1 endpoint

Not bad. Most of our endpoints, however, don't emit only an HTTP status code; in case of a successful request, they also return a JSON object with a well-defined, predetermined structure. Wouldn't it be nice to describe those return types to our API users as well, to let them know what to expect? To achieve such a goal, we need to add some samples to these descriptions. In the next section, we'll see how.

11.2.6   Add request and response samples

Ideally, each API operation should include a request and response sample so that users will understand how each one is expected to work. As we already know, our beloved SwaggerUI takes care of that task for the request part; it shows an Example Value tab containing a sample input data-transfer object (DTO) in JSON format whenever we use it, as shown in figure 11.5.

To the right of the Example Value tab is a neat Schema tab showing the object's schema and a lot of useful information, such as the maximum size, nullability, and underlying type of each field. Unfortunately, this automatic feature doesn't always work for JSON response types, requiring some manual intervention.

NOTE   Sometimes, the SwaggerUI manages to autodetect (and show an example of) the response type. If we expand the GET /BoardGames endpoint's SwaggerUI panel, for example, the RestDTO<BoardGame> object is shown properly

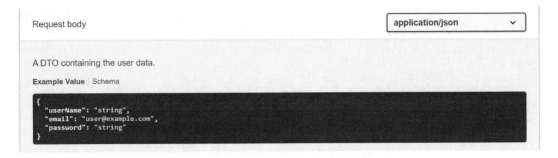

Figure 11.5   **Response sample for the** `/Account/Register` **endpoint**

in the Responses section. Sadly, when the method has multiple return types, this convenient feature often fails to autodetect most of them. The method described in the next section takes care of those scenarios.

Let's see how we can tell SwaggerUI to show a response sample whenever we want it. The `[ProducesResponseType]` attribute comes with the `Microsoft.AspNetCore.Mvc` namespace and isn't part of Swashbuckle. But because we configured the component to take annotations into account, SwaggerUI will use it to determine the response type(s) of each method and act accordingly.

The main parameters to use with the `[ProducesResponseType]` attribute are the response type and the status code returned by the method. Again, because endpoints can return different response types and status codes, it can be added to each method multiple times. We already know that SwaggerUI is unable to autodetect the return types of the `/Account/Register` and `/Account/Login` endpoints, which makes them the perfect candidates for this attribute.

Open the `/Controller/AccountController.cs` file, and locate the `Register` action method. Then add the following attributes below the existing ones, right before the method's declaration (new lines in bold):

```
[HttpPost]
[ResponseCache(CacheProfileName = "NoCache")]
[ProducesResponseType(typeof(string), 201)]
[ProducesResponseType(typeof(BadRequestObjectResult), 400)]
[ProducesResponseType(typeof(ProblemDetails), 500)]
```

HTTP Status Code 201 description

HTTP Status Code 400 description

HTTP Status Code 500 description

Do the same with the `Login` action method, using the following attributes:

```
[HttpPost]
[ResponseCache(CacheProfileName = "NoCache")]
[ProducesResponseType(typeof(string), 200)]
[ProducesResponseType(typeof(BadRequestObjectResult), 400)]
[ProducesResponseType(typeof(ProblemDetails), 401)]
```

HTTP Status Code 200 description

HTTP Status Code 400 description

HTTP Status Code 401 description

To test what we've done, launch the project in Debug mode, and check out the Responses section of the `/Account/Register` and `/Account/Login` endpoints panels in SwaggerUI to ensure that they look like those in figure 11.6.

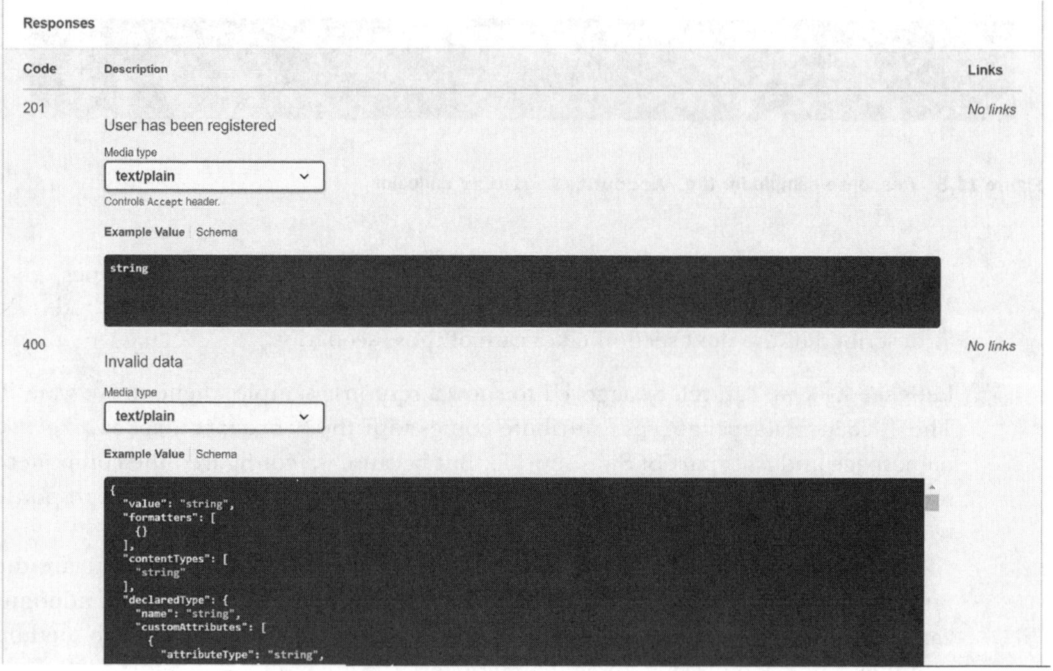

Figure 11.6   JSON samples for the `/Account/Register` return types

The screenshot depicted in figure 11.6 has been cropped because the JSON representation of the `BadRequestObjectResult` returned in case of `HTTP Status Code 400` is long. But the figure should give us an idea of what we've done. Now that we know how to force SwaggerUI to provide a sample of our response types, we're ready to master another good practice: endpoint grouping.

11.2.7   *Group endpoints into sections*

If a web API has lots of endpoints, it can be useful to group them into sections corresponding to their role/purpose. In our scenario, it could be wise to group the authentication endpoints, those that operate on the board-game entities, and so on. We could say that we've already done that because we used a controller for each of these groups, following the ASP.NET Core default behavior in this matter. As we've known since chapter 1, ASP.NET Core controllers allow us to group a set of action methods that have a common topic, meaning, or record type. We adopted this convention in our `MyBGList` scenario by using the `BoardGamesController` for the endpoints related to board games, the DomainsController for the domain-based endpoints, and so on.

This approach is enforced automatically by our current Open API implementation. If we look at our SwaggerUI dashboard, we see that the API endpoints handled by action methods pertaining to the same controller are grouped as shown in figure 11.7.

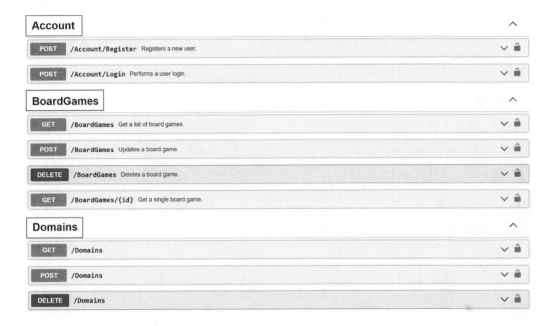

Figure 11.7 SwaggerUI group names for endpoints handled by controllers

As we can guess, these groups are generated automatically by Swashbuckle. This trick is performed by adding the controller's name to the swagger.json file via the tags property, which is designed to handle grouping tasks.

TIP For additional information about Swagger's tags property, check out http://mng.bz/5178.

To check, open the swagger.json file by clicking the hyperlink below the SwaggerUI main title, or navigate to https://localhost:40443/swagger/v1/swagger.json. The tags property for the /Account/Register endpoint is located near the beginning of the file:

```
{
  "openapi": "3.0.1",
  "info": {
    "title": "MyBGList",
    "version": "1.0"
  },
```

```
"paths": {
  "/Account/Register": {              /Account/Register
    "post": {                         endpoint description
      "tags": [
        "Account"                     "Account" tag taken
      ],                              from controller's name
```

Unfortunately, this automatic behavior doesn't work for Minimal API methods because they don't belong to a controller. The only thing Swashbuckle can do is list them all in a generic group with the name of the app (MyBGList, in our scenario), as shown in figure 11.8.

Figure 11.8   Generic group for endpoints handled by Minimal API

The result of such a fallback behavior isn't bad. But because our current Minimal API endpoints handle different sets of related tasks, we may want to find a better way to group them.

If we want to improve Swashbuckle's default tagging behavior, we can use the Tags property provided by the [SwaggerOperation] attribute to override it. Let's test it. Suppose that we want to group the three endpoints, starting with the /auth/ segment, in a new SwaggerUI section called "Auth". Open the Program.cs file; locate those methods; and make the following change to their existing [SwaggerOperation] attribute, starting with the /auth/test/1 endpoint (new lines in bold):

```
app.MapGet("/auth/test/1",
    [Authorize]
    [EnableCors("AnyOrigin")]
    [SwaggerOperation(                       Adds the Tags
        Tags = new[] { "Auth" },            property
```

```
Summary = "Auth test #1 (authenticated users).",
Description = "Returns 200 - OK if called by " +
"an authenticated user regardless of its role(s).")]
```

Do the same with the /auth/test/2 and /auth/test/3 methods, and then run the project in Debug mode to see the new Auth group (figure 11.9).

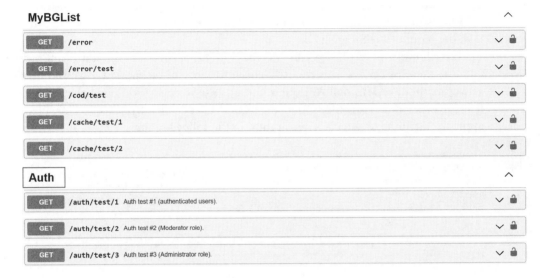

Figure 11.9   New Auth group for authorization-related endpoints

We can use the same technique to override Swashbuckle's default behavior for the action methods belonging to a controller. Whenever the Tags parameter is present with a custom value, Swashbuckle will always use it to populate the swagger.json file instead of falling back to the controller's or action method's name.

NOTE   This override feature can be handy if we want to customize the end-point's group names instead of using the controller names. It's important to keep in mind, however, that this level of customization violates one of the most important development best practices enforced by ASP.NET Core: the *convention over configuration* design paradigm, which aims to limit the number of decisions that a developer is required to make, as well as the amount of source code, without losing flexibility. For that reason, I strongly suggest adhering to the ASP.NET Core grouping and tagging conventions for controllers, leaving the Tags property customization practice for the Minimal API methods and a limited amount of exceptions.

11.2.8 Exclude reserved endpoints

The `ApiExplorer` service Swashbuckle uses to find all the controller's action methods and Minimal API methods in our project's source code automatically and describe them in the `swagger.json` file, is a great feature in most cases. But we may want to hide some methods (or whole controllers) that we don't want to show to our audience.

In our current scenario, this case could apply to the `SeedController`, which contains a couple of methods meant to be called and known only by administrators. It could be wise to exclude these operations from the `swagger.json` file, which will also take them out of the SwaggerUI.

To achieve this result, we can use the `[ApiExplorerSettings]` attribute, which contains a useful `IgnoreApi` property. This attribute can be applied to any controller, action method, or Minimal API method. Let's use it to exclude our `SeedController` from the `swagger.json` file. Open the `/Controllers/SeedController.cs` file, and apply the attribute to the class declaration in the following way:

```
[Authorize(Roles = RoleNames.Administrator)]
[ApiExplorerSettings(IgnoreApi = true)]         ◁——  Excludes the
[Route("[controller]/[action]")]                       controller from the
[ApiController]                                         swagger.json file
public class SeedController : ControllerBase
```

To test what we did, run the project in Debug mode; navigate to the SwaggerUI main dashboard; and confirm that the whole `Seed` section, which was present when we visited that page earlier, isn't visible anymore.

> **WARNING** It's important to understand that the `IgnoreApi = true` setting will only prevent the controller and its action methods from being included in the `swagger.json` file; it doesn't prevent users from calling (and potentially executing) it. That's why we also restricted it to administrators by using the `[Authorize]` attribute in chapter 9.

Up to this point, we've learned how to configure the content of the `swagger.json` file and the resulting SwaggerUI layout by working on individual methods, using either XML documentation or data annotation attributes. In the next section, we'll see how to perform these kinds of changes with a more structured and centralized approach, based on the use of Swashbuckle's filters.

11.3 Filter-based Swagger customization

As we know from chapter 6, Swashbuckle exposes a convenient filter pipeline that hooks into the `swagger.json` file-generation process, allowing us to create and add our own filters to customize the file's content according to our needs. To implement a filter, all we need to do is extend one of the built-in interfaces made available by Swashbuckle, each of them providing a convenient `Apply` method for customizing the autogenerated file. Here's a comprehensive list of the filter interfaces made available by Swashbuckle:

- IDocumentFilter–To customize the whole swagger.json file
- IOperationFilter—To customize operations/endpoints
- IParameterFilter—To customize the operations' query string input parameters
- IRequestBodyFilter—To customize the operations' request body input parameters
- ISchemaFilter—To customize the input parameters' default schema

We used this feature in chapter 6 when we added a SortColumnFilter and SortOrder-Filter (extending the IParameterFilter interface) to provide SwaggerUI some regular-expression-based patterns to validate some input parameters. Swashbuckle uses those filters, which we implemented in the /Swagger/ folder and then added to the Swashbuckle's filter pipeline in the Program.cs file, to add the pattern JSON key selectively to all parameters decorated with the [SortColumnValidator] and [Sort-OrderValidator] custom attributes. What we did was a simple yet perfect example of how the filter pipeline works.

In this section, we'll learn how to use the other filter interfaces provided by Swash-buckle to further configure our autogenerated swagger.json file, thus also updating the SwaggerUI accordingly. As always, we'll assume that we've been asked to imple-ment some credible new-feature requests.

11.3.1 Emphasizing the authorization requirements

In chapter 9, when we learned how to use the [Authorize] attribute, we added a secu-rity definition and a security requirement to our existing Swagger configuration set-tings. We did that to make the Authorize button appear in the SwaggerUI, which now allows us to set a bearer token and test our authorization-restricted endpoints. But this addition had a secondary effect that we deliberately overlooked at the time: it also added an odd padlock icon next to all our endpoints, as shown in figure 11.10.

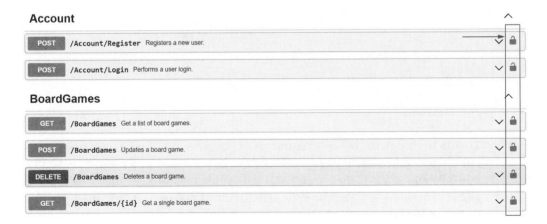

Figure 11.10 The padlock icons in SwaggerUI

When clicked, those icons make the Authorization pop-up window appear, like the Authorize button near the top-right corner of the page that we used several times in chapter 9. The padlock icon is always shown as open, however, regardless of the endpoint's authorization requirements, which isn't the behavior we expect. Ideally, we want that padlock icon to appear only next to endpoints that require authorization of some sort. The next section explains how to achieve this result.

Before delving into the source code, let's see how the padlock icon feature works under the hood. The SwaggerUI renders those icons automatically if the endpoint has a security requirement of some sort—in other words, if it requires some level of authorization. This information is taken from the swagger.json file, which assigns a security property to those endpoints:

```
"security": [{
        "Bearer": [ ]
    }]
```

In chapter 9, when we configured Swagger to support our token-based authorization mechanism, we added a global security requirement to the swagger.json file-generator service, using a dedicated configuration option in our project's Program.cs file:

```
// ...existing code

options.AddSecurityRequirement(new OpenApiSecurityRequirement
{
    {
        new OpenApiSecurityScheme
        {
            Name = "Bearer",
            In = ParameterLocation.Header,
            Reference = new OpenApiReference
            {
                Type=ReferenceType.SecurityScheme,
                Id="Bearer"
            }
        },
        new string[]{}
    }
});

// ...existing code
```

Thanks to this global security requirement, the security property is being set on all our endpoints because they're considered to be protected by a token-based authorization scheme—even if they aren't. To patch this behavior, we need to replace that global requirement with a specific rule that will trigger only for methods that are restricted by such a scheme.

The most effective approach is to create a custom filter by using the IOperation-Filter interface, which can extend the swagger.json generator service to provide additional info (or modify the existing/default info) for the affected operations. In our scenario, we want a filter that can set the same security requirements that we currently assign to all operations, but only for those with an [Authorize] attribute applied. To implement this requirement, create a new AuthRequirementFilter.cs class file inside the /Swagger/ root-level folder, and fill its content with the source code in the following listing.

Listing 11.3 /Swagger/AuthRequirementFilter.cs file

```
using Microsoft.AspNetCore.Authorization;
using Microsoft.OpenApi.Models;
using Swashbuckle.AspNetCore.SwaggerGen;

namespace MyBGList.Swagger
{
    internal class AuthRequirementFilter : IOperationFilter
    {
        public void Apply(
            OpenApiOperation operation,
            OperationFilterContext context)          Checks for the
        {                                            [Authorize]
                                                     attribute
            if (!context.ApiDescription
                .ActionDescriptor
                .EndpointMetadata
                .OfType<AuthorizeAttribute>()
                .Any())
                return;

            operation.Security = new List<OpenApiSecurityRequirement>
            {
                new OpenApiSecurityRequirement
                {
                    {
                        new OpenApiSecurityScheme
                        {
                            Name = "Bearer",
                            In = ParameterLocation.Header,
                            Reference = new OpenApiReference
                            {
                                Type=ReferenceType.SecurityScheme,
                                Id="Bearer"
                            }
                        },
                        new string[]{}
                    }
                }
            };
        }
    }
}
```

If not present, does nothing → return;

If present, secures the operation → operation.Security = new List<OpenApiSecurityRequirement>

As we can see, our new operation filter internally performs the same tasks that are currently being done in the Program.cs file. The only difference is that it skips the operations that don't have the [Authorize] attribute, because we don't want them to have any security requirement documented in the swagger.json file (or a padlock icon).

Now that we have our AuthRequirementFilter, we need to update the Swagger generator configuration options to use it instead of the global scale requirement we currently have. Open the Program.cs file; scroll down to the AddSwaggerGen method; and replace the existing AddSecurityRequirement statement with a new AddOperationFilter statement, as shown in the following code listing. (The previous code lines are commented out; new code lines are bold.)

Listing 11.4   `Program.cs` file: `AddSwaggerGen` configuration update

```
using MyBGList.Swagger;              ◄──┐  Required
                                        │  namespace
// ... existing code...

//options.AddSecurityRequirement(new OpenApiSecurityRequirement    ◄──┐
//{
//    {                                                                │  Previous
//        new OpenApiSecurityScheme                                    │  code to
//        {                                                            │  remove
//            Name = "Bearer",
//            In = ParameterLocation.Header,
//            Reference = new OpenApiReference
//            {
//                Type=ReferenceType.SecurityScheme,
//                Id="Bearer"
//            }
//        },
//        new string[]{}
//    }
//});                                                    ┐  New code
options.OperationFilter<AuthRequirementFilter>();    ◄──┘  to add

// ... existing code...
```

> **TIP**   In the GitHub repository for this chapter, I've commented out the previous code lines instead of deleting them.

To test what we did, we can launch the project in Debug mode and take another look at the same endpoints that previously had a padlock icon (figure 11.11). As we can see, the padlock icon has disappeared for the publicly accessible endpoints, but it's still there for those that require authorization of some sort. Our custom IOperationFilter allowed us to do what we wanted to do.

11.3.2 *Changing the application title*

Suppose that we want to change the application's title in the SwaggerUI, which is currently set to MyBGList—the same name as the ASP.NET Core project, per Swashbuckle's default behavior. If we look at the swagger.json file, we can see that the

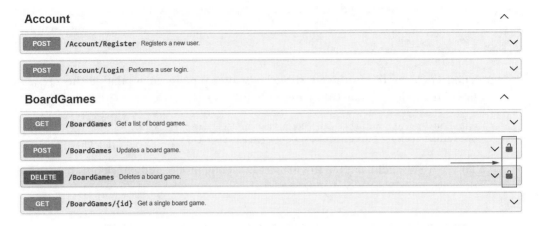

Figure 11.11 The new behavior of padlock icons in SwaggerUI

JSON property hosting that value is called `title` and is part of a parent `info` property set at document level:

```
{
  "openapi": "3.0.1",
  "info": {
    "title": "MyBGList Web API",
    "version": "1.0"
  },
```

This means that if we want to override it, we need to create a custom filter that allows us to customize the document-level parameters of the `swagger.json` file. The most effective way to achieve our goal is to create a custom `DocumentFilter` (by extending the `IDocumentFilter` interface) and add it to the filters pipeline. Create a new `Custom-DocumentFilter.cs` file in the /Swagger/ root-level folder, and fill it with the content of the following listing.

Listing 11.5 /Swagger/CustomDocumentFilter.cs file

```
using Microsoft.AspNetCore.Authorization;
using Microsoft.OpenApi.Models;
using Swashbuckle.AspNetCore.SwaggerGen;

namespace MyBGList.Swagger
{
    internal class CustomDocumentFilter : IDocumentFilter
    {
        public void Apply(
            OpenApiDocument swaggerDoc,
            DocumentFilterContext context)
        {
```

```
            swaggerDoc.Info.Title = "MyBGList Web API";
        }
    }
}
```
◁ ── Sets a custom title

Then hook the file to the Swashbuckle's filter pipeline by updating the `Program.cs` file in the following way (new lines in bold):

```
options.OperationFilter<AuthRequirementFilter>();
options.DocumentFilter<CustomDocumentFilter>();
```
◁ ── Existing filter
◁ ── New filter

To test what we did, launch the project in Debug mode, and check out the new title of the SwaggerUI dashboard (figure 11.12).

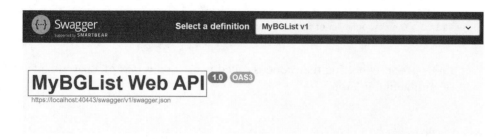

Figure 11.12   SwaggerUI title changed with the `CustomDocumentFilter`

Not bad. Let's see what we can do with the `IRequestBodyFilter` interface.

11.3.3   *Adding a warning text for passwords*

Suppose that we want to set up a custom warning text for our users whenever they need to send a password to our web API. By looking at our current endpoint, we can easily determine that for the time being, such a warning would affect only the `Account-Controller`'s `Register` and `Login` methods. By taking that fact into account, we could insert this message into the operation's `Summary` or `Description` property, using either the XML documentation comments (section 11.2.3) or the `[SwaggerOperation]` attribute (section 11.2.4), as we learned to do earlier. Alternatively, we could work at parameter level by using the `<param>` XML tag or the `[SwaggerParameter]` attribute.

Both approaches have a nontrivial downside. If we add endpoints that accept a password in the future, we'll have to repeat the XML tag or data annotation attribute there as well, which would mean replicating a lot of code—unless we forget to do that, because such a method would be error-prone.

To overcome such problems, it would be better to find a way to centralize this behavior by creating a new filter and adding it to Swashbuckle's pipeline. We need to determine which filter interface to extend among the available ones. Ideally, the `IRequestBodyFilter` interface would be a good choice, considering that we want to target a specific parameter with a name equal to "password", which currently comes (and will likely always come) with POST requests. Let's proceed with this approach. Create a new PasswordRequestFilter.cs file in the /Swagger/ root folder, and fill it with the code in the following listing.

Listing 11.6   /Swagger/PasswordRequestFilter.cs file

```
using Microsoft.OpenApi.Models;
using Swashbuckle.AspNetCore.SwaggerGen;

namespace MyBGList.Swagger
{
    internal class PasswordRequestFilter : IRequestBodyFilter
    {
        public void Apply(
            OpenApiRequestBody requestBody,
            RequestBodyFilterContext context)          Input
        {                                              parameter
            var fieldName = "password";      ←        name

            if (context.BodyParameterDescription.Name
                .Equals(fieldName,
                    StringComparison.OrdinalIgnoreCase)
                || context.BodyParameterDescription.Type
                .GetProperties().Any(p => p.Name                Property
                    .Equals(fieldName,                          check
                        StringComparison.OrdinalIgnoreCase)))  ← (complex type)
            {
                requestBody.Description =
                    "IMPORTANT: be sure to always use a strong password " +
                    "and store it in a secure location!";
            }
        }
    }
}
```

Name check (primitive type) → (points to `if (context.BodyParameterDescription.Name .Equals(fieldName, StringComparison.OrdinalIgnoreCase)`)

As we can see by looking at this code, we check whether the input parameter name is equal to "password" (for primitive types) or contains a property with that name (for complex types, such as DTOs). Now that we have the filter, we need to register it in Swashbuckle's filter pipeline in the following way, below the AuthRequirementFilter and CustomDocumentFilter that we added earlier:

```
options.OperationFilter<AuthRequirementFilter>();       Existing filters
options.DocumentFilter<CustomDocumentFilter>();
options.RequestBodyFilter<PasswordRequestFilter>();  ←  New filter
```

As always, we can test what we did by executing our project in Debug mode and checking the SwaggerUI for the expected changes (figure 11.13).

The changes seem to work. Thanks to such an approach, our password warning message will cover our two existing endpoints and any future endpoints that accept a password parameter in their request body.

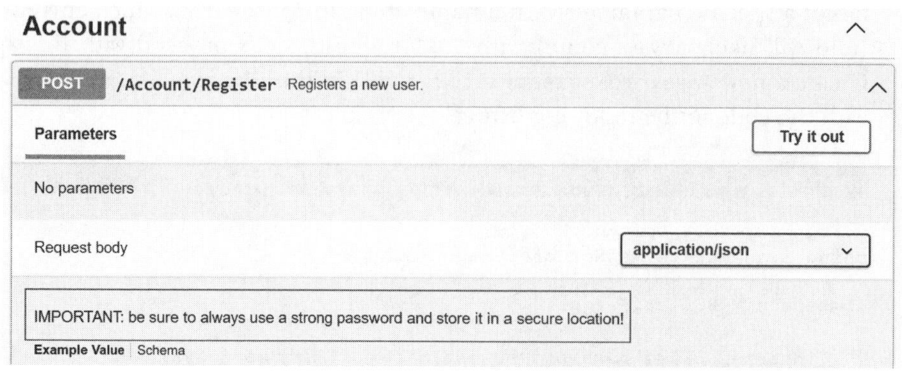

Figure 11.13   The new description added by the `PasswordRequestFilter`

> **NOTE** If we want to extend our coverage to query string parameters, we need to add another filter that extends the `IParameterFilter` interface and does the same job, and then register it in the `Program.cs` file by using the `Parameter-Filter` helper method.

All that's left to do now to complete our filters overview is the `ISchemaFilter` interface.

11.3.4 *Adding custom key/value pairs*

Let's take another look at the `SortColumnFilter` and `SortOrderFilter` classes that we implemented in chapter 6. Extending the `IParameterFilter` interface was a good idea, because we only had to handle some specific input parameters coming from the query string. In other words, we wanted to add the `pattern` key to the JSON schema of those parameters in the `swagger.json` file, taking the value from the same data annotation attribute—`[SortColumnAttribute]` or `[SortOrderAttribute]`—used to identify them.

Suppose that we want to extend that approach to implement a new filter that's capable of adding any arbitrary JSON key (and value) to any property, whether it's a request parameter, a response parameter, or anything else. In this section, we'll achieve this goal by implementing the following:

- A custom data annotation attribute, which will allow us to set one or more custom JSON `Key` and `Value` pairs to any property
- A custom `SchemaFilter` that extends the `ISchemaFilter` interface, adding those `Key` and `Value` pairs to all parameters, responses, and properties that have those data annotation attributes applied to them

The `ISchemaFilter` interface is the perfect choice to deal with this task, as it's specifically designed to postmodify the JSON schema generated by Swashbuckle's `Swagger-Gen` service for every input and output parameter and complex types exposed by controller actions and Minimal API methods. Now that we've chosen our route, let's put it into practice.

IMPLEMENTING THE CUSTOMKEYVALUEATTRIBUTE

In Visual Studio's Solution Explorer panel, right-click the /Attributes/ folder in the MyBGList project's root, and add a new CustomKeyValueAttribute.cs class file with two string properties: Key and Value. The following listing provides the source code for the new class.

Listing 11.7   CustomKeyValueAttribute

```
namespace MyBGList.Attributes
{
    [AttributeUsage(
        AttributeTargets.Property | AttributeTargets.Parameter,
        AllowMultiple = true)]
    public class CustomKeyValueAttribute : Attribute
    {
        public CustomKeyValueAttribute(string? key, string? value)
        {
            Key = key;
            Value = value;
        }

        public string? Key { get; set; }

        public string? Value { get; set; }
    }
}
```

Notice that we've decorated our new class with the [AttributeUsage] attribute, which allows us to specify the use of the attribute. We did that for two important reasons:

- To allow the attribute to be applied to properties and parameters, using the AttributeTargets enum.
- To allow the attribute to be applied multiple times because the AllowMultiple property is set to true. This setting is required because we want the chance to apply multiple [SwaggerSchema] attributes (thus setting multiple custom key/value pairs) to a single property or parameter.

Now that we have the attribute, we're ready to implement the filter that will handle it.

IMPLEMENTING THE CUSTOMKEYVALUEFILTER

Add a new CustomKeyValueFilter.cs class file within the /Swagger/ folder. The new class must implement the ISchemaFilter interface and its Apply method, which is where we'll handle the [CustomKeyValue] attribute lookup and JSON key/value pair insertion process. The following listing shows how.

Listing 11.8   CustomKeyValueFilter

```
using Microsoft.OpenApi.Any;
using Microsoft.OpenApi.Models;
using Swashbuckle.AspNetCore.SwaggerGen;
```

```
namespace MyBGList.Attributes
{
    public class CustomKeyValueFilter : ISchemaFilter
    {
        public void Apply(
            OpenApiSchema schema,
            SchemaFilterContext context)
        {
            var caProvider = context.MemberInfo
                ?? context.ParameterInfo
                as IcustomAttributeProvider;

            var attributes = caProvider?
                .GetCustomAttributes(true)
                .OfType<CustomKeyValueAttribute>();

            if (attributes != null)
            {
                foreach (var attribute in attributes)
                {
                    schema.Extensions.Add(
                        attribute.Key,
                        new OpenApiString(attribute.Value)
                        );
                }
            }
        }
    }
}
```

Determines whether we're dealing with a property or a parameter

Checks whether the parameter has the attribute(s)

If one or more attributes are present, acts accordingly

This code should be simple to understand. We're checking the context provided by the ISchemaFilter interface by using Language Integrated Query (LINQ) to determine whether our property or parameter has one or more [CustomKeyValue] attributes applied and act accordingly. All we need to do now is add the new filter to Swashbuckle's filter pipeline. As always, we can update the Program.cs file in the following way:

```
options.OperationFilter<AuthRequirementFilter>();
options.DocumentFilter<CustomDocumentFilter>();
options.RequestBodyFilter<PasswordRequestFilter>();
options.SchemaFilter<CustomKeyValueFilter>();
```

Existing filters

New filter

Now that our two classes are ready and the filter has been registered, we can test the [CustomKeyValue] attribute by applying it to a property of one of our existing DTOs. Let's pick the LoginDTO used by the AccountController's Login action method. Open the /DTO/LoginDTO.cs file, and apply a couple of these attributes to the existing UserName property in the following way:

```
[Required]
[MaxLength(255)]
[CustomKeyValue("x-test-1", "value 1")]
[CustomKeyValue("x-test-2", "value 2")]
public string? UserName { get; set; }
```

First CustomKeyValue attributes

Next, run the project in Debug mode, access the SwaggerUI dashboard, and click to the swagger.json file link below the main title (figure 11.14) to open it in a new tab.

Figure 11.14 swagger.json file URL

Use the browser's Search feature to look for the "x-test-" string within the swagger .json file. If we did everything properly, we should see two entries of this string in the JSON schema of the LoginDTO's username property, as shown in the following listing.

Listing 11.9 swagger.json file (LoginDTO schema)

```
"LoginDTO": {
  "required": [
    "password",
    "userName"
  ],
  "type": "object",
  "properties": {
    "userName": {
      "maxLength": 255,
      "minLength": 1,
      "type": "string",
      "x-test-1": "value 1",     |   Custom
      "x-test-2": "value 2"      |   key/value pairs
    },
    "password": {
      "minLength": 1,
      "type": "string"
    }
  }
}
```

So far, so good. Let's perform another test to ensure that the same logic will work for a standard GET parameter of a primitive type. Open the /Controllers/BoardGames-Controller.cs file, scroll down to the Get action method accepting a single id parameter of int type, and add a [CustomKeyValue] attribute to that parameter in the following way:

```
[HttpGet("{id}")]
[ResponseCache(CacheProfileName = "Any-60")]
[SwaggerOperation(
```

```
    Summary = "Get a single board game.",
    Description = "Retrieves a single board game with the given Id.")]
public async Task<RestDTO<BoardGame?>> Get(
    [CustomKeyValue("x-test-3", "value 3")]        ◁────┐  Adds a new
    int id                                              │  [CustomKeyValue]
    )                                                   │  attribute
```

Next, run the project in Debug mode, access the swagger.json file contents as we did earlier, and check again for the presence of the of the "x-test-" string within it. This time, we should locate three entries, the last of which is the one we added (see the following listing).

Listing 11.10   swagger.json file (/BoardGames/{id} endpoint schema)

```
"/BoardGames/{id}": {
  "get": {
    "tags": [
      "BoardGames"
    ],
    "summary": "Get a single board game.",
    "description": "Retrieves a single board game with the given Id.",
    "parameters": [
      {
        "name": "id",
        "in": "path",
        "required": true,
        "schema": {
          "type": "integer",           Custom
          "format": "int32",           key/value
          "x-test-3": "value 3"    ◁──┘ pair
        }
      }
    ],
```

Our custom key/value feature seems to be working well. This last task concludes our journey through Swashbuckle's filter pipeline and our API documentation overview. The only thing left to do now is learn to deploy our web API project to production, which is the topic of chapter 12.

11.4   Exercises

It's time to challenge ourselves with a new streak of hypothetical task assignments given by our product owner. As always, dealing with these tasks will greatly help us memorize and remember the concepts covered and the techniques learned throughout this chapter.

> **NOTE**   The solutions of the exercises are available on GitHub in the /Chapter_11/Exercises/ folder. To test them, replace the relevant files in your MyBG-List project with those in that folder, and run the app.

11.4.1 Use XML documentation

Describe the GET /Domains endpoint in the following way, using the XML documentation approach:

- Summary—Gets a list of domains
- Description—Retrieves a list of domains with custom paging, sorting, and filtering rules
- Parameter—A DTO object that can be used to customize some retrieval parameters
- Returns—A RestDTO object containing a list of domains

TIP The description can be added with the <remarks> XML element.

11.4.2 Use Swashbuckle annotations

Describe the GET /Mechanics endpoint in the following way, using the Swashbuckle annotations approach:

- Summary—Gets a list of mechanics
- Description—Retrieves a list of mechanics with custom paging, sorting, and filtering rules
- Parameter—A DTO object that can be used to customize some retrieval parameters
- Returns—A RestDTO object containing a list of mechanics

11.4.3 Exclude some endpoints

Use the [ApiExplorerSettings] attribute to hide the following endpoints from the swagger.json file:

- POST /Domains
- DELETE /Domains

Then ensure that these endpoints are also excluded from the SwaggerUI dashboard.

11.4.4 Add a custom filter

Extend the IRequestBodyFilter interface to implement a new UsernameRequestFilter that will add the following description to any input parameter with a name equal to "username". Then register the new filter within Swashbuckle's filter pipeline, and test it in the SwaggerUI dashboard by checking the sername parameter used by the POST Account/Login and POST Account/Register endpoints.

WARNING Be sure to remember your username, as you'll need it to perform the login!

11.4.5 *Add custom key/value pairs*

Use the [CustomKeyValue] attribute to add the following key/value pairs to the existing id parameter of the DELETE Mechanics endpoint:

- Key: x-test-4, Value: value 4
- Key: x-test-5, Value: value 5

Then check for the presence of the new properties in the endpoint's JSON schema within the swagger.json file.

Summary

- Well-written documentation can greatly increase or speed the adoption of a web API.
  - For that reason, it's important to identify the API documentation best practices and learn to follow them, using ASP.NET Core built-in and third-party tools.
- Identifying the potential audience for our web API—the stakeholders who are expected to choose and/or use it—can help us write compelling documentation. Ideally, we need to satisfy
  - Early adopters who are eager to try what we did (prospectors).
  - IT solution architects who aim to evaluate our work (contractors).
  - Software developers who will be asked to implement our web API's endpoints (builders).
- Focusing on the needs of the builders without forgetting the other two audience groups (prospectors and contractors) is almost always the way to go.
- Developers are analytical, precise, and demanding. To meet their expectations, it's important to adhere to some well-known documentation best practices widely adopted by the IT industry, including
  - adopting an automated description tool.
  - describing endpoints, input parameters, and responses.
  - providing request and response samples.
  - grouping endpoints into sections.
  - emphasizing the authorization requirements.
  - customizing the documentation context.
- The Swagger/OpenAPI framework provides a standardized approach for documenting and describing APIs, using a common language that everyone can understand.
  - We can use Swagger to create the documentation for our web API thanks to Swashbuckle: a set of services, middleware, and tools that allows us to implement the OpenAPI specification within ASP.NET Core while following the best practices that we identified earlier.

- Swashbuckle exposes a convenient set of data attributes, as well as a powerful filter pipeline, that can be used to postmodify the autogenerated `swagger.json` file, thus customizing the API documentation to suit our needs.
  - Swashbuckle's features allow us to improve the description of operations, input parameters, and output parameters, as well as add custom key/value pairs to the existing JSON schemas.

Release and deployment

This chapter covers

- Getting the web API ready for release
- Adopting a security by design approach
- Setting up a content-delivery network (CDN)
- Creating a Windows Server virtual machine (VM) in Microsoft Azure
- Installing and configuring Internet Information Services (IIS)
- Deploying the web API to Windows Server with Visual Studio

We're close to the end of our journey. Our ASP.NET Core web API project is mature enough to be classified as a potentially shippable product (PSP), a definition used by most Agile methodologies to indicate that the application, although still incomplete, has reached a level of maturity solid enough to be shown to product owners, beta testers, and/or end users.

It's important to understand that this status doesn't mean the app is ready to be delivered to customers. *Potentially shippable* is a state of confidence from a development perspective; actual shipping is a business decision that should take other data into account.

In this chapter, we'll suppose that the IT project manager assigned to our development team, after carefully reviewing the results of our work, has decided that our web API is ready for its first release. To comply with this decision, we need to publish it somewhere to enable the interested parties—ideally, product owners and testers—to access and evaluate it.

After a brief introductory part, where we'll perform some required steps to ensure that our ASP.NET Core application is ready for the deployment phase, we'll learn how to publish our project to a Windows Server machine. ASP.NET Core is platform agnostic, so although we'll target a Windows OS, we could use the same process, with minor differences, to deploy our app on a Linux machine, a Docker container, or any other publishing target.

> **WARNING** The topics covered in this chapter concern different skills from those required in the previous chapters. Most of the tasks are typically assigned to deployment engineers and/or system administrators, not to software—at least, in large organizations. But being able to release, deploy, and publish a project is a required learning path for anyone who aims to become a full-stack developer or to work on a small, DevOps-oriented team—a rather common scenario for small companies and startups.

12.1 Prepublishing tasks

In this section, we'll learn how to get our ASP.NET Core web API ready to publish in a production environment. Here's what we're about to do:

1 Define the overall security approach that will guide us through implementation of the various required tasks.
2 Determine the domain name that we'll use to make our app publicly available on the World Wide Web.
3 Set up a content-delivery network (CDN) to achieve Transport Layer Security (TLS) and caching capabilities, as well as protect our web API from distributed denial of service (DDoS) attempts, brute-force attacks, and other web-related threats.
4 Configure our project to make it ready for production.

We'll also review our current caching and security settings to ensure that the app is ready to be accessed by external users (including potentially malicious parties) while minimizing the risks of request-based attacks, data breaches, and other harmful scenarios.

12.1.1 Considering security

The depth and scope of the prepublishing review we're about to perform are strictly determined by our scenario. We're bringing into production a (yet) unknown web API, which is meant to be accessed by a limited panel of users and beta testers, and which doesn't contain restricted or sensitive data. Based on these premises, we can reasonably expect that we won't be subject to sophisticated attacks, at least not for some time.

This expectation, however, must not lead us to take the risk of attack lightly. According to the *2022 Imperva Bad Bot Report* (http://mng.bz/v1Dx), 27.7 percent of internet traffic is made up of automated threats. These bots can be instructed to attack specific websites, as well as to scan the internet for potentially vulnerable IP addresses and/or TCP ports. When a suitable target is found, these bots will likely carry out some automated attacks on it and signal the outcome to their "master"—a person or organization that might orchestrate even worse malicious activities.

For that reason, whenever we're commissioned to bring one of our web-based projects into production, we should adopt a security by design approach: to take the most secure route to fulfill each of our tasks as long as we maintain a decent cost/benefit (and/or risk) tradeoff. Now that we've defined our overall security approach, let's deal with the first of our prepublishing tasks: obtaining a suitable domain name.

12.1.2 Choosing a domain name

In information technology, a *domain name* is a string of text that uniquely maps to a numeric Internet Protocol (IP) address, which can be used to access a web resource (typically, a website). We can think of it as a human-readable alias of the IP address we want to connect to, which is also machine-readable and understood by all web browsers and web servers.

> **NOTE** For reasons of space, I'll take for granted that you know most of the basic networking and TCP/IP-related concepts that are used throughout this section. If not, I strongly suggest improving your knowledge by reading *HTTP/2 in Action*, by Barry Pollard (Manning; https://www.manning.com/books/http2-in-action).

For deployment purposes, we'll register a dedicated mybglist.com domain so that we'll be able to create custom subdomains and use them to create public endpoints for our users. I won't guide you through the domain-purchase process; I take for granted that you'll complete it before continuing to the next section. If you don't want to purchase a dedicated domain, you're free to use a subdomain and follow the same instructions, replacing the subdomain we're going to use in our deployment sample (win-01.mybglist.com) with your chosen subdomain.

12.1.3 Setting up a CDN

Now that we've determined our domain name, we have another important decision to make: whether to set up a direct binding to the IP address of our web server or set up an intermediate layer (such as a CDN service). Each option has advantages and drawbacks. Configuring a CDN will inevitably require additional configuration efforts and will complicate our overall architecture, but it will also grant us valuable caching and security benefits.

TIP In the unlikely case that you don't want (or are unable) to set up a CDN, you can skip this section and go to the next one.

Based on what we learned in chapter 8, which was about intermediate caching, we already know that adding a CDN service to our network stack will increase the performance of our web API. But we should take into account some relevant security benefits, assuming that we want to stick to the security-by-design approach that we chose to adopt. Those benefits may vary depending on the CDN service and/or the subscription plan, but some of them are usually available, such as the following:

- *IP address masking*—The CDN acts as a proxy, hiding the IP address of the origin server (the web server hosting our web API). All requests go to the CDN first and then are forwarded to our origin server.
- *Web Application Firewall (WAF)*—CDNs typically use a dedicated WAF that checks the incoming HTTP requests and filters potentially malicious traffic based on a given set of rules, blacklists, and other industry-standard security measures.
- *DDoS protection*—Most CDNs automatically detect and mitigate DDoS attacks by using rate-limiting rules and other advanced techniques.

These features alone, which would be difficult (and costly) for any software development team to implement, are more than enough to make the CDN worth the effort. For that reason, we're going to set it up. Before choosing a provider, however, let's consider the result we want to achieve.

USING THE EDGE-ORIGIN PATTERN
In chapter 3, which introduced CDNs, I briefly mentioned the edge-origin architectural pattern, an infrastructure in which a proxy or CDN service (the edge) publicly serves the content by taking it from a source web server (the origin) that isn't exposed directly. Figure 12.1 illustrates this concept.

Figure 12.1 Edge-origin architectural pattern

As we can see, the end user points the browser to our web API's public (sub)domain, which is handled by the CDN service (edge). The CDN serves the content back, taking it from its intermediate cache or requesting it from the web server (origin) using its dedicated (and not exposed) IP address.

That process is precisely what we want to implement for our web API. With that in mind, let's start by choosing a CDN service provider.

CHOOSING A CDN SERVICE PROVIDER

In general terms, there are four main features to look for when choosing a CDN service provider:

- *Capability*—A good CDN should have a decent network size (number of servers) and distribution (worldwide coverage). More servers will likely lead to less buffering, greater redundancy, and more scalability, and a good geographic distribution will ensure the same level of services for all members of our potential audience, regardless of where they're connecting from.
- *Performance*—Performance is often related to (and mostly dependent on) capability. The most important key metrics to measure include Domain Name System (DNS) response time, connect time, wait time, overall latency, packet loss rate, and bandwidth throughput.
- *Reliability*—When it's set up, the CDN becomes the only gateway of our web application. If something bad happens to it or to its configuration settings, our users will be unable to connect. For that reason, we need to ensure that the service guarantees near-100 percent uptime/availability and good (and fast) customer support.
- *Pricing*—A good CDN should offer an affordable, transparent pricing model. Most CDNs use modular subscription plans based on custom negotiated contracts, depending on the customer's bandwidth and feature needs. Another common model relies on use, with a per-GB pricing that typically goes down as volume rises. Some CDNs even offer free plans for small-scale projects. Any of these approaches can be viable, depending on specific needs and—most important—the expected (or known) traffic volume of the web application.

Because we have a small-scale project with a limited budget, we should choose a CDN provider with a great cost-benefit ratio. Starting from this premise, our choice will be Cloudflare, an extremely popular CDN service provided by Cloudflare, Inc. since 2010. According to a W3Techs.com survey (http://mng.bz/41EB), Cloudflare CDN is used by 19.1 percent of websites worldwide, with a CDN market share of 79.7 percent. This popularity is easily explained by the fact that Cloudflare is one of the few CDN services to offer an unlimited and unrestricted free plan, which makes it perfect for our needs. Another great reason to choose Cloudflare is the fact that it provides two free SSL/TLS certificates:

- *The edge certificate*—The edge certificate will be generated automatically and used by the CDN itself when serving the content to our visitors, ensuring full HTTPS support for our web API.
- *The origin certificate*—We can manually generate and install the origin certificate on the web server(s) hosting the web API to ensure an encrypted connection between the CDN (edge) and the host (origin) server.

In the following sections, we'll learn how to create a Cloudflare account and set up this service.

CREATING A CLOUDFLARE ACCOUNT

The first thing we need to do is create a Cloudflare account. I won't go into details here, because the registration process is straightforward. At the end of it, perform the login by using the credentials (email and password) that we set up. Then click the Add Site button (figure 12.2), which takes us to a page where we can add our domain.

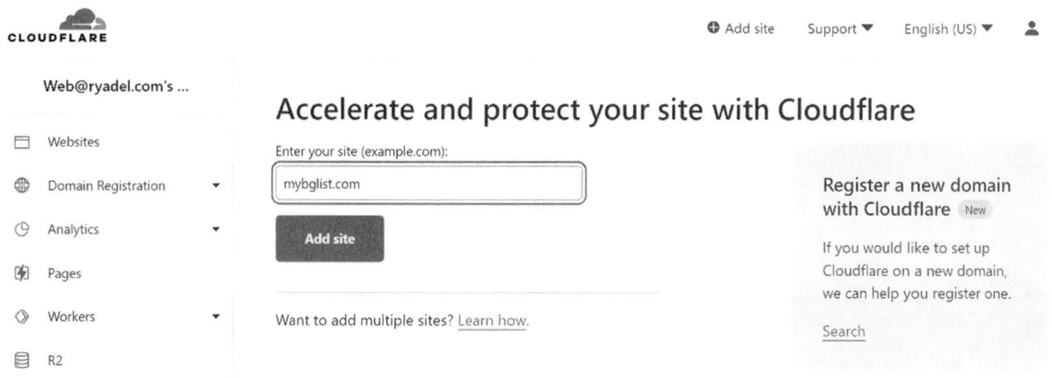

Figure 12.2   Adding a domain to Cloudflare

We can't add a subdomain here, however. If we plan to use a subdomain of an existing domain instead of a dedicated domain, we still need to type the "parent" domain in this text box unless it's already configured with Cloudflare. We'll be given the chance to choose domain configuration options later. Right after we add the domain and click the Add Site button, we'll be prompted to select a subscription plan (figure 12.3).

The paid plans (Pro, Business, and Enterprise) are stuffed with interesting features. But because we're aiming for a budget-friendly solution, we'll start with the free plan, which guarantees the core features we require (at least for the time being).

The free plan requires us to configure Cloudflare as the primary DNS provider for our domain, so we'll use the Cloudflare nameservers and manage our DNS records on Cloudflare. This configuration option is known as Full Setup. In case we want to use a subdomain of an existing domain that we don't want to move to Cloudflare, we should consider purchasing the Business or Enterprise plan instead. These plans include the CNAME set-up feature, also known as Partial Setup. We're going to choose the Full Setup option, which allows us to select the free plan.

> **TIP**   For more information about the Full Setup and Partial (CNAME) Setup configuration options, see http://mng.bz/Q86m and http://mng.bz/X5yY.

After we click Continue, Cloudflare performs a scan of the existing DNS records of our domain (which will take a few seconds). These records will be used to populate a DNS management panel. Cloudflare will try to copy (or clone) the current DNS

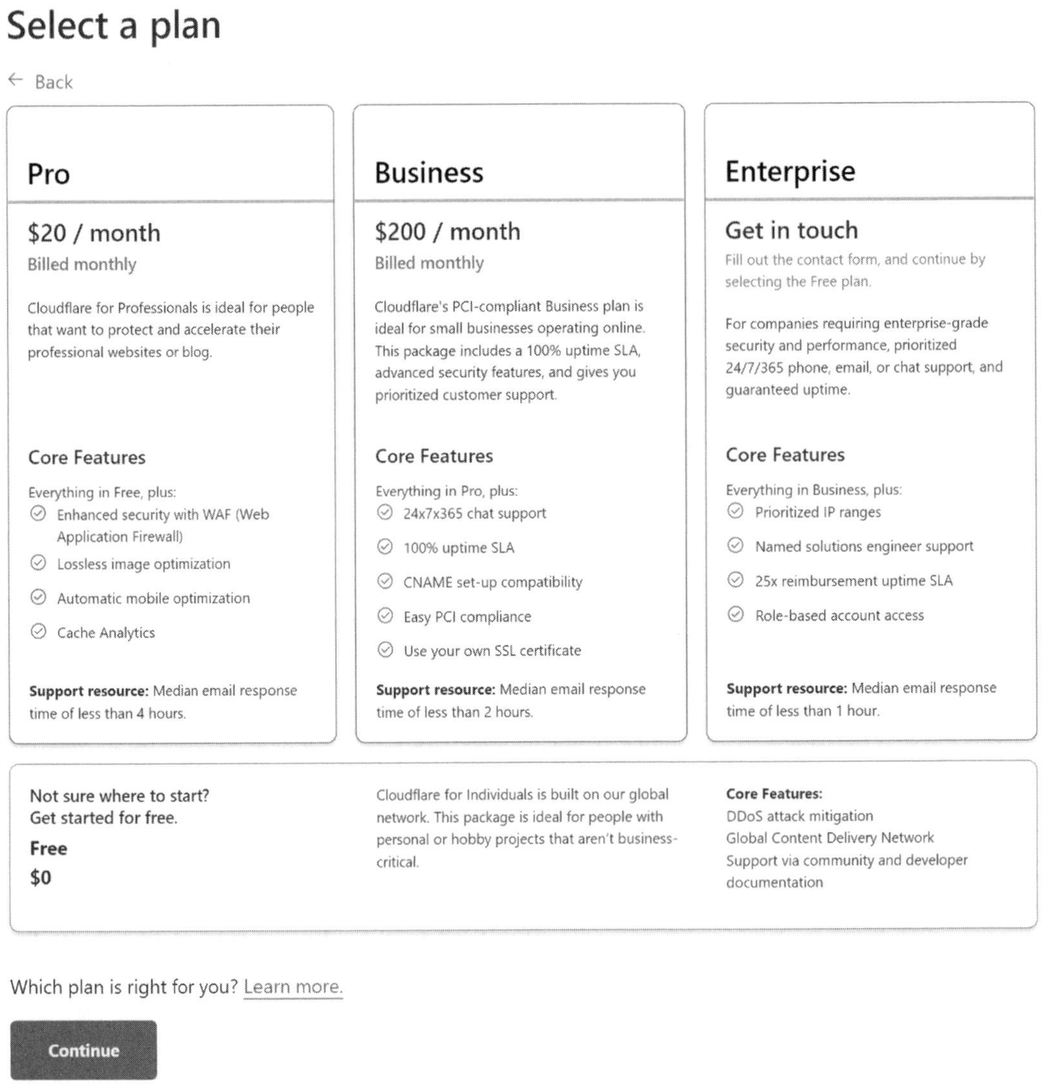

Select a plan

← Back

Pro

$20 / month
Billed monthly

Cloudflare for Professionals is ideal for people that want to protect and accelerate their professional websites or blog.

Core Features

Everything in Free, plus:
- ⊘ Enhanced security with WAF (Web Application Firewall)
- ⊘ Lossless image optimization
- ⊘ Automatic mobile optimization
- ⊘ Cache Analytics

Support resource: Median email response time of less than 4 hours.

Business

$200 / month
Billed monthly

Cloudflare's PCI-compliant Business plan is ideal for small businesses operating online. This package includes a 100% uptime SLA, advanced security features, and gives you prioritized customer support.

Core Features

Everything in Pro, plus:
- ⊘ 24x7x365 chat support
- ⊘ 100% uptime SLA
- ⊘ CNAME set-up compatibility
- ⊘ Easy PCI compliance
- ⊘ Use your own SSL certificate

Support resource: Median email response time of less than 2 hours.

Enterprise

Get in touch
Fill out the contact form, and continue by selecting the Free plan.

For companies requiring enterprise-grade security and performance, prioritized 24/7/365 phone, email, or chat support, and guaranteed uptime.

Core Features

Everything in Business, plus:
- ⊘ Prioritized IP ranges
- ⊘ Named solutions engineer support
- ⊘ 25x reimbursement uptime SLA
- ⊘ Role-based account access

Support resource: Median email response time of less than 1 hour.

Not sure where to start?
Get started for free.

Free
$0

Cloudflare for Individuals is built on our global network. This package is ideal for people with personal or hobby projects that aren't business-critical.

Core Features:
DDoS attack mitigation
Global Content Delivery Network
Support via community and developer documentation

Which plan is right for you? Learn more.

Continue

Figure 12.3   Choosing a Cloudflare subscription plan

configuration of our domain to get ready to handle it by using its own nameservers. Unsurprisingly, we'll eventually have to update our domain's existing nameservers to use Cloudflare's nameservers.

UPDATING THE NAMESERVERS

After the DNS scan, we'll access a gridlike view showing the various DNS records currently registered for our domain in Cloudflare. But that configuration won't become active until we update the nameservers currently used by our domain with the one provided by Cloudflare. The required steps are summarized on Cloudflare's Overview page, accessible through the menu on the left side of the page (figure 12.4).

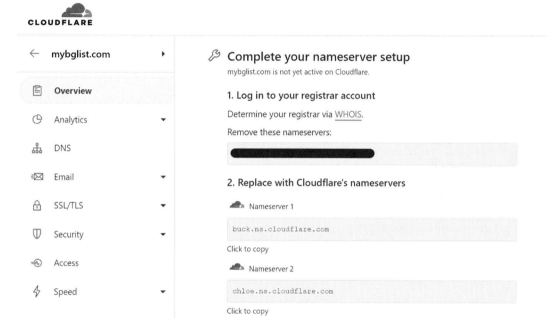

Figure 12.4 Cloudflare's nameservers setup guide

The nameservers update process is straightforward and shouldn't pose significant problems. We need to access the domain management dashboard of the domain service provider that we used to purchase the domain and replace the content of a couple of text boxes with the values provided by Cloudflare.

> **TIP** First, it may be wise to do a detailed check to ensure that the automatic DNS scan performed by Cloudflare fetched all the existing A, CNAME, TXT, and MX records and to add the missing ones (if any) in the Cloudflare DNS management panel. If we fail to do that, the nameservers update process could compromise some of the existing domain services; they would no longer be resolved.

Next, we'll need to wait for DNS propagation (the timeframe it takes for DNS changes to be updated across the internet). This process can take up to 72 hours, depending on several factors, including the time-to-live (TTL) values of our existing DNS records.

When the process completes, Cloudflare will send us an email notification saying that our domain is active on Cloudflare. If we don't want to wait, we can click the Check Nameservers button at the end of the nameserver setup guide (partly visible in figure 12.4) to perform a real-time check.

> **NOTE**   For reasons of space, we've only scratched the surface of Cloudflare's features and capabilities. To learn more about the service, read the official docs at https://developers.cloudflare.com.

While we wait for the nameserver update to propagate, we can proceed to the next step: deploying our ASP.NET Core web API by using Visual Studio's publishing capabilities.

12.1.4 Fine-tuning our APP

In this section, we'll take care of the following tasks:

1 Get our project ready for production by reviewing the `appsettings.json` file(s) and the `Program.cs` file.

2 Improve the web API's security posture by adding some specific HTTP response headers (better known as security headers) that will help mitigate or prevent some common attacks.

3 Create a static API documentation interface (client) instead of exposing our Swagger definition file and SwaggerUI directly.

REVIEWING THE APPSETTINGS.JSON FILE(S)

Our project's `appsettings.json` files should be OK for production because we adopted the good practice of creating multiple versions of them, one for each environment we need to support. We have the following "cascading" files:

- `appsettings.json`—Contains the default settings
- `appsettings.Development.json`—Contains development-specific settings and overrides (for all developers)
- `secrets.json`—Contains development-specific settings and overrides (for our own private development environment)

Ideally, we need to create a new `appsettings.Production.json` file containing the equivalent of the `secrets.json` files for the production environment. Adding this file in our Visual Studio project (and/or sharing it among developers) would be a bad idea, however, because it could easily end up in some publicly accessible repositories (such as GitHub) and/or unprotected storage devices.

For that reason, we'll create the `appsettings.Production.json` file directly on the production server during the deployment phase. This approach may not always be practical, depending on the overall complexity of that file and the working practices of the IT development team, but it's viable enough in our scenario. We'll see how to do that when we deploy our web API in production. For now, we have nothing to do with these files.

REVIEWING THE PROGRAM.CS FILE

As we've known since chapter 2, the `Program.cs` file allows us to set up middleware for each available runtime environment (development, staging, and production) by using the `app.Environment` property. Two good examples are the Swagger and SwaggerUI middleware, configured to be available only in development:

```
if (app.Environment.IsDevelopment())
{
    app.UseSwagger();
    app.UseSwaggerUI();
}
```

Hiding Swagger in staging production environments is good security practice. Publicly documenting our API might give potential attackers some valuable hints on ways to abuse our endpoints. We can lessen these risks by implementing a restrictive Cross-Origin Resource Sharing (CORS) policy (chapter 3), as well as adding HTTP security headers that could mitigate or prevent other attacks.

Using HTTP security headers

As we know all too well, each time a browser navigates to a website, it issues an HTTP Request to the web server hosting that site. The server typically responds with an HTTP Response, which usually contains a status code, some response headers and often some content in HTML, JavaScript Object Notation (JSON), or other browser-compatible formats.

Another thing we know well is that the response headers contain useful info that the client will use to handle several tasks, such as content caching, language and localization, and character encoding. Some of this (meta)data can affect the website's security posture, as it controls the browser's behavior with regard to the received content. It can force the client/browser to communicate over HTTPS only, for example, or force the browser to block any FRAME, IFRAME, or other source (SRC) content from third-party servers.

The response headers that contain these client policies are called *security headers*. Adding them to our web applications is widely considered to be one of the most convenient security best practices in terms of cost-benefit ratio, for the following reasons:

- They're easy to implement.
- It's easy to understand how they work (and what attacks they help mitigate).
- They require minimum configuration changes.
- They have a negligible effect on performance.

Security headers are required nowadays to pass any penetration test, vulnerability scan, risk assessment, data security checklist, and decent IT audit and/or certification process. Here's a list of the most important HTTP security headers that we might consider implementing in our web API project:

- *HTTP Strict Transport Security (HSTS)*—Tells the web browser to access the web server over HTTPS only, ensuring that each connection will be established only through secure channels.
- *X-Frame-Options*—Protects against clickjacking (http://mng.bz/51y4) by preventing FRAMEs and IFRAMEs from specific sources (such as different web servers) from loading on your site.

- *X-XSS-Protection*—Protects against cross-site scripting (XSS) by enabling a specific filter built into most modern browsers. Although XSS filtering is active by default in most modern browsers, it's advisable to enable (and configure) it explicitly to strengthen our website even more.

- *X-Content-Type-Options*—Prevents the browser from downloading, viewing, and/or executing a response that differs from the expected and declared content type, thus reducing the risk of executing malicious software or downloading harmful files.

- *Content security policy*—Prevents attacks such as XSS and other code-injection-based attacks by defining which content the browser should and shouldn't load.

- *Referrer policy*—Determines whether the URL of the web page that linked to the requested resource has to be sent along with the request (using the `Referer` HTTP Header). The default behavior, if no value is specified, is to strip that header (and hence the referrer info) when going from a page using HTTPS to a page using unsecure HTTP and leaving it in all other cases.

Now that we know what these security headers are and what they do, let's see how to implement them. As we might guess, the best place to handle this task is the `Program.cs` file. Open that file, scroll down to this point,

```
if (app.Environment.IsDevelopment())
{
    app.UseSwagger();
    app.UseSwaggerUI();
}
```

and replace it with the code shown in lithe following listing.

Listing 12.1 `Program.cs` file: HTTP security headers

```
if (app.Environment.IsDevelopment())
{
    app.UseSwagger();
    app.UseSwaggerUI();
}
else
{
    // HTTP Security Headers                    Strict-Transport-
    app.UseHsts();                              Security header
    app.Use(async (context, next) =>
    {
        context.Response.Headers.Add("X-Frame-Options",      X-Frame-Options
            "sameorigin");                                   header
        context.Response.Headers.Add("X-XSS-Protection",
            "1; mode=block");
        context.Response.Headers.Add("X-Content-Type-Options",
            "nosniff");                                       Content-
        context.Response.Headers.Add("Content-Security-Policy",  Security-Policy
            "default-src ' self' ;");                            header
```

X-XSS-Protection header

X-Content-Type-Options header

```
        context.Response.Headers.Add("Referrer-Policy",
            "strict-origin");                          Referrer-
        await next();                                  Policy
    });                                                header
}
```

Notice that the HTTP Strict Transport Security (HSTS) header has its own built-in middleware; the others require a manual implementation using custom middleware. We chose to add the header only in nondevelopment environments—a wise choice, because some of headers (especially HSTS) might create some inconvenient problems when we run our app on localhost.

> **NOTE** I won't cover security headers in detail. We'll add them by using their most common settings, which are good enough to protect our MyBGList web API. Plenty of websites offer information about how they work and how to configure them. A good place to start is the OWASP HTTP Security Response Headers Cheat Sheet at http://mng.bz/ydDJ.

Although the security headers we implemented can prevent or mitigate some attacks, exposing Swagger in a nondevelopment environment would still be risky. The best thing we can do to comply with the security-by-design approach is to keep adding Swagger middleware in the development environment only.

Unfortunately, this approach will also prevent our audience from accessing the API documentation we worked with in chapter 11, including the SwaggerUI. Is there a way to preserve what we did there without exposing Swagger directly? Luckily, several code-generator tools can seamlessly create static, HTML-based web user interfaces from Swagger JSON definition files. In the next section, we'll learn how to use one of them.

> **TIP** First, be sure to inspect the Program.cs file thoroughly for other middleware that shouldn't be used in nondevelopment environments, and use the app.Environment property to prevent them from being added to the HTTP pipeline. Our sample project has none of this middleware, but it's a good practice to perform this check before the publishing phase.

CREATING A STATIC API DOCUMENTATION INTERFACE

The first thing we must do to create static API documentation interface is choose a code-generator tool. Plenty of those tools are available, made, developed, and maintained by the Swagger team or third parties. For simplicity, we'll limit our choices to the following:

- *Swagger Codegen*—An open source command-line interface (CLI) tool available on GitHub at https://github.com/swagger-api/swagger-codegen.
- *Swagger Editor*—A web-based, open source online editor providing a Generate Client feature that uses Swagger Codegen to achieve the same results. This tool is available at https://editor.swagger.io.

- *SwaggerHub*—An integrated API design and documentation platform that includes the preceding tools and a lot of additional configuration and productivity features. It's available at https://swagger.io/tools/swaggerhub.

The first two options are free, and the third one requires a subscription plan (with a 14-day free trial available). All things considered, the Swagger Editor is the most practical free choice, as it doesn't require us to install anything. To use it, navigate to https://editor.swagger.io, and wait for the main page to load (figure 12.5).

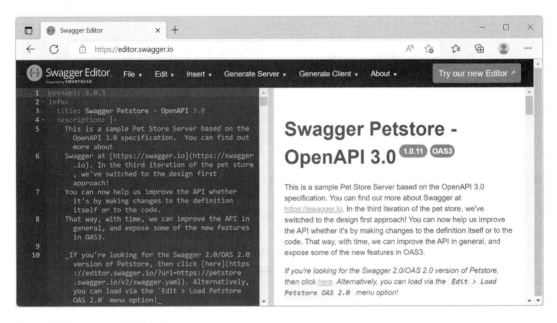

Figure 12.5   Swagger Editor's home page

The editor already contains a sample Swagger definition file (left panel), which is rendered in real time to a HTML-based user interface (UI; right panel). To replace the sample file with ours, perform the following steps:

1 Launch the `MyBGList` project in Debug mode, and access the SwaggerUI main dashboard.
2 Click the https://localhost:40443/swagger/v1/swagger.json link below the title to access our web API's Swagger definition file, and save that file locally.
3 Go back to the Swagger Editor's home page.
4 Choose File > Import File Option to import the saved `swagger.json` file.
5 When the file is loaded, choose Generate Client > HTML2 to download a zip archive containing a single HTML file.

That HTML file is our autogenerated, HTML-based UI. To see what it looks like, unzip and execute it in a browser (figure 12.6).

Figure 12.6 Static API documentation generated by Swagger Editor using Swagger Codegen

Not bad, right? Now that we have this static HTML file, we can choose how to release it to our audience—via email, a partner-only website, or any other secure method—without having to expose our Swagger definition file and/or the SwaggerUI directly.

> ### Alternative API documentation tools
> The static documentation we've obtained by using the Swagger Editor and Swagger Codegen is one of many options for creating a suitable reference for our web API. Several other open source and commercial tools can help us to achieve the same result, offering different UI/UX templates, additional customization features, and so on. I also encourage you to try the additional Generate Client options provided by the Swagger Editor, which include more advanced (and visually appealing) clients built with C#, TypeScript, Angular, PHP, Dart, Go, Scala, and the like.

We're ready to move to our next topic: choosing a suitable .NET publishing mode.

12.1.5 Understanding the .NET publishing modes

The first thing we need to learn is that .NET applications can be published in two modes:

- *Framework-dependent*—This publishing mode requires the presence of the .NET Framework, which must be installed and available on the target system. In other words, we'll build a .NET application that can run only on a hosting server that has been configured properly to support it.

- *Self-contained*—This publishing mode doesn't rely on the presence of .NET components on the target system. All components, including the .NET libraries and runtime, will be included in the production build. If the hosting server supports .NET, the app will run in isolated mode, separating itself from other .NET applications. Self-contained deployment (SCD) builds include an executable file (an .exe file on Windows platforms) as well as a dynamic link library (DLL) file containing the application's runtime.

NOTE The framework-dependent mode produces a platform-specific executable and a cross-platform binary (in the form of a DLL file). The self-contained mode produces a platform-specific executable only.

Let's try to understand the pros and cons of each publishing mode.

FRAMEWORK-DEPENDENT MODE

The framework-dependent mode grants the developer several advantages:

- *Small package size*—The deployment bundle is small because it contains only the app's runtime and the third-party dependencies. .NET itself won't be there because we expect it to be present on the target machine by design.
- *Latest version*—Per its default settings, the framework-dependent mode will always use the latest runtime and framework version installed on the target system, with all the latest security patches.
- *Improved performance in multihosting scenarios*—If the hosting server has multiple .NET apps installed, the shared resources will enable us to save some storage space and, most important, reduce memory use.

This publishing mode also has several weaknesses:

- *Reduced compatibility*—Our app will require a .NET runtime compatible with the one used by our app (or later). If the hosting server is stuck to a previous version, our app won't be able to run.
- *Stability problems*—If the .NET runtime and/or libraries change their behavior (in other words, if they have breaking changes or reduced compatibility for security or licensing reasons), our app would potentially be affected by these changes.

SELF-CONTAINED MODE

Using the self-contained mode has two big advantages that could easily outweigh the disadvantages in some scenarios:

- *Full control of the published .NET version*—Regardless of what is installed on the hosting server (or what will happen to it in the future)
- *No compatibility problems*—Because all the required libraries are provided within the bundle

Unfortunately, there are also some relevant disadvantages:

- *Platform dependency*—Providing the runtime with the production package requires the developer to select the target building platforms in advance.

- *Increased bundle size*—The additional presence of the runtime resources will eventually take its toll in terms of disk space requirements—a heavy hit if we plan to deploy multiple SCD .NET Core apps to a single hosting server, as each of them will require a significant amount of disk space.

The bundle-size problem was mitigated in .NET Core 3.0 with the introduction of the app trimming feature (also called *assembly linker*), which trims the unused assemblies. This approach was further improved in subsequent .NET versions; assemblies were cracked open and purged of the types and members not used by the application, further reducing the size.

> TIP For further info about the .NET app trimming feature, check out this post by Sam Spencer (program manager, .NET Core team): http://mng.bz/MlK2.

CHOOSING A PUBLISHING MODE

As we can guess, both publishing modes can be viable depending on several factors, such as how much control we have of the production server, how many ASP.NET Core apps we plan to publish, the target system's hardware/software/size capabilities, and so on. As a general rule, as long as we have access to the production server (and permission to install and update system packages such as .NET and ASP.NET Core), the framework-dependent mode is often an ideal choice. Conversely, if we host our apps on a cloud-hosting provider that doesn't have our desired .NET runtime, the self-contained mode probably would be a more logical choice (if not the only way to go). Available disk space and memory size will also play major roles, especially if we plan to publish multiple apps.

> NOTE The requirement to install and update the packages on the server manually should no longer be a hindrance, because all .NET updates are now released through the regular Microsoft Update channel, as explained in this post by Jamshed Damkewala (principal engineering manager, .NET): http://mng.bz/aMzJ.

Now we must make a decision. For our `MyBGList` project, we're going to use the framework-dependent publishing mode, because we plan to have full access to all the hosts where we'll release and deploy our web API. But we still need to choose where we're going to perform those release and deployment tasks.

CHOOSING THE RELEASE AND DEPLOYMENT TARGET

Let's go back to the scenario introduced at the start of this chapter: our IT project manager asked us to release and deploy our web API to a public server to make it publicly accessible on the World Wide Web. To comply with this request, we need to make some important decisions, carefully evaluating the pros and cons of each option. Here's a breakdown of the most relevant questions we should ask before proceeding, assuming that we're a member of a full-stack development team or the deployment manager of a structured IT team:

- Should we use a physical or virtualized server?
- Should we host the server on our own data center (assuming that we have one) or on an external data center, or should we use a cloud service platform?
- If we choose the cloud, should we opt for an Infrastructure as a Service (IaaS) environment, which would allow us to set up, access, and configure the web server(s) directly, or should we use a Platform as a Service (PaaS) alternative, in which all the machine, OS, and runtime-related tasks are handled and managed by the service provider?
- If we opt for the server (or service) OS, should we pick Windows or Linux?

As always, the answer to each question depends on several factors: the budget; the skills, know-how, and composition of the IT team; and the performance we expect. Luckily, regardless of the choices we make, the publishing, release, and deployment tasks won't change much. Physical and virtualized servers work in the same way, and .NET and ASP.NET Core, due to their cross-platform foundation, work well on both Windows and Linux systems.

After taking all those questions into account, we decide to release and deploy our web API to a Windows Server virtual machine (VM). In the following sections, we'll create and configure those hosts, starting with the Windows VM.

12.2 *Creating a Windows VM server*

Creating a Windows VM on the cloud is easy these days, thanks to the fact that most cloud service providers platforms—such as Azure, Amazon Web Services (AWS), and Google Cloud Platform—offer a wide set of fully managed, GUI-based configuration tools that allow users to create a VM within minutes. This UI-based approach has greatly simplified setup of a VM, allowing any willing developer or IT enthusiast, even with limited technical know-how, to create and manage a web server host. But this hyper-simplification has also increased performance, stability, and security risks due to an incorrect configuration of the underlying machine, OS, services, and core apps, including the web server software itself.

For reasons of space, we will not delve into the subject of system hardening, a collection of tools, techniques, and security best practices to minimize the vulnerabilities of a given infrastructure, server, or service. But we'll reduce the risks of creating a weak VM by choosing a cloud platform that grants good levels of performances, reliability, and security. We'll create our VM in Microsoft Azure, the public cloud platform managed and operated by Microsoft.

Reasons for choosing Azure

We opted for Azure not only for security reasons, but also because it fully integrates with .NET, .NET Core, and Visual Studio publishing features, which will greatly simplify our deployment. You're free to choose any other suitable physical, virtualized, or cloud-based alternative. Most release and deployment techniques explained in this chapter will also work for any other infrastructure, platform, or solution.

In the following sections, we're going to set up a brand-new VM on the Azure platform and then perform the release and deployment tasks on it. Here's what we'll do:

1 Create a new VM in Azure, using the Windows 2022 Datacenter Edition template and configure it to accept inbound calls to the required TCP ports.

2 Configure the VM by downloading and/or installing all the necessary services and runtimes to host our ASP.NET Core web API, including Internet Information Services (IIS).

3 Publish the `MyBGList` web API and deploy it to the web server we've set up.

4 Test the `MyBGList` web API, using a remote client/browser.

NOTE If you already have a production-ready Windows Server, you're free to skip the VM setup sections and go directly to the publishing and deployment topics.

12.2.1 Accessing Azure

To use the Azure platform, we need to create a new account or use an existing account. The good part about creating a new account is that it comes with a welcome offer that grants $200 in credits, more than enough to do everything we're about to do in this chapter.

NOTE If you've read chapter 7 and followed the required steps to implement the `ApplicationInsights` logging provider, you should have an Azure account (and the credits). In case you didn't, point your browser to https://azure .microsoft.com/en-us/free and click the Start Free button.

When you have an account, navigate to https://portal.azure.com to access the Azure administration portal, where we're going to spend some of our $200 credit to create our new VM.

12.2.2 Creating and setting up the Windows VM

On the main Azure administration portal dashboard, click the Virtual Machines icon, as shown in figure 12.7 (or just search for *virtual machine* in the top search bar).

Figure 12.7 Create a new VM in Azure.

On the next page, click Create (near the top-left corner of the page), and select the Azure Virtual Machine option to access a new page called Create a Virtual Machine, which is where most of the magic happens. The Create a Virtual Machine page is a wizardlike form that we use to create and configure our VM. The various configuration settings are grouped in several panels, each one dedicated to a specific set of options:

- *Basics*—Subscription type, VM name, deployment region, image, login credentials, and so on
- *Disks*—Number and capacity of drives that will be assigned to the VM
- *Networking*—Network-related configuration settings
- *Management*—Antimalware settings, autoshutdown capabilities, backup, OS updates, and the like
- *Monitoring*—Diagnostic and system monitoring features
- *Advanced*—Agents, scripts, extensions, and other advanced settings
- *Tags*—Key/value pairs that can be used to assign Azure resources to different logical groups

Most of the default settings are good enough for tutorial purposes. For the sake of simplicity, we'll change something here and there. Here's a short list of what we need to change in the Basics tab:

- *Subscription*—Select the active subscription that you want to use for this VM. If you have a new free account, you should have your free trial subscription available.
- *Resource group*—Create a new resource group with a suitable name. (We'll use `Manning` in our screenshots and samples.)
- *VM name*—Choose a suitable name to assign to the VM. (We'll use `MyBGList-Win-01`.)
- *Region*—Choose the region closest to your geographical position.
- *Availability options*—No infrastructure redundancy is required.
- *Image*—We'll choose Windows Server 2022 Datacenter: Azure Edition – Gen 2.
- *VM architecture*—Choose X64.
- *Run with Azure Spot discount*—Select Yes to create the VM by using the Azure Spot feature, which allows us to take advantage of Azure's unused capacity at a significant cost saving. But because these VMs can be evicted at any time when Azure needs the capacity back, such a feature should be used only for short-term testing purposes. If we want to create a permanent, production-like VM, we should choose No and create a standard pay-as-you-go machine. Note that the Azure Spot option isn't available for all VM series and/or sizes (including the B2ms that we're going to use in this tutorial).
- *Size*—Choose Standard B2ms (2 vCPU, 4 GB memory) or anything similar. Feel free to choose a different size if you're willing to spend more. B2ms is an entry-level machine featuring a limited set of resources that will suffice for this deployment sample. It won't perform well in production, however.

- *Administrator account*—Select the Password authentication type and then create a suitable username and password set. Remember to write these credentials in a secure place because we'll need them to access our machine in a while.

TIP For additional info about the Azure Spot feature, check out http://mng.bz/gJDR.

Click the Next button at the end of the form to move to the Disk tab, where we need to configure the OS disk type settings. Select Standard HDD if you want to save credits, as it is the cheapest available choice and good enough for our tutorial. For nontutorial purposes, however, it's strongly advisable to choose a solid-state disk. All other settings, including the Advanced options panel near the end of the page, can be left at their default values. Next, move to the Networking tab and change the following settings:

- *Virtual network*—Create a new one called `<ResourceGroupName>-vnet` (should be the default option).
- *Public inbound ports*—Choose Allow Selected Ports and then select the HTTP (80) and HTTPS (443) ports, leaving ports 22 and 3389 closed for security reasons.

Skip the Management tab (the default settings are fine), and access the Monitoring tab, where we're given the option to disable the Diagnostics > Boot Diagnostics settings. Doing that is not recommended for production servers, but it can be a good idea for our tutorial purposes (to save some credits). Leave all other settings in the next tabs at their defaults, and go straight to the Review + Create tab (figure 12.8),

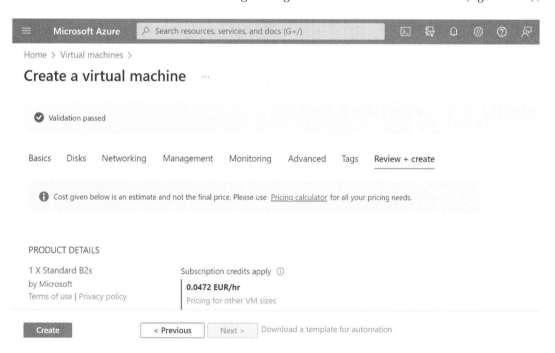

Figure 12.8   Reviewing the VM settings

where we'll review our configuration settings and confirm them by clicking Create in the bottom-left corner of the screen.

Check out the VM settings to ensure that they're OK; then click Create to start the VM deployment process, which will likely take a few minutes. Eventually the page will refresh, informing us that the VM deployment is complete and giving us the chance to access its main configuration panel by clicking to the Go to Resource button, which is precisely what we're going to do.

12.2.3   *Working with the VM public IP address*

The VM configuration panel is where we can review and change all the VM's main settings. The panel is split into several pages, all accessible from the left menu. If we accessed it from the Go to Resource button, we should be looking at the Overview page (figure 12.9), which is a dashboard showing a summary of the current settings. From there we should be able to retrieve the VM's public IP address, which is located in the right part of the screen.

Figure 12.9   Retrieving the VM's public IP address

ADDING AN AZURE DNS NAME

While we're here, we configure a unique DNS name that will resolve to that IP address by clicking the DNS Name option below it. We'll gain access to a new settings page where we'll be able to input an optional DNS name label, as shown in figure 12.10.

As we can see, we used the lowercase VM name (`mybglist-win-01`) to set the DNS name label. This will create the following Azure-managed unique subdomain, which will resolve to our VM's IP address: `mybglist-win-01.westeurope.cloudapp.azure.com`.

But we don't want to use this subdomain to access our web API directly. We want to have our HTTP incoming request be handled by the Cloudflare CDN that we set up earlier. For that reason, in the next section we're going to configure our VM's public IP address on our CDN by creating a dedicated A record (and subdomain) for it.

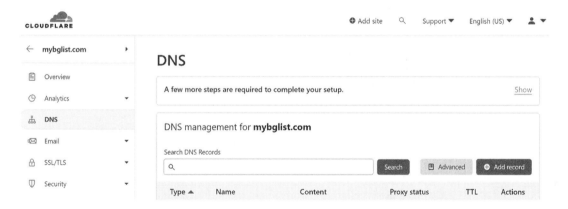

Figure 12.10   Setting a unique DNS name

Adding a new A record

Open another tab in the browser (without closing the VM Overview page) and use it to access Cloudflare (https://www.cloudflare.com). Log in with the account we created earlier; select the relevant domain (mybglist.com in our sample); and click the DNS page on the left menu to access the domain's DNS configuration settings, as shown in figure 12.11.

Figure 12.11   Cloudflare DNS management page

Click the Add Record button to create a new record, specifying the following options, as shown in figure 12.12:

- *Type*—A
- *Name*—win-01
- *IPv4 address*—Azure VM public IP address (20.123.146.191 in our sample)
- *Proxy status*—Proxied
- *TTL*—Auto

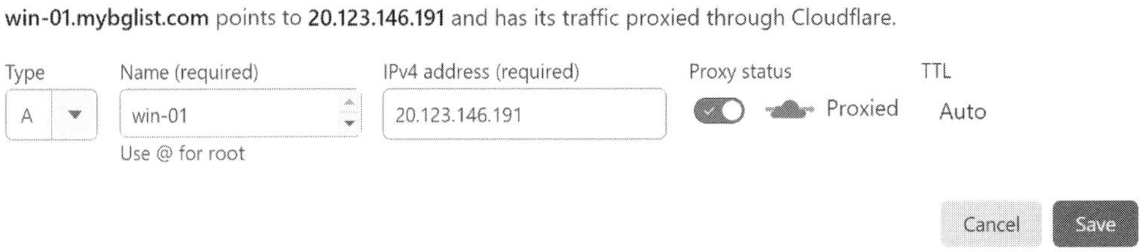

win-01.mybglist.com points to 20.123.146.191 and has its traffic proxied through Cloudflare.

Type	Name (required)	IPv4 address (required)	Proxy status	TTL
A ▾	win-01	20.123.146.191	⬤◯ ☁ Proxied	Auto
	Use @ for root			

Cancel   Save

Figure 12.12   Cloudflare Add Record settings for `win-01.mybglist.com`

These settings create a new `win-01.mybglist.com` subdomain that will point to the IP address of our Windows VM, like the Azure unique DNS name that we created earlier.

Azure DNS name vs. custom subdomain

There is an important difference between how the Azure DNS name and our custom `win-01.mybglist.com` subdomain will work in practice: the Azure-managed subdomain will resolve directly to our VM server's IP, and the Cloudflare subdomain will not because we activated Cloudflare's proxying (and IP masking) feature. More precisely, the `win-01.mybglist.com` subdomain will resolve to Cloudflare's proprietary IP, which will internally forward all requests to our VM's public IP without exposing it to the public. Such a difference might seem trivial, but it could be relevant in terms of security as long as we use only the Cloudflare subdomain, keeping the Azure one hidden from public eyes.

Moreover, notice that we intentionally chose to not use the `www.mybglist.com` domain name for this deployment tutorial. We preferred to use a subdomain that uniquely identifies the Windows VM that we'll create later, so that we'll be able to create additional VMs/hosts in future editions of this book. You're free to use `www` (or any other suitable subdomain name) instead.

Click the Save button to persist the newly created A record to the domain DNS configuration so that we can test it.

TESTING THE A RECORD

The new subdomain will start working immediately, because our domain's DNS configuration is already handled by Cloudflare and the internal proxying feature doesn't need to propagate. But even if our Windows VM is already up and running, it doesn't have a web server listening to the HTTP (80) and/or HTTPS (443) TCP ports.

If we try to navigate to `http://win-01.mybglist.com/` or `https://win-01.mybglist.com/` with our browser, we hit a `522 - Connection timed out` error (see figure 12.13). Notice that the error is clearly coming from Cloudflare, meaning that the connection problem occurs between the CDN (working) and the Host (error), as shown by the informative icons displayed by the error page. There's no need to worry. The error will disappear as soon as we configure a web server to handle the incoming HTTP

Connection timed out _{Error code 522}

Visit cloudflare.com for more information.

2022-10-01 01:39:21 UTC

You	Milan	win-01.mybglist.com
Browser	Cloudflare	Host
Working	Working	**Error**

Figure 12.13   Cloudflare returning a `522 – Connection timed out` **error**

requests. First, let's fulfill another important task in Cloudflare: create an SSL/TLS certificate that we will configure to our origin server.

12.2.4   Creating an SSL/TLS origin certificate

One of the main reasons why we chose Cloudflare as our CDN service provider is that it grants two free SSL/TLS certificates for our domain, one for the edge server (valid for everyone) and one for the origin server (valid only for Cloudflare servers). The edge certificate is automatically generated, renewed, and served by Cloudflare; the origin certificate must be created manually and then installed on the origin hosts.

> **Why do we need an origin certificate?**
> Setting up the origin certificate is optional. We need it only if we want Cloudflare to connect to the origin server using HTTPS, thus using the Full SSL/TLS encryption mode instead of the default one (which uses HTTP). However, if we want to adhere to our security-by-design approach, we definitely need to switch to that encryption mode to ensure that all transferred data will be always encrypted from the origin server to the end users' browsers, and vice versa.

Because we're going to configure our newly created Windows VM, now is a good time to generate the origin certificate. From Cloudflare domain's configuration page, expand the SSL/TLS panel in the left menu and then select the Origin Server option to access the Origin Certificates section (see figure 12.14).

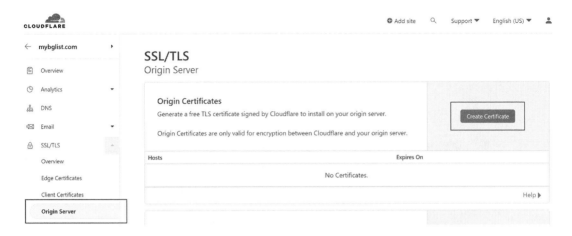

Figure 12.14   Create an origin certificate in Cloudflare.

Click the Create Certificate button to start the generation process. We access a dedicated form, which we can fill with the following values:

- *Generate private key and CSR with Cloudflare*—Yes.
- *Private key type*—RSA (2048).
- *Hostnames*—Leave the default values.
- *Choose how long before your certificate expires*—15 years.

Then click the Create button to generate the certificate. After a couple of seconds, we access a page with two text boxes containing, respectively, our origin certificate and its private key. Copy and paste the content of each text box into a text editor of your choice (such as Windows Notepad) and then save both in a safe local folder using the following names:

- `mybglist.com-origin.pem`—For the origin certificate
- `mybglist.con-origin.key`—For the private key

We're going to need these files when we configure our Windows VM to be the origin host. Before moving on to that, let's switch the Cloudflare SSL/TLS encryption mode from Flexible to Full to take advantage of what we did.

12.2.5 *Setting Cloudflare Encryption Mode to Full*

From Cloudflare domain's configuration page, expand the SSL/TLS panel in the left menu and then select the Overview option to access the SSL/TLS Encryption Mode section (figure 12.15). Then change the encryption mode from Flexible to Full.

The Full encryption mode ensures that Cloudflare will always use (and require) the origin certificate when connecting to our origin host, thus granting full encryption capabilities to our architecture's HTTP stack. We need to configure that host, which is what we're about to do.

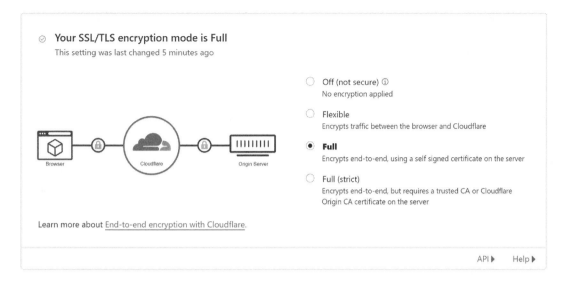

Figure 12.15 Cloudflare's SSL/TLS Encryption Mode settings

12.3 Configuring the Windows VM server

Now that we have created our Windows VM server, we need to connect to it. Azure gives us several ways to do that, the most secure of them being Azure Bastion, a fully managed service providing secure and seamless Remote Desktop Protocol (RDP) and Secure Shell Protocol (SSH) access to VMs without any exposure through public IP addresses.

> **TIP** For additional info about Azure Bastion features and pricing, check out http://mng.bz/eJjJ.

The only "bad" thing about Azure Bastion is that it's a paid service with an hourly rate that might be too costly for our actual scenario. For the purpose of this chapter we'll use a standard RDP connection by (securely) opening the 3389 TCP port on our Azure VM.

> **NOTE** To open the 3389 TCP port for inbound traffic on Azure, follow the instructions detailed in the appendix, using 3389 for the port number and RDP for the service name. It's important to remember that the 3389 TCP port is a common target for network-related attacks performed by malicious third parties, as it's used by a protocol (RDP) that allows attackers to take control of the VM remotely. Keeping that port open for everyone is hardly good practice in terms of security. To mitigate these risks, it's strongly advisable to restrict the inbound rule to the IP address(es) of our development machine(s), as explained in the appendix.

Now that we have the 3389 TCP port open, we can connect with our new server using the RDC tool from our local Windows-based development machine. Type the public

IP address of the Azure VM that we retrieved earlier and click Connect to initiate an RDP session with our remote host. Once connected, the first thing we must do is install and configure IIS, a flexible, secure, and manageable HTTP server that we'll use to serve our ASP.NET Core web API over the web.

> **NOTE** For reasons of space, we're not going to explain how IIS works or explore its functionalities. We'll use the settings strictly required to host our app. For additional information regarding IIS, check out https://www.iis.net/overview.

Together with IIS, we will install Web Deploy, an extensible client-server tool that can be used to publish and deploy web apps directly from Visual Studio, thus avoiding the need to implement other data-transfer alternatives (such as FTP). Last, but not least, we're going to install a local instance of SQL Server to host our `MyBGList` web API's production database.

12.3.1 *Installing IIS*

To install IIS, follow the instructions detailed in the appendix. Be sure to do that in the Windows VM using the established RDP connection, not on your local development machine.

12.3.2 *Installing the ASP.NET Core hosting bundle*

When IIS has been installed, we can proceed with downloading and installing the ASP.NET Core Windows Hosting Bundle, a convenient bundle that includes the .NET runtime, the ASP.NET Core runtime, and the ASP.NET Core IIS module. That's all we need to run our ASP.NET Core web API using the framework-dependent publishing mode.

> **TIP** The instructions for installing the ASP.NET Core Windows hosting bundle are detailed in the appendix.

After the installation, be sure to restart the IIS service by following the appendix instructions.

12.3.3 *Installing the Web Deploy component*

Web Deploy (formerly msdeploy) is a IIS-related component that greatly simplifies the deployment of web applications to IIS servers. For our release and deployment tutorial, we're going to use it to create a one-click publishing profile that will allow us to deploy our `MyBGList` web API from Visual Studio to the VM server in a fast and seamless way (as we'll see in a short while).

It's important to understand that Web Deploy is not the only deployment option offered by Visual Studio; it's the one we have chosen for this book. If you prefer to use a more "classic" deployment approach based on a different data transfer method/protocol such as FTP, XCOPY, RoboCopy, SCP, and the like, feel free to skip the Web

Deploy installation. You will also need to create a different Visual Studio publishing profile (and deal with the file upload tasks manually).

> **TIP**   Web Deploy installation instructions are detailed in the appendix.

After installing it, we also need to open the 8172 TCP port for inbound traffic, which is required by the IIS management service (and Web Deploy).

12.3.4   *Opening the 8172 TCP port*

The 8172 TCP port must be open at OS level (using the Windows Firewall) and network level (using the Azure VM configuration panel). The Windows Firewall configuration should be OK, assuming we have already installed IIS with the management service optional role feature, as it's automatically handled by that component during the installation process. We need to open that port on Azure.

> **TIP**   To open the 8172 TCP port for inbound traffic on Azure, follow the instructions detailed in the appendix, using 8172 for the port number and Web Deploy for the service name.

With that done, we can move to the next step: configuring IIS to host our web API.

12.3.5   *Configuring IIS*

Let's start by launching the IIS Manager app, a management tool that gets installed with IIS and can be used to configure most IIS settings through an intuitive, easy-to-use GUI (figure 12.16).

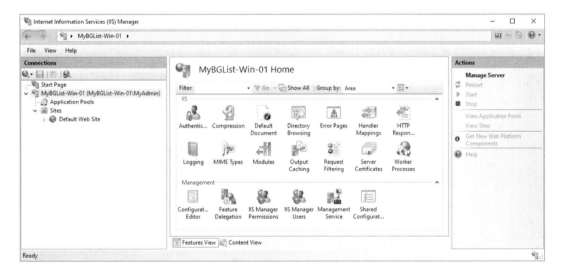

Figure 12.16   The IIS Manager main dashboard

The first thing to do here is install the SSL/TLS origin certificate that we got from Cloudflare a short while ago. However, the PEM/KEY certificate format that we have saved to our local disk cannot be directly imported to IIS. To do that, we need to convert them to a PFX (PKCS#12) file.

CONVERTING THE PEM CERTIFICATE TO PFX

To quickly convert our PEM Certificate to a PFX file we suggest using OpenSSL, an open source command-line tool that can be used to perform a wide variety of cryptography tasks, such as creating and handling certificates and related files. Most information about OpenSSL, including the updated GitHub link to the project's source code, can be retrieved from its official website (https://www.openssl.org). However, the Windows binaries (and installer packages), which is what we need to install it, are available at the following third-party URL, courtesy of Shining Light Productions (http://mng .bz/pdDP).

More precisely, we need to download the Win64 OpenSSL v3.0.5 Light edition. The light edition is lightweight (5MB) and contains only the tool's basic features, which are more than enough for our purposes.

The installation process is straightforward; we'll be asked only to copy the required DLLs to the Windows folder or to a separate folder (both will work) and to make an optional donation to the authors. After installing it, the tool will be available at the following path:

```
C:\Program Files\OpenSSL-Win64\bin
```

To use it, open a command prompt, navigate to the folder where we put the `.pem` and `.key` files, and execute the following one-line command:

```
"C:\Program Files\OpenSSL-Win64\bin\openssl.exe" pkcs12
   -export -out mybglist_origin.pfx
   -in mybglist_origin.pem -inkey mybglist_origin.key
```

> **TIP** In case you installed the tool on a different path and/or used different filenames, change the command accordingly.

The tool will ask us to enter an export password. Choose one (and remember it, as we'll need it in a short while); then confirm it by typing it again, and click Enter to generate the `mybglist_origin.pfx` file.

> **TIP** Now we can safely delete the `.pem` and `.key` files from our local machine, as we don't need them anymore.

Now that we have the `.pfx` file, we can install it on our Windows VM's IIS.

INSTALLING THE SSL/TLS ORIGIN CERTIFICATE

Go back to the Windows VM desktop. Then copy the `mybglist_origin.pfx` file from our local machine to the remote VM, using the RDP copy/paste capabilities.

Switch to (or open) the IIS Manager main dashboard, locate the Server Certificates icon, and click it to access that section. Next, click the Import link button in the Actions menu on the right to access the Import Certificate modal window (figure 12.17).

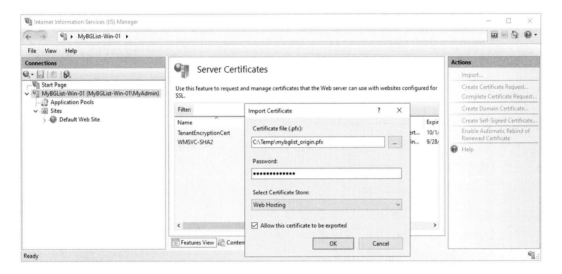

Figure 12.17   The IIS Manager's Import Certificate window

Fill the form with the following values, shown in figure 12.17:

- *Certificate file (.pfx)*—The `.pfx` file path on the remote VM
- *Password*—The export password we chose earlier
- *Select Certificate Store*—Web hosting
- *Allow this certificate to be exported*—Yes

Click OK to import the certificate.

> **TIP**   Again, we can safely delete the `.pfx` file from our local machine and from the remote server right after importing it. We can always export it from the IIS Manager certificate store if we ever need to.

With that done, we can finally configure our ASP.NET Core web API to IIS.

ADDING THE MYBGLIST WEBSITE TO IIS

Keeping the IIS Manager GUI open, locate the Sites folder node in the left tree view; right-click it and choose the Add Website option to access the modal window, which we will use to add a new website entry for our `MyBGList` web API. Fill the form with the following values:

- *Site name*—MyBGList
- *Content directory*
  - *Application pool*—MyBGList
  - *Physical path*—C:\inetpub\MyBGList
- *Binding*
  - *Type*—https
  - *IP Address*—All unassigned
  - *Port*—443
  - *Host name*—win-01.mybglist.com
  - *Require Server Name Indication*—Yes
  - *SSL Certificate*—CloudFlare origin certificate
- *Start Website immediately*—Yes

After we click OK, a new `MyBGList` website entry should appear in the left tree view, right below the default website.

> **TIP** Let's take this chance to disable the default website (right-click, Manage Website, Stop), as we don't need it.

We're almost done. We need to start the web management service.

STARTING THE WEB MANAGEMENT SERVICE

In the IIS Manager GUI, left-click the main server's root note (it should be called `MyBGList-Win-01`, like the VM name), locate the Management Service icon in the central panel, and click it to access another configuration window (figure 12.18).

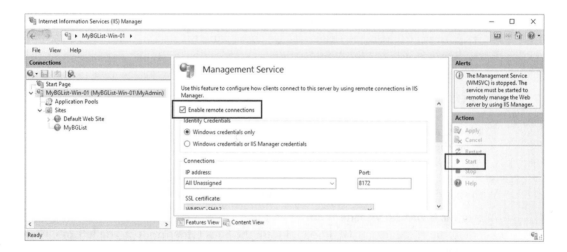

Figure 12.18   The IIS Manager's Management Service window

From here, we need to do the following:

1   Activate the Enable Remote Connections check box.
2   Start the service by clicking the Start button to the right.

> ### Web Management Service startup mode
> The Web Management Service is configured with a manual startup mode, meaning that it won't automatically start when the VM boots (or reboots). If we plan to consistently use the Web Deploy component to publish and deploy our app, we might think of changing the startup behavior of this service, as it's required to be running for that feature to work. This can be done using the Control Panel > Administrative Tools > Services app.

Now that IIS has been properly configured, we can deal with the database.

12.3.6   Creating the production database

In chapter 4 we hosted our development database on a local instance of SQL Server installed on our development machine; more precisely, we opted for that route instead of using a cloud-based solution such as the SQL database provided by Azure. Now that we are releasing our web API in production, we are faced with that same choice: on-premise or cloud-based?

For reasons of space, in this deployment tutorial we're going to pick the on-premise option again so that we can replicate what we have already learned and got used to. However, readers who want to challenge themselves with a different alternative (such as the previously mentioned Azure SQL Database service) are strongly encouraged to do that.

> **NOTE**   For additional info, documentation, and installation guides about the Azure SQL Database service and other Azure SQL-related available products, check out https://learn.microsoft.com/en-us/azure/azure-sql.

Now that we have chosen our path, here's what we need to do:

1   Install SQL Server.
2   Install SQL Server Management Studio (SSMS).
3   Create a new instance of the MyBGList database.

All of these tasks can be easily dealt with by repeating the same steps we took in chapter 4.

When creating the MyBGList database, be sure to also create its login and user structure, as we're going to need them for the production connection string.

> **NOTE**   For obvious security reasons, be sure to set a different password for the production login. Using the same passwords for development and production environments is a bad practice that could lead to severe data breaches.

Should we install SSMS on the VM server?

Technically speaking, we could avoid installing the SQL Server Management Studio tool on the server and connect to the remote database using the SSMS local instance that we installed on our development machine. However, this would require us to open the 1433 TCP port (as we did with 3389 and 8172 earlier), which would lead to additional security problems. In case we want to do that, we should definitely restrict the inbound rule to the IP address(es) of our development machine(s), as explained in the appendix.

Once the `MyBGList` production database is up and running, we can finally create the `appsettings.Production.json` file on the Windows VM.

12.3.7   Creating the appsettings.Production.json file

When we added the `MyBGList` website entry to IIS, we were asked to specify a physical path, which we filled with `C:\inetpub\MyBGList` earlier; that's the filesystem path where IIS expects our web API artifacts to be deployed, including the `appsettings.json` files.

Open that folder using the remote VM's File Explorer (or command prompt), and create a new `appsettings.Production.json` file within it using a text editor of your choice (such as Windows Notepad). That's the file that will be used by our ASP.NET Core web API to override the `appsettings.json` values in the production environment.

Ideally, the `appsettings.Production.json` file should contain the same keys and values that we currently have in our local `secrets.json` file, with the sole difference of the `ConnectionStrings`'s `DefaultConnection` value, which we must replace with the values required to connect to our `MyBGList` production database. If we followed the same naming conventions that we used when creating the development database, we'll have to change the user ID and/or password values, leaving the rest as is.

> **WARNING** For the sake of simplicity, we're not going to change the Azure Application Insight `Connection String` and the Redis `Configuration` values, because they are not that relevant to our sample tutorial scenario. But assuming we want to use those services, we should definitely create different instances for development and production environments as we did with the `MyBGList` database.

We can quickly deal with this task by using the RDP client to copy and paste the content of our local `secrets.json` file to the `appsettings.Production.json` file and then perform the required value change(s) on the new file and then save it to disk. While doing that, ensure that the `appsettings.Production.json` file has the correct extension (`.json` and not `.json.txt`, which is a common problem when using Notepad).

With this last step, our Windows VM configuration is complete. Now it's finally time to publish, release, and deploy our web API. However, before doing this, we need to learn more about the Visual Studio built-in publishing capabilities and how this feature actually works.

12.4 Publishing and deploying

In this section we'll learn how to publish our app. More specifically, we'll create the output artifacts (framework libraries, project binaries, static contents, and the like) that will then be deployed to the production server(s) to release our app over the World Wide Web. Here's what we're going to do in detail:

1 Choose a suitable .NET publishing mode among the four available ones, which will be done after learning the pros and cons of each of them.

2 Create a Windows publishing profile using Visual Studio's publishing capabilities to publish and deploy our web API project on the production server.

Are we ready? Let's start!

12.4.1 Introducing Visual Studio publish profiles

The Publish feature is one of the greatest advantages of Visual Studio (and VS Code) over the other IDE alternatives: a built-in set of capabilities that allow developers to build, publish, and sometimes even deploy a web application directly from the GUI, thus greatly simplifying the whole release and deployment process.

The publish feature is basically a wizard that guides the developer to build a profile, a set of configuration settings about the project and the deployment target. Once created, the profile is saved to a dedicated .pubxml file on a dedicated /Properties/ PublishProfiles/ folder, which is created together with the first profile (if it doesn't exist already). Such a file/folder structure allows applications to have multiple publishing profiles, meaning that we can pre-configure its release and deployment settings over several different locations. To create a new publish profile, right-click the MyBGList project's root node in Solution Explorer and select Publish.

> **TIP** Alternatively, we can select the Publish MyBGList option from the Build section of the menu.

Once we do that, we'll be greeted by a modal window that will ask us to select one of several available publish targets, as shown in figure 12.19.

Each available target provides a short description explaining how it works. The important thing to notice here is that most targets will create a profile that will perform the publishing and deployment tasks together, meaning that our app will also automatically go live at the end of the publishing process. However, a few of them (such as the folder target) allow us to only publish the artifacts locally, thus requiring us to manually perform the deploy using different techniques.

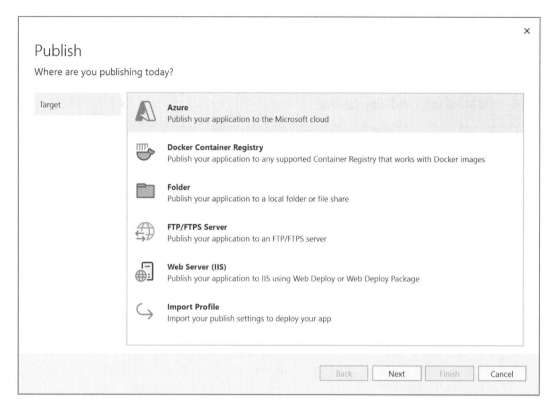

Figure 12.19   Visual Studio Publish feature

Publish and deploy requirements

As we can easily expect, the "publish and deploy" profile targets require the hosting server to support (or be compatible with) a specific deployment module, package, or component, be it a FTP server, the Web Deploy component that we have installed a short while ago, or other services supported by Visual Studio. This requirement is quite easy to fulfill when dealing with Windows-based hosts Microsoft services (such as the Azure App Service). However, it can be difficult for Linux servers, where these techniques are not supported. For that reason, publishing profiles for Linux hosts typically targets a local folder or an FTP server preinstalled on the host.

Because we installed the Web Deploy component to our Windows VM server, our best option here would be creating a publishing profile based on the Azure target. Let's do this.

12.4.2   *Creating an Azure VM publish profile*

From the Visual Studio's Publish modal windows, choose the Azure target, select the Azure Virtual Machine option from the next screen (figure 12.20), and click Next to proceed.

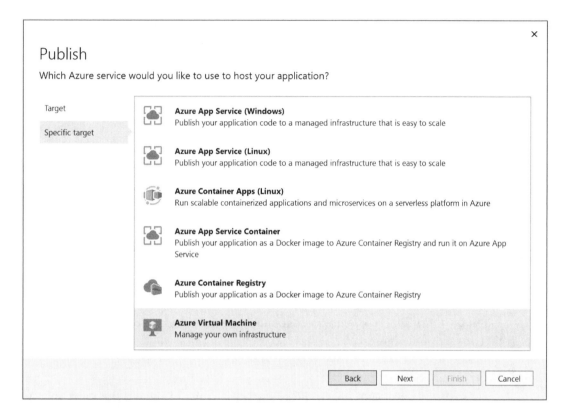

Figure 12.20   Publishing from Visual Studio to an Azure VM

In the following panel we'll be asked to select (and/or connect) an Azure account and a Subscription name. After completing that part with our relevant info, we should be able to select our Windows VM, as shown in figure 12.21.

Click the Finish button to create the publish profile, which will be saved in the /Properties/PublishProfiles/ folder. From now on, if we right-click the MyBGList root node in the Solution Folder's tree view and select the Publish option again, Visual Studio will open a dedicated MyBGList: Publish tab (figure 12.22) that can be used to visually edit and configure the publishing profile we have created. Let's take the chance to do that, because we need to change a couple of default settings that Visual Studio took for granted while creating the profile.

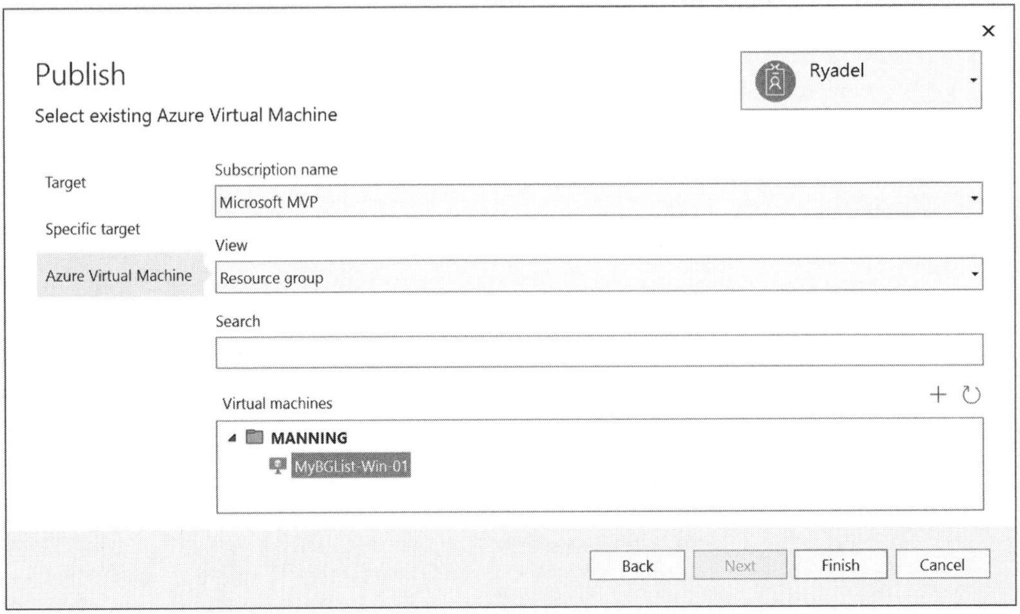

Figure 12.21   Selecting the Windows VM where we want to publish and deploy our app

12.4.3   *Configuring the publish profile*

From the MyBGList: Publish tab, click the Show All settings link button (or More Actions > Edit) to access a modal containing the publish profile's configuration settings, as shown in figure 12.22.

From there, change the following settings:

- *Connections*
  - *Site name*—MyBGList (it must match the name of the website entry that we created on IIS).
  - *User name*—Insert the VM Administrator's user name.
  - *Password*—Insert the VM Administrator's password (it will make sense only if you activate the Save Password check box below).
  - *Save password*—Choose Yes if you want to save it and No if you prefer to type it every time.
  - *Destination URL*—https://win-01.mybglist.com.
  - *Validate Connection*—Click this button to ensure that the connection can be performed successfully with these parameters.
- *Settings*
  - *Configuration*—Release
  - *Target Framework*—net6.0
  - *Deployment Mode*—Framework-dependent
  - *Target Runtime*—win-x64

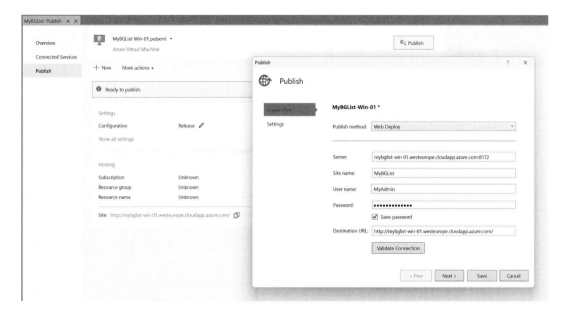

Figure 12.22   Visual Studio's Publish Profile configuration settings

Right after doing that, click Save, we can finally hit the Publish button near the top-right of the `MyBGList`: Publish tab to finally start the publish, deployment, and post-deployment testing tasks.

12.4.4 Publishing, deployment, and testing

If everything goes well, the publishing (and deployment) process will successfully complete without problems. Once it completes, we should receive a `Publish Succeeded on <CurrentDateTime>` message with an Open Site link button that we can click to launch the https://win-01.mybglist.com website.

Let's click the button to see if our web API is working. If we did everything correctly, we should be welcomed by... an `HTTP 400 - Not Found` error page.

We might be surprised by this error, but if we think about it, we can see how it's absolutely normal. When we were launching our project in Debug mode (and from a development environment), we had the SwaggerUI dashboard configured as the startup page in the `launchSettings.json` file. Now that we are in production, there is no such file and no SwaggerUI either, as we have chosen to disable it for security reasons.

However, we still have some `GET` endpoints that we can call with our browser to test that the app is working, such as the following:

- https://win-01.mybglist.com/error/test
- https://win-01.mybglist.com/cod/test

The `error/test` endpoint should work without problems, showing the same RFC7231-compliant JSON error we implemented in chapter 6. Conversely, the `cod/test` endpoint that we added in chapter 3 will likely output a blank page. Where's the JavaScript alert pop-up that is expected to appear? To answer this question, press Ctrl+Shift+I (or F12) to access the browser's developer console and take a look at the red message that should be there:

```
Refused to execute inline script because it violates the following Content
Security Policy directive: "default-src ' self' ". Either the 'unsafe-inline'
keyword, a hash ('sha256-j3kW1ylRRXx1+pINyR/6EW435UHoxKSlU6fhd5xVSSk='), or a
nonce (' nonce-...' ) is required to enable inline execution. Note also that
' script-src' was not explicitly set, so ' default-src' is used as a
fallback.
```

As we can see, the JavaScript alter window was negated by the content security policy that we set with one of our HTTP security headers at the start of this chapter. That's great news, as now we have the visual proof that they work! Let's take this chance to slightly relax that policy to allow this (and only this) script to be accepted (and executed) by the requesting browsers.

UPDATING THE CONTENT-SECURITY POLICY

Open the `Program.cs` file and scroll down to the HTTP security headers block. Locate the line of code that adds the `Content-Security-Policy` header and change its value in the following way:

```
context.Response.Headers.Add("Content-Security-Policy",
    "default-src ' self' ; script-src ' self'  ' nonce-23a98b38c' ;");
```

The nonce that we have set here is a random alphanumeric identifier that instructs cloud service providers to only allow scripts having that same nonce in their `<script>` element. Unsurprisingly, this also means we need to set that same nonce value in our script. To do that, open the `Program.cs` file, scroll down to the Minimal API method that handles the cod/test endpoint, and update its current implementation in the following way (new code is marked in bold):

```
app.MapGet("/cod/test",
    [EnableCors("AnyOrigin")]
[ResponseCache(NoStore = true)] () =>          ┐  Adds the
    Results.Text("<script nonce='23a98b38c'>" +  ←┘  nonce value
```

> **WARNING** From a security perspective, enabling inline scripts negates the whole purpose of the content security policy. For that reason, I strongly recommend avoiding doing what we did here in a real production web app unless we really need these kinds of code on demand endpoints.

Once done, execute again the publish profile to redeploy the web app to the production server, then try again to call the cod/test endpoint. The JavaScript alert pop-up should now appear without problems.

CHECKING THE LOGS TABLE

The second thing to do is test if the logging capabilities of our app are properly working. As we've known since chapter 7, our web API is expected to log its events to the [MyBGList].[LogEvents] database table using the Serilog SQL Server sink.

Let's open that table using the VM server's SSMS tool to ensure that it exists (it should have been created automatically by Serilog) and that it contains some startup-related log entries. If we can confirm these assumptions, it means that the logging feature is working as expected.

While we are there, let's also take the chance to thoroughly check the existing log entries to ensure that the app is running without errors. As we learned in chapter 7, keeping this table under control will be a crucial activity to prevent or promptly react to most runtime and application-related problems that might affect the production environment over time.

CREATING THE DATABASE STRUCTURE

The next thing we should do is to create the board-game-related tables, as they are still missing from the MyBGList production database. There are several methods to do that, including

- Generating a SQL script from the development machine using the dotnet-ef CLI, and then execute the scripts on the production DB
- Creating a migration bundle from the development machine using the dotnet-ef CLI, and then execute them on the production machine
- Using the dotnet-ef CLI directly from the production machine
- Using a programmatic approach, such as the dbContext.Database.Migrate() helper method from within the Program.cs file

The following article explains these alternatives in detail, highlighting the pros and cons of each: http://mng.bz/Y6M7.

In a nutshell, SQL script and migration bundle (introduced in .NET 6) are the recommended approaches, as they offer some unique advantages without significant downsides. More specifically, SQL scripts can be reviewed by an experienced DBA that could fine-tune the raw SQL commands to fit production-specific requirements and/or prevent accidental data losses before applying them; however, they require a dedicated SQL management tool (such as SSMS) to execute them. Conversely, migration bundles are self-contained executables that can be launched in production without any software requirement (no SQL management tool, NET SDK, or the dotnet-ef CLI).

> **TIP** Alternatively, we could avoid any of these approaches and copy the whole development database structure in production using the SSMS import/export tools. This approach would basically have the same effect of the EF Core SQL script method that we will adopt here.

For our specific scenario, because we have installed the SSMS tool on the server, we're going to use the SQL script approach. To generate the script, execute the following tasks:

1   Open a command prompt from the development machine.
2   Navigate to the project's root folder (the one containing the `Program.cs` file).
3   Execute the following `dotnet-ef` CLI command:

```
> dotnet ef migrations script -o ./Migrations/script.sql
```

After doing that, we'll end up with a `script.sql` file in the project's `/Migrations/` folder. We just have to open that file, copy its content, paste it to a new SSMS query window and execute it there to re-create our database model structure in the `MyBG-List` production database—minus the `[AppCache]` table, that we have created without relying to EF Core migrations and hence requires a separate script.

CREATING THE APPCACHE TABLE

The quickest way to generate the SQL script for the `[AppCache]` table is to use the SSMS tool installed on our development machine. From the tree view on the left, right-click on the `[AppCache]` table, then Select Script Table As, Create To, New Query Editor Window to generate the script in a new tab. Once done, copy and paste the script to a new query window on the SSMS tool installed on the production server, then execute it to create this last table. Now that we have re-created the whole DB structure on our production server, we just need to populate it with actual data.

POPULATING THE PRODUCTION DATABASE

Our `MyBGList` production database is almost ready, except it's empty. To populate it, we have two choices:

- Copy the data from the development database.
- Import the data source (the board games CSV file) from scratch.

The former approach could be doable, as long as we are 100 percent sure we want the exact same data that we currently have in our development database—including all the insert, delete, and update tests we did throughout this book; in practical terms, this is often a bad practice, as we would likely end up with altered info—not to mention some sensitive data that we hardly want to deploy to production, such as the passwords of the users that we created in chapter 9. For that reason, we will proceed with a brand-new CSV data import using our `SeedController`. More precisely, here's what we need to do:

1   From Visual Studio's Solution Explorer, select the `/Data/bgg_dataset.csv` file by left-clicking it.
2   From the Properties window, change the Copy to Output Directory value from Do Not Copy to Copy Always or Copy if Newer (both will work), as shown in figure 12.23.

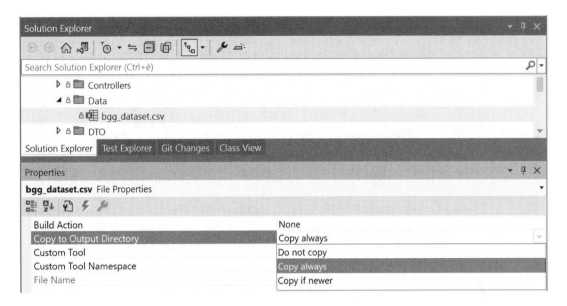

Figure 12.23 Changing the Copy to Output Directory settings from the Visual Studio Properties window

Doing this will ensure that the /Data/bgg_dataset.csv file will be copied in the MyBGList web app's production folder, thus allowing the SeedController's Board-GameData method to find and use it to populate the database. We have to temporarily comment out the [Authorize] attribute that we placed on that controller in chapter 9 to be able to call it, as it is currently restricted to administrators.

After having temporarily commented and/or enabled what we need, we can execute the publishing profile again to re-publish and redeploy the web app; once done, we can perform the seeding tasks. Right after that, we can take the chance to also create some users using the POST /account/register endpoint, as well as assign them to the roles of our choice using the POST /Seed/AuthData endpoint, possibly changing its current implementation to match our new users' names.

Once we do that, we will be able to perform as many code and configuration changes as we want, republishing our project at will to have them instantly deployed in production until we are done. That's a great way to experience the advantages of the one-click deployment mechanic we've worked so hard to implement.

How to test our endpoints without SwaggerUI
Calling non-GET endpoints (such as the PUT /Seed/BoardGameData and the POST /Seed/AuthData) in production can be a rather difficult task, considering we don't have the SwaggerUI client available; to do that, I suggest using Postman (https://www.postman.com), a great web API client platform that allows to easily execute all kinds of HTTP requests.

> **(continued)**
>
> Alternatively, we could choose to temporarily enable the SwaggerUI in production; there won't be security problems in doing that, assuming we'll promptly disable it after performing the seeding tasks. However, if we opt for that route, we will also have to temporarily comment out the `SeedController`'s `[ApiExplorerSettings]` attribute which we added in chapter 11 to prevent that controller from being ignored by SwaggerUI.

When we are done with the database seeding tasks, we shouldn't forget to roll back the temporary changes that we did. More precisely, we need to

1 Delete the `/Data/bgg_dataset.csv` file from the remote VM's production folder (it should be `c:\inetpub\MyBGList\`).

2 Uncomment `SeedController`'s `[Authorize]` and/or `[ApiExplorerSettings]` attributes.

3 Disable the SwaggerUI in production in the `Program.cs` file (if we chose to temporarily enable it to execute the seed/ endpoints).

Doing this will restore our app's security posture back to its former, production-ready state.

12.4.5 *Final thoughts*

Now that our `MyBGList` app has been published and deployed in production together with its database, our journey through ASP.NET Core web API development has finally come to an end. Rest assured, through these chapters we dedicated ourselves to laying down a solid foundation and learning the core concepts, while scratching only the surface of several long and complex topics that would have probably deserved much more time and space. Still, we have plenty of reasons to be satisfied with what we did; the results obtained and the lessons learned will definitely help us to build even better web APIs in the future. Most importantly, we hope you enjoyed this book. Many thanks for reading it!

Summary

- Before thinking about publishing, releasing, and deploying our web API, it's important to define the overall security approach we want to stick to, as it will determine the whole architectural design of the production infrastructure.

- Choosing the domain name, the presence of intermediate proxies (such as a CDN service), and the SSL/TLS posture, are some of the decisions we must make before committing to the publishing tasks.

- A good practice when dealing with these choices is to adopt a security by design approach, meaning that we should always take the most secure route to fulfill our tasks while keeping a decent cost/benefit (and/or risk) tradeoff.

- Before publishing and deploying our web API, we need to ensure that it's ready for release.
  - Reviewing the configuration files, removing the unnecessary (or potentially vulnerable) middleware, and adding additional security countermeasures (such as the HTTP security headers) can greatly help to minimize the risk of malicious attacks, DDoS attempts, and data breaches.
- Using a content-delivery network (CDN) to serve our content instead of directly exposing our web hosting server has several advantages, not only in terms of caching and performance yet also for security reasons.
  - Among other things, most CDNs allow us to implement a secure edge-origin architectural pattern based upon a full encryption mode from our web hosting server to the end users' browsers, thus further improving the overall security posture of our infrastructure.
- Creating a VM on the cloud is a rather easy task, especially if we can count on the powerful GUI-based configuration tools provided by most market-leading cloud platforms (such as Azure) that allows us to build and configure a VM in few minutes.
  - However, before doing that it's important to acquire the required know-how to avoid some common security pitfalls, especially when dealing with some network-related tasks such as opening the TCP ports required by services like RDP and Web Deploy.
- Visual Studio allows to easily release and deploy a web app thanks to its built-in publishing features and GUI-based, wizard-like tools that can greatly simplify the whole release and deployment process.
- As for the database, the `dotnet-ef` CLI offers a wide set of alternatives to replicate the development database structure in production.
- Last but not least, the data seeding tasks can be handled by our `SeedController`, which can be temporarily tweaked to work in production by taking advantage of the one-click deployment capabilities of the Visual Studio publish profile.

appendix

Installing SQL Server

The SQL Server installer for Windows can be downloaded from http://mng.bz/GRmN. This page also provides detailed instructions for installing SQL Server on Linux, with specific guides for RHEL, Ubuntu, and SUSE.

> **NOTE** For this book, we're going to install the Express edition, which comes with no usage limitation. If you want to use the Developer edition, download it instead; the editions behave in the same way for all our needs.

Installing SQL Server on Windows is a wizard-guided, straightforward process that should pose no problems. Be sure to allow the installation tool to update the machine's firewall rules or prevent it from doing that, depending on whether you want the database management system (DBMS) to be accessible to the outside. When the first part of the installation completes, the wizard will ask some additional questions that can be answered in the following way:

- *Instance Name*—I suggest setting it to SQLExpress, the name we'll be using throughout this book.
- *Instance ID*—I suggest setting it to SQLEXPRESS for the same reason. If you want to change it, be sure to remember your choice. We're going to need this value when we write our connection string.
- *Authentication Mode*—Choose one of the following options:
  - *Windows authentication*—If we want unrestricted access to the database engine only from the local machine (using our Windows credentials). This option is better for security purposes but lacks some versatility because it won't allow us to administer the database remotely.
  - *Mixed Mode*—To enable the SQL Server system administrator (the sa user) and set a password for it.

SQL Server installation references

If you need a more comprehensive guide to installing the SQL Server local instance on a Windows or Linux machine, take a look at the following tutorials:

- http://mng.bz/zmDZ
- http://mng.bz/0yJz

Installing Internet Information Services

Internet Information Services (IIS) is an optional Windows component, part of the software shipped with the OS but typically not installed by default. The IIS installation process can be started in one of the following ways:

- Opening the Server Manager and selecting Add Roles and Features
- Opening the Control Panel, selecting Program and Features, and turning Windows features on and off

Both paths will take us to the Add Roles and Features wizard, which we need to follow to the Server Roles panel, where we can select Web Server (IIS) (figure A.1).

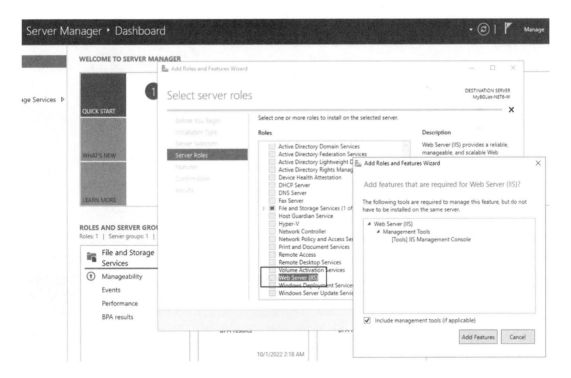

Figure A.1 Adding the Web Server (IIS) role

Ensure that the Include Management Tools check box is checked, and click Add Features to continue.

Installing the IIS Management Service

Advance the wizard up to the Role Services tab, and select the Management Service check box before continuing (as shown in Figure A.2). This service is required for the Web Deploy component to work.

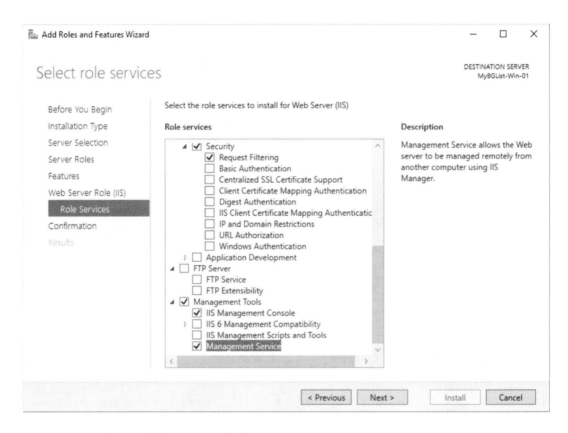

Figure A.2   Installing the IIS Management Service

Click Next, and complete the wizard, leaving the other options at their default values until reaching the Confirmation tab. Then click the Install button and wait for the IIS installation to complete.

Installing the ASP.NET Core Windows hosting bundle

The ASP.NET Core Windows hosting bundle is available as a free download at http://mng.bz/Klzn. Be sure to pick the ASP.NET Core 6.0.11 Runtime—Windows Hosting Bundle installer package for Windows x64, as shown in figure A.3.

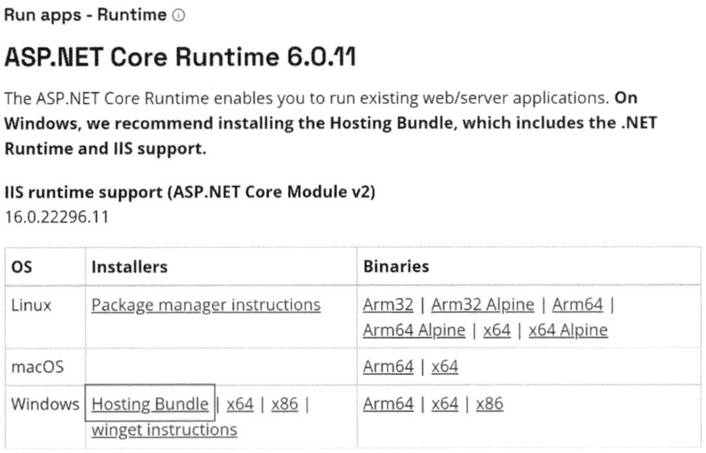

Run apps - Runtime ⓘ

ASP.NET Core Runtime 6.0.11

The ASP.NET Core Runtime enables you to run existing web/server applications. **On Windows, we recommend installing the Hosting Bundle, which includes the .NET Runtime and IIS support.**

IIS runtime support (ASP.NET Core Module v2)
16.0.22296.11

OS	Installers	Binaries
Linux	Package manager instructions	Arm32 | Arm32 Alpine | Arm64 | Arm64 Alpine | x64 | x64 Alpine
macOS		Arm64 | x64
Windows	Hosting Bundle | x64 | x86 | winget instructions	Arm64 | x64 | x86

Figure A.3   Downloading the ASP.NET Core Hosting Bundle for Windows

> **NOTE** It's strongly advisable to install the .NET runtime after installing IIS because the package bundle will perform some modifications to the IIS default configuration settings.

The installation process is straightforward and should pose no problems, but it's strongly advisable to restart the IIS service after it completes to ensure that it will load the newly added settings. To do this, open a command prompt window with administrative rights and execute the following console commands:

```
> net stop w3svc /y
> net start w3svc
```

These commands will stop and restart the World Wide Web publishing service.

Installing Web Deploy

To install the Web Deploy component, download the installer from http://mng.bz/ 91E8. The installation process is straightforward and should pose no problems. Be sure to select the Complete installation option to ensure that all the required components and prerequisites are installed as well, as the required IIS Deployment Handler feature is not selected by default.

> **NOTE** We can download the installer directly on the virtual machine (VM) server or download it locally and then copy/paste it using the RDP client.

Adding an inbound port rule in Azure

From the Azure Portal, access the VM configuration panel, and navigate to the Networking page (figure A.4).

Figure A.4   Azure VM's inbound port rules

On that page, we see the inbound and outbound port rules currently configured for our Azure VM; as shown in the figure, the Windows VM created in chapter 12 starts with TCP ports 80 (HTTP) and 443 (HTTPS) open to inbound traffic for anyone, and nothing more. To add a TCP port to that list, click the Add inbound port rule and set up a new rule with the following settings:

- *Source*—Your development machine's public IP address or mask (Any is not recommended for security reasons)
- *Source port ranges*—*(Asterisk—meaning that we will accept any source port)
- *Destination*—Any
- *Service*—Custom
- *Destination port ranges*—The number of the port we want to open for inbound traffic (3389 for RDP, 8172 for the management service used by Web Deploy)
- *Protocol*—TCP
- *Action*—Allow
- *Priority*—Leave the default number
- *Name*—The name of the service (RDP or Web Deploy)

WARNING   Publicly exposing a TCP port such as 3389 or 8172 to the internet is a nontrivial security problem that is recommended only for short-lived testing purposes. For production environments, it's highly recommended to keep those ports closed or restrict their source to the IP addresses of a few authorized deployment machines.

When ready, click the Add button to add the new rule, thus making the TCP port accessible from the internet.

index